THE CARLETON LIBRARY SERIES

A series of original works, new collections and reprints of source material relating to Canada, issued under the supervision of the Editorial Board, Carleton Library Series, Carleton University Press Inc., Ottawa, Canada.

General Editor
Michael Gnarowski

Editorial Board

Valda Blundell (Anthropology)
Irwin Gillespie (Economics)
Naomi Griffiths (History)
Robert J. Jackson (Political Science)
David B. Knight (Geography)
Michael MacNeil (Law)
Stephen Richer (Sociology)

The leader of his church: John Strachan as bishop of Toronto, 1847 (J. Ross Robertson Collection, Metropolitan Toronto Library, T15000).

THE ANGLICAN EXPERIENCE
IN UPPER CANADA, 1791-1854

Curtis Fahey

CARLETON UNIVERSITY PRESS
OTTAWA, CANADA

1991

©Carleton University Press Inc. 1991

ISBN 0-88629-124-0 (paperback)
ISBN 0-88629-125-9 (casebound)

Printed and bound in Canada

Carleton Library Series 163

Canadian Cataloguing in Publication Data
Fahey, Curtis, 1951-
  In His name : the Anglican experience in Upper Canada, 1791-1854

(The Carleton Library ; CLS 163)
ISBN 0-88629-125-9 (bound)
ISBN 0-88629-124-0 (pbk.)

  1. Church of England in Canada. 2. Church of England--Missions--Ontario. 3. Ontario--Church history--19th century. I. Title. II. Series.

BX5610.F341991   266'.3   C90-090265-5

Distributed by   Oxford University Press Canada,
                 70 Wynford Drive,
                 Don Mills, Ontario,
                 Canada. M3C 1J9
                 (416) 441-2941

Cover design: Aerographics Ottawa

Acknowledgement

Carleton University Press gratefully acknowledges the support extended to its publishing programme by the Canada Council and the Ontario Arts Council.

This book has been published with the help of a grant from the Social Science Federation of Canada using funds provided by the Social Science and Humanities Research Council of Canada.

*To my father,
the memory of my mother,
and my son, Matthew*

CONTENTS

Preface xiii

Chapter One
Establishment and Survival 1

Chapter Two
Preaching the Word 37

Chapter Three
Building a Church 61

Chapter Four
The End of Harmony 89

Chapter Five
The Defence of the Old Order 113

Chapter Six
Defeat 163

Chapter Seven
The Seeds of Independence 197

Chapter Eight
A House Divided 239

Conclusion 289

Bibliography 301

Index 337

ABBREVIATIONS

ADO	Archives of the Diocese of Ontario (Kingston)
AO	Archives of Ontario (Toronto)
BRMTL	Baldwin Room, Metropolitan Toronto Library
CHAR	Canadian Historical Association Report
CHR	Canadian Historical Review
DCB	Dictionary of Canadian Biography
GSA	General Synod Archives (Toronto)
JCCHS	Journal of the Canadian Church Historical Society
NAC	National Archives of Canada
OH	Ontario History
OHSPR	Ontario Historical Society Papers and Records
SCCIPGDS	Society for Converting and Civilizing the Indians and Propagating the Gospel Among the Destitute Settlers (of Upper Canada)
SPCK	Society for Promoting Christian Knowledge
SPG	Society for the Propagation of the Gospel (in Foreign Parts)
TDA	Toronto Diocesan Archives (St. James's Cathedral)

PREFACE

In the writing of Upper Canadian religious history, there has been a tendency either to concentrate on the lives of individuals and the institutional evolution of particular churches,[1] or to examine, almost to the exclusion of all else, the role of various denominations in political affairs.[2] Both these approaches have severe limitations. The first makes the mistake of isolating religious groups from the society in which they functioned, and in so doing obscures rather than illuminates their historical experience. The second has the merit of underlining the role of religious institutions in the secular world, but the picture it presents is rendered superficial by a lack of attention to the social and ideological factors that determined the churches' response to political issues.

The limitations of the narrowly political approach to Upper Canadian church history are well illustrated in the case of the Church of England. It is generally recognized that, under the forceful leadership of John Strachan, the Church of England was a moving force behind Upper Canada's conservative political tradition. Yet only one scholar, S.D. Clark, has related Anglican conservatism to the Church of England's position in Upper Canadian society, and his conclusions rest more on an uncritical acceptance of the assumptions of Turnerian frontierism than on a careful examination of the colony's religious life.[3] Further, aside from S.F. Wise[4] and, more recently, William Westfall[5] and John Webster Grant,[6] historians have shown little interest in the intellectual content of Upper Canadian Anglicanism. Studies that document in painstaking detail the history of church-state relations in Upper Canada ignore completely or give only a passing glance to the philosophical principles underlying the Anglican defence of church establishment. The result is that much of the literature on the Anglican experience in Upper Canada suffers from a glaring weakness: an inability to see the forest for the trees. We are told what Anglican clergymen did, but not why they did it.

This book, for its part, has something to say about the institutional evolution and political fortunes of the Church of England in Upper Canada. However, its central concern is to place these issues in the

In His Name

context of the church's social and intellectual experience in the community. In terms of the church's record as a religious organization, emphasis is placed not only on its response to New World conditions at the level of missionary activity, but also on the connection between its position in Upper Canada and the plans conceived by Strachan to establish an Anglican-controlled university and to increase the profitability of the clergy reserves. Similarly, with regard to its role in politics, attention is devoted to a wide range of subjects, including the philosophical principles at the heart of the Anglican world view and the idea of church establishment, the ideological response of Anglican clergymen to political reverses, the importance of the church's sense of mission in carrying it through the turbulent 1820s and 1830s, and the effects on the Anglican mind of the voluntarist victories of the post-union period. Lastly, the Church of England's transformation in the 1840s and 1850s into a self-governing institution is tied to the Anglican clergy's changing view of their church's place in Upper Canadian society, and the High Church-Evangelical feuding of these years is examined as part of the church's growing confusion about its role as a religious organization.

There is no need to apologize for the narrow denominational focus of this study. Although the major religious groups of Upper Canada had various things in common, the Church of England's experience had a number of distinctive characteristics, so many, in fact, that a social and intellectual analysis of the Anglican record is bound to reveal much that is fundamental to the history of the colony as a whole. The Church of England was the principal exponent both of the idea of church establishment and of the conservative doctrines which that idea implied. At the same time, while the basic tenets of Anglican conservative thought were shared by other churches, only the Church of England had the power to transform its vision of the good society into concrete government policies, as witnessed by Strachan's success in the 1820s in obtaining a royal charter for King's College and persuading the imperial government to accept his plan for the sale of the clergy reserve lands. Another peculiar feature of the Church of England was the fact that its ideological perspective went hand in hand with a distinctive brand of messianism. From the 1790s Anglican clergymen were inspired by the conviction that their church was entrusted with the responsibility of maintaining social stability and

Preface

defending the imperial connection. This messianic outlook remained strong until disestablishment became a reality in the late 1840s and early 1850s. And even then, clergymen and laymen alike responded to defeats in the temporal sphere by taking refuge behind a new view of the Church of England's mission. They put forward the notion — a notion that had no counterpart among other denominations — that the church should withdraw into itself, turn its back on the social and political activities that had previously occupied so much of its time, and act as a beacon of purity in the midst of a corrupt society.

This book does not examine the views of the laity in any detail, partly because Anglican laymen played a largely passive role in church affairs until well into the 1830s, but also because studying both clergy and laity for a period of over sixty years would result in a work of unmanageable proportions. Yet Anglican laymen are not ignored entirely. The laity's reluctance to support the church financially is examined, and the chapters dealing with the Anglican experience after the rebellion look at the growing importance of laymen in the institutional and intellectual life of the church, specifically in the work of the Church Society and in the movement for synodical government. An attempt is also made to analyze the position of the laity in the High Church-Low Church warfare that plagued the Church of England throughout the 1840s and 1850s.

A word of explanation is in order regarding the phrase "church establishment." Some scholars have claimed that, technically speaking, the Church of England was never legally established in Upper Canada. They explain that the Constitutional Act of 1791 provided the Church of England not with legal status as an establishment but only with a landed endowment in the form of the clergy reserves; that several denominations in addition to the Church of England had access to state financial aid, including, after 1840, proceeds from the sale of the clergy reserves; and that, on the whole, the few special rights the Church of England did enjoy — such as a monopoly on the position of chaplain to the House of Assembly — were more a matter of custom than of law.[7] While this interpretation is correct in strict legal terms, it should not be taken too far. Whatever the Church of England's status in law, Anglican clergymen themselves held steadfastly to the view that the principle of church establishment was enshrined in the Constitutional Act, and indeed this view lay at the core of their social and

In His Name

political philosophy. Furthermore, the Church of England's opponents, whether they wanted to extend the boons of church establishment beyond the Church of England or to destroy church establishment completely, accepted the fact of Anglican establishment in the very act of campaigning against it. For these reasons, my analysis refers repeatedly to the "policy of church establishment," the Church of England's "established status," and "disestablishment." Such phrases are appropriate in the context of a study that focuses less on politics and the law than on perceptions of the world. They are meant to describe intellectual reality, not legal facts.

A few comments should also be made concerning the place of Strachan in the book. As the leading Anglican clergyman in Upper Canada and a key figure in the colony's oligarchical government, Strachan is, by any standards, a giant in the Canadian past. This fact alone makes it difficult, if not impossible, to avoid concentrating on him in a study of the Anglican experience in Upper Canada. What compounds the problem is that Strachan left behind a body of material, published and unpublished, that is without parallel in pre-Confederation Ontario. Still, the Church of England was not a monolith carved under the guiding hand of Strachan, but a large, disparate group of individual clergymen responding in their uniquely personal ways to developments in Upper Canadian society. In the pages that follow, therefore, an effort has been made to rescue many clergymen from the obscurity to which they have been customarily relegated. The first two chapters deal with the Church of England's experience as a religious organization in the pre-1820 period. The next three study Strachan's role in Upper Canada's religious and political life in the pre-rebellion years, but in chapters six, seven and eight a number of issues — the separation of church and state, the achievement of responsible government, the church's struggle to become self-supporting and self-governing, and the conflict between High Churchmen and Evangelicals — have been analyzed from the standpoint not of Strachan alone but of the entire clergy. To provide this broad focus, a variety of hitherto neglected sources has been used, including sermons and pamphlets, letters and editorials published in the Anglican press, and reports to missionary organizations.

Two final points. Firstly, the boundary dates of this study are not as arbitrary as they might first appear: 1791 marks the formation of the

Preface

province of Upper Canada, and 1854 was the fateful year that witnessed, with the secularization of the clergy reserves, the destruction of the Church of England's vision for Upper Canadian society. Secondly, examining the Anglican experience during these years presents one structural difficulty — the fact that Upper Canada was part of the diocese of Quebec until 1839. That difficulty, however, is unavoidable. To have studied the Church of England in the two Canadas would have been an impossibly ambitious task. Besides, Upper Canada and Lower Canada were two distinct political cultures and presented the church with radically different problems. The Church of England in Lower Canada operated in a society that was overwhelmingly Catholic. As a result, whereas the church in Upper Canada was profoundly influenced by the Tractarian movement, its Lower Canadian counterpart, far more conscious of the threat of "popery," was solidly Low Church in its theological orientation. Furthermore, since the Lower Canadian church was on the periphery of the colony's religious life, its clergymen were not driven by the same sense of mission that inspired their brothers beyond the Ottawa River. For them, the Church of England in Lower Canada resembled more a tolerated sect than a church legally established under the Constitutional Act. Put simply, their major concern was not charting the course of their society's evolution, but survival.

This study began life as a doctoral dissertation, and several debts have been incurred during its transformation into a book. I am deeply obliged to Professor S.F. Wise of Carleton University, whose work on religious and political life in British North America has illuminated what would otherwise be a murky, impenetrable world. Professor Wise provided invaluable guidance during the writing of my thesis, and more recently he has offered the encouragement I needed as I began the laborious process of turning the thesis into a book. Another historian at Carleton, J.K. Johnson, is also deserving of my sincerest thanks, both for the encouragement he too has offered and for his shrewd editorial advice. Kind words and intelligent criticism were offered as well by two anonymous readers of the Social Science Federation of Canada, and the final draft of the manuscript has benefited greatly from their comments. Last but not least, I wish to thank Jane Graham of the *Dictionary of Canadian Biography*. Over the last several years, Jane has acted as a sounding-board for all my

In His Name

historical ideas, even the most outlandish ones. Without her support and inexhaustible patience, this book would not have been written.

My principal debts — to those who shaped the writer if not the book — are acknowledged elsewhere.

Curtis Fahey
Toronto, May 1990

Preface

NOTES

1 In the case of the Church of England, good examples of the biographical\institutional approach are: C.W. Vernon, *The Old Church in the New Dominion* (London, 1929); C.H. Mockridge, *The Bishops of the Church of England in Canada and Newfoundland* (London, 1896); and J. Langtry, *History of the Church in Eastern Canada and Newfoundland* (London, 1892). The culmination of institutional surveys was reached with the publication of W. Perkins Bull's *From Strachan to Owen: How the Church of England was Planted and Tended in British North America* (Toronto, 1937). Philip Carrington's *The Anglican Church in Canada: A History* (Toronto, 1963) showed that this approach was not something of the distant past but was still thriving in the 1960s. The most recent example of the same kind of historical writing is Alan L. Hayes, ed., *By Grace Co-workers: Building the Anglican Diocese of Toronto, 1780-1989* (Toronto, 1989).

2 For the political approach to the writing of Upper Canadian religious history, see Alan Wilson, *The Clergy Reserves of Upper Canada: A Canadian Mortmain* (Toronto, 1968); J. S. Moir, *Church and State in Canada West: Three Studies in the Relation of Denominationalism and Nationalism, 1841-67* (Toronto, 1959); and Goldwin French, *Parsons and Politics: The Role of the Wesleyan Methodists in Upper Canada and the Maritimes from 1780 to 1855* (Toronto, 1962). George Spragge and J.D. Purdy can also be seen as practitioners of this approach, while T.R. Millman and J.L.H. Henderson combine the political and institutional approaches. For the writings of these historians, see bibliography.

3 S.D. Clark, *Church and Sect in Canada* (Toronto, 1968).

4 See especially Wise's "God's Peculiar Peoples," in W.L. Morton, ed., *The Shield of Achilles: Aspects of Canada in the Victorian Age* (Toronto, 1968), pp. 36-61; and "Sermon Literature and Canadian Intellectual History," *United Church Bulletin*, no. 18 (1965), pp. 3-18.

5 William Westfall, *Two Worlds: The Protestant Culture of Nineteenth-Century Ontario* (Kingston and Montreal, 1989).

6 Grant's recent book, *A Profusion of Spires: Religion in Nineteenth-Century Ontario* (Toronto, Buffalo and London, 1988), ranges over all facets of the province's religious experience. Because of its nature as an overview, the book cannot explore in depth the intellectual contours of Anglican history, but it does take this subject seriously and offers a number of interesting comments on it.

7 See the following: A.H. Young, "The Church of England in Upper Canada, 1791-1841", *Queen's Quarterly* (1930), pp. 145-66; A.H. Young,

"A Fallacy in Canadian History," *CHR*, XV (December 1934), pp. 351-60; James J. Talman, "The Position of the Church of England in Upper Canada, 1791-1840," *CHR*, XV (December 1934), pp. 361-74; and Mark C. McDermott, "The Theology of Bishop John Strachan: A Study in Anglican Identity," Ph.D. thesis, St. Michael's College, University of Toronto, 1983, p. 15.

CHAPTER ONE

ESTABLISHMENT AND SURVIVAL

No period in the Church of England's history in Upper Canada has been more neglected than that from the founding of the colony in 1791 until the years immediately following the War of 1812. This neglect of the formative era of Upper Canadian Anglicanism is particularly regrettable since a review of it illuminates both the elements that would remain constant in the Anglican experience and those that would change. Driven by a deep belief in its mission as the established church of Upper Canada, the Church of England in these years found itself in a religiously diverse society that mocked the lofty notions it had of its status. It also discovered, much to its dismay, that many of its own members were less than enthusiastic in its support. Yet, even while reality intruded on the Church of England's perception of the world, there was a surprising degree of optimism in Anglican circles concerning the church's future in Upper Canada. Additionally, this optimistic spirit was accompanied by a remarkable amount of good will towards the Church of England's denominational rivals. In later years the essence of the church's world view would survive intact, but its optimism and naivety would not. The years before 1820 were the age of innocence for Upper Canadian Anglicanism.

* * * * *

The Church of England transplanted in Upper Canada was the product of a long period of historical evolution, and the ideas and values it had accumulated shaped its experience in the colony. None of its beliefs would be of greater significance than the principle of the union of church and state. The roots of this idea went far back in the church's history. Its origins can be traced to the Henrician reformation of the sixteenth century, which established the union of church and state by making King Henry VIII head of the new Church of England. Under the Elizabethan settlement, the alliance between church and state was reinforced, with both parties agreeing to uphold the authority of the other against the hostility of foreign states and the threat of religious dissent at home. In the age of the Stuarts the same church-state alliance played an important role in combating the growing influence of English puritanism. The Cromwellian Revolution upset the apple cart for a time, but the Glorious Revolution of 1688 restored the old order. Through the reigns of William and Mary, Anne and the first two Georges, there was again a widespread belief that the Church of England had a vital part to play in the governing of the nation and also in maintaining social and political stability, while the state, in turn, had an obligation to defend the church's special position as the "established" church of the realm. This belief became even stronger during the early years of the reign of George III, when theories about the alliance of church and state were increasingly balanced by a view which saw the two bodies as inseparable. Upholding the church's established status in the eighteenth century were a range of special privileges: Anglican bishops sat in the House of Lords; the Test Act and Corporation Acts prevented Catholics and dissenters from holding offices of any kind; the universities of Oxford and Cambridge were under Anglican control; all Englishmen, regardless of denominational affiliation, were obliged to contribute tithes in support of the Church of England.[1]

Given the central place of the union of church and state in English political culture, it is not surprising that, from an early date, efforts were made to establish the Church of England in the colonies of Nova Scotia and Quebec. In Nova Scotia the Church of England's established status was recognized in royal instructions to successive governors and also in an act passed by the local legislature in 1758.[2] Similarly, in the old province of Quebec, the establishment of the Church of England was a central part of the imperial government's strategy of preparing the way, gradually but inexorably, for the assimilation of the French Canadians. While the Treaty of Paris in 1763 granted the Crown's new Roman Catholic subjects the liberty of religious worship "as far as the laws of Great Britain permit,"[3] instructions issued to the first two governors, James Murray and Guy Carleton, gave them the power to reserve land throughout the colony for the support of Protestant clergymen and schools[4] — a power which, as Murray was told in 1763, would ensure "that the Church of England may be established both in Principle and Practice, and that the said Inhabitants may by Degrees be induced to embrace the Protestant Religion, and their Children be brought up in the Principles of it."[5] Even the Quebec Act of 1774, supposedly the Magna Carta of French Canadian liberties, was emphatic in its declaration that while the Roman Catholic Church was to be granted its accustomed dues and rights, it would nevertheless be lawful for the Crown to make provision for "the Encouragement of the Protestant Religion, and for the Maintenance and support of a Protestant Clergy within the said Province, as he or they shall, from Time to Time, think necessary and expedient."[6] That the phrase "Protestant Clergy" was meant to apply only to the Church of England became plain in the following year, when Carleton was informed that "it is a toleration of the free exercise of the religion of the Church of Rome only, to which they are entitled, but not to the powers and privileges of it, as an established Church, for that is a preference which belongs only to the Protestant Church of England."[7]

Of course, enshrining the principle of church establishment in law was one thing, and actually establishing the Church of England was another. The importance of this distinction was well illustrated in Quebec and Nova Scotia, for in each of these colonies the Church of England's *de facto* position bore little resemblance to its *de jure* status. To take the case of Nova Scotia, when the American Revolution broke out in 1775, the Church of England's insignificant privileges as the established church — namely its right to marry by licence and the power of its congregations to function, in a legal sense, as corporate bodies — hardly compensated for its weakness as a religious force: at that point there were only six Church of England missions in the colony, and Anglicans were greatly outnumbered by the members of other denominations.[8] Worse still was the situation in Quebec, where a combination of factors, notably a severe shortage of clergymen, a lack of substantial immigration from the British Isles, and the attitude of successive governors, confined the Church of England to the periphery of the colony's religious life. When civil rule was inaugurated in 1764 there were only two Anglican clergymen in the colony, John Ogilvie and John Brooke, and they were military chaplains who restricted their ministrations to the garrisons of Montreal and Quebec City.[9] This state of affairs, which in the eyes of one witness encouraged "the French inhabitants to look upon their conquerors in an odious light, and to become more impatient of the English yoke,"[10] might have been remedied if the governors of the colony had followed their instructions to support the Church of England. But Murray, Carleton and Frederick Haldimand, taking the view that the imperial government's plans for the assimilation of the French Canadians were both misguided and impractical, ignored all injunctions to strengthen the position of the Anglican establishment. The result was that, at the conclusion of the American Revolution, Quebec did not possess a single Anglican church building; services were performed in various military barracks or Recollet chapels borrowed for the purpose.[11] There were then only four Anglican clergymen in the colony, and three of these, David Chabrand Delisle, David-François de Montmollin and Léger-Jean-Baptiste-Noël Veyssière, were French clerics unable to speak English intelligibly.[12] Something might have been salvaged had the few clergymen resident in the colony been men of sincerity and dedication. But these were precisely the characteristics that Delisle, de Montmollin and Veyssière lacked. Carleton accused de Montmollin of "levity and folly, both before and after his renouncing the errors of the Church of Rome."[13] An anonymous individual reported that Delisle, stationed in Montreal, performed service only on Sunday mornings, Christmas day and Good Friday.[14] Veyssière was described as "almost useless as a clergymen" by Charles Inglis, the first Anglican bishop in British North America, and as an essentially "bad character" by Jacob Mountain, first bishop of the diocese of Quebec.[15]

The state of the Church of England in Quebec and Nova Scotia was a matter of vital concern in Britain. In the 1780s, the American Revolution sparked considerable reflection in British political circles on what had gone wrong in the Thirteen Colonies. It was widely believed that the revolt had been caused in part by the weakness of colonial Anglicanism — an unsurprising view given the intellectual climate of the age. By the late eighteenth century, the old belief in the union of church and state had become fundamental to a conservative ideology that dominated British political culture. This ideology, drawing on Anglican theology and the conservative elements of the Whig tradition, stressed the divine origins of government, the necessity of obedience to the powers that be, the divinely sanctioned nature of the social hierarchy, and the role of the Church of England as an agent of social and political control.[16]

One man who embodied the intellectual currents of the age was William Knox, Under-Secretary for the Colonies between 1770 and 1782. During the last years of the American revolutionary war, Knox concluded that British North America, then becoming the home of thousands of Loyalist exiles, would have to be provided with a strong Anglican establishment if a second colonial revolution was to be avoided. This point of view was advanced in a number of reports drawn up by Knox in the 1780s. In the first of these, described as "a general plan for the introduction and establishment of the Church of England and thro' it combatting and repressing the prevailing disposition of the colonies to republicanism, and exciting in them an esteem for Monarchy," Knox argued that British North America would follow the example of its revolutionary neighbours if the imperial government did not immediately lay the foundations of a colonial church establishment by appointing a bishop, deans and archdeacons, and by arranging for the payment of all clerical salaries out of the quit rents.[17] In later reports presented after the end of the war, Knox again emphasized the need for a local ecclesiastical hierarchy and a state-supported clergy in British North America. He also put forward two recommendations that had not been mentioned earlier — the creation of an Anglican college in Nova Scotia, and the setting aside of two or three thousand acres in each township in British North America for Anglican glebes and schools.[18]

In the years just after the Revolution, the British government also took the view that the time had come to place the colonial church on a sounder footing. Besides sharing Knox's belief that the future of the empire depended upon church establishment,[19] the imperial authorities were convinced that the presence of large numbers of Anglican Loyalists in British North America would provide the Church of England with a solid base of popular support.[20] Acting on these twin assumptions, the imperial government adopted a number of measures designed to bolster the position of the Anglican establishment. In 1783 the Colonial Office instructed the governor of Nova Scotia to set aside one thousand acres of glebe lands for the support of Anglican clergy

In His Name

and schools.[21] In 1787 Charles Inglis, a Loyalist who had served as assistant rector of Trinity Church, New York, was appointed bishop of Nova Scotia, a diocese that included, besides Nova Scotia itself, New Brunswick, St John's (Prince Edward) Island, Newfoundland, Quebec and Bermuda.[22] In 1787 and 1788 the Church of England in Nova Scotia was provided with imperial government grants totalling £3,000 to assist in the construction of churches in new settlements.[23] Finally, in 1790 a grant of £1,000 was made to one of Inglis's favourite projects, the Windsor Academy, an institution whose central purpose was to create a body of locally educated Anglican clergymen.[24]

This new awareness of the need to strengthen the colonial church establishment was also at the heart of the Constitutional Act of 1791, a measure which, more than any other, bore witness to the widespread perception of the Church of England as the most effective safeguard against the forces of revolution. The origins of the Act dated to the mid-1780s, when the Loyalists who had settled west of the Ottawa River in the old province of Quebec began petitioning for a separate representative government and freehold land tenure, two essential British rights which they had enjoyed in the American colonies but which were now denied them. In responding to these appeals, Prime Minister William Pitt and Colonial Secretary William Grenville, the main authors of the Constitutional Act, adhered to a set of basic principles. Neither man had any doubt whatsoever that the imperial government had an obligation to redress the legitimate grievances of the Loyalist exiles. Nor had they any doubt that a sympathetic response to the Loyalists' demands would be in the best interests of the empire, for, in their view, a Loyalist community that saw itself as well treated would remain a stalwart defender of the imperial connection. Yet, in working out their ideas on the changes needed in the province of Quebec, Pitt and Grenville were primarily motivated not by a desire to placate the Loyalists, but by a determination to avoid the mistakes that had led to the American Revolution. According to their analysis of the period before 1775, the movement for independence had gained momentum because of the overwhelming strength of the "democratic element" in each of the Thirteen Colonies. It followed, therefore, that if Quebec was to be granted representative government, care must be taken to ensure that the new colonial constitution made provision for the three checks on the popular will that had been noticeably absent in the American colonies — a landed aristocracy, an executive branch that was financially and politically independent of the House of Assembly, and an established Church of England. Ignoring the need for these institutional safeguards would not only sow the seeds of social and political instability. It would also lead directly to another colonial revolution, a result that would be calamitous both for the Loyalists and for the empire as a whole.[25]

Seen in this light, the provisions of the Constitutional Act relating to the Church of England were merely one aspect of a larger project in counter-revolution. An Order in Council that followed the passage of the Act divided the province of Quebec into the colonies of Upper and Lower Canada, thus meeting the demand of the Loyalists for a government of their own. Under the Act itself, the executive branch was rendered independent by the extensive sources of revenue placed at its disposal and by its lack of constitutional responsibility to the Assembly, the members of the legislative and executive councils being appointed by the governor. To encourage the growth of a landed aristocracy, crown reserve lands were set aside, appointments to the Legislative Council were to be made for life, and — under a provision that was never implemented — the king was authorized to issue hereditary titles of honour which could be coupled with hereditary membership in the Legislative Council. Finally, one-seventh of the public lands of the two Canadas — soon to become known as the clergy reserves — was set aside for the maintenance of a "Protestant Clergy."[26]

The ambiguity of that phrase would haunt Upper Canadian politics in the years ahead, with the Church of Scotland in particular arguing that the words "Protestant Clergy" entitled it to a share of the reserves. While there is some evidence to support the Church of Scotland's claim to co-establishment under the Constitutional Act,[27] the Church of England took the view that it alone was intended to be the beneficiary of the reserves. The church's case was not unreasonable. Supporting it was the fact, already mentioned, that in the old province of Quebec instructions to governors drew a direct correlation between "Protestant Clergy" and the Church of England. There was in addition the clause of the Constitutional Act authorizing the endowment of rectories according to the "Establishment of the Church of England."[28] Further support could be found in the whole thrust of the British government's position after the American Revolution. That position revolved around the need to establish the Church of England in the remaining colonial possessions; neither the Church of Scotland nor any other "Protestant" bodies were mentioned. In brief, although the Constitutional Act did not specifically establish the Church of England, Upper Canadian Anglicans could easily argue that this was the Act's intention.

A couple of additional points should be made with regard to the Constitutional Act. First of all, whether or not the words "Protestant Clergy" referred exclusively to the Church of England, there is no doubt that the imperial government saw the clergy reserves as an endowment designed to enable the Church of England to fulfill its mission as a bastion of the social and political order. As well, although it is tempting to see the creation of the clergy reserves as an outlandish innovation destined to cause only grief, the truth is that the church's acquisition of a landed endowment under the Constitutional Act was entirely in keeping with privileges it enjoyed in England and with prevailing assumptions about the relationship of church and state. Thus, when Anglican clergymen in Upper Canada supported the policy of church establishment, they were only defending something that had been part of the British tradition for centuries. It was the advocates of disestablishment who were calling for a radical break with the past.

The conservative ideological perspective underlying the Constitutional Act was personified in the man chosen to head the civil administration of the new colony of Upper Canada. John Graves Simcoe, throughout his five years as lieutenant-governor, bristled with an astonishing variety of schemes for the development of a colony whose cause he adopted as his own. Having fought in the American Revolution, Simcoe retained to the end an unwavering conviction that "the most scandalous and swindling Transaction that has disgraced the Annals of Mankind"[29] had been instigated by a devious, conspiring minority. It was his view that if Upper Canada could be fashioned into a stable, contented, prosperous community, with an institutional and social structure patterned in the minutest detail on that of England, the majority of Americans would soon begin to appreciate the blessings showered down upon those fortunate enough to live under British rule. The reconstruction of the empire would then be only a matter of time.[30]

Establishment and Survival

This plan to make Upper Canada an "image and transcript" of the British constitution accorded a central place to the Church of England. Simcoe campaigned incessantly for the erection of the two Canadas into a separate diocese, the appointment of archdeacons and the founding of a church-controlled university. He was equally vigorous in suppressing any incipient dissatisfaction with the Church of England's privileged status in the colony. Before Simcoe had even seen Upper Canada, he was convinced that "every establishment of Church and State that upholds the distinction of ranks and lessens the undue weight of the democratic influence, ought to be introduced.[31] After a year's residence in Upper Canada he had not changed his mind. He was adamant in his insistence that "all just Government ... is founded on the Morality of the People, and that such Morality has no true basis but when placed upon religious Principles." It was for these reasons, he added, that "I have always been extremely anxious, both from political as well as more worthy motives that the Church of England should be essentially established in Upper Canada."[32] With his fervent commitment to church establishment, Simcoe did not hesitate to take a leading part in the passage of the restrictive Marriage Act of 1793. Under this measure, the power to solemnize marriages was confined to Anglican clergymen, and civil marriages were permitted only when neither partner lived within eighteen miles of an Anglican clergyman.[33] When Baptists and Presbyterians in eastern Upper Canada complained that the Act made them "aliens in their own country," Simcoe responded that their petition was "the Product of a wicked Head and a most disloyal heart."[34]

It was not long before one of Simcoe's proposals for strengthening the colonial church — the formation of the two Canadas into a diocese — was accepted by the British government. In the summer of 1793 the imperial authorities, revealing once again their heightened awareness of the importance of church establishment in British North America, created the diocese of Quebec, which encompassed both Upper and Lower Canada. That November, Jacob Mountain, the first occupant of the new see, arrived in Quebec City to begin an episcopate that was to last until his death in 1826. From one point of view, Mountain, a scholarly, ambitious and rather austere divine of the Hanoverian church, was ill suited for a diocese that sprawled over a vast territory of nearly 2,000 miles, from the Gaspé coast in the east to the western tip

In His Name

of Lake Erie. Yet if the imperial government was searching for a churchman who, as bishop of Quebec, would act as an uncompromising champion of the interests of the colonial church, a stronger candidate than Mountain could not have been selected. Throughout his episcopate Mountain remained constant in the belief that the established Church of England in the diocese of Quebec, and indeed in all of British North America, was entrusted with the task not only of disseminating the principles of sound religion but also of checking the spread of sectarian "enthusiasm," maintaining social and political stability, and defending the imperial connection. He lobbied tirelessly on behalf of the Anglican establishment, pleading again and again for additional clergymen and waging an unrelenting campaign for an increase in the imperial government's financial assistance to the colonial church. He also repeatedly criticized the civil administration of Lower Canada for encouraging the claims of the Church of Rome and, equally serious, failing to make adequate provision for the established Church of England, whose prosperity, as he told the colonial secretary in 1804, was absolutely vital "not only for the Interests of His Majesty's Government, & of his Protestant subjects in this Province, but for the progressive improvement & happiness of his Canadian subjects also."[35]

Although Mountain spent most of his time in the lower province, he did visit Upper Canada on several episcopal tours between 1794 and 1820.[36] After the first of these visits, Mountain had few illusions about the Church of England's position in Upper Canada. In September 1794 he emphasized to Henry Dundas, the secretary for war, that in terms of "Religious Instruction, the state of these settlers is, for the most part, truly deplorable." He wrote:

> from Montreal to Kingston, a distance of 200 miles, there is not one clergyman of the Church of England, nor any house of Religious Worship, except one small Chapel belong'g to the Presbyterians. The Public Worship of God is entirely suspended or performed in a manner that can neither tend to improve the people in Religious Truth, nor to render them useful members of Society .... The great bulk of the people have and can have no instruction but such as they receive occasionally from itinerant & mendicant Methodists, a set of ignorant Enthusi-

asts whose preaching is calculated only to perplex the understanding & corrupt the morals, to relax the nerves of industry, and dissolve the bonds of Society.

Things were much better in Kingston itself, where Mountain was pleased to report that "there is a small but decent church: a respectable congregation (much too numerous to be properly seated in it:) and a Minister greatly and justly esteemed by the people." But in the area between Kingston and Niagara, religious destitution of appalling proportions was again the order of the day. Here, Mountain wrote, there were only two clergymen, and the buildings set aside for religious worship were totally inadequate. One of these clergymen ministered to settlements along the Bay of Quinte, conducting services in "3 or 4 small log huts which are used as churches, but which are altogether insufficient for the decent accommodation of their respective congregations." The other clergyman was responsible for a "numerous & respectable congregation" in Niagara, where "service is performed sometimes in the chamber of the L[egislative] C[ouncil] and sometimes at Free Mason's Hall, a house of Public Entertainment."[37]

So much for the Church of England's established status under the Constitutional Act. Its problem in putting down roots in Upper Canada was to be the dominant theme of its experience in the colony from the 1790s until the years just after the War of 1812. Yet Anglican clergymen never despaired; in fact, they were incredibly optimistic, apparently oblivious to the facts of Upper Canadian religious life. Understanding the difficulties they faced — as well as the attitudes they displayed in confronting those difficulties — requires a detailed examination of the Church of England's record in the first three decades of Upper Canada's history.

* * * * *

In His Name

A few words must be said at the outset about the religious complexion of the Upper Canadian Loyalists. Throughout the first half of the nineteenth century there seemed to be a general assumption amongst Anglican clergymen that most of the Loyalist settlers in Upper Canada were members of the Church of England. For instance, John Strachan wrote in 1827 that "the Province of Upper Canada was settled by Loyalists from the United States, formerly British colonies, soon after the termination of the American Revolution, the greater part of whom were Episcopalians, and sincerely attached to the Church of England."[38] Although such claims reinforced the Church of England's image as a bulwark of social stability and the imperial tie, they were not true. The Loyalists represented a cross-section of American society, and in the case of Upper Canada they came from a variety of religious, ethnic and class backgrounds.[39] During the revolutionary war and in the years immediately after the signing of the Treaty of Paris in 1783, approximately 6,000 Loyalists settled in what was to become the colony of Upper Canada. The vast majority, contrary to the assertions of nineteenth-century purveyors of loyalist mythology, were not educated "gentlemen" but farmers from the frontier regions of New York and Pennsylvania.[40] What is more, this same group of Loyalist exiles belonged to a number of different denominations. Apart from the Church of England, no fewer than seven denominations — Roman Catholics, Presbyterians, Lutherans, Mennonites, Quakers, Baptists and Methodists — were planted in Upper Canada during the period of Loyalist settlement.[41]

Religious pluralism was reinforced in the period between the early 1790s and the War of 1812, when roughly 90,000 "late Loyalists" from the United States were lured into Upper Canada by the promise of free land grants.[42] The denominations that benefited most from this second wave of immigration were the Baptists and Methodists. By 1812 over fifteen Baptist congregations had been formed in the Niagara region and along the north shore of Lake Ontario,[43] and these congregations were served by nine resident ministers and several travelling missionaries from the United States.[44] Even more remarkable was the strength of the Methodists. The turning-point for this denomination came in 1790 with the appointment of William Losee of the New York Conference to a circuit that embraced Kingston, Ernesttown, Fredericksburgh, Adolphustown, Marysburgh and Sophiasburgh.[45]

The success of Losee and other preachers in sparking a religious revival led in 1794 to the formation of Upper Canada into a separate district under the New York Conference, the appointment of Darius Dunham as Presiding Elder and the creation of the Niagara circuit.[46] Progress would now be rapid. According to one source, by 1797 there were 795 members and 5 preachers; in 1800, 936 members and 7 preachers; in 1805, 1,787 members and 10 preachers; and in 1810, the year that the Genesee Conference was founded to tend to the spiritual welfare of western New York state and Upper Canada, there were 2,603 members and 13 preachers.[47] These figures are of uncertain accuracy, but they do indicate general trends.

While the War of 1812 temporarily halted the growth of some denominations, it did little to reverse the growing pluralism of Upper Canadian society. Before 1820 the Roman Catholic Church, which made significant strides after the arrival in 1804 of a large flock of Highlanders under the leadership of the Reverend Alexander Macdonell,[48] had become firmly entrenched: in 1817 there were seven priests serving a flock which, in Macdonell's estimate, numbered roughly 17,000.[49] As for the Presbyterian, Baptist and Methodist denominations, all of which had suffered serious reverses during the war, the return of peace in 1815 inaugurated an era of steady progress. In the period from 1815 to 1820 the Baptists and Presbyterians grew significantly in popular support as a result of immigration from the British Isles; equally important, by 1820 both had succeeded in increasing their clerical manpower to the level that had been achieved before the war.[50] The Methodists — again, these figures should be viewed cautiously—saw their membership dwindle to 1,635 in 1815,[51] but they regained lost ground with the burst of revivalism that followed the 1817 meeting of the Genesee Conference in Elizabethtown. In 1820 Upper Canadian Methodism numbered over 5,000 members and 24 preachers, and the colony was divided into 19 circuits, from the Ottawa River circuit in the east to the Thames River circuit in the west.[52]

The diversity that characterized Upper Canada's religious landscape in the pre-1820 period becomes even more apparent when the position of the Church of England is considered. Throughout the 1790s there were only three Anglican clergymen in Upper Canada, John Stuart in Kingston, Robert Addison in Niagara, and John Langhorn in Ernesttown, Fredericksburgh and Adolphustown. Despite the assistance of the Society for the Propagation of the Gospel in Foreign Parts (SPG)[53] — the British missionary body which, from its founding in 1701, played a critical role in paying the the salaries of colonial clergymen and fostering the growth of the church throughout the empire — the number of Anglican clergy in Upper Canada increased only gradually, reaching a total of six in 1812 and nine in 1819.[54]

More serious still was the lack of substantial support for the church in all parts of the province, including those served by Anglican clergymen. In 1787 John Stuart claimed that Upper Canada's inhabitants were "principally Presbyterians, Anabaptists, Dutch Calvinists, & New England Sectaries,"[55] and in his own parish of Kingston he was not long in concluding that Anglicans were greatly outnumbered by the members of other denominations.[56] In the Niagara district Robert Addison reported in 1796 that the majority of settlers were Presbyterians,[57] and eight years later he warned that many of the settlers flocking over the border into his mission were dissenters.[58] To the East, in Langhorn's parishes of Ernesttown, Fredericksburgh and Adolphustown, a similar situation prevailed. In 1788 Langhorn informed the SPG that only 300 of the 1,500 people in his mission were Anglicans, the rest being Moravians, Quakers, Baptists, Lutherans, Presbyterians and "New Lights."[59] Things deteriorated still further a few years later when William Losee of the New York Methodist Conference began his work in the Bay of Quinte region. By 1802 Langhorn was describing Ernesttown, which then possessed the services not only of a Methodist preacher but also of one Presbyterian and one Lutheran minister, as "a sore refractory town against the Church of England,"[60] and in the following year he estimated that this settlement contained 160 Anglicans, 398 Methodists, 250 Lutherans, 498 Presbyterians, 11 Quakers, 63 Universalists, 16 "Papists," 33 Deists, 10 Baptists and 688 people who professed no religion.[61] With good reason did Langhorn complain in 1806: "What a tedious piece of ground Providence has cast me upon and what great opposition there is made to me .... The people here encourage them [American Presbyterian ministers], and such like trash to come hither, and run after them with great eagerness."[62] In 1811, two years before Langhorn's departure from the colony, Fredericksburgh was "much better affected." But Ernesttown by this time could boast only 37 Anglicans in a population he now estimated at 509.[63]

The men who entered the ranks of the Anglican clergy in the first decade of the nineteenth century echoed Addison's and Langhorn's comments. In 1803 George Okill Stuart informed the SPG that Presbyterians, Roman Catholics and Methodists abounded in the parish of York.[64] John Strachan was confronted with the same sort of problem in Cornwall. "My flock is not numerous," he wrote to Dr. Brown, an old friend in Scotland, soon after his ordination in 1803. "A great part of my Parish belongs to the Lutheran persuasion, a greater has no religion at all. A number of the people are Catholics, and plenty of Presbyterians, with a few Methodists &c. You see I am in a pickle."[65] His concern was shared by Richard Pollard, the Anglican clergyman in Sandwich. Although there were few dissenters in Sandwich itself, the state of the church in the surrounding district was far from rosy. Nathan Bangs established a Methodist mission on the Thames River in 1803 and six years later ignited a religious revival that swept through the settlements on the shorelines of Lake St. Clair and the western end of Lake Erie.[66] Pollard, only too aware of the spiritual dangers facing the large number of Anglicans in this area, warned that the absence of Church of England clergymen was allowing the Methodists to gain converts.[67] In 1810 he made a journey to York to see Lieutenant-Governor Francis Gore. He noted that:

> my route to the Capitol being among people connected with my Mission I endeavoured to make my voyage, a ministerial visit to the inhabitants as I had reason to think the Methodists had made great progress (by the means of the most illiterate teachers), I distribute Sermons, explaining the Orthodox faith of our Church ... calling the families together of an evening and endeavouring to establish our holy faith ... stript of the fascinating garb, of Superstition & Enthusiasm.[68]

After the War of 1812 Anglican clergymen continued to complain about the Church of England's enfeebled condition in relation to other denominations. John Wilson, headmaster of the Midland District Grammar School and chaplain to the naval forces in Kingston, took time off from his official duties between 1818 and 1819 to serve the vacant mission of Ernesttown on alternate Sunday afternoons. His labours went unappreciated. He reported in 1817 that Presbyterians

In His Name

vastly outnumbered the few Episcopalians in Ernesttown, and that at a recent meeting dissenters outvoted churchmen and prohibited the purchase of Anglican prayer books.[69] Similar stories were told by other clergymen. In 1818 John Gunther Weagant of Williamsburg and Osnabruck attributed the diminished number of baptisms and communicants to the activities of Lutheran, Presbyterian and Methodist "Itinerants" in the vicinity of his mission.[70] William Sampson claimed that Grimsby and its neighbourhood were "almost wholly composed of Dissenters who have left the Church from want of a regular Minister."[71] Ralph Leeming, stationed in Ancaster, estimated that there were 600 Methodists, 200 Presbyterians and only 200 Anglicans in his parish.[72]

In addition to the church's numerically weak position in a religiously pluralistic society, Anglican clergymen also had to worry about the negligible revenues yielded by the clergy reserves — that landed endowment which, in theory at least, formed the basis of the policy of church establishment. While the clergy reserves were set aside in surveys conducted between 1794 and 1798, only 650 reserve lands had been leased by 1819 and only 100 of the lessees were bothering to pay their rent.[73] This failure to turn the reserves into a lucrative source of income was attributable in part to the difficulty of collecting land rents from a small population scattered over an immense territory. But the main problem was that few settlers were willing to lease clergy reserves as long as other lands were granted free of charge to anyone who applied. This basic flaw at the heart of the government's plans for the development of the reserves meant that, until the policy of free land grants was brought to an end in the mid-1820s, the Church of England's landed endowment would remain of little monetary value. It also meant, as a necessary consequence, that in the pre-1820 period the church was unable to rely on the clergy reserves for the revenue it needed to build up a larger supply of clerical manpower—the very thing it could not do without if it was to improve its fortunes in Upper Canadian society. Throughout these years the unproductiveness of the clergy reserves made the church totally dependent for its financial support on the SPG and the local government.[74]

Compounding these problems was the reluctance of the Anglican laity to contribute to the financial support of their church. Soon after he

Establishment and Survival

arrived in the colony in 1787, John Langhorn was forced to perform service in his own lodgings when one of his congregations refused to contribute the necessary £10 for church expenses.[75] Several years later, in 1806, he observed that, despite their greatly improved material circumstances, his people were unmoved in their selfishness,[76] and again, in 1812, he reflected that "these people here seemingly have a notion they do me a huge favour, if I am permitted to do anything for them."[77] The fate of Robert Addison in Niagara was no better. When Addison assumed charge of his mission in 1792, he was assured by some of his more prominent parishioners that they would contribute £100 annually to his support.[78] Their promise proved barren. Not having received a shilling by 1795, Addison contemplated moving to Oswegatchie or Nova Scotia.[79] In 1799 he informed the SPG that over the past eight years his people had contributed the paltry sum of £200 in all, and in the last two or three years even these meagre donations had been withheld.[80] By 1801 he certainly had cause to complain that "he expected better things when he came out, & he thinks it hard to spend nine of the best years of his life in Canada, in the humble, but honest discharge of his duty, & most of that time without any competent support." [81]

John Stuart, a New York Loyalist, also decried the stinginess of his flock. When in 1785 he settled in Kingston, or Cataraqui as it was then known, he immediately informed the SPG that his kind-hearted but impoverished flock would be unable to contribute to his support for seven years.[82] By the late 1780s, he was less charitably disposed. Having received only £13 of the £22 subscribed on his arrival, Stuart now confessed that he never expected to see the remainder. In a letter to Bishop Inglis in 1788, he wrote bitterly that "my parish consists chiefly of the New York, Loyal Refugees, a description of Men, not remarkable for either Religion, Industry or Honesty, — they are careless in their attendance on public worship, dissolute in their morals, and in general, not industrious in providing even for their own families."[83] Two years later in another letter to Inglis he claimed that the unwillingness of his flock to assist him financially was the result not of their "want of ability" but of their selfishness.[84] In 1791 an impatient SPG dismissed the pleas of poverty in a memorial from Stuart's churchwardens and ordered them to fulfill their obligations. Unfortunately, as Stuart pointed out, this interference only increased the

In His Name

stubbornness of the Kingston laity.[85] For the rest of his ministry, which lasted until his death in 1811, Stuart laboured without the financial assistance of his people. He informed Bishop Mountain in 1795 that "I may be permitted to end my Days here in Quietness, — provided always, that I ask or expect nothing from my Parishioners."[86]

There were several reasons for the laity's niggardliness, which crippled the church not only in the pre-1820 period but throughout the first half of the nineteenth century. Unlike the members of other denominations, Anglican laymen until the 1830s and 1840s had little incentive to develop habits of financial generosity in their dealings with the church, since in their case the services of religion were provided *gratis* by the state and the SPG. It is also probable that many Anglican immigrants from the British Isles took it for granted that the church in the colonies, like the church at home, was supported by the government. Yet another factor was the policy of church establishment, which inevitably gave rise to the belief that the Church of England had abundant financial resources and therefore had no need to depend upon the voluntary contributions of its own members. This belief manifested itself most clearly in the 1830s and 1840s, when the growing profitability of the clergy reserves convinced many laymen that the revenue accruing therefrom was more than sufficient to meet the church's expenses.[87] But even in earlier years, there is reason to conclude that the church-state connection was more of a hindrance than a help to the Church of England. In 1789 John Stuart told Inglis that, "as they [the laity] formerly had Pork & Pease ... a general opinion prevails in this country, that as the Clergy receive Salaries from Government, they ought not to have anything from the people."[88]

Considering the church's problems in these years — its precarious position in relation to other denominations, the uselessness of the reserves as a source of church revenue, the laity's slowness in contributing to their church's support — Anglican clergymen could have been pardoned had they despaired. In fact, however, throughout the pre-1820 era they saw signs of hope where others would have seen only gloom. To them, one of the most encouraging signs for the Church of England's future was the absence of inter-denominational barriers at the parish level. Again and again they proudly informed the SPG that the members of other denominations were quite friendly towards the Church of England and that in many areas, especially those communities without rival churches, non-Anglicans regularly attended Church of England services. John Stuart, for example, reported in 1787 that "several of the principal Inhabitants of Cataraqui, though educated Dissenters, constantly attend Divine Service, and in every respect concur in promoting the interest of the Church, though not actual members,"[89] and two years later he estimated that only one-eighth of his flock were members of the Church of England.[90] In 1805 Richard Pollard wrote of his parishes of Sandwich and Amherstburgh that, "as there is no establishment of dissenters (except the Roman Church,—) I am willing to place those that come to our church, under the head of Members."[91] Ralph Leeming prided himself on the fact that most people in Ancaster, a stronghold of Methodism, were "well-disposed towards the Church of England."[92] William Sampson claimed in 1819 that Grimsby dissenters were his "most steady supporters."[93]

These conditions at the parish level — evidence of the fluid nature of denominational loyalties in early Upper Canada[94] — were at the root of a wildly optimistic view of the Church of England's prospects in the colony. In spite of massive and seemingly overwhelming problems, two Anglican clergymen, Richard Pollard and John Strachan, expressed the belief that, if their church had a larger supply of clerical labourers, it would be able to capitalize on the friendliness of rival denominations and transform Upper Canada into a predominantly Anglican society. This kind of talk was not just a passing fancy. The vision of an Anglican Upper Canada rested on old assumptions concerning the unity of church, state and society, and also on the sincerely held conviction that Upper Canadian society was in a state of flux. Furthermore, this vision had a long life, providing the intellectual underpinnings for Strachan's plans in the 1820s to strengthen the Church of England's institutional foundations. To be sure, it would always have practical uses, particularly in attracting British support for the Upper Canadian church, but it was never just a convenient tool. For Strachan in particular, but also for others, the dream of a religiously homogeneous Upper Canada was, at least until the 1830s, the standard by which the Church of England's performance was judged.[95]

Richard Pollard gave concrete expression to the vision of an Anglican Upper Canada in 1818, when he asserted that "the people in every part of the District are willing to assist the Establishment ... the result of regular ministers and regular worship would be the bringing in the Greatest part of the people within the pale of the Church ...."[96] Strachan was equally sanguine in his 1808 report to the SPG, in which he claimed that Methodism, despite its appearance of strength as a result of recent camp meetings, was on the decline and would gradually disappear if there were more Anglican clergymen in the colony.[97] He expressed similar sentiments in an 1815 report on the state of religion in Upper Canada,[98] and in an 1818 letter to Charles Stewart, who later succeeded Mountain as Bishop of Quebec.[99]

One of the most interesting statements on the prospects of the Anglican cause is found in an article by Strachan in the *Christian Recorder*, an Anglican journal which he edited in York for the three years of its brief existence. Writing in March 1819, he made it clear that the Anglican clergy's perception of the religious future of Upper Canada was closely related to their own belief in the Church of England's intrinsic superiority over all other religious groups. Claiming that the church commanded considerable moral influence by reason of its doctrinal purity, inspiring liturgy and status as the established church of the colony, Strachan announced that its position would be further strengthened by the sale of the clergy reserves and by the measures being adopted for the local education of ministerial candidates.[100] He also confidently predicted that the transformation of Upper Canada into a religiously homogeneous society was close at hand, for, in his view, as soon as the Church of England had the necessary financial resources and manpower to make its services available throughout the colony, the members of other faiths would eagerly embrace a church widely known as one of the purest branches of the catholic and apostolic Church of Christ. He declared:

> the prospect of obtaining a respectable Clergyman, would certainly unite neighbourhoods together, and though differing in their religious views, or remembering that their Parents were attached to different principles, they may be at first unwilling to give them up, yet settle a Minister among them to answer their doubts and remove their scruples, to accustom them to the form of worship, and to explain the doctrines of the Gospel, and they will soon collect around him and consider themselves his flock.[101]

Although such a utopian perspective was hopelessly out of touch with the realities of Upper Canadian religious life, it did have positive results in the realm of inter-denominatinal relations. With the exception of John Langhorn, Anglican clergymen in the pre-1820 period did not become involved in sectarian bickering and even cooperated with other denominations at the parish level, particularly in the work of Bible societies. Their attitude was partly a reflection of the liberal Anglicanism of the age — a brand of churchmanship noted for its emphasis on questions of morality rather than on obscure issues of theology, its hazy conception of the Church of England's doctrinal character, and its "softness" on dissent.[102] But the Anglican clergy's good will towards other denominations also had roots closer to home. We can do little more than speculate — Anglican clergymen did not always spell out the assumptions that determined their behaviour — but it seems reasonable to argue that the vision of a religiously homogeneous Upper Canada influenced the clergy's decision to avoid giving offence to other denominations. After all, since the goal of an Anglican Upper Canada seemed to be within reach, the clergy had no reason to become involved in religious wars with their rivals. On the contrary, sectarian strife was to be avoided at all costs because the distrust and rancour produced by such feuding would make Anglicanism less attractive to those outside the fold. By the same token, a church that cooperated fully and enthusiastically with other religious groups in meeting the spiritual needs of Upper Canadians would enhance its popular appeal and thus prepare the way for its eventual triumph.

Mountain, as a resident of Catholic Lower Canada, was never dazzled by visions of a triumphant colonial church. Still, as a churchman with deep intellectual roots in the liberal Anglicanism of the eighteenth century, he too believed in the value of inter-denominational harmony. In his episcopal charge of 1803, for example, Mountain's criticisms of "self-appointed Teachers" who propagated "pernicious error" amongst the credulous multitude[103] went hand in hand — curious though it may seem — with an eloquent plea to Anglicans to show good will towards all. Urging Anglican clergyman to display "charity, meekness, long suffering, forgiveness of injuries" in their relations with other Christians,[104] Mountain argued passionately that "nothing can be more palpably unreasonable and absurd, than to persecute and hate each other because we differ ... nothing can be more preposterous, than to condemn men without mercy, merely because we are persuaded that they err!"[105]

Equally revealing was a conflict that pitted Mountain and Stuart against John Langhorn, the one clergyman in the pre-1820 period who had no use for the principle of inter-denominational harmony. The underlying cause of this internal split in Upper Canadian Anglicanism was the personal character of Langhorn himself. During his twenty-six-year ministry in Upper Canada, Langhorn was an object of curiosity to Anglicans and non-Anglicans alike. Apart from his obesity, two of Langhorn's most striking peculiarities were his habit of bathing daily in Lake Ontario, even in the depths of winter, and his insistence on walking rather than riding between his various missions, with a rucksack containing all his earthly possessions slung over his back.[106] But Langhorn attracted attention in other ways as well. Although he was a good-hearted soul, loved by many for his acts of personal kindness, he could be exasperating. An old-fashioned High Churchman in an age dominated by theological liberalism, Langhorn was obsessed — the word is not an overstatement — with rubrical regularity. For instance, he had nothing but contempt for what he regarded as Stuart's negligence in observing the rubrics of the marriage ceremony.[107] When Stuart's son, George Okill, dared to officiate without a surplice, Langhorn informed the SPG that he would have nothing further to do with this "presbyterian preacher," adding that "if I could get safely to England, I could wish I was there to tell the people what use their charity is applied to."[108] In his own parishes, Langhorn decided not to church two women when they expressed their unwillingness to kneel during the ceremony;[109] he solemnized marriages only in buildings set aside for religious worship and only within certain specified hours;[110] he refused to comfort and pray with a sick person unless his prayer book was ready at hand.[111] In sum, considering his unusual behaviour, Langhorn had no reason to be startled when his Hallowell and Fredericksburgh congregations decided in 1805 that they no longer wanted his services.[112]

The same inflexibility was evident in Langhorn's relations with dissenters. Believing they were sinful schismatics who were doomed in the world to come,[113] Langhorn would go to any lengths to avoid coming into contact with them. He would not walk on the same side of the road as a dissenter,[114] and he refused to enter the house of a woman who had been married by a Presbyterian minister.[115] When this same minister offered him a ride in his buggy, Langhorn self-righteously replied: "Sir, you are a promoter [of] Schism in the flock of Christ. I cannot therefore have any intercourse with you, much less accept any favour from you. Please keep at your side of the road & go your way."[116] In order to ridicule Methodism, Langhorn composed a satirical ditty which he circulated throughout his mission and on occasion even sang himself.[117] More seriously, in the late 1790s he took the ludicrous position that all marriages performed by non-Anglican clergymen before the passage of the Marriage Act of 1793 were invalid and the parties concerned living in a state of adultery — a state from which he would gladly help them escape by remarrying them, to each other or to any other partner they might desire.[118] When two couples who had been married by a Lutheran minister actually announced their wish to exchange partners, Langhorn was willing to accommodate them. The Church of England was saved from embarrassment only by the decision of the couples themselves to abandon their prank.[119]

As Mountain's ecclesiastical commissary in Upper Canada, Stuart had the job of enforcing discipline amongst the clergy. In Langhorn's case, his hands were full. Stuart was always contemptuous of Langhorn, clearly regarding him as an uneducated simpleton who conspicuously lacked the qualities of a civilized gentleman — qualities much prized by Anglican clergymen throughout the first half of the nineteenth century.[120] Yet, despite his dislike of the man, his initial attitude was indulgent. In a letter to Inglis in 1788, Stuart began by noting that Langhorn "has so many Singularities in Manner & Dress that the real Friends to the Interest of our Church have often wished him in England again," but he then added that "nothing can be objected to his moral character, or his attention to Church Rituals" and that "his Neighbours, being now accustomed to his Oddities & Absurdities & discovering Honesty & Simplicity at Bottom are more and more reconciled to their Fate."[121] However, as time passed, it became increasingly difficult for Stuart to dismiss Langhorn as an annoying but harmless eccentric. By the late 1790s it had become apparent to Stuart that Langhorn's antics were not only alienating members of the Anglican communion but also driving a wedge between the Church of England and dissenting denominations. Accordingly, he began writing angry letters to Mountain calling attention to the behaviour of Langhorn, whom he now regarded as an "incorrigible animal,"[122] and stressing the importance of bringing him into line. In 1797 he reported that Langhorn's offer to remarry couples not originally married by Anglican clergymen "has made much Noise, and given Occasion to Dissenters to use great Freedom of Speech."[123] In 1801 he expressed his opinion that "Mr. Langhorn's uncouth Manners and illiberal Conduct, have given the Methodists, and a dissenting Minister in his Neighbourhood, an Opportunity of drawing away many of his former Congregation."[124] When he learned of Langhorn's musical parody of Methodism, he angrily complained that "he is untaught, unteachable, & incorrigible...his conduct... has been such, as to bring a scandal not only on the clerical dignity, but on our profession as Churchmen ... unless he alters his conduct, he will be forsaken & left to himself without the appearance of a Congregation."[125]

These reports on Langhorn's conduct placed Mountain in an awkward position. Like Stuart, Mountain was convinced that Langhorn's misguided zeal and simple-minded bigotry posed a serious threat to the interests of the church. In 1797 he told Stuart that Langhorn's behaviour with regard to non-Anglican marriages was "unquestionably impolitic, injudicious, & absurd ... tell him that I hope he will conduct himself with greater circumspection & decorum for the future."[126] A few years later he sadly stated that "I wish with all my heart he were removed from a situation for which he is so utterly unqualified & from the exercise of functions which he disgraces."[127] Yet at the same time Mountain was only too aware that he was powerless to do more than admonish and rebuke, since Langhorn's actions, as Stuart himself admitted, were legally unimpeachable.[128] Of course, with any other clergyman the mere expression of episcopal displeasure would have been regarded in a serious light. But in Langhorn's case, things were not so simple. When the SPG, on information supplied by Mountain and Stuart, severely reprimanded Langhorn for his endless bickering with Methodists, he responded with one of the strangest *ad hominem* attacks ever delivered by an Anglican clergyman in Upper Canada. In his 1805 report to the SPG he wrote bitterly that "I hope you did not send me here to be railed at and abused by the Methodists, and that I should be still, and hold my tongue." How could he be expected to obey the orders of his bishop when that individual was "a free mason, and converses by masonic signs, and expects that his meaning is to be understood by his mumping?" Given Mountain's conduct, Langhorn concluded, "it is no wonder if I oftentimes transgress."[129]

Oddly enough, Mountain's and Stuart's commitment to interdenominational harmony was shared by John Strachan, who in the 1820s and 1830s was to lead the Anglican crusade against "sectarianism." Before 1820 Strachan's prejudices against dissent were always balanced by his awareness that the progress of the Church of England depended upon the maintenance of amicable relations with other denominations. During these years his attacks on dissent were relatively few in number and restrained in tone.[130] In addition, he felt little hesitation in publicly professing his own belief in the ideal of interdenominational harmony, since from his point of view the preservation of such good will was a vital part of the Church of England's strategy as it struggled to become the "national" church of Upper Canada. In a sermon of 1804, Strachan denounced those self-righteous and narrow-minded zealots who thought that their church alone was holy in the sight of God. If such persons were sincere in their faith, he noted, they "would perceive that God had servants among every denomination of Christians and that it was not for them to pass judgment upon their brethren."[131] Similarly, in an article he wrote in 1811 for the *Kingston Gazette* under the pseudonym of "The Reckoner," he specifically criticized religious bigotry as one of the manifestations of that spirit of exclusiveness which was so prevalent in society.[132]

The pages of the *Christian Recorder* also revealed Strachan's belief in the importance of fostering good-will among rival denominations at this critical point in the Church of England's history. Outlining his plans for the *Recorder* to Mountain, Strachan remarked that "I will gradually lead my readers in favour of the Church taking care to insert nothing particularly offensive to Dissenters; as the work gains ground we can be more explicit, but caution is necessary as the whole of the population not of our Church is ready to join against us."[133] Caution was certainly the keynote of the first issue of the *Recorder*. In an article on the "History and Present State of Religion in Upper Canada," Strachan was lavish in his praise of the Presbyterian and Catholic clergy.[134] The Methodist itinerants, against whom "serious political objections" could be raised, were extolled for "preserving a religious feeling in many parts of the Province, where it was becoming dead" and for "undergo-

In His Name

ing many fatigues and privations to reclaim the vicious, and to soften the hardened." After stating that "such benevolent exertions ought to be applauded ... they are entitled to the respectful consideration of their fellow Christians," Strachan ended by urging all denominations to cooperate in the dissemination of the Gospel.[135]

Perhaps the best example of the strategy of moderation pursued by the Church of England in the pre-1820 period was the work of the Bible and Common Prayer Book Society of Upper Canada. This organization had its origins in November 1816, when Robert Addison established a Niagara auxiliary of the British and Foreign Bible Society, an inter-denominational body founded by Anglican Evangelicals in protest against the exclusively Church of England character of the Society for Promoting Christian Knowledge (SPCK). In his address on this occasion, Addison announced that Britain, recently the divine instrument of preserving the "blessings of civil government" in Europe, was now to be the divine instrument of spreading the word of God through Upper Canada. He also praised the cooperation between various denominations which had characterized the parent Society's work, and expressed the hope that the widespread possession of bibles would effectively combat drunkenness among the lower orders.[136]

Addison's initiative may have been responsible for the formation in York, one month later, of the Bible and Common Prayer Book Society of Upper Canada.[137] The decision to make the dissemination of the Prayer Book one of the responsibilities of the new Society was not meant to discourage the involvement of dissenters, for subscribers could confine their financial support to the distribution of bibles — a provision which, as Strachan declared, opened the door "to all denominations of Christians, to all who are anxious to extend the limits of vital religion."[138] The Upper Canadian body, moreover, was formally connected with the inter-denominational British and Foreign Bible Society, which Strachan lauded for its success in extinguishing "all party spirit and narrow views" and infusing "into all ranks such a charitable zeal for the general interests of Christianity, as cannot fail to produce the happiest effects."[139]

In 1818 the Bible and Common Prayer Book Society was divided into two sections, one distributing bibles and the other prayer books, and in the following year the new Prayer Book Society became a branch committee of the SPCK.[140] These changes, however, far from being a reflection of increasing tension between Anglicans and dissenters, were actually defended as a means of allaying the suspicion that the Bible and Common Prayer Book Society was a Church of England organization. Under the altered arrangements the Bible Society, while open to all denominations, permitted dissenters to distribute the Scriptures unaccompanied by the Anglican Prayer Book.[141] The Church of England had thus been instrumental in forging an inter-denominational structure that accommodated sectarian differences, an achievement which at least two of its clergymen regarded with pride. In November 1819 a British missionary named Fenton declared that he saw the work of the Upper Canada Bible Society as evidence of the enlightened atmosphere of the age: "We live in days of candour, when party distinction is lost, when sectarian opposition is absorbed by Christian charity, when all are uniting and assimilating into one spirit and making a simultaneous effort for the distribution of the Bible, and that without comment."[142] Strachan echoed these remarks at a meeting of the District Committee of the SPCK, the very meeting at which the dissolution of the Prayer Book Society was announced. With reference to the creation of a separate Bible Society, Strachan said:

> we are taught to have respect to the weakness of a brother, and his scruples, should we think them wrong, are entitled to favour, as they indicate the force of conscience. In this country, where all the various denominations of Christians meet together, far from their native homes and the lively and interesting scenes of their childhood, there is generally a disposition to be kindly and affectionate one towards another. This spirit should be cherished, and no society can promote this more than one for disseminating the Scriptures.... this is the age of religious and moral improvement .... Christianity is extending on every side, it is breaking down the walls of partition, and it calls for all its friends to assist in the gracious work.[143]

In His Name

Underlying the Anglican clergy's good will towards other denominations was a set of very special circumstances. While the Church of England had more than its share of problems in the first few decades of Upper Canada's history, it also retained its supreme self-confidence, which was rooted in its historic role as the established church of the mother country and its special status in Upper Canada under the Constitutional Act, the fluctuating state of the colony's denominational balance, and the lack of divisive issues in inter-church relations. Reflecting this mood, Anglican clergymen, with visions of religious homogeneity dancing in their heads, could afford to be broadminded in their dealings with their church's rivals. Later decades, however, would see a very different Upper Canada, where religious loyalties were more fixed and inter-denominatonal hostility a basic fact of life. These changes led the Anglican clergy to re-evaluate their perspective on their church's prospects, and also to modify some of the ways in which their church functioned. The results for Upper Canadian Anglicanism — and the colony as a whole — would be momentous.

NOTES

1. This discussion of Church of England history draws upon several secondary sources. The point about the changing view of the church-state connection during the reign of George III is taken from J.C.D. Clark, *English Society, 1688-1832: Ideology, Social Structure and Political Practice During the Ancien Regime* (Cambridge, U.K., 1985). The most important of the other sources used are: John R.H. Moorman, *A History of the Church of England* (New York, 1954); Norman Sykes, *Church and State in England in the Eighteenth Century* (Cambridge, 1934); Gerald R. Cragg, *From Puritanism to the Age of Reason* (Cambridge, 1950); Gerald R. Cragg, *The Church and the Age of Reason, 1648-1789* (London, 1960); William Haller, *Foxe's Book of Martyrs and the Elect Nation* (London, 1963); E.G. Rupp, *Studies in the Making of the English Protestant Tradition* (Cambridge, 1947); W.H. Hutton, *The English Church from the Accession of Charles I to the Death of Anne* (London, 1903); Christopher Hill, *The Century of Revolution, 1603-1714* (London, 1961).

2. Judith Fingard, *The Anglican Design in Loyalist Nova Scotia* (London, 1972), pp. 114-15.

3. Adam Shortt and Arthur Doughty, eds., *Documents Relating to the Constitutional History of Canada, 1759-1828*, 3 vols., I (Ottawa, 1907), p. 86.

4. Ibid., pp. 139-40 and 217. In the 1780s, similar instructions were issued to Haldimand. See ibid., p. 475.

5. Ibid., pp. 139-40.

6. Ibid., p. 403.

7. Ibid., p. 425.

8. Fingard, *The Anglican Design in Loyalist Nova Scotia*, pp. 41-42 and 116.

9. H.C. Stuart, *The Church of England in Canada, 1759-1793, from the Conquest to the Establishment of the See of Quebec* (Montreal, 1893), p. 14.

10. Ibid., pp. 24-25.

11. T.R. Millman, *Jacob Mountain, First Lord Bishop of Quebec: A Study in Church and State, 1793-1825* (Toronto, 1947), pp. 36-37.

12. These three clergymen, all of whom were Europeans, had been sent to Quebec by the British government. Curious though it may seem, imperial administrators were convinced that French-speaking clerics were much needed in Quebec to serve that colony's large population of French Protestants. See Stuart, *The Church of England in Canada*, pp. 24-35.

13   Stuart, *The Church of England in Canada*, p. 29.
14   Ibid., p. 84.
15   Ibid., p. 83.
16   On the intellectual response to the American Revolution, see Vincent T. Harlow, *The Founding of the Second British Empire, 1763-93*, 2 vols., II (London, 1964). On conservative ideology in the late eighteenth century, see J.C.D. Clark, *English Society, 1688-1832*.
17   Harlow, *The Founding of the Second British Empire*, II, p. 736.
18   See the following: John M. Norris, "Proposals for Promoting Religion and Literature in Canada, Nova Scotia, and New Brunswick," *CHR*, XXXVI (1953), pp. 335-401; William Knox, *Extra Official State Papers* (London, 1789); Fingard, *The Anglican Design in Loyalist Nova Scotia*, pp. 2-3 and 9-11; Alan Wilson, *The Clergy Reserves of Upper Canada: A Canadian Mortmain* (Toronto, 1968), pp. 9-10.
19   Harlow, *The Founding of the Second British Empire*, II, pp. 735-42 and 755.
20   Fingard, *The Anglican Design in Loyalist Nova Scotia*, pp. 3-4.
21   Ibid., p. 83.
22   Ibid., p. 74. For information on the life of Bishop Inglis, see also Reginald V. Harris, *Charles Inglis: Missionary, Loyalist, Bishop (1734-1816)* (Toronto, 1937); and Brian Cuthbertson, *The First Bishop: A Biography of Charles Inglis* (Halifax, 1987).
23   Fingard, *The Anglican Design in Loyalist Nova Scotia*, p. 74.
24   Ibid., pp. 149-51.
25   For Pitt's and Grenville's ideas on these issues, see Harlow, *The Founding of the Second British Empire*, II, pp. 735-42 and 755-73.
26   The terms of the Constitutional Act may be found in Shortt and Doughty, *Documents Relating to the Constitutional History of Canada*, I, pp. 694-708 (clauses 35-42 related to the Church of England and are found between pp. 702-6).
27   See Gerald Craig, *Upper Canada: The Formative Years, 1784-1841* (Toronto, 1963), pp. 16-17. Craig quotes (p. 278, note 34) a letter from Colonial Secretary Henry Dundas to Lord Dorchester in 1794. In that letter Dundas wrote that "temporary and discretionary" allowances might be made to Presbyterian ministers, "for your Lordship will recollect, in framing the Canada Act, that the reservation for the Church and the Crown in all Grants of Land, was fixed at a larger proportion than was originally intended, with a view to enable the King to make from those Reservations, such an Allowance to Presbyterian Ministers, Teachers and Schools, as His Majesty should, from time to time, think proper."

28 Shortt and Doughty, *Documents Relating to the Constitutional History of Canada*, I, p. 704.

29 E.A. Cruikshank, ed., *The Correspondence of Lieut. Governor John Graves Simcoe*, 5 vols., IV (Toronto, 1926), Simcoe to Portland, 30 Oct. 1795, p. 116.

30 On the career and thought of Simcoe, see Craig, *Upper Canada, 1784-1841: The Formative Years*, pp. 20-41; S.R. Mealing, "The Enthusiasms of John Graves Simcoe," *CHAR*, 1958, pp. 50-62; and S.R. Mealing, "John Graves Simcoe," *Dictionary of Canadian Biography*, V (Toronto, 1983), pp. 754-59.

31 Quoted in Wilson, *The Clergy Reserves*, p. 17.

32 Cruikshank, *The Correspondence of John Graves Simcoe*, I (Toronto, 1923), Simcoe to Dundas, 6 Nov. 1792, p. 251.

33 J.S. Moir, *Church and State in Canada, 1627-1867: Basic Documents* (Toronto, 1967), pp. 142-43.

34 Ibid., pp. 144-45.

35 Millman, *Jacob Mountain*, p. 15. The above interpretation of Mountain is based on this work.

36 Ibid., p. 51.

37 Richard A. Preston, ed., *Kingston before the War of 1812* (Toronto, 1959), Mountain to Dundas, 15 Sept. 1794, p. 292.

38 John Strachan, *Observations on the Provision Made for the Maintenance of a Protestant Clergy* (London, 1827), p. 37.

39 The best study of the Loyalists in the Thirteen Colonies is W.H. Nelson's *The American Tory* (New York, 1961). For a good introduction to the Loyalists in Ontario, see Bruce Wilson, *As She Began: An Illustrated Introduction to Loyalist Ontario* (Toronto and Charlottetown, 1981).

40 Craig, *Upper Canada: The Formative Years*, pp. 7-8.

41 See J.S. Moir, *Enduring Witness: A History of the Presbyterian Church in Canada* (Toronto, n.d.), pp. 48 and 52-53; Stuart Ivison and Fred Rosser, *The Baptists in Upper and Lower Canada before 1820* (Toronto, 1936), pp. 105-7; C.R. Cronmiller, *A History of the Lutheran Church in Canada* (1961), pp. 73-76, 82-83 and 87-88; C.J. Burkholder, *A Brief History of the Mennonites in Ontario* (1935), pp. 29-30 and 43-52; A.G. Dorland, *A History of the Society of Friends (Quakers) in Canada* (Toronto, 1927), pp. 50-52; George F. Playter, *History of Methodism in Canada* (Toronto, 1862), pp. 10 and 15; and H.A. Scott, "The Roman Catholic Church East of the Great Lakes, 1760-1917," in Shortt and Doughty, eds., *Canada and Its Provinces*, XI (Toronto, 1913), pp. 24-27.

42 A good account of the development of religious pluralism in Upper Canada before the War of 1812 can be found in Grant, *A Profusion of Spires*, pp. 20-35.

43 Ivison and Rosser, *The Baptists in Upper and Lower Canada*, pp. 82-120.

44 Ibid., pp. 121-54 and 34-55.

45 Playter, *History of Methodism*, pp. 20-25.

46 Ibid., pp. 44-45.

47 Ibid., pp. 54, 67, 84 and 98.

48 For the life of Macdonell, see J.E. Rea, *Bishop Alexander Macdonell and the Politics of Upper Canada* (Toronto, 1974).

49 Scott, "The Roman Catholic Church East of the Great Lakes," p. 50.

50 See Moir, *Enduring Witness*, pp. 48-53 and 66-68; and Ivison and Rosser, *The Baptists in Upper and Lower Canada*, pp. 82-120.

51 Playter, *History of Methodism*, p. 143.

52 Ibid., p. 193. Included in the total of twenty-four preachers were a few British Wesleyan missionaries stationed in eastern Upper Canada.

53 On the SPG, see H.P. Thompson, *Into All Lands: The History of the Society for the Propagation of the Gospel in Foreign Parts, 1710-1950* (London, 1951).

54 The clergymen stationed in Upper Canada in 1819 were Robert Addison, John Langhorn, George Okill Stuart, John Strachan, Richard Pollard, John Gunther Weagant, Ralph Leeming, Salter Mountain and William Sampson.

55 NAC, MG 17, B1, SPG Journals, vol. 27, 16 Nov. 1787.

56 Preston, *Kingston Before the War of 1812*, Stuart to Inglis, 6 July 1788, pp. 133-38. Preston claims that during Stuart's ministry Kingston was an island of Anglicanism in a sea of dissent, but he fails to advance convincing evidence to support this assertion. It is true that Stuart was quite successful in repulsing the incursions of the Methodists into his mission, and that Anglicans were more numerous in Kingston than in other parts of the province. However, other denominations, particularly Presbyterians, were extremely powerful in Kingston. As noted earlier in this chapter, Stuart estimated that only one-eighth of his flock were Anglicans.

57 SPG Journals, vol. 27, 18 March 1796.

58 Ibid., vol. 29, 18 Nov. 1804.

59 NAC, MG 17, B1, SPG Letters, Series C, Box IVA/38, no. 439, 14 Aug. 1788.

Establishment and Survival

60 SPG Journals, vol. 28, 19 Nov. 1802.
61 Ibid., 8 Nov. 1803.
62 SPG Letters, Series C, Box IVA/38, no. 439, 10 Oct. 1806.
63 Ibid., 18 April 1811.
64 SPG Journals, vol. 28, 18 Feb. 1803.
65 AO, Strachan Papers, Strachan to Brown, 27 Oct. 1803.
66 Playter, *History of Methodism*, pp. 80-83 and 160.
67 SPG Journals, vol. 30, 19 Jan. 1810.
68 SPG Letters, Series C, Box IVA/38, no. 441, 20 March 1810.
69 SPG Journals, vol. 31, 18 July 1817.
70 Ibid., 16 Jan. 1818.
71 Ibid.
72 Ibid., 20 June 1817.
73 Wilson, *The Clergy Reserves*, pp. 18-25 and 37.
74 For the role of the state and the SPG in the payment of the Upper Canadian clergy, see Chapter Seven.
75 SPG Letters, Series C, Box IVA/38, no. 439, 14 Aug. 1788.
76 Ibid., 15 May 1806.
77 Ibid., 6 Oct. 1812.
78 H.P. Thompson, *Into All Lands*, p. 142.
79 SPG Journals, vol. 27, 18 March 1796. See also Preston,*Kingston before the War of 1812*, Stuart to Mountain, 1 Nov. 1795, pp. 308-9.
80 SPG Journals, vol. 28, 22 Nov. 1799.
81 Ibid., 16 Feb. 1801.
82 SPG *Report*, 1785, pp. 47-51.
83 Preston, *Kingston before the War of 1812*, Stuart to Inglis, 6 July 1788, pp. 133-38.
84 SPG Journals, vol. 27, 21 May 1790.
85 Preston, *Kingston before the War of 1812*, Stuart to Inglis, 11 March 1792, pp. 283-84.
86 Ibid., Stuart to Mountain, 1 Nov. 1795, pp. 308-9.
87 See Chapter Seven.
88 Preston, *Kingston before the War of 1812*, Stuart to Inglis, September 1789, pp. 149-51.

In His Name

89 SPG Journals, vol. 27, 16 Nov. 1787.

90 Preston, *Kingston before the War of 1812*, Stuart to Inglis, September 1789, pp. 149-51.

91 SPG Letters, Series C, Box IVA/38, no. 441, 26 Sept. 1805.

92 SPG Journals, vol. 31, 20 June 1817.

93 SPG *Report*, 1819, pp. 71-72.

94 This point is commented upon in Grant, *A Profusion of Spires*, pp. 52-53 and 67.

95 The decline of Anglican optimism in the 1820s and 1830s is traced in Chapters Two to Five.

96 SPG Journals, vol. 31, 18 July 1818.

97 Ibid., vol. 29, 28 May 1808.

98 AO, Strachan Papers, 1 March 1815.

99 Ibid., Strachan to Stewart, 16 Feb. 1818.

100 "History and Present State of Religion in Upper Canada," *Christian Recorder*, March 1819, p. 11.

101 Ibid., p. 12.

102 For studies of liberal Anglicanism in the eighteenth and early nineteenth centuries, see: Sykes, *Church and State in England in the 18th Century*; Abbey and Overton, *The English Church in the Eighteenth Century*; Cragg, *The Church and the Age of Reason*; Roland N. Stromberg, *Religious Liberalism in Eighteenth-Century England* (Oxford, 1954); Yngve Brilioth, *The Anglican Revival: Studies in the Oxford Movement* (London, 1933).

103 Jacob Mountain, *A Charge Delivered to the Clergy of the Diocese of Quebec in August, 1803* (Quebec, 1803), pp. 26-27.

104 Ibid., p. 13.

105 Ibid., pp. 11-12.

106 Ernest Hawkins, *Annals of the Diocese of Toronto* (London, 1848), pp. 30 and 43.

107 SPG Letters, Series C, Box IVA/38, no. 439, 8 May 1810.

108 Ibid., 6 Oct. 1812.

109 Ibid., 14 Aug. 1788.

110 Ibid., "Memorandum of ... Rev. John Langhorn," Series C, Box V/46, no. 545.

111 ADO, Stuart Papers, Folio 2, Stuart to Inglis, 8 Oct. 1791.
112 SPG Journals, vol. 29, 15 Nov. 1805.
113 Preston, *Kingston before the War of 1812*, Stuart to Mountain, 29 Oct. 1802, pp. 321-23.
114 Hawkins, *Annals of the Diocese of Toronto*, p. 40.
115 SPG Letters, "Memorandum of Rev. John Langhorn," Series C, Box V/46, no. 545.
116 Ibid.
117 SPG Journals, vol. 29, 17 Jan. 1805.
118 Preston, *Kingston before the War of 1812*, Stuart to Mountain, 18 April 1797, pp. 312-13.
119 Ibid.
120 See Chapter Seven for a discussion of the class attitudes of the Anglican clergy.
121 Preston, *Kingston before the War of 1812*, Stuart to Inglis, 6 July 1788, pp. 133-38.
122 ADO, Stuart Papers, Folio 2, John to James Stuart, 11 Oct. 1802.
123 Preston, *Kingston before the War of 1812*, Stuart to Mountain, 18 April 1797, pp. 312-13.
124 Ibid., Stuart to Mountain, 11 May 1801, p. 319.
125 SPG Journals, vol. 29, 17 Jan. 1805.
126 Preston, *Kingston before the War of 1812*, Mountain to Stuart, 21 May 1797, pp. 313-14.
127 Ibid., Mountain to Stuart, 10 Oct. 1804, pp. 324-25.
128 ADO, Stuart Papers, Folio 2, Stuart to Inglis, 8 Oct. 1791.
129 SPG Letters, Series C, Box IVA/38, no. 439, 4 Oct. 1805.
130 See Chapter Four.
131 AO, Strachan Sermons, "So the last shall be first and the first last" (23 Dec. 1804). This date refers to the first time the sermon in question was preached. The same applies to all subsequent references to the Strachan Sermons.
132 *Kingston Gazette*, "The Reckoner," 29 Jan. 1811.
133 BRMTL, Strachan Papers, Scadding Collection, Strachan to Mountain, 12 March 1819.

In His Name

134 *Christian Recorder*, March 1819, pp. 14-15.
135 Ibid., pp. 15-16.
136 *Christian Recorder*, March 1819, pp. 36-37.
137 Ibid., p. 37.
138 Ibid., p. 39.
139 Ibid.
140 Ibid., December 1819, pp. 377-81. In these pages an address by Strachan clarifies the complicated structural evolution of the Bible and Common Prayer Book Society of Upper Canada.
141 Ibid., pp. 378-79.
142 Ibid., November 1819, p. 360.
143 Ibid., December 1819, pp. 378-79. Significantly, it also appears that Strachan remained actively involved with the Bible Society of Upper Canada. See the *Christian Recorder*, December 1820, pp. 357-63. For Strachan's changing attitude towards this organization in the 1830s, see Chapter Four.

CHAPTER TWO

PREACHING THE WORD

For the Church of England, one of the most striking and distressing features of Upper Canadian life in the 1820s and 1830s was the entrenched position of its denominational rivals. Religious diversity, of course, was nothing new, but in the post-1820 period it became even more pronounced. In spreading its message in this pluralistic society, the Church of England set out in a new direction, adopting an energetic approach to evangelization and modifying its institutional structure to meet the needs of a rapidly growing society. Its efforts enjoyed a fair measure of success, certainly far more than has been generally recognized. Yet, despite the Church of England's accomplishments, the religious conditions of the 1820s and 1830s — with dissent growing by leaps and bounds, and countless Anglicans inadequately served, if served at all, by their church — were a bitter disappointment to the Anglican clergy. In the main, they retained their optimism in the 1820s, when the dream of an Anglican Upper Canada was still alive, but not in the 1830s. By the time of the rebellion, their view of the Church of England's future was no longer naive. The anxiety they displayed, the fears they expressed as they surveyed the religious landscape of the province, made it clear that the vision of a triumphant Church of England was about to become a thing of the past.

* * * * *

The religiously pluralistic nature of Upper Canada in the 1820s and 1830s is documented in several secondary works and also in censuses conducted in 1839 and 1842. As noted in the earlier discussion of the

In His Name

religious diversity of Upper Canada in the pre-1820 period, some of these sources, a few of the secondary works in particular, are not the last word in accuracy, but the general patterns they highlight are beyond dispute.

The Methodists, with their shrewd revivalist techniques and superbly efficient organizational structure, continued to make impressive strides: in 1825 there were 35 preachers and 6,875 members;[1] in 1830, 55 preachers and 11,348 members;[2] and in 1835, two years after the union of the Upper Canadian Methodist Conference and the English Wesleyans, 77 preachers and 15,056 members.[3] Three other denominations, the Baptists, Presbyterians and Roman Catholics, received an immense boost with the influx of thousands upon thousands of English, Scottish and Irish immigrants. By 1835 the Baptist cause, greatly strengthened by the settlement of large numbers of Scottish Baptists in eastern Upper Canada, was represented by 40 resident ministers and 60 to 70 churches, a dramatic increase from the 10 clergymen and 15 congregations of 1820.[4] The Church of Scotland and its various secessionist offshoots, also strengthened by immigration, had more than 40 clergymen and 60 congregations by the time of the rebellion.[5] The Roman Catholic Church, which by 1820 had only 7 priests and 15,000 members, could by 1840 boast 34 priests, 48 parishes and approximately 60,000 members, most of whom were from the south of Ireland.[6]

The Church of England also made significant progress. In the 1820s and 1830s Anglican immigration from the British Isles transformed it from the beleaguered denomination of earlier years into one that surpassed all its rivals in popular support. In 1839 a religious census of Upper Canada showed that the Church of England was the single largest denomination in the London, Niagara, Home, Newcastle and Johnstown districts. In the Eastern, Prince Edward and Bathurst districts, Anglicans were outnumbered by Presbyterians and Methodists, but the various denominational divisions within these two religious groups were not taken into account. No statistics were provided for the Western, Gore, Midland and Ottawa districts.[7] The accuracy of this census was corroborated by the census of 1842, which revealed that in the colony as a whole Anglicans outnumbered the adherents of any other denomination. In that year the Church of England counted 107,291 members, while its closest rivals, the Church of Scotland, the

Roman Catholic Church and the Methodists, had only 77,929, 65,203 and 55,667 members.[8]

Thanks to the efforts of the SPG, which after 1813 found its financial position greatly improved as a result of annual parliamentary grants,[9] the Upper Canadian church also had the advantage of more clergy. The first sign of better days came in 1818 and 1819, when five clergymen, Joseph Thompson, Michael Harris, Romaine Rolph, William Stoughton and William Macaulay, were appointed to Upper Canadian parishes, bringing the total in the colony to thirteen.[10] In subsequent years the position of the church was further bolstered by a steady stream of clergymen from the British Isles, and by SPG financial assistance to ministerial candidates who were receiving their divinity training under clergymen already stationed in Upper Canada.[11] The resulting increase in the church's supply of clerical manpower was so great that by the 1830s a force of Anglican clergymen had been built up which was almost equal in strength to the army of itinerant preachers employed by the Methodists: in 1833 there were forty clergymen in the colony,[12] and by 1836 this figure had increased to sixty-eight.[13]

Yet the Church of England's success in the Upper Canada of the 1820s and 1830s cannot be attributed exclusively to the arrival of Anglican immigrants from the British Isles and to a substantial increase in the number of clergy. It was also partly the result of a new perspective, detectable both at the parish level and in the upper echelons of the church, on the value of missionary activity.

Initially, in the 1790s, the three clergymen resident in the colony — John Stuart, John Langhorn and Robert Addison — had shown considerable energy and determination in spreading the Anglican message. Stuart occasionally visited the Iroquois settled on the far distant Grand River in the Niagara district; he made semi-annual trips to the Mohawk settlement on the Bay of Quinte; once a year he made a missionary tour of the "lower settlements" in the vicinity of Cornwall, a journey that covered 140 miles; and these extra-parochial labours were in addition to his annual travels in the Kingston area, a demanding trip of 200 miles. Similarly, while Langhorn's sphere of missionary work was restricted by his refusal to ride a horse, he too served a district that was by no means small: excluding Fredericksburgh and Ernesttown, which he visited on alternate Sundays, and Adolphustown, which he visited on a less regular but still frequent basis, Langhorn had eight stations, each of which he visited approximately ten times a year; these pastoral tours meant gruelling walks of fifty to seventy miles. Even the scholarly Addison was something of an itinerant. Although Stuart claimed that Addison was ill-equipped, by reason of his "temper and qualifications," to minister effectively to the "generality of the vulgar" on the Upper Canadian frontier,[14] Addison in the years before 1820 was far from lazy as a clergyman. Besides serving his Niagara congregation, he made a point in the 1790s of undertaking an annual circuit of 150 miles, and also of visiting the Grand River Mohawks, seventy miles from his own parish, a few times each year.[15]

Curiously, the Anglican clergy's missionary zeal declined sharply in the first two decades of the nineteenth century. The reasons for the decline are obscure; the personalities of some of the clergymen involved, a complacency born of fanciful visions of an Anglican Upper Canada, and a continuing attachment to the traditional ideal of compact parishes may all have had something to do with it. Whatever the reasons, however, the facts themselves are clear. During these years John Stuart generally restricted his labours to Kingston and the Mohawk settlement on the Bay of Quinte, while Robert Addison abandoned his missionary journeys and instead contented himself with visiting "neighbouring villages" once a month and making the occasional trip to the Mohawk mission on the Grand River. In the case of both men, advancing age may have accounted for their increasing lethargy, but age was no excuse for the clergymen appointed after 1800. John Gunther Weagant did not venture beyond his two missions of Osnabruck and Williamsburgh. Salter J. Mountain seldom left the secure confines of Cornwall. Ralph Leeming remained entrenched in Ancaster until 1818, when he began assisting Addison in serving the Grand River Mohawks. Richard Pollard, though performing only a weekly service in Sandwich and a monthly service in Amherstburg, did not pay regular visits to the Anglican settlements on Lake Erie and the Thames River until 1816. George Okill Stuart, during his twelve years as the incumbent of York, had virtually no duties outside of his immediate parish, and after his appointment to Kingston in 1812 he waited until 1815 before undertaking his first missionary journey, a 160-mile trip to the vacant parish of Elizabethtown and Augusta. While John Strachan was stationed in Cornwall from 1803 to 1812 he made only the occasional visit to Oswegatchie and Augusta, and he itinerated even less after his move to York in 1812. Indeed, in 1821 he was relieved of his "country church" at York Mills when he complained that it detracted from his responsibilities in the parish of York.[16]

This decline of missionary zeal makes the Church of England's crusading spirit in the 1820s and 1830s all the more striking. The unparalleled growth of rival denominations in this period, together with the problems posed by the hordes of Anglican immigrants from the British Isles, convinced Anglican clergymen that the Church of England's future depended not only on an increase in clerical manpower, but also on its own willingness to exert itself to the utmost in furthering its own interests. On the political front, this new perspective on the church's position would underlie Strachan's efforts to place the clergy reserves on a sounder footing and to establish an Anglican-controlled university.[17] In the religious sphere, the same determination to improve the church's fortunes gave rise to a renewed interest in missionary activity. An indication of this interest was the Anglican clergy's willingness, in contrast to the attitude of their counterparts in earlier years, to pay regular visits to those neighbouring settlements which lacked the services of a resident minister. By the time of the rebellion the average Anglican clergyman, much in the manner of John Stuart in the 1790s, served two or three parishes in addition to his own immediate charge, and all these stations were separated by distances of anywhere from five to fifty miles.

A few examples will serve to illustrate. Joseph Thompson had four congregations in his parish of Cavan, and besides visiting these stations every Sunday and occasionally on weekdays, he also paid monthly visits to Port Hope, Monaghan, Smith's Creek, Emily and Ops. From 1819 to 1827, when he was transferred to Hallowell, William Macaulay made occasional visits to the Carrying Place, Belleville, Cavan and Darlington, stations which were twenty to forty-eight miles distant from his own parish in Hamilton township. Michael Harris's territory encompassed Perth and its back-settlements, Lanark, Richmond, Beckwith and March, the last of these being fifty miles from Perth. Robert Blakey held regular services in Prescott, Four Corners, the Blue Church and Maitland, and he also paid occasional visits to the

In His Name

townships of Oxford and Scarborough. John Grier claimed with some justice that his mission, which embraced the Carrying Place, Pleasant Bay, Murray, Cold Creek, Frankford, Hillier and Ameliasburg, could employ four clergymen. A.N. Bethune conducted services in Cobourg on Sunday mornings and evenings, on festivals and fastdays, and on weekdays during the Lenten season. He also served the Cobourg gaol and courthouse, Grafton, Hamilton township and Haldimand; from November to April he paid monthly visits to a schoolhouse five miles distant from Cobourg; during the same months he held weekday lectures in houses. His mission covered forty miles, and he estimated that he performed 240 services a year, or an average of four every week.[18]

The Anglican clergy's heightened awareness of the importance of proselytizing also led to a growing demand for itinerant missionaries. In the 1820s the Upper Canadian church enjoyed the services of two: Charles Stewart held the position of visiting missionary in the two Canadas from 1819 until his elevation to the episcopacy in 1826;[19] and George Spratt was a travelling missionary in the townships of Yonge and Bastard from 1824 until his departure for the United States in 1826.[20] Shortly after Spratt left the colony, Stewart, now bishop, informed the SPG that the appointment of another such missionary was imperative if the Church of England was ever to take root in the more isolated settlements of the colony.[21] These representations had the desired effect, for in 1827 George Archbold became travelling missionary in the diocese of Quebec.[22] The continued influx of immigrants in the late 1820s, however, created an impossible burden for the unaided Archbold, and in 1828 John Strachan suggested that additional travelling missionaries be appointed to Upper Canada so that Anglican ministrations might be frequently offered to isolated and religiously destitute settlements. "In every township in this province," he wrote to the SPG after the completion of his first archdiaconal visitation,

> ... the travelling Missionary discovers here and there scattered episcopal families, some times one or two, some times a more considerable number, who are entirely deprived of the ministrations of the Church. Their children are growing up ignorant of our Church, and wandering from her communion. These families were many of them emi-

grants from England and Ireland, and were formerly attached to the doctrines, constitution, and worship of that Church, under whose nurturing care they were born and brought up. In every district there is ample room for one or more additional Missionaries, but there are few places where a congregation can be collected at once sufficiently numerous to employ his undivided services. Yet frequent visits of a month or two at a time, would preserve their attachment to the worship of their fathers. At present they labour under the most serious disadvantages in a new and thinly settled country: many of them will be lost, if Missionaries come not among them.... It is not meant by this, that there should be any delay in settling clergymen so far as our means permit, wherever congregations can be formed. But as we are not always able to place clergymen in every township where they might be useful, the next step is to do all we can, by sending some one round from time to time to greet them in the Lord.[23]

The formation of the Society for Converting and Civilizing the Indians and Propagating the Gospel Among Destitute Settlers of Upper Canada (SCCIPGDS)[24] was the direct result of the Anglican clergy's belief that the religious needs of the colony's immigrants could best be met by a force of itinerant missionaries. The origins of this body dated to 29 October 1830, when a group of Anglican clergy and laity founded the Society for Converting & Civilizing the Indians, an organization whose sole concern was spreading the Anglican message among Indian communities on the Bay of Quinte, the Grand River, Lake St. Clair and the north shore of Lake Huron.[25] At the Society's next meeting on 22 November a decision of major importance was taken: it was then resolved that missionaries would be sent not only to various Indian settlements but also among the religiously destitute white people of the colony. In taking such a step, the Society announced that its objective was to provide the "British Emigrant" with "a continuance of the ministrations to which he is attached — (thus, to him, divesting the wilderness of half its terrors, and preserving unimpaired in his

In His Name

bosom the fear of God and submission to lawful authority, so sincerely inculcated and faithfully exemplified by that communion)."[26]

Although the SCCIPGDS never flourished financially (in 1838 its funds from all sources amounted to only £411[27]), it was able to appoint a number of missionaries in the course of the 1830s. Four were sent to Indian missions: J.D. Cameron served Sault Ste. Marie from 1831 to 1832; J. O'Brian was stationed at the Indian mission on the St. Clair River for an indeterminate length of time; William McMurray replaced Cameron at Sault Ste. Marie in 1832 and remained there until 1840; Saltern Givins was sent to the Mohawk village on the Bay of Quinte in 1833, and he retained this charge until 1850, eight years after the SCCIPGDS had been supplanted by the Church Society.[28] Another four clergymen appointed by the Society served as travelling missionaries: Adam Elliot worked in the Home District from 1832 to 1835, when he moved to the Grand River to take up a permanent charge at the Six Nations mission; W.F.S. Harper was first in the Midland District and then in the Newcastle District before being transferred to the parish of March in 1838; C.T. Wade served in the Newcastle District from 1836 to 1838; G.C. Street was appointed as Wade's replacement in the Newcastle District in 1839, and there he remained until his transfer to the parish of Emily some time in 1840 or 1841.[29]

Elliot, Harper, Wade and Street were assisted by other travelling missionaries in the 1830s. When the imperial government decided in 1831 to terminate its annual grant to the SPG — a decision whose ramifications for the Upper Canadian church will be explored later[30] — Bishop Stewart published an address calling on the British public to come to the assistance of the Canadian church.[31] In response to this appeal, one of Stewart's English relations, the Reverend W.J.D. Waddilove, promptly established a fund to provide the church in the Canadas with additional clerical manpower.[32] In the 1830s the Upper Canadian Travelling Missionary Fund supported Richard Flood as a missionary to the Lake St. Clair Indians, John Gibson as a missionary at Georgiana, Ebenezer Morris as a travelling missionary in the Bathurst, Johnstown and Eastern districts, and Thomas Green and George Petrie as travelling missionaries in the London District. It also contributed to the support of W.F.S. Harper in the Midland District, James Padfield in March and Huntley, Frederick Mack in Amherstburg, James Usher in Brantford, R.V. Rogers in Richmond and J.G. Geddes in Hamilton.[33]

Preaching the Word

Another British organization responsible for the support of travelling missionaries was the Upper Canada Clergy Society. Founded in 1835 by a group of lay Evangelicals,[34] this Society appointed H.H. O'Neill as travelling missionary in the Niagara, Gore and Home districts, F.L. Osler as missionary in Tecumseth, West Gwillimbury and the surrounding countryside in 1837, Frederick O'Meara as travelling missionary in the Home District in 1838, B.C. Hill as travelling missionary in the sprawling Grand River tract in 1838, William Morse as missionary in the town of Paris in 1839, and T.M. Bartlett as missionary at Shanty Bay on Lake Simcoe. As a further proof of its generosity, the Upper Canada Clergy Society supported Dominick Blake after his appointment to the parish of Adelaide in 1833.[35]

The labours of Anglican travelling missionaries in the 1830s equalled those of any Methodist itinerant. Adam Elliot's charge in the Home District embraced thirty-six townships, a sphere of duty that necessitated almost daily sermons and services in houses, barns and fields.[36] W.F.S. Harper had seventeen stations in the Midland District, and he, like Elliot, was compelled by the very size of his mission to preach sermons and perform services virtually every day of the week and in any building that was available, including dissenting schools and meeting houses.[37] Thomas Green had sixteen stations in the London District, and at fourteen of these he conducted services every third week; he also preached sermons daily, and on many Sundays he performed services at three stations which were ten to fifteen miles apart.[38] In the Grand River tract B.C. Hill served thirteen stations which were eight to forty-nine miles distant from his residence in Hamilton, and he held frequent scripture classes to supplement his daily sermons and services.[39] Ebenezer Morris's mission covered nineteen townships and 370 miles.[40] George Petrie had eighteen stations scattered throughout an almost equal number of townships, and some of these stations were from thirty to sixty miles apart.[41] F.L. Osler, a travelling missionary (in fact, if not in name) in a huge 240-mile mission with the parishes of Tecumseth and West Gwillimbury as its nucleus, served twenty townships and twenty-eight congregations.[42]

Many of the congregations of these travelling missionaries, like the congregations of so many Methodist circuit riders, assembled in surroundings which were hardly conducive to spiritual contemplation. F.L. Osler, for example, regularly preached in a stable at Bond

In His Name

Head. He noted that during one of his services in this stable "a calf was tied up in the stall, at the front of which, on a barrel, I was standing, and by frequent bleating would drown my voice. These things at first used almost to distress me, but now I am almost accustomed to them."[43] On another occasion he remarked that in one of his barely finished frame churches "we were much disturbed by the barking of numerous dogs who had followed their owners, the screaming of babies, and the chattering of many swallows disturbed in their resting places."[44]

It was the distance between various missions, however, rather than the primitive facilities for religious worship that Anglican missionaries found most trying. Osler provided this description many years later in his autobiography:

> ... the more distant places were from six to twelve miles apart and in these I used to manage to have two services a day, except in Winter. All my journies were taken on horseback and alone, at times riding from one hundred to one hundred and fifty miles during the week and holding services five or six times. In many places the roads were little more than cattle tracks leading through the woods, many miles without a house or clearing.[45]

Such exertions took their toll. In 1838 Osler informed an English clerical friend that

> ... during the last three months especially my duties have been almost too much for me. I have risen on the Sunday Mornings with a feeling of almost overpowering weariness, yet could not rest for who was to take my duties? and on reaching home between 10 and 11 o clock, it has required an exertion to sit up for a few moments ... but there never having been a clergyman settled here before, every thing I establish will be a precedent, and all may not be strong in body as myself indeed I may not be capable of enduring as much fatigue in a little time as at present.[46]

Underlying this willingness to endure tremendous hardship were a remarkable spirit of dedication and an unwavering faith in divine providence. These qualities were revealed in a story related by Thomas Green, travelling missionary in the London District, in 1836. He wrote in his journal that on a trip to Woodhouse he

> ... found much difficulty in passing, with the cutter, some of the streams which were swollen by the thaw, and the ice so weakened as not to support the horse. How uncertain are all the things in this life! When I hoped that I had overcome all my difficulties, and to reach the end of my journey, I was upset; the ice broke in one place, upon which the horse became so much frightened, that in endeavouring to free himself, he became so hampered with the sleigh and harness, that he was dragged under the ice by the stream; my life was in imminent danger, and I was struck down twice by his plunges amid the broken ice and water. After some danger and much difficulty, I succeeded in raising his head above the water, and resting it upon a piece of broken ice, so as to prevent his being smothered; and after some delay, I procured the assistance of an old man, who was living at no great distance from the place. With his help I contrived at last to free the horse; but had he remained only a few minutes longer in the water, he must have died from the extreme cold. I was apprehensive that my own legs were frozen; but happily, through the care and keeping of the Most High, I suffered no further inconvenience than what I endured at the time—May I show forth my gratitude for this preservation, by a life devoted to the honour and glory of God my saviour.[47]

* * * * *

In His Name

There is a striking contrast between the Church of England's fairly impressive record as a religious organization in the post-1820 period and the scholarly argument concerning the failure of "church types" on the Upper Canadian frontier. According to this argument, the Church of England's character as an old world church type hindered the Anglican cause in two basic ways: its organizational rigidity, particularly its devotion to the parish system, prevented it from ministering effectively to a population that was scattered over an immense stretch of territory; and, since the formal and structured nature of Anglican religious services was totally unsuited to a frontier society, the Church of England's popular appeal was confined almost exclusively to the ranks of the urban gentility. In contrast, the argument goes, Methodism gained widespread support in Upper Canadian society because of its natural resourcefulness as a "sect." Its organizational structure, complete with class meetings, societies, circuits, districts, conferences, local preachers and itinerants, enabled it to spread its message with unrivalled efficiency, while its emotional religious "style" was perfectly adapted to the tastes and needs of isolated and culturally deprived backwoods settlers.[48]

This argument, a combination of North American frontierism and the church-sect typology of sociological theorists,[49] has basic flaws. To begin with, since by the late 1830s the Church of England was the single largest denomination in Upper Canada, it can hardly be described as an example of the failure of traditional church types in a frontier environment. Just as dubious are claims about the failure of the Anglican religious style. While Methodist camp meetings were indeed a powerful mode of evangelization in early Upper Canada, sweeping generalizations concerning the ineffectiveness of more traditional religious services rest on the assumption that frontier societies, by their very nature, are anti-intellectual, suspicious of tradition and hostile towards anything savouring of the cultural elitism of the old world. This assumption, besides being totally unproven, is sharply at variance with the conclusions of recent historical scholarship.[50] In any case, even if one has a frontierist perspective, the possibility remains that the formalism and intellectualism of the Church of England's religious style was a positive advantage in the more urbanized and commercially oriented Upper Canada of the 1820s and 1830s.[51]

Preaching the Word

As for criticism of the Church of England's inflexible organizational structure, the situation is more complicated. In one sense, this perception is clearly off the mark. The appointment of travelling missionaries and the revival of extra-parochial missionary activity in the 1820s and 1830s indicate that, at the very least, the Church of England's organizational inflexibility has been greatly exaggerated. Yet the issue points to something important. The Anglican clergy always subscribed to the position that the spiritual well-being and social stability of Upper Canadian society depended on the maintenance of a parish system. In 1838 the *Church*, an Anglican newspaper established the previous year, put it as follows:

> ... among the various links and connexions which, in the order of Providence, bind society together, there is none of a more amiable and endearing nature than that of a PASTOR AND FLOCK. The former may be regarded as the head of a large and extended family, over whose temporal and spiritual interests he is appointed to watch with a kind of parental care; and although there must unavoidably be, in this extended range, various grades and classes, — some rich, some poor, separated by different shades of intellectual endowment or of secular occupation, — yet there seems a common centre to which all the radiated lines converge; one person upon whom the eyes of all are fixed with equal regard and affection; one who is alike looked up to as the rich man's counsellor and the poor man's friend; and through whom all the blessings of heaven are alike conveyed to all without distinction; as the purchase of a common Redeemer's blood; — and that one is the PASTOR OF THE PARISH. He is the link by which all are joined together in one bond of Christian brotherhood, the spiritual teacher by whom they are instructed in those divine lessons which 'make wise unto salvation,' — the regularly commissioned guide who points to heaven and leads the way.[52]

As indicated earlier, this attachment to the parish system may help to explain why Anglican clergymen in the pre-1820 period displayed such a conspicuous lack of missionary zeal. It might also explain why the Anglican missionary campaign of the 1820s went no farther than it did. No one ever suggested that travelling missionaries should outnumber resident clergymen or that resident clergymen themselves should itinerate through entire districts; nor did anyone suggest that extra-parochial missionary activity would always be necessary in the religious conditions of Upper Canada. As a matter of fact, the Anglican clergy's commitment to the parish system seemed to go hand in hand with the hope that the church would one day be able to dispense with travelling missionaries and transform all Anglican circuits into closely knit parishes. Strachan explained in 1840, just after his consecration as first bishop of Toronto, that "intervening stations will be taken up, so as gradually to make the field of each Missionary smaller and smaller, till such fields approach towards very large parishes instead of counties, and even districts, which many of them resemble at present."[53]

Nevertheless, the Anglican attachment to the parish system should not be seen as proof of the Church of England's character as an old world church type. In point of fact, the parish system, far from being an intrinsic characteristic of the church type, enjoyed the support of most Upper Canadian "sects," including the Baptists and secessionist offshoots of the Church of Scotland. Furthermore, a denomination's approach to missionary activity must be viewed in relation to religious and social factors which are largely irrelevant to the theoretical framework of frontierism and the church-sect typology. To take the case of Methodism, the organizational structure of that denomination was a product neither of the influence of the frontier nor of the natural missionary zeal of sectarian religion; on the contrary, Methodism had originated in eighteenth-century Britain, and the development of its circuit system had been a pragmatic response to the religious needs of a country where urbanization and industrialization were rendering the Anglican parochial system obsolete. Similarly, since the Church of England displayed considerable institutional flexibility in the 1820s and 1830s, and since both churches and sects in Upper Canada supported the idea of a resident clergy, the Anglican commitment to the parish system cannot be blamed on the blindness of the church type to the needs of the frontier. It must rather be ascribed to an inability to transcend ideas and values which had deep roots in the Anglican historical experience, and which were entirely independent of the Church of England's character as a church type.

All in all, then, the Church of England's record in the 1820s and 1830s can be described as a qualified success — while the church might have achieved more than it did, it still had significant accomplishments to its credit. For Anglican clergymen themselves, however, the Church of England's accomplishments were no cause for celebration. Indeed, as dissent continued to grow and the Church of England itself encountered severe difficulties in ministering to the needs of its own flock, the Anglican clergy displayed a curious ambiguity when reflecting on their church's place in the colony's religious life.

On the one hand, there was still a belief in Anglican circles that, if the Church of England built up a larger supply of clerical labourers, it would soon attract the allegiance of the vast majority of Upper Canadians. In an 1830 letter to the SPG, A.N. Bethune wrote that, "where the church has a fair trial in Canada, it will universally gain a preeminence [over] every other religious sect & denomination merely on its own foundation & by its own inherent strength."[54] The same point of view was expressed in the *Church*. In an 1837 editorial the paper argued that a well-manned Church of England would inevitably become the church of the Upper Canadian majority.[55] Three years later one of the *Church's* correspondents wrote that, if the Church of England was "faithfully exhibited in her Scriptural doctrines and worship, and in her Apostolic Ministry, by zealous and laborious Missionaries," dissent would "vanish before her as noxious vapours before the genial sun."[56]

Still, this kind of rhetoric sounded increasingly hollow by the time of the rebellion — a ritualistic acknowledgment of hopes for an Anglican Upper Canada which could not be abandoned completely, but which few people, deep in their hearts, took seriously. More and more, as the 1830s progressed, visions of a triumphant Anglicanism were gradually supplanted by a growing fear that the Church of England was still far too undermanned to meet the needs of its own members, let alone to draw dissenters into its fold. Anxiety over the plight of Anglicans who, deprived of the services of their church, were lapsing into infidelity, or — just as bad — drifting into the arms of the "sectaries," was a recurrent theme in the missionary reports of the 1830s. In July 1834, for instance, Adam Elliot informed the SCCIPGDS that Anglicans were constantly complaining of the inability of their church to make its ministrations generally available. "Many persons," he said, "who originally belonged to our communion, have joined other persuasions, on account of their destitution of the public means of grace."[57] He was just as depressed about the state of the church in 1835. In that year he reported that he often heard people "observe with deep regret that though they belong to the Established Church, they are the most neglected and destitute denomination of Christians in this flourishing country. They are, indeed, at present an unhappy and scattered flock."[58]

Similar statements on the religious deprivation of the Anglican community were made by other clergymen. W.F.S. Harper wrote in 1835 that, in the township of West Loughboro in the Midland District, the absence of a "regular Ministry" made the settlers susceptible to "every kind of doctrine that may chance to come among them." Like Elliot, Harper too warned that many Anglicans in his district had "been induced to leave our Communion and to join other denominations, from being unable to obtain the ministrations of their own."[59] H.H. O'Neill claimed that, in the Niagara, Gore and Home districts, "the children of hundreds of Emigrants, who are members of our Church, are growing up in perfect ignorance of her doctrines, discipline and government, from the want of Clergymen, and the parents are gradually becoming lukewarm and indifferent."[60] George Petrie asserted that the religious destitution of the London District, where there were only two Anglican clergymen for thirty-six townships and 7,000 people, was "appalling."[61] On 3 August 1837, a disconsolate Thomas Green informed Waddilove that "gloomy, dark, and lowering is the scene around: very many possessing and boasting of the name of Christian, yet live and die in Pagan darkness."[62] Green claimed on another occasion that "the total want of sound and evangelical teaching" in the London District allowed "the seeds of Socialism [sic] and Universalism" to be "disseminated and cherished."[63] The lack of Anglican clergymen in townships such as Biddulph, McGillivray, Osborne and Nissouri, he noted, "leaves them most lamentably open to the pernicious and anti-christian doctrines which are daily and actively disseminated by the busy agents of Satan."[64]

In 1837 F.L. Osler related an anecdote which starkly underlined the Church of England's failure to meet the needs of many of its own members. He wrote that at Bolton Mills,

> ... a granary was filled with seats. Whilst waiting for the people to assemble, many having to come a considerable distance, an old man named Pringle accosted me. After some conversation he said, 'I was always brought up a member of the Church. Twenty years I have been in this country, and but four times during that period have I seen the face of a minister.' The reflection that he was thus deprived of the means of grace seemed to overpower him, for he covered his face with both his hands and turned away to conceal the tears which trickled down his furrowed cheeks. I told him that he still had his Bible and that God was to be found even in the wilderness. 'I know it, Sir, I know it,' he replied, 'and I well know that being a member of the Church of England will not save me; but we want a minister to guide and direct us, we want God's word preached to us.' I deeply felt for the old man, and, indeed for the destitute state of Canada, for hundreds, nay thousands, like him mourn over the blessings of the Gospel which they once enjoyed in their native land.[65]

Predictably, concern about the religious destitution of Upper Canadian Anglicans went side by side with a violently hostile attitude towards the imperial government's policy of withdrawing financial assistance from the SPG. Throughout this period travelling missionaries, the clergymen most intimately acquainted with conditions at the local level, complained angrily that the niggardliness of the British government was preventing the Church of England from fulfilling its responsibilities to Upper Canada's growing immigrant community. They also warned that, by depriving the church of the support it needed to spread its message throughout Upper Canada, Britain had seriously undermined the one institution that could have preserved the colony's social and political stability. Typical were statements by Thomas Green in an 1838 report to Waddilove. After noting that "the

In His Name

cruel aggressions of *ruthless and infidel* marauders from the States, have once more disturbed the peaceful firesides and happy homes of the loyal Canadians," Green declared that, "had those who have presided over the destinies of the Kingdom ... acted faithfully towards the emigrants ... many, if not all, of our present dangers and disturbances would never have occurred." He went on to state:

> ... sending out annually such an enormous mass of poor emigrants, without making even the slightest provision for their religious instruction — what in the name of common sense, could Statesmen expect? This state of things is but the natural, the inevitable, result; and it cannot surprise any thinking man to find that, (themselves neglected, and their children left entirely without instruction,) all alike forget the obedience due to the 'Powers that be,' as ordained of God, when the 'Powers that be' set them the example of thus forgetting God .... what have we else to expect than that if we persist in the same system of neglecting the true interests of the Colony, at no very distant day, a majority may be found (if not seeking it) at least quietly acquiescing in a change of Government ....[66]

Another travelling missionary, George Petrie, was even more blunt. In an 1839 report he denounced Britain's policy of sending out twenty to sixty thousand emigrants annually without making any provision for their religious and educational needs. He also claimed that the imperial government's abandonment of the SPG had weakened the Upper Canadian church to such an extent that designing demagogues from the United States had been able to spread their revolutionary ideas without resistance. As he put it:

> ... the Americans, shrewdly perceiving the advantage to be obtained by this blind and infatuated neglect of the English Government, and what a favourable opportunity it presented ... both in Religion and Politics, amongst these poor and neglected British Settlers, soon pounced upon the Prey spread to their hand by Christian England ....

> Yankee Teachers, and Preachers were soon poured into Canada, under the pretext of this neglect. I need not tell you they were received with open arms — by these forlorn people, who comparing their apparently disinterested benevolence, with the cruelly parsimonious conduct of the British Government — viewed them, AS THE BENEFACTORS OF MANKIND.

To Petrie, it was clear that Britain should repent for its past errors and take immediate steps to plant "throughout the two Provinces proper Churches, Schools, Preachers and Teachers, so that instead of a system of Mischief ... the people being nourished and brought up in principles based on Religion, Peace and Tranquility may once more be established in Canada." If this course of action was not taken, and if the Church of England continued to labour under "the mark of Pestilence," Britain would have to contend with a social and political upheaval "which, ere long, shall shake the throne to its foundation, and scatter Royalty, and Title, and Property, and Peace, and every social comfort to the four winds of Heaven."[67]

In expressing their feelings on the strength of other denominations and the "sects" in particular, the problems of the Church of England in ministering to the needs of its members, and the perfidy of the imperial government in withdrawing its support from the church, Anglican clergymen provided more than sufficient evidence of the importance of the 1820s and 1830s as a turning-point in Anglican history — a time when naive optimism about the Church of England's prospects gradually gave way to disappointment, anger and profound bitterness. Yet these features of the Anglican mind were not caused solely by the church's problems in competing as a religious organization for the allegiance of Upper Canadians. During these same years John Strachan was to find himself enormously frustrated in his efforts to bolster the church's institutional foundations. His case makes it clear that the church's defeats in the world of politics, as well as the general deterioration in the colony's political climate, were key contributing factors to the increasingly black mood of the Anglican clergy.

In His Name

NOTES

1. Playter, *History of Methodism*, p. 271.
2. J.E. Sanderson, *The First Century of Methodism in Canada*, 2 vols. (Toronto, 1908), I, pp. 241-42.
3. Ibid., pp. 355-56.
4. S.D. Clark, *Church and Sect in Canada* (Toronto, 1948), pp. 101-2.
5. These figures are based on a collation of data found on pp. 55-86 of Moir's *Enduring Witness*.
6. Scott, "The Roman Catholic Church East of the Great Lakes," pp. 53-54.
7. This census was published in the *Church* in instalments on 25 May, 1 June, 15 June, 22 June, 13 July, 14 Sept. and 12 Oct. 1839. The compilers are unknown.
8. This census has been reprinted in Moir's *Church and State in Canada West*, p. 185.
9. See Thomas R. Millman, *The Life of Charles James Stewart* (London, Ont., 1953), p. 114.
10. See Ibid., pp. 186-223 for short biographical sketches of these clergymen.
11. From 1815 to 1834 SPG scholarships were granted to twenty-nine ministerial candidates in the two Canadas. See Millman, *Jacob Mountain*, pp. 186-92, and Millman, *Stewart*, pp. 93-94.
12. SPG *Report*, 1833, p. 10.
13. The *Church*, 30 Dec. 1837.
14. ADO, Stuart Papers, folio 2, Stuart to Inglis, 22 Oct. 1792 and 25 June 1793.
15. These conclusions with regard to the missionary labours of Stuart, Langhorn and Addison are based on a collation of data included in the SPG *Reports*, Journals and Letters.
16. Once again, all the above conclusions are based on material found in the SPG *Reports*, Journals and Letters.
17. See Chapter Three.
18. See SPG *Reports*, Journals and Letters.
19. Millman, *Stewart*, pp. 44-59.
20. SPG *Report*, 1827, pp. 105-6; SPG Letters, Series C, Box IVA/39, no. 454.
21. SPG *Report*, 1827, pp. 105-6; SPG Letters, Series C, Box IVA/39, no. 454.

Preaching the Word

22　Ibid., 1828, pp. 50-51. Archbold travelled 3,000 miles in a missionary tour of Upper Canada in 1829.

23　Ibid., 1829, pp. 159-60.

24　The following account of the SCCIPGDS draws exclusively on the organization's annual reports, found at the AO.

25　*First Annual Report of the Society for Converting & Civilizing the Indians, and Propagating the Gospel Among Destitute Settlers in Upper Canada, for the Year Ending October, 1831. To which is Prefixed an Introductory Account of the Particulars Attending the Formation of the Society* (York, 1832), pp. 7-8.

26　Ibid., p. 16.

27　See the Society's reports for the 1830s.

28　For a discussion of the Church Society, see Chapter Seven.

29　For the appointments and activities of these clergymen, see the Society's reports for the 1830s. Wade and Street are not mentioned in these reports; still, since a Newcastle District branch had been established in 1835 to collect funds for the support of a travelling missionary, it is likely that both Wade and Street were supported by the Society.

30　See Chapter Seven.

31　*Address from the Bishop of Quebec to the British Public in behalf of the Church of England in Canada, received in July 1834.* Included in W.J.D. Waddilove, ed., *The Stewart Missions* (London, 1838), pp. 137-40.

32　Millman, *Stewart*, pp. 128-30.

33　*The Stewart Missions*, pp. 141-43. See also the photocopies of the Upper Canadian Travelling Missionary Fund reports located in the GSA, especially the letters dated 6 March, 10 June and 9 July 1839 (included in the report for 1838).

34　Millman, *Stewart*, pp. 131-34; AO, Osler Family Papers, Series II-I, F.L. Osler Diaries and Journals, "Sketch of My Life," p.4.

35　Millman, *Stewart*, p. 134; *The First Report of the Upper Canada Clergy Society* (London, 1838); *The Third Report of the Upper Canada Clergy Society* (London, 1840). The Upper Canada Clergy Society merged with the SPG in 1840.

36　*Third Annual Report* of the SCCIPGDS (1833), p. 42. See also the *Fourth Annual Report* of the Society (1834).

37　*Fifth Annual Report* of the SCCIPGDS (1835), pp. 20-93. See also Harper's journal in the *Sixth Annual Report* (1837).

In His Name

38 *The Stewart Missions*, Green to Waddilove, 4 July 1836, pp. 152-53; 21 Oct. 1836, pp. 154-56; 23 Feb. 1837, pp. 157-61.

39 SPG Letters, Series C, Box IVB/42, no. 452, Hill to Upper Canada Clergy Society. See also Series G, vol. 3, journal no.2.

40 Upper Canada Travelling Missionary Fund report, 1840, letter from E. Morris, 19 Nov. 1839.

41 Ibid., 1841, letter from George Petrie, 26 Jan. 1841.

42 Osler, "Sketch of My Life," p. 10.

43 Ibid., p. 104.

44 Ibid., p. 7.

45 Ibid., p. 11.

46 Osler Family Papers, Series I-I, vol. 2, Osler to Proctor, 27 July 1838.

47 *The Stewart Missions*, p. 190.

48 This argument is set out by S.D. Clark in *Church and Sect in Canada*. See especially pages 102-32.

49 The church-sect typology is elaborated in Ernst Troeltsch, *The Social Teachings of the Christian Churches*, translated by Olive Wyon, with an introductory note by Charles Gore, 2 vols. (London, 1931); and in H. Richard Niebuhr, *The Social Sources of Denominationalism* (Connecticut, 1929).

50 A good introduction to the controversy surrounding the frontier thesis is Michael Cross, ed., *The Frontier Thesis and the Canadas: The Debate on the Impact of the Canadian Environment* (Toronto, 1970).

51 Of course, Clark himself is keenly aware of the changing nature of Upper Canadian society in these decades: one of the central themes of *Church and Sect in Canada* is the connection between the social and economic developments of the post-1820 era and the transformation of Upper Canada's sects, including the Methodists, into church types. Yet, curiously enough, this awareness of the importance of social and economic change is the element most notably lacking in Clark's treatment of the historical experience of the Church of England. Even when dealing with the impact of Tractarianism on the Church of England in the post-rebellion period, Clark barely mentions the changing socio-economic life of the colony, and merely reiterates the argument that Anglican ritualism had little appeal for the great mass of Upper Canadians. See *Church and Sect in Canada*, pp. 123-25.

52 The *Church*, 18 Aug. 1838.

53 SPG *Report*, 1840, p. lxii.
54 SPG Letters, Series C, Box IVA/40, no. 462, 1 July 1830.
55 The *Church*, 7 Oct. 1837.
56 Ibid., 5 Sept. 1840.
57 *Fourth Annual Report* of the SCCIPGDS (1834), p. 62.
58 *Fifth Annual Report* (1835), p. 64.
59 Ibid., pp. 73 and 91.
60 *Seventh Annual Report* of the SCCIPGDS (1838), p. 16.
61 Upper Canadian Travelling Missionary Fund report, 1839, letter from George Petrie, 10 Sept. 1839.
62 *The Stewart Missions*, p. 170.
63 Ibid., Green to Waddilove, 21 Oct. 1836, p. 155.
64 Ibid., p. 252.
65 Osler, "Sketch of My Life," pp. 99-100.
66 Upper Canadian Travelling Missionary Fund report, 1838, letter from Thomas Green, 24 Nov. 1838.
67 Ibid., 1840, letter from George Petrie, 23 Dec. 1839.

CHAPTER THREE

BUILDING A CHURCH

Like other Anglican clergymen, John Strachan came to believe after the War of 1812 that the rapid growth of the Church of England's rivals demanded a vigorous response. In his case, however, determination to promote the Anglican cause took the form not only of a renewed commitment to missionary activity, but also of a concerted effort to strengthen the church through political action. By taking measures to turn the clergy reserves into a profitable endowment, and by attempting to create an Anglican-controlled university, Strachan set his sights on bolstering the position of the Anglican establishment. Achieving this goal would, he thought, ensure the survival of the colony's social and political order, and pave the way for the transformation of Upper Canada into a predominantly Anglican society.

Strachan's schemes were ambitious, but they soon drew fire from opponents who saw in them the spectre of an Anglican ascendancy in Upper Canada. The growing momentum of their campaign against the Church of England's privileged status left Strachan in a rage. In his darker moments, which became ever more frequent, he could only wonder whether the world he had always known — a world he had thought most right-thinking people cherished — had been turned upside down.

* * * * *

Strachan's resort to politics after the War of 1812 was perfectly understandable, for no clergyman was in a better position than he to use the resources of government in the interests of the Church of England.

In His Name

After arriving in Upper Canada on the last day of the eighteenth century, Strachan had spent three years working as a private tutor to the family of Kingston merchant Richard Cartwright. Upon his ordination in 1803 he moved to Cornwall, where he served both as parish clergyman and as master of a grammar school which he founded. Although he gained considerable respect in Cornwall — among his students were many who would become leading members of the colonial elite — the tranquil life of a country parson and schoolteacher was not for him. Intensely ambitious, he longed for a larger stage on which to display his talents, and his opportunity came with his transfer to York in 1812. During the American occupations of York in 1812 and 1813 Strachan caught the eye of the powerful for the courage he displayed in his dealings with the invaders. He was rewarded shortly after the conflict ended, with appointments to the Executive Council in 1817 and the Legislative Council in 1820; he was to remain an Executive Councillor until 1836, and a Legislative Councillor until the union of the Canadas in 1841. In the 1820s his influence in the councils of church and state grew quickly: he was made Archdeacon of York in 1827, by which time he was also one of the most important figures of the local oligarchy. He used his political power throughout this period for a variety of ends, but two closely related goals underlay all his political activities: defending Upper Canada's character as a stable, loyal British colony; and doing everything possible to strengthen the Church of England, which he viewed as the guardian of social order and the imperial tie.

From the start, Strachan's determination to foster the interests of his church, and hence the interests of the conservative society he cherished so profoundly, lent added weight to his fierce desire for influence and power. Discussing his possible appointment to the Legislative Council in an 1816 letter to Solicitor General John Beverley Robinson, Strachan — ever anxious to conceal his ambitions under a cloak of humility — explained that "I have little or nothing personal to expect but I have plans to prepare which I think useful & expedient for the temporal & eternal Interests of the people."[1] His desire to serve Upper Canada from a position of authority received an added fillip when in 1817 the Legislative Council defeated a bill intended to appropriate £500 annually for the education of ministerial candidates. Strachan, in a letter to Bishop Mountain, expressed his disappointment with the Council's action and noted that "the time is come when the

Church ought to have in the Legislative Council several Friends judiciously alive to her Interests." Claiming that the Church of England could count on the vote of only one Councillor, he concluded that his own presence in the Council would be of invaluable assistance to the cause of the church establishment. He further asserted that a seat in the Council would enable him to make use of his influence with those of his former pupils who were now members of the House of Assembly, which, judging by the recent passage of resolutions against the clergy reserves, was becoming increasingly hostile to the Church of England.[2]

With the realization of his political ambitions, Strachan led the way in formulating measures designed to strengthen the Church of England's structural foundations. In the early 1820s he began reminding the Colonial Office that the creation of a separate Upper Canadian diocese, with himself as its first bishop, was both "essential and pressing" if the Church of England was "to be placed on anything like an equality with the Roman Catholics, or to acquire a decided superiority over the Sectaries."[3] He also conducted a vigorous campaign against the projected union of the two Canadas in 1824, arguing that such a union would produce an assembly dominated by Lower Canadian Roman Catholics, who, in league with the "sectaries" of Upper Canada, would succeed in despoiling the Church of England of its landed endowment. He suggested a number of amendments to the proposed bill, but emphasized that the wisest course for the imperial authorities would be to shelve this project and instead establish a general union of the British North American colonies — a measure which would effectively curtail the influence of the Roman Catholic Church and thus improve the position of the established Church of England.[4]

Strachan's desire to strengthen the Church of England was also revealed in his efforts to increase the profitability of the clergy reserves. He first commented upon the clergy reserves in an 1817 letter to Mountain, in which he emphasized the importance of turning the reserves into a more lucrative source of income but offered no suggestions as to how this could be accomplished.[5] The following year he became more specific, proposing in a memorial to Lieutenant Governor Francis Gore that the clergy reserve fund be used to endow parsonages, and that the reserves themselves be placed under the

In His Name

management of a corporation — a step he hoped would result in a more efficient leasing system and the punctual payment of rents.[6] This led to the creation in 1819 of the Clergy Reserves Corporation, one of the most notable of whose members was Strachan himself.

When the policy of free land grants was brought to an end in the 1820s Strachan became convinced that the Church of England could best augment its financial resources by selling rather than renting its clergy reserve lands. In May 1824, in a letter that revealed the connection in Strachan's mind between a stronger church establishment and the goal of an Anglican Upper Canada, he informed Robert Wilmot Horton of the Colonial Office that "an authority to sell [the clergy reserves] would I am persuaded enable us to get in a few years so much ahead of the Sectaries, that they could never again become formidable."[7] Two years later, after blocking single-handed the transfer of a portion of the reserves to the Canada Company, he persuaded the imperial government to authorize the sale of one half of the reserves at a maximum yearly rate of 100,000 acres. According to his calculations, this measure would after a period of twenty-one years produce an annual revenue of £38,000 — an income sufficient to support two or three hundred Anglican clergymen.[8]

Turning the clergy reserves into a profitable landed endowment was one way of strengthening the Anglican establishment. Another was establishing an Anglican-controlled educational system. As early as 1815 Strachan submitted a memorial to the lieutenant governor proposing the establishment of a university at some future date; the creation of a scholarship fund to support needy students at the grammar schools that had been erected in each district by an act of 1807; annual government grants to common schools; and the formation of a board of education which would be responsible for regulating all common and grammar schools in the colony and whose members might include the judges of the Court of King's Bench, the members of the Executive Council, and the school trustees and Anglican clergy of the Home District.[9] One of Strachan's goals — the creation of state-supported common schools — was achieved in 1816 with the passage of the Common School Act, which provided the annual sum of £6,000 for the support of common schools. The Act did not create a general board of education; instead, responsibility for the superintendence of the schools was given to non-elective district boards whose members were appointed by the lieutenant governor, and to locally elected trustees answering to the boards. The Act also stipulated that teachers had to be British subjects.[10]

Over the next few years, the educational system established in 1816 was consolidated and modified in a few important respects so as to achieve greater centralized control. In 1817, upon his appointment to the Executive Council, Strachan was given the responsibility of providing textbooks for the common schools,[11] and in 1823 he was made superintendent of the newly created Board of the General Superintendence of Education. This body had six members, including Strachan, all of whom were Anglican.[12] The following year an amendment to the Common School Act curtailed the authority of elected trustees by providing that, in order to receive a government grant, a teacher had to be approved by at least one member of the district board.[13]

For Strachan, one of the most important objectives of this state-supported school system was to make the Church of England the supreme authority in the field of education. He told Bishop Mountain in March 1816 that the Common School Act would give the Church of England "the power of directing the books to be used, and the qualifications of the Masters."[14] Later the same year he explained to Mountain that his own appointment as "inspector of Education" would establish the principle that this post should always be filled by the Anglican clergyman stationed in York. "By this means," he wrote, the Church of England would possess "a paramount influence over the education of the people."[15]

Naturally, an Anglican-controlled educational system would be of great assistance in advancing the interests of the Church of England. Throughout this period Strachan believed that a properly designed school system would serve as a vehicle for the inculcation of sound religious principles in Upper Canadian society. On 19 February 1821 he informed Mountain that "the most effectual method of supporting our Establishment is by getting the Education of the rising generation to be placed under the direction and control of the regular Clergy."[16] Another letter to Mountain written shortly afterwards made the point that the "true foundation of the prosperity of our Establishment must be laid in the Education of Youth the command and direction of which must as far as possible be concentrated in our Clergy." Strachan added, "this hitherto [has] been the silent policy of all the measures taken for the Education of Youth adopted in this Province."[17]

In Strachan's mind, an educational system under the control of the Church of England would play a vital political role. After the War of 1812 he felt certain that the security of Upper Canada hinged upon the ability of religious and political authorities to discredit republican ideology. Closely linked to this conviction was the view that the loyalty of Upper Canadians would be virtually guaranteed if responsibility for the operation of the educational system was vested in the Church of England, a denomination known for its devotion to the imperial tie. In 1815 Strachan insisted that McGill College, which he hoped would make the young men of the Canadas "friendly to our different establishments and attached to the Parent State," should retain a religious character, and with this end in mind he recommended that its principal should always be an Anglican clergyman.[18] Five years later his praise of the "great excellence" of an education "flowing naturally from a regular establishment" was coupled with the warning that a university was essential if Upper Canada was to survive as a British colony.[19]

Curiously, perhaps because he was too occupied with other duties or perhaps because he realized that his plans were impractical, Strachan did little to translate his intentions for the school system into government policy. Admittedly, the Church of England did have considerable influence in the colony's network of grammar schools—until the 1840s grammar school teachers were predominantly Anglicans[20] — and reform politicians also claimed that Anglicans represented a disproportionately high number of the trustees on the non-elective district boards. But there is no evidence whatsoever that Anglicans were over-represented among common school teachers; on the contrary, a recent history of the Ontario school system in the nineteenth century indicates that these teachers were an extraordinarily varied lot.[21] Nor does the evidence suggest that the General Board played an active role in determining what was taught in the common schools — the same recent study has concluded that the board met infrequently and paid little attention to the operation of the common schools, concentrating instead on the administration of the colony's reserved school lands and on the realization of Strachan's goal of establishing an Upper Canadian university.[22] After 1827, authority over the common schools was informally exercised by the newly formed council of King's College,[23] of which Strachan was president, but it seems to have been no more interested than the General Board in expanding Anglican influence in the school system. In an 1829 report on the educational system, Strachan commented on its lack of uniformity and proposed, as a remedial measure, greater provincial control over the curriculum. Nothing came of it.[24] On the whole, then, while the local government did exercise authority over the schools through its power of appointment to the district boards, this power does not appear to have led to undue Anglican influence in the classrooms.[25]

Strachan's ideal of an Anglican-controlled educational system came closer to realization in his plan for a provincial university. The origins of this institution date from just after the war, when on three separate occasions Strachan attempted to prod the legislature into founding a college at York that would be under his personal control.[26] Some years later, in February 1826, he drafted an Executive Council report emphasizing that tutors in an Upper Canadian university should be "not merely eminent for their learning, but for their attachment to the British Monarchy and to the Established Church." Moreover, the university itself should be allied with the Church of England, and one of its main purposes would be to produce a larger supply of Anglican clergymen.[27]

The lieutenant governor, Sir Peregrine Maitland, shared Strachan's dream of an Upper Canadian university, and in 1826 he sent Strachan to England to lobby on behalf of the project. That June, Strachan submitted a draft charter for the university to the colonial secretary, Lord Bathurst. While this document, in recognition of Upper Canada's religious pluralism, did not require religious tests for professors and non-divinity students, it did lay down other conditions that underlined Strachan's commitment to the principle of Anglican control: the president and vice-president of the university were to be Anglican clergymen, the Bishop of Quebec was to be the official visitor, and only Anglican professors could be members of the governing council.[28] Strachan's lobbying bore fruit the following March, when King's College, Upper Canada, received a royal charter and was endowed with 225,944 acres of crown lands and annual payments of £1,000 from the Canada Company.[29] As it happened, opposition to King's College was to block its establishment for many years to come, but in 1827 all

In His Name

this was in the future. Strachan was now at the pinnacle of his political career, and from his point of view, the King's College charter was one of the most splendid feathers in his cap.

There are several misconceptions about the founding of King's College. One of these concerns the royal charter of 1827. It has been claimed that the 1827 charter required all professors to be Anglican, that Lord Bathurst was the person responsible for this requirement, and that Strachan regarded the restriction as "injudicious."[30] The truth is more complex. At the outset of their negotiations, Bathurst did indeed insist upon an Anglican teaching staff and Strachan, though he disliked the idea, gave it his approval.[31] But matters did not rest there, for the final charter required only professors on the college council to subscribe to the Church of England's Thirty-Nine Articles.[32] It thus appears that, in the end, Bathurst was swayed by Strachan's arguments in favour of a more liberal university. This is borne out by Strachan's declaration in 1831 that "it cost me more trouble than I can well express to get the students freed from any test, and still more to get the professors relieved from signing the Standards."[33]

Another misconception is that the Anglican council of King's College was the handiwork of a colonial secretary who ignored Strachan's liberal vision for the institution. In 1831, Strachan claimed that the provision for an Anglican council had been forced upon him by the imperial authorities,[34] but the facts seem to be otherwise. The draft charter of 1826 indicates that Strachan had always supported the idea of an all-Anglican council, and his June 1826 correspondence on the subject of a university clearly reveals that he and Bathurst disagreed not over the composition of the council but over the need of religious tests for professors.[35] Moreover, as president of the college council, Strachan was responsible in 1832 for proposing a series of amendments to the 1827 charter which did little to curtail Anglican influence. One of these amendments, while abolishing the requirement that appointment to the college council was conditional upon a subscription to the Thirty-Nine Articles, maintained the principle that all professors on the council were to be members of the Church of England.[36] Strachan adopted a similar position in 1837, when a bill was introduced into the Assembly stipulating that members of the council should not have to be Anglicans or to subscribe to the Thirty-Nine

Articles.[37] He was on the select committee of the Legislative Council which was established to study this bill, and which recommended in its report that professors on the college council should be members of either the Church of England or the Church of Scotland. When the Assembly passed the bill in its original form, Strachan supported it in the Legislative Council.[38] His reversal, however, was not prompted by a conversion to the idea of religious equality. Strachan later explained that he supported the 1837 bill not because he was convinced of its intrinsic merits but because he was anxious to end the wrangling that for the past ten years had blocked the establishment of King's College.[39]

The charter of 1827 has been misunderstood in still another sense. It has been argued that Strachan's rejection of religious tests for professors and non-divinity students was testimony to his tolerance and his progressive philosophy of education.[40] This interpretation of the evidence is not without foundation. Apparently influenced by the egalitarian model of the Scottish school system,[41] Strachan accepted youngsters of all religious persuasions in his Cornwall school,[42] and, as noted, later adopted the same policy in his plans for the arts program at King's College. Without a doubt, the lack of restrictions on non-divinity enrolment in the King's College charter made that document remarkably liberal by contemporary British standards, and historians are quite right in emphasizing this point. All that said, however, descriptions of the liberal nature of the King's College charter tend to be misleading. For one thing, the provision in the charter restricting enrolments in divinity was not insignificant in an era when ministerial candidates comprised the bulk of students in institutions of higher learning.[43] In addition, the portrayal of Strachan as a liberal-minded educator swimming against the current of the times is hard to reconcile with what is known of his broader ideological outlook. In the 1820s Strachan was an uncompromising defender of the privileges of the established church and a violent critic of dissenters, whom he saw as sinful schismatics from a branch of the Church of Christ and as fanatics determined to destroy Upper Canada's social and political order.[44] It seems unlikely, therefore, that Strachan, the personification of Anglican hostility towards dissent, was inspired in his educational endeavours by an attachment to the principle of religious equality. A far more convincing explanation is that Strachan's liberality as an educator was a strategic act of policy designed to promote his vision of Upper

Canada's future. In his early years as a teacher, and later as the chief architect of Upper Canada's educational system, Strachan's aim was to mould as many minds and train as many characters as he could. That goal, of course, necessarily ruled out any attempt at religious exclusion, whether in his Cornwall school or at the King's College. When he attempted to launch the college, he operated on the principle that since it was to play a central role in the creation of a stable, loyal and Anglican community, it could not, by its very nature, confine its influence to the members of a single denomination. In Strachan's mind, dissenters admitted to King's College — where the teachings of all professors, be they Anglican or non-Anglican, were supervised by Anglican administrative authorities — would obviously be encouraged to become God-fearing citizens, eager to maintain social stability and to defend the imperial tie. The King's College charter of 1827, therefore, far from embodying the "liberality and breadth of Strachan's views on higher education,"[45] reflected instead his belief in the relationship between education, loyalty and the Church of England.

Strachan never made a secret of the fact that King's College was to act as a guardian of the imperial connection. In his report for the Executive Council in 1826, he emphasized the role of an Anglican-controlled university in disseminating British values and sound political principles throughout the colony, declaring that such a university "from its natural relation with an increasing Clergy would gradually infuse into the whole population, a tone and feeling entirely English and by a judicious selection of Elementary Books issuing from its Press render it certain that the first feelings, sentiments, and opinions of the youth should be British." In the same document he proclaimed that the students of an Upper Canadian university, drawn from "the most opulent Families," would in later years constitute a political and professional elite which, by the mere force of its example, would foster patriotism amongst all sectors of the community. "The effects of the university," he wrote,

> would soon be visible in the greater intelligence and more confirmed principles of Loyalty of those who would be called to the various public duties of Magistrates, and Legislators, and in the Members of the learned Professions, whose principles and conduct have inevitably so great an influence in

> Society .... It is quite evident that such an institution, in alliance with the Church, would tend to establish a most affectionate connexion between this Colony and the Parent State ....[46]

This argument was repeated almost verbatim in an 1827 pamphlet urging the British public to contribute financially to the support of King's College. In his *Appeal to the Friends of Religion and Literature* Strachan asserted that the youth of Upper Canada, lacking a university of their own, were forced to complete their education in the United States, where they were encouraged to renounce their British heritage and embrace the destructive theories of American republicanism. He was thus convinced that a university was indispensable if Upper Canadians were to love Great Britain and appreciate the merits of the British constitution; if men in public life were to be noted for their intelligence and their sound political views; and if lawyers, doctors and clergymen — the three groups which, as the elite of colonial society, formed the values of the entire population — were to have loyalty "implanted upon their hearts."[47] Believing that Upper Canada could never be secure as long as its young men received their higher education in a country characterized by social anarchy and the rule of the multitude, Strachan warned that any delay in the creation of a university "may be attended with evil consequences, which may never be retrieved." In the United States, he declared,

> politics pervade the whole system of education; the school books from their very first elements are stuffed with praises of their own institutions and breathe hatred to everything English .... To such a country our youth may go strongly attached to their native land and to all its establishments, but by hearing them continually depreciated and those of America praised, this attachment will in many be weakened, and some may become fascinated with that liberty which has degenerated into licentiousness, and imbibe, perhaps unconsciously, sentiments unfriendly to things of which Englishmen are proud .... Nor can it be expected that any of them on their return will give up their hearts and

In His Name

affections to their Parent State with the same cordiality nurtured within the British Dominions. What indeed can be more important to the true prosperity of the Province, than the careful education of its youth? In what other way can we ever obtain a well-instructed population by which to preserve our excellent constitution and our connexion with the British Empire, and give that respectable character to the country which arises from an intelligent magistracy and from having public situations filled by men of ability and information. [48]

The same pamphlet also revealed Strachan's perception of the relationship between King's College and the cause of the Church of England. Announcing that twenty-four Anglican clergymen served a population scattered over 28,260 square miles,[49] Strachan argued that the limited manpower of the Church of England had produced a state of religious and political anarchy. "Nothing can be more manifest," he wrote, "than that Upper Canada has not yet felt the advantage of a religious establishment. What can twenty-four clergymen do scattered over a country of nearly six hundred miles in length? Can we be surprised that under such circumstances ... sectaries of all descriptions have increased?"[50] Strachan estimated that 112 additional clergymen were needed immediately, and that a total of 272 clergymen would be required by 1846 to tend to a population which would by then number in the vicinity of 400,000.[51] The newly chartered King's College was to provide the Church of England with the clergymen it needed if it was to defend Upper Canada against the designs of disloyal and subversive dissenting preachers who came from the "republican states of America."[52] More important still, the clergymen provided by King's College would enable the Church of England to embark on a campaign of missionary expansion which would not only save the souls of "our brethren who are perishing or falling away for lack of instruction,"[53] but also return dissenters to the Anglican fold. Strachan predicted that Upper Canada would one day possess a population of twelve to sixteen million, and he asserted that "it is impossible to set limits to the influence which the University of the Province, if wisely and piously directed, may acquire over this vast population — the greater portion

Building a Church

of which may, through the Divine blessing, be brought up in the Communion of the Church of England."[54] This belief in the capacity of King's College to create an Anglican Upper Canada prompted Strachan to emphasize that "it is chiefly on religious grounds that this appeal for the University of Upper Canada is made, which, while it offers its benefits to the whole population, will, for a century to come, from the peculiar circumstances of the country be essentially a Missionary College...."[55]

Strachan made the same argument in a letter to the SPCK soliciting financial assistance for King's College. "In the Canadas," he wrote in reference to the purpose of an institution he again described as a "Missionary College,"

> there are about three hundred thousand British Protestants without any seminary beyond a Grammar School. Of this number only a portion are Churchmen — but all may become so under good management .... the demand for Clergymen is at this moment so great in Upper Canada and from the rapid increase in population continually becoming greater that the College will have for a long period to furnish more candidates for the Church than for all the other professions put together ....[56]

Portraying King's College in this light may have been part of a strategy to rally British support for the institution. Yet it seems unlikely that Strachan's talk of a "missionary college" was just empty rhetoric. The statements he made on King's College for British consumption were perfectly consistent with his earlier remarks, offered in government reports and private correspondence, concerning the role of an Anglican-controlled university in advancing the interests of the Church of England and maintaining the stability of the entire colony.[57]

* * * * *

In His Name

Strachan's plans for strengthening the Church of England were not destined to succeed. Their failure was the direct result of the growing opposition to church establishments of any kind, opposition that was evident not only in Upper Canada but across the world. In the first half of the nineteenth century, the combined influence of religious pluralism and increasingly powerful nation-states led to a fundamental alteration in the relation between churches and secular authorities in several countries, including Britain, the essential feature of which was the replacement of church establishments by non-denominational political regimes.[58] In Britain, where the Anglican estabishment had been fundamental to political life for so long, the Church of England found itself increasingly beleaguered, surrounded by religious and political forces that were pledged to a new order in church and state. The first blows for religious equality were struck in the late 1820s with the granting of Roman Catholic emancipation and the repeal of the Test and Corporation Acts. Thereafter Anglican privileges were gradually whittled away until, by the 1870s, little of substance was left.[59]

The Anglican church in Upper Canada was to fall victim to the same kinds of forces. There, the assault on the Anglican citadel began tentatively in the early 1820s and quickly gained momentum as part of a more general campaign of religious and social protest. During the 1820s and 1830s an increasingly vocal and powerful reform movement focused its guns on a wide range of issues touching the social, political and religious fabric of Upper Canadian society. One of the most significant features of the Reformers' crusade was the growing demand for the secularization of the clergy reserves, a demand echoed by many of the Church of England's denominational rivals.

Criticism of the Church of England's landed endowment was first voiced in 1817, when the Assembly adopted resolutions condemning the reserves as "unsurmountable obstacles" to settlement and calling on the imperial government to authorize the sale of all clergy reserve lands.[60] Two years later the reserves once again became the subject of controversy when a Church of Scotland congregation in Niagara-on-the-Lake petitioned the colonial authorities for a government grant, from the clergy reserves or any other source, to assist in the restoration of their church and in the maintenance of a resident clergyman.[61] Lieutenant Governor Maitland forwarded this petition to the Colonial Office, but not without adding his own opinion that the congregation's

Building a Church

claim was inadmissible.[62] To his astonishment, however, the Law Officers of the Crown ruled that the religious clauses of the Constitutional Act made provision for the endowment of the Church of Scotland, and that on this basis Church of Scotland congregations were entitled to a share of clergy reserve revenues. Although this decision, so damaging to the Church of England, was kept secret by Maitland,[63] the clergy reserves continued to be a principal cause of religious discord. In 1823 resolutions were passed in the provincial legislature recognizing the Church of Scotland as a co-established church of Upper Canada and upholding its claim to a share of the reserves.[64]

Ironically, Strachan himself was primarily responsible for transforming discussion of the possibility of "co-establishment" into a vigorous attack on the idea of establishment itself. In a sermon preached after the death of Bishop Mountain in 1825, Strachan set forth an aggressive defence of the established Church of England and cast aspersions on the loyalty of "itinerant preachers."[65] Other denominations now entered the fray, and in the process the terms of the debate were fundamentally altered. In a lengthy letter published in William Lyon Mackenzie's *Colonial Advocate*, Egerton Ryerson, newly appointed Methodist preacher on the Yonge Street circuit, refuted Strachan's claims about Upper Canadian Methodism and, more importantly, advanced a detailed philosophical critique of the principle of church establishment.[66] The controversy escalated further in 1827, when the calumnies and inaccuracies of Strachan's *Ecclesiastical Chart*, a document purporting to be an analysis of the Church of England's position in relation to other denominations, became public knowledge.[67] The following year a select committee of the Assembly and the Canada Committee of the British House of Commons criticized the policy of church establishment as totally impractical in a religiously pluralistic society, and recommended that the clergy reserves be devoted to education and internal improvements.[68] The local and imperial authorities turned a deaf ear to these appeals, but the crusade for the separation of church and state continued to gain momentum over the next decade. Indeed, when the clergy reserves finally began to yield revenue in the early 1830s, the drive to abolish the Church of England's endowment became more intense than ever. In 1830 an organization known as the Friends of Religious Liberty was founded to spread the "voluntarist" message — namely that churches should be supported not by the state, but "by the people among whom they labour and by the voluntary contributions of benevolent Societies in Canada and Great Britain."[69] Subsequently, bills providing for the secularization of the reserves were passed annually by the Assembly but rejected by the Legislative Council.[70]

The voluntarist campaign for the separation of church and state also focused on the Church of England's privileges in the field of education. In 1828, the Assembly's select committee denounced the proposed King's College for its close connection with the Church of England, the Assembly itself petitioned the king to revoke the college's charter, and the Canada Committee of the imperial parliament recommended that religious tests for council members be abolished and that provision be made for a Church of Scotland divinity professorship.[71] The new lieutenant governor, Sir John Colborne, used his authority as chancellor to block the establishment of the controversial university, and in its place he laid the groundwork of a preparatory school, soon to be in operation as Upper Canada College, which he believed was far better suited to the needs of a primitive frontier colony.[72]

Strachan's hopes for the development of higher education in Upper Canada received yet another setback in 1831, when the colonial secretary, believing that a more liberal university was essential if public discontent was to be placated, asked the council of King's College to surrender the charter of 1827. Strachan and his fellow council members refused to comply with this request,[73] but their truculence served only to strengthen the resolve of the college's opponents. In 1832 a select committee of the Assembly introduced a bill abolishing all religious tests in the college. Although this bill and a similar one in 1835 were rejected by the Legislative Council,[74] it was now apparent even to Strachan that adherence to the terms of the 1827 charter was untenable. In 1837 the Legislative Council bowed to popular pressure and accepted a King's College bill passed by the Assembly, a measure which, in addition to abolishing religious qualifications for members of the college council, stated that visiting rights were to be transferred from the Bishop of Quebec to the Court of King's Bench, that the president did not have to hold any ecclesiastical office, and that doctrinal tests were unnecessary for degrees in divinity.[75] Even these concessions, however, failed to quell the controversy over the university. There was still no provision in the projected King's College for a non-Anglican divinity professorship — a fact which led many to conclude that such a narrowly denominational institution had no right to a lavish public endowment. Thus, voluntarist denominations, such as the Baptists, continued to denounce the policy of state support for sectarian education, while denominations such as the Roman Catholic Church, the Church of Scotland and the Methodists demanded a share of the King's College endowment. This opposition to the revised charter, combined with financial difficulties, was to postpone the establishment of King's College until 1843.[76]

Criticism of the colony's grammar and common schools was equally intense. Although the school system could not be described as Anglican-controlled in any meaningful way, it was nevertheless perceived as a creature of the local government and consequently was subjected to uninterrupted abuse. As for Strachan, while the schools in no way reflected his vision of an educational system controlled by the Church of England, he nevertheless supported them against their opponents. His reasons for doing so are not entirely clear; he seems to have taken this stand principally because the existing educational order confined the operation of democracy to the election of local trustees. But he may also have championed that order because, unlike the one that would replace it in the 1840s, it at least did not proscribe denominational religious teaching.

The first victim in the campaign for educational reform was the Board of the General Superintendence of Education, a body that was deeply resented by the Assembly partly because it was beyond the reach of legislative supervision, and partly because Strachan was at its head. In 1833 the Assembly passed a bill abolishing the Board, and, more important, that same bill made it through the Legislative Council of which Strachan was a member — a clear indication of Strachan's waning influence in the Council by the early 1830s. This accomplishment inspired Reformers to greater efforts, and during the remainder of the decade they attacked every facet of the educational system whose foundations had been laid with the Grammar School Act of 1807 and the Common School Act of 1816. The grammar schools were denounced for their preponderance of Anglican teachers and their high tuition and boarding fees, while the common schools were attacked for their anti-democratic administrative structure and their

In His Name

low educational standards. Reformers insisted that the educational system would flourish and gain the general acceptance of the Upper Canadian community only when power was wrested from appointed boards and given to locally and annually elected trustees, and when the schools themselves were supported with funds accruing from the sale of clergy reserve and school reserve lands.

The educational proposals advanced by Reformers were rejected by Strachan and his fellow Conservatives, who tended to favour a continued restriction of the democratic principle, and, on the financial side, a combination of local assessment and government grants. While Reformers and Conservatives gradually reached a consensus on the manner in which schools were to be financed—through a combination of government grants and local assessments — the issue of structure remained as contentious as ever. For Conservatives, placing ultimate authority over the schools in the hands of locally elected trustees was a republican innovation which, besides being awkward and expensive to implement, would make it impossible to maintain a centralized educational system. Reformers, for their part, were no less convinced that the appointed trustees of the district boards were the mainstay of a system which vested control over education in a York oligarchy, and which enabled this oligarchy to extend its influence throughout the colony.

These opinions hardened as Upper Canadian political life became more tumultuous. In 1835 the Legislative Council rejected a bill to promote education because of its democratic features, and the following year another bill with similar features suffered an identical fate. Such obstruction, however, could not continue indefinitely. By the late 1830s it was evident that Upper Canadians of all political persuasions were becoming increasingly discontented with the existing educational system. In 1839 a commission that included two conservative Anglican clergymen, John McCaul and H. J. Grasett, and one Reformer, S.B. Harrison, called for the election of township directors of common schools. Their report, while not turned into legislation, was an indication of a non-partisan commitment to the ideal of a more democratic educational system. This ideal would soon be embodied in the Common School Act of 1841, a measure regarded by Strachan as a repudiation of his plans for the educational development of Upper Canada.[77]

Building a Church

Predictably, these reversals for the Anglican cause made Strachan more determined than ever to defend the Church of England's interests. A good example of his belligerent, inflexible attitude was his position on King's College. In the 1830s Strachan was prepared, as his support of the Act of 1837 indicates, to open the council and administrative posts of King's College to non-Anglicans. But he was not prepared to agree to any proposal for the division of the college's endowment, because in his eyes such a proposal would be a futile concession to unscrupulous and subversive agitators. When A.N. Bethune claimed in 1831 that the Church of England should accept the colonial secretary's suggestion that the endowment of King's College be shared between two separate institutions, one under Anglican control and the other inter-denominational, he was reproved by Strachan for acting "quite contrary to what I consider the true interest of the Province as well as of the Church ... to agree to two Universities of different religious principles is to entail the curse of division in the Province for ever."[78] Strachan expressed an identical point of view in 1839, when he learned of proposals to divide the King's College endowment between the Church of England and the Church of Scotland. "If the Church tries to bribe the Kirk by offering it a share of the Univ endowment," Strachan warned, "other denominations will demand their share & we shall be left with nothing ... [the Church of England] ... can never be served by compromising her principles or by consenting to what is unjust either directly or indirectly it were far better to lose all."[79]

Yet, if Strachan was belligerent in defending the Church of England's privileged status, he also became increasingly bitter and frustrated as he followed the course of religious and political life in the 1820s and 1830s. On a number of occasions during these years he reflected angrily that local "incendiaries" were being encouraged by British radicals and the British government itself, and that the end result would be the destruction not only of the Church of England, but also of the constitutional fabric of the empire as a whole. In 1828 he claimed that the effect of the Canada Committee's report would be to "prostrate everything British to nourish discontent — to depress the Friends of Good Govt and to strengthen levellers & Democrates."[80] Similarly, in 1831 he criticized the imperial government for pandering to Upper Canadian "grievance Mongers," while the "steady and

In His Name

enlightened supporters of good Govt" were slighted and sometimes insulted.[81]

Strachan's disgust with Britain's colonial policy even threatened to undermine his loyalty to the imperial connection. He told his old friend John Macaulay in 1832 that a deputation should be sent to England to warn the government that "if they continue to attend to such persons as Ryerson & Mackenzie & to break down the Constitution the Conservative Party will turn round upon them & first trample on the necks of those miscreants and then govern themselves."[82] Strachan expressed similar sentiments in a memorandum of 1828, a particularly bitter piece of writing that formed the basis of his 1830 *Letter to Thomas Frankland Lewis* on the subject of the recommendations of the Canada Committee. In this document Strachan declared that he was striving to defend the established status of the Church of England, "but the progress of liberalism is bringing everything into disorder." The liberalism he had in mind was at work in Upper Canada, where the Church of England, assailed both by Roman Catholics and dissenters, was being accused of "bigotry persecution & Intolerance." It was also at work in Britain, where the government appeared anxious to scorn supporters of the Upper Canadian church and to discard the constitution "which used in former days to be the envy of the world the model for Politicians the theme of the Eloquent & the meditation of the Philosopher." This apostasy on the part of a nation chosen by God to act as a barrier against subversive ideas led Strachan to the edge of despair. "Of late years," he lamented, "there appears in England a merit in giving up all principles ... the Protestant Church & State which used to be the glory of our Ancestors is now considered an antiquated thing .... It is sickening to the heart to read the language of Ministers of State & Members of the House of Commons."[83]

These views were echoed in the *Letter to Thomas Frankland Lewis*. Emphasizing to Lewis, a British Member of Parliament, that "the policy which has been adopted towards the Canadas for some years past is producing a similar state of things to that which existed in America before the Revolution," he warned that acceptance of the Canada Committee's "levelling recommendations" would destroy the constitution in Britain itself and establish a "ruthless democracy." He then denounced those British politicians who were supporting the campaign of Upper Canadian revolutionaries against the established Church of England. The majority of Upper Canadians, he wrote,

> have peculiar claims to protection and indulgence. Driven from their homes by rebellion, or emigrating from the Parent State in quest of comfort and tranquility, they find all hopes blasted by a turbulent and clamorous minority.... This small, but ferocious minority, is encouraged by the attention paid to their representations, and the more they shew themselves the enemies of British principles, and the Church of England, the more are they caressed by the opposition in Parliament, and sometimes even by the Ministry themselves, while the true friends of the Constitution are treated with scorn and neglect. Thus encouraged, and restrained by no principle, they are busily employed in poisoning the minds of the people by a regular system of deception, calumny and slander.... And after all, how can we condemn them, when we see a Report by a Select Committee of the House of Commons, as deserving of all these remarks as any which they have promulgated.[84]

From Strachan's vantage point, of course, there was good reason to feel angry and embittered. By the early 1830s it had become painfully clear that his most beloved plans for strengthening the Church of England were in a shambles, subverted by enemies both in Upper Canada and in the mother country. The reverses he suffered from the late 1820s on were a bitter pill to swallow for a man as proud as Strachan, and the vitriol he hurled at his opponents reflected, in part, his outrage over the defeats he had suffered. Yet his fury did not spring from wounded pride alone. For Strachan, the political developments of the time were nothing short of a disaster. The campaign against the common and grammar schools reflected the growing influence of republican ideology in Upper Canada, while demands for the secularization of the clergy reserves threatened to deprive the church of the money it needed if it was to prosper as a religious organization and attract the allegiance of a majority of Upper Canadians. Similarly, the failure to establish King's College severely handicapped the Church

In His Name

of England's attempts to build up a larger supply of clergy — another essential pre-condition to Strachan's plans both to strengthen the church's position and to achieve the goal of an Anglican Upper Canada. All this was bad enough; infinitely worse was the fact that, for Strachan, the woes of the church had serious implications for Upper Canada as a whole. Regarding the Church of England's interests as closely intertwined with the social and political fabric of Upper Canadian society, Strachan felt certain that every blow to the Anglican cause seriously jeopardized the colony's future as a bastion of stability and British patriotism on the North American continent. It was this conviction that fuelled his rage as he watched the events of 1820s and 1830s unfold.

NOTES

1. AO, Robinson Papers, Strachan to Robinson, 7 May 1816.
2. George Spragge, ed., *The John Strachan Letter Book, 1812-34* (Toronto, 1946), Strachan to Mountain, 12 May 1817, pp. 129-32.
3. Strachan Papers, Strachan to Horton, 10 July 1824.
4. Ibid., Strachan to Horton, 25 May and 25 June 1824.
5. Spragge, *Strachan Letter Book, 1812-34*, Strachan to Mountain, 10 Nov. 1817, p. 142.
6. Strachan Papers, Draft of a memorial to Lieutenant Governor Gore, 1818.
7. BRMTL, Strachan Papers, Scadding Collection, Strachan to Horton, 15 May 1824.
8. John Strachan, *Observations on the Provision Made for the Maintenance of a Protestant Clergy* (London, 1827), pp. 9-10.
9. See Spragge, *Strachan Letter Book, 1812-34*, Strachan to Drummond, 26 Feb. 1815, pp. 75-80; and Susan E. Houston and Alison Prentice, *Schooling and Scholars in Nineteenth-Century Ontario* (Toronto, 1988), pp. 27-28.
10. For the terms of the Common School Act, see George W. Spragge, "Elementary Education in Upper Canada, 1820-1840," *OH*, XLIII (July 1951), p. 109; and Houston and Prentice, *Schooling and Scholars*, pp. 28-30. Contrary to the conventional wisdom, Strachan was not the *eminence grise* behind the Common School Act; the initiative for it came from within the Assembly itself. See John C. Weaver, "James Durand," *DCB*, VI (Toronto, 1987), pp. 228-30; and Robert Lochiel Fraser, "John Willson," *DCB*, VIII (Toronto, 1985), pp. 945-47.
11. George W. Spragge, "John Strachan's Contribution to Education, 1800-23," *CHR*, XXII (June 1941), p. 154.
12. Spragge, "Elementary Education in Upper Canada," p. 111.
13. Houston and Prentice, *Schooling and Scholars*, pp. 28-30.
14. Strachan Papers, Scadding Collection, Strachan to Mountain, 19 March 1816.
15. Spragge, *Strachan Letter Book, 1812-34*, Strachan to Mountain, 30 Sept. 1816.
16. Ibid., Strachan to Mountain, 19 Feb. 1821, p. 210.
17. Ibid., Strachan to Mountain, 26 Feb. 1821, p. 212.

In His Name

18. Ibid., Strachan to Sam Sherwood, Andrew Stuart and James Stuart, 14 Feb. 1815, p. 68. See also the draft version of this letter, p. 69.
19. *A Visit to the Province of Upper Canada in 1819. By James Strachan* (Aberdeen, 1820), pp. 128-31. John Strachan was the real author of this book; James was the name of his brother.
20. Houston and Prentice, *Schooling and Scholars*, p. 44.
21. Ibid.
22. Ibid., p. 30.
23. Susan E. Houston, "Politics, Schools, and Social Change in Upper Canada," *CHR*, LIII (September 1972), p. 252.
24. Houston and Prentice, *Schooling and Scholars*, pp. 30-31.
25. Ibid., passim.
26. Spragge, "Strachan's Contribution to Education," p. 153.
27. Strachan Papers, "Extract from a Report of the Executive Council relative to the founding of an University in Upper Canada," 3 Feb. 1826. The tone of this report bears a close resemblance to *An Appeal to the Friends of Religion and Literature, in Behalf of the University of Upper Canada. By John Strachan, D.D. Archdeacon of York, Upper Canada* (London, 1827).
28. Strachan Papers, Strachan to Bathurst, 15 June 1826.
29. Craig, *Upper Canada, 1784-1841* p. 184.
30. See J.L.H. Henderson, *John Strachan, 1778-1867* (Toronto, 1969), p. 41; and Moir, *Church and State in Canada West*, p. 83. Henderson's error in claiming that all professors had to be Anglicans is all the more glaring since it contradicts his own statements and the material quoted in his *John Strachan: Documents and Opinions* (Toronto, 1969), pp. 123-27. In this work Henderson correctly states that religious tests were required only of council members.
31. Strachan Papers, Bathurst to Strachan, 22 June 1826; and Strachan to Bathurst, 26 June 1826.
32. *The Charter of the University of King's College, at York, in Upper Canada* (London, 1827).
33. AO, Strachan Letter Book, 1827-34, Strachan to John McLaurin, 3 Oct. 1831.
34. Ibid.
35. See, once again, Strachan Papers, Bathurst to Strachan, 22 June 1826; and Strachan to Bathurst, 26 June 1826.

36 J.G. Hodgins, ed., *Documentary History of Education in Upper Canada, vol. III: 1836-40* (Toronto, 1895), pp. 34-35.

37 See ibid., pp. 66-70, for the provisions of this bill.

38 Ibid.

39 Ibid., p. 185.

40 See J.D. Purdy, "Strachan and Education in Canada, 1800-51," Ph.D. Thesis, University of Toronto, 1962, pp. 194-203; and Moir, *Church and State in Canada West*, p. 83. For the perception of Strachan as a liberal educator, see also Houston and Prentice, *Schooling and Scholars*, p. 95; J. Donald Wilson, "The Pre-Ryerson Years," in Neil McDonald and Alf Chaiton, eds., *Egerton Ryerson and His Times* (Toronto, 1978), pp. 31-32; and Douglas Owram, "Strachan & Ryerson: Guardians of the Future," *Canadian Literature*, 83 (Winter, 1979), pp. 21-29.

41 Purdy, "Strachan and Education in Canada," pp. 11, 45-46 and 53.

42 George W. Spragge, "The Cornwall Grammar School under John Strachan, 1803-12," *OHSPR*, XXXIV (1947), p. 66.

43 J. W. Grant makes this point in *A Profusion of Spires*, p. 90.

44 See Chapter Four.

45 Moir, *Church and State in Canada West*, p. 83.

46 Strachan Papers, "Report of Executive Council relative to the founding of an university," 3 Feb. 1826.

47 John Strachan, *An Appeal to the Friends of Religion and Literature*, pp. 5-11.

48 Ibid., pp. 5-6.

49 Ibid., p. 12.

50 Ibid., p. 10.

51 Ibid., p. 13.

52 Ibid., pp. 10 and 18.

53 Ibid., p. 22.

54 Ibid., p. 17.

55 Ibid., p. 12.

56 Strachan Papers, Strachan to SPCK, 1827.

57 Purdy and J. Donald Wilson take a contrary view, but, in the mind of this writer, their arguments are unconvincing. See Purdy, "Strachan and Education in Canada," p. 207; and Wilson, "The Pre-Ryerson Years," pp. 31-32.

In His Name

58 See E.R. Norman, *The Conscience of the State in North America* (Cambridge, U.K., 1968).

59 The campaign against the Anglican establishment in Britain can be traced in S.C. Carpenter, *Church and People, 1789-1889: A History of the Church of England from William Wilberforce to "Lux Mundi"* (London, 1933); Owen Chadwick, *The Victorian Church*, 2 vols., (London, 1966); J.C.D. Clark, *English Society, 1688-1832*; F. W. Cornish, *The English Church in the Nineteenth Century*, 2 vols. (London, 1910); W.L. Mathieson, *English Church Reform, 1815-40* (London, 1923); John R.H. Moorman, *A History of the Church of England*; E.R. Norman, *Church and Society in England, 1770-1970: A Historical Study* (London, 1976); J. H. Overton, *The English Church in the Nineteenth Century* (London 1894); and Richard A. Soloway, *Prelates and People: Ecclesiastical Thought in England, 1783-1852* (London, 1969).

60 John S. Moir, *Church and State in Canada, 1627-1867: Basic Documents* (Toronto, 1967), p. 160.

61 Ibid., p. 161.

62 Wilson, *The Clergy Reserves*, p. 67.

63 For the terms of the Law Officers' decision and Maitland's reaction, see Moir, *Church and State in Canada*, pp. 161-62; and Wilson, *The Clergy Reserves*, p. 67.

64 Moir, *Church and State in Canada*, pp. 164-65.

65 John Strachan, *A Sermon, preached at York, Upper Canada, third of July, 1825, On the Death of the late Lord Bishop of Quebec* (Kingston, 1826).

66 Craig, *Upper Canada*, pp. 173-74.

67 Ibid., p. 174.

68 Moir, *Church and State in Canada*, pp. 173-77.

69 Ibid., pp. 180-81.

70 Ibid., pp. 181-82.

71 Craig, *Upper Canada*, p. 184.

72 Ibid., p. 185.

73 For the relevant documents on this episode, see Hodgins, *Documentary History of Education*, III, 32-37.

74 See ibid., pp. 62-65 for the provisions of these two bills.

75 Ibid., pp. 60-70.

76 See Chapter Six for a study of the university question in the 1840s.

77 This above analysis of the politics of education in the 1830s is based on: Spragge, "Elementary Education in Upper Canada"; Houston, "Politics, Schools, and Social Change in Upper Canada"; Purdy, "Strachan and Education in Canada," and "John Strachan's Educational Policies, 1815-1841," *OH*, LXIV (March 1972), pp. 45-64; Craig, *Upper Canada*, pp. 186-87; and Houston and Prentice, *Schooling and Scholars*, pp. 97-107.

78 Strachan Letter Book, 1827-39, Strachan to Bethune, 5 Nov. 1831.

79 AO, Macaulay Papers, Strachan to John Macaulay, 28 Dec. 1839.

80 AO, Strachan Letter Book, 1827-39, Strachan to Hall, 29 Dec. 1828.

81 Ibid., Strachan to Hargreave, 7 March 1831.

82 Macaulay Papers, Strachan to Macaulay, 12 March 1832.

83 Strachan Papers, "Church Establishment," *circa* 1828.

84 John Strachan, *A Letter, to the Right Honorable, Thomas Frankland Lewis, MP.* (1830), pp. 97-99.

CHAPTER FOUR

THE END OF HARMONY

There was more to Strachan in the 1820s and 1830s than rage and bitterness. Just as significant was the profound change in his attitude towards other denominations. Defeats and disappointments on various fronts — the difficulties encountered in the Church of England's missionary crusade, the growing momentum of the campaign against the clergy reserves, and the success of the church's opponents in blocking the opening of King's College — shattered the commitment to inter-denominational harmony that had inspired Strachan in earlier, more tranquil times. Furious over the blows being suffered by his church, and convinced that the colony's social and political order was unravelling before his eyes, he launched a wide-ranging and violent assault on the "sectaries," who, from his standpoint, were the root cause of the turbulence of Upper Canadian life. This ideological crusade was largely a one-man show, but the ideas underlying it were not Strachan's alone. Indeed, there is good reason to believe that, when Strachan lashed out against the practitioners of "enthusiasm," he was giving expression to values and prejudices that were widely shared among the entire Anglican clergy. John Langhorn would have been pleased.

* * * * *

In Upper Canada, sectarian religion was first denounced publicly in an episcopal charge delivered by Bishop Mountain in Kingston on 25 July 1820. Unlike his 1803 charge, in which he had urged Anglican clergymen to maintain good relations with other Christians,[1] the 1820 charge left no doubt that the growing strength of the sects, particularly the

In His Name

Methodists, had undermined his belief in the importance of interdenominational harmony. On this occasion Mountain began by expressing his disgust with "self-appointed Teachers"[2] who prided themselves on their lack of knowledge. "Observe how rapidly they proceed from error to error," he remarked, "how boldly they discuss, and how confidently they decide upon questions of the deepest, and most difficult research, and which they possess no single qualifications that can enable them fairly to examine ...."[3] Such conduct, inseparable as it was from that "extravagance of enthusiasm, which, however acceptable it may be to the multitudes, is but a miserable excuse for the mischiefs introduced, by ignorance, and folly,"[4] was having a highly destructive effect on the spiritual life of the Canadas. Mountain urged the Upper Canadian clergy to guard their flocks against the infection of "enthusiasm" by instilling in them a respect for the articles, rubrics and liturgy of the Church of England, preaching the fundamental doctrines of Christianity, and insisting upon the importance of good works, which "self-stiled Evangelist Preachers" overlooked.[5] He also stressed that the Church of England had every right to defend itself against the attacks of sectarian religious groups.

> We are, for the most part, the persons attacked. Where is the fold, into which, under the pretence that the appointed Shepherd is not faithful to his trust, unauthorized, and instructed Teachers, do not endeavour to intrude themselves; calumniating the conduct of the regular Clergy, and tearing asunder, the bonds of union, between the Pastor, and his People? .... When our Doctrine is misrepresented, and our mode of teaching vilified; when our people are not only seduced from us, but taught to believe that we do not preach the Gospel of Christ; can we if we contend against the mischief, be justly censured, as narrow-minded bigots? — No surely: Censure can only justly attach to those, who compel us to the contest.[6]

John Strachan agreed with his bishop on the need for an aggressive response to the challenge of sectarianism. Before 1820 Strachan had been circumspect in his attitude towards dissenters: he seldom commented publicly on the errors of dissent, and when he did he only occasionally made specific reference to the strongest dissenting denomination in the colony, the Methodists.[7] But after 1820 the turbulence of Upper Canadian religious and political life led him to change his strategy. Much like defenders of the Anglican establishment in Britain, who were also lashing out at their church's opponents, Strachan began levelling a variety of charges against sectarian religion in general and Upper Canadian Methodism in particular. While some of these charges had first surfaced in earlier years, they received frequent and passionate expression only in the 1820s and 1830s. Others, moreover, had never been raised in Upper Canada, either by Strachan or by any of his fellow Anglican clergymen.

Theologically, there was nothing original in Strachan's critique of sectarianism — its central tenets were deeply rooted in Anglican tradition. One of these tenets concerned the respective roles of faith and good works in the process of salvation. Frequently during his career as a clergyman Strachan put forward the position that salvation was attained through faith *and* virtuous conduct, the latter being the concrete manifestation of faith in the present life.[8] This position, both in its simplicity and ambiguity, was the quintessence of orthodox Anglicanism. To Strachan it was inconceivable that a man of bad habits and morals could possess faith. Good works were the necessary consequence of faith, "the proofs or results of our justification,"[9] and without them faith could only be a sham. Similarly, good works that did not proceed from a love of God could not lead to salvation. In an 1847 sermon, Strachan claimed that there was no contradiction between the gospels and the Pauline epistles. A straightforward doctrine had been needlessly obscured through the determination of some men to avoid reading the scriptures with "humility" and to perplex themselves with "unnatural explanations and artificial rules."[10] For those sincere Christians who wished to remain faithful to the doctrine of faith expounded by Christ and his apostles, Strachan offered the following advice:

> Faith then is not a temporary or impetuous emotion, but a habit, a state of mind, lasting and consistent .... Christian faith is essentially practical. Is it belief in God's truth, then it keeps his commandments, for God's truth is practical. Is faith a belief in the teaching and life of Christ? — then it is practical

> — for his teaching and his life were all living breathing active benevolence .... Faith may be considered the Soul opening itself to receive the Divine Spirit for the recovery of that purity which consists in obeying the Law of God. Again, Faith is the yielding up of ourselves to the obedience of Christ — but to obey Christ is to live the life which Christ lived a life pre-eminently of good works. Under whatever aspect therefore we choose to place Gospel Faith it will appear the very element and power of good works or obedience.[11]

This view of the close relationship between faith and good works made Strachan harshly critical of Methodist revivalism. For Strachan, the grace necessary to salvation was obtained through a life-long struggle to trust in God and to live in accordance with Christian teachings. He therefore had little use for the Methodist notion that conversion could occur in a single instant of blinding revelation and in the midst of emotional hysteria. In his mind such a notion struck at the very heart of the Christian message, for its ultimate effect was to downplay the importance of virtuous conduct in the achievement of salvation. In 1803 he informed Dr. Brown that in Cornwall, "the Methodists make some progress, and as they despair to get to heaven by works, they hope to get there by grace." He added that "I intend next sunday to attack and expose the notions of sudden inspirations, to which the Methodists pretend, not mentioning them by name as that would be to lose my labour."[12] Many years later, in an article published in the *Kingston Gazette* in 1812, he emphasized that the "enthusiasm" of the sects bore little resemblance to the holiness on which man's salvation depended. While he defended the place of emotion in religious worship, he also stressed that "reason must always be the guiding and ruling faculty — the affections must not lead but follow," that the emotions themselves were the "attention and order of mind which consists in the exercise of strong and lively sentiments of virtue and piety," and that good works were the only true test of "rational devotion." He then declared that

> enthusiasm is the fruit of deplorable ignorance of pride and presumption. The loud vociferations, the absurd contortions and the vehement language

The End of Harmony

> which many use in prayer arise from the little knowledge which they have of true religion, and from their wish to seem pious in the eyes of the world. And tho' some weak persons may be carried away by uncommon transports inward persuasions that they are under the peculiar influence of the divine spirit, they cannot be so easily excused since a little attention on their parts would prove that all these are the effects of blind zeal, and ought to be suppressed as dangerous.[13]

The charge that "enthusiasm" ignored the importance of good works was reiterated in the 1820s and early 1830s, when the holding of Methodist camp meetings led to a sharp increase in the number of Upper Canadians claiming to be "converted." In an 1829 sermon Strachan argued thus:

> altho' we cannot say that good works entitle us to salvation yet we are supported by reason as well as by Scripture in asserting that they are the necessary sign of our Justification .... Let us not wait indolently for the inletting of the Spirit. Let us not expect that we shall be able to mark the very moment of our conversion or that our reformation shall be effected by some miraculous interposition. This is the unmanly and deplorable consequence of a distempered imagination — repugnant to reason — unsupported by the scriptures and most prejudicial to the interests of true religion.

He then went on to state that the notion of instantaneous conversion, by encouraging men to turn a blind eye to the importance of good works in the salvation of the human soul, threatened to destroy the foundations of the social order. "By vilifying good works," he declared, "the bonds of Society are torn asunder — religion and morality are set at variance all motives to action are destroyed and those under their influence become enemies to God as well as to man. Let us not then imagine that the works of the Law [observance of the commandments] are rendered of no effect by the grace of God."[14]

In His Name

Again, in 1835, Strachan criticized the idea that conversion could occur suddenly under intense emotional pressure. Insisting that "turning from sin to holiness from darkness to light from the dominion of evil passions to gospel humility is not to be accomplished in a few minutes or hours or days as it were a miracle," he argued that a true conversion was "the work of time of mature reflexion of continued industry of steady perseverance." At the same time, he emphasized again that society would disintegrate if everyone accepted the idea that conversion had nothing to do with good works. He declared that those who were attempting to divorce "the relative and social duties of life from Christianity would deprive men of the only sure basis of rational freedom & happiness the only pure standard of morals the only effectual restraint on the bad passions and the true consolations for the miseries incident to human nature while we remain in this lower world." Although this truth seemed to be scorned by many dissenters, Strachan was confident that, "as the Gospel is better understood," Christians would "seek rather to fulfill more nobly than others their various duties in life than to busy themselves with internal feelings & severe judgements of their neighbours sudden conversions morbid anticipations of future scenes and rapturous imaginations."[15]

Strachan had other objections to "enthusiasm." As a clergyman who prided himself on his rationality, Strachan was disgusted by the more primitive aspects of sectarian religion. His own brand of piety derived from the Hanoverian church, and he had nothing but contempt for those who failed to appreciate the essentially rational nature of Christian faith. Preferring a form of religious worship characterized by restraint and aesthetic beauty, he frequently made it clear that the frenzied outbursts common at Methodist revivals offended his sensibilities and violated those standards of decorum to which, in his view, all civilized men subscribed. In 1806, for instance, he told Dr. Brown that "the Methodists are making great progress among us and, filling the country with the most deplorable fanaticism. You can have almost no conception of their excesses. They will bawl twenty of them at once, tumble on the ground, laugh, sing, jump and stamp ...."[16] Similarly, in a sermon preached throughout the 1820s, Strachan drew a distinction between commendable religious zeal and "mysterious raptures which the sober minded may call enthusiasm and which are hardly to be separated from natural constitution and animal fervour."[17]

For Strachan, the emotionalism of Methodist religion could be primarily attributed to the poor educational training of most of its preachers. As he saw it, since Christianity was a rational religion, those chosen to teach its principles had to be men of learning and cultivated tastes. When such was not the case, there could be only one result, the dissemination far and wide of false religious doctrines. In an 1804 sermon Strachan attacked those who "step forward boldly and without preparation to expound the darkest mysteries of our religion and which the most learned tremble to touch. Of all the Enemies religion ever had those ignorant expounders are the worst." The sinful pride of such imposters had effects that extended far beyond the immediate circle of their disciples. "To them," Strachan asserted, "we are indebted for almost all that variety of opinions which distract the Christian world." Their "deluded followers," told that "human learning was not necessary to expound them [the scriptures] but on the contrary that the same inspiration that dictated them at first would be present to explain them," regarded "every wild and uncommon reverie a beam of divine illumination which should be carefully treasured up." Religion in the hands of these individuals "became a visionary system without solidity and without morals."[18]

When Methodist religious revivals swept the entire colony in the 1820s and 1830s, Strachan's criticisms of "ignorant expounders" of the Christian faith became even more impassioned. In his 1825 sermon on the death of Mountain, Strachan denounced "uneducated itinerant Preachers, who leaving their steady employment betake themselves to preaching the Gospel from idleness, or a zeal without knowledge, by which they are induced without any preparation, to teach what they do not know, and which, from their pride, they disdain to learn."[19] In another sermon, preached in 1832, Strachan argued that uneducated preachers were endangering the future of Christianity itself. Noting that the New Testament description of Peter and Paul as "unlearned and ignorant men" had given rise to misunderstanding, Strachan was at pains to point out that this description could hardly be taken literally. Both these apostles, he argued, had mastered the scriptures and had been guided by the Holy Spirit; hence, they could be classed as ignorant only in the sense of not being versed in the learning of the Scribes and Pharisees. Strachan was astounded that such a straightforward interpretation of the words "ignorant and unlearned" had eluded

In His Name

the grasp of so many: "thousands taking it for granted that the translation of the Bible is every word and sentence perfectly correct ... think that no preparation is necessary for preaching the Gospel and assume the duties of the Christian Ministry without being acquainted in any accurate manner even with their own native tongue." It was Strachan's conviction that these pretenders to the ministry had succeeded in spreading distorted views of the gospel message and in rending the Church of Christ into a collection of warring factions. To make matters worse, in the process of disgracing the Christian religion, these same preachers had marred the clergy's distinguished reputation as a social class. As he put it:

> Do we not see many persons whose opportunities of mental improvement have been exceedingly limited who are unable either to speak or write correctly in their own language much less possessing any knowledge of those in which the revelations of God are written deciding without hesitation upon the most difficult doctrines of Christianity taking upon themselves the office of Evangelists and consigning to eternal misery all who differ from them in opinion — it is to such men that we owe most of the divisions that rend Christ's Church, and that deplorable ignorance of the true spirit of the Gospel which so widely prevails .... If therefore any persons assume the sacred office without due preparation they stand guilty before God .... Under the Christian dispensation till of late years when a disposition seems to prevail among some to level all distinctions social intellectual and spiritual the Ministers of Christ have stood conspicuous in every age among their fellow men ... who can look upon those who have prostituted the authority of the Gospel Ministry degraded its dignity and polluted its holiness without shame and indignation and alas there have been and still are many such .... [20]

Strachan also objected to the American ties of Upper Canadian Methodism. To the end of his days, he was intensely hostile to the factionalism and disorder which, in his eyes, characterized American society.[21] Not unexpectedly, therefore, he concluded that American-born Methodist preachers in Upper Canada were the main driving force behind the religious and political discord afflicting the colony. His feelings on this subject were made evident in 1825, when he warned in his sermon on the death of Mountain that Upper Canada's religious teachers, excluding Anglican clergymen and "a very few respectable Ministers" of the Church of Scotland, "come almost universally from the Republican States of America, where they gather their knowledge and form their sentiments." He then added that, if measures were not immediately taken to strengthen the Church of England, "the mass of the population will be nurtured and instructed in hostility to our Parent Church, nor will it be long till they imbibe opinions anything but favourable to the political Institutions of England."[22] Two years later in his *Ecclesiastical Chart*, besides reiterating his claim about the American origins of most of Upper Canada's preachers, Strachan emphasized that "the Methodist teachers are subject to the orders of the Conference of the United States of America," and that the number of "established clergy" would have to be immediately increased if the local government was to stand any chance of preventing Methodist preachers "from gradually rendering a large portion of the population, by their influence and instruction, hostile to our institutions, both civil and religious."[23] These assertions were repeated almost verbatim in his *Appeal in Behalf of the University of Upper Canada*, and in a slightly modified form in a pamphlet designed to enlighten imperial statesmen on the contentious subject of the clergy reserves.[24]

As recounted earlier, Strachan's aspersions on the Church of England's rivals provoked a violent religious controversy in Upper Canada. Eventually, on 6 March 1828, Strachan responded to his critics in a lengthy speech to the Legislative Council. Few dissenters could have been placated by the sentiments he expressed on this occasion. Certainly not in an apologetic mood, Strachan began his speech with a defence of the *Ecclesiastical Chart* and then congratulated the Methodists on their decision to establish an independent Canadian conference: "at this I rejoice and am so pleased to think that my observations have not been in vain, and that angry as they are, they find it expedient to act in conformity to my advice ... but it is rather hard that I should become the object of their enmity for urging measures which they find it necessary to adopt." He also stressed that his prime concern was not

In His Name

the actual number of American preachers in Upper Canada but rather the extent to which Methodism, as a denomination with close ties to the United States, had actively fostered the spread of republican principles. In this respect, he noted, the demand of Methodists for the separation of church and state revealed their wholehearted support of the infidelity and social insubordination which were the distinguishing characteristics of all experiments in revolution. The inference in this argument was unmistakable: the goal of Methodism was the propagation of American democratic philosophy and the destruction of the Upper Canadian social order. As Strachan declared,

> my remarks were confined to those Teachers and Preachers who came from the United States where they gather their knowledge and form their sentiments, and so far am I from being able to soften them that I must extend them to the present Teachers and Preachers, so long as they are found proposing the most slanderous resolutions at public meetings, and going round the country persuading ignorant people to sign the petitions which contain them, and so long as any of them continue to exhibit a rancorous spirit against other denominations. Have not the Methodists in this Province in connexion with the American Conference ever shewn themselves the Enemies of the Established Church? Are they not at this moment labouring to separate religion from the State, with which it ought ever to be firmly united, since one of its greatest objects is to give stability to good Government, nor can it be separated with impunity in any Christian country? — Is not Christianity a continual lesson of obedience to the laws and submission to constituted authorities, and has it not been the primary object of all enemies to regular Government to destroy the influence of religious principles, and to pull down religious establishments? To effect this, they have ever considered the consummation of victory.[25]

The End of Harmony

Another facet of Strachan's critique of sectarianism — his increasingly "High Church" view of the Anglican mission and, as a necessary corollary, of the folly of dissent — cannot be understood without an appreciation of his theological development. Although his father had introduced him as a boy to the teachings of the profoundly traditionalist Episcopal Church of Scotland,[26] which did not accept the Hanoverian succession until 1788, Strachan in the years before 1820 remained faithful to the temper and principles of the liberal Anglicanism of the eighteenth century. He displayed no familiarity with the writings of the Hackney Phalanx, an informal association of High Church divines which had arisen towards the end of the eighteenth century. His sermons, like the sermons of the "moderate men" he so much admired, were moralistic in tone, less concerned with explaining complex theological questions than with portraying Christianity as a set of rational inducements for virtuous conduct in the present life. During these years he never addressed himself to the question of church government, an abiding concern of High Church divines, and only once did he echo the High Church principle that the Church of England's greatness was rooted in the "primitive purity of her worship and discipline."[27]

All this changed in the 1820s. Abandoning the liberal Anglicanism he had espoused for so long, Strachan now became an enthusiastic proponent of High Church doctrines. Long before the Oxford movement of the 1830s made such doctrines fashionable, Strachan used his pulpit time and time again to proclaim the High Church "line" — the Church of England, he told his congregation repeatedly in the 1820s and early 1830s, was a branch of the catholic and apostolic church, its episcopal government was sanctioned by tradition, and its liturgy touched man's innermost spiritual instincts and imposed a degree of uniformity and order on religious worship. This conversion to High Church theology may have been partly prompted by intellectual currents emanating from outside Upper Canada; for example, Strachan was undoubtedly influenced by Bishop John Henry Hobart of New York, a leading High Churchman in the Episcopal Church whose principles he greatly admired.[28] Nevertheless, there seems good reason to believe that Strachan's growing concern over the fortunes of the Upper Canadian church played an important role in determining the course of his theological evolution. In a period when the Church of England was engaged in a fierce struggle to spread its message and stem the tide of religious "enthusiasm," Strachan was naturally drawn to a brand of theology that offered a clear and messianic view of the Anglican doctrinal position. At the same time, High Church theology had the advantage of strengthening Strachan's case against many of the Church of England's denominational rivals. Inspired by the High Church principle that the Church of England was the guardian of the true faith, Strachan could denounce all dissenters for splitting from the Church of Christ and thereby inflicting a severe blow against the Christian religion. He could also argue that, unless dissenters repented of their sins and returned to the Anglican fold, they would soon suffer the consequences of divine wrath.

Strachan first expressed his High Church views in the *Christian Recorder*. In the November 1820 issue he wrote an editorial asserting that the Church of England's government "claims, and most justly claims a Divine origin. It is sanctioned by the practice of the Apostles, which is the Law of Christ." He then advanced the classic High Church defence of the liturgy and doctrinal position of the Church of England. Contrasting the Church of England's unity with the internal divisions of sectarian religion, he stressed that, among the Anglican clergy, "there is no discordance in doctrine, precept or discipline. The people whom they address are not bewildered with a variety of opinions, all is simple, clear and beautiful ...." To him it was obvious that dissent from such a church was a grievous sin, for "all that our religion requires as necessary to salvation is concentrated in its ordinances, and consequently those who forsake or remove from its ordinances endanger their immortal souls."[29]

These ideas were reiterated in the *Recorder* in February 1821. At the time Strachan argued that the sermon, if not accompanied by the sacraments and forms of prayer, gave excessive power to the individual preacher; in support of his contention he pointed to the intolerance with which "sectaries" expounded their ever-changing opinions.[30] While this argument could have been made clearer, he was certainly straightforward in another article dealing with a charge by Bishop Hobart: here Strachan expressed his enthusiastic agreement with Hobart's view that the only way to restore "purity and unity to that Christian family, which is now deformed and distracted by heresies and schisms," was to gain general acceptance of "the great principle that we are saved from the guilt and dominion of sin by the merit and grace of the Lord Jesus Christ received ... in union with his church, by the participation ... [in] its sacraments and ordinances from the hands of her authorized ministry."[31] At another point in the same issue of the *Recorder* Strachan claimed that the absence of a liturgy in sectarian religious worship turned the congregation into passive hearers of prayers spoken by the preacher.[32]

The *Christian Recorder* ceased publication in 1821, but this did not prevent Strachan from publicizing his new attachment to High Church ideas. Setting aside the journalist's pen for the clergyman's pulpit, he preached numerous sermons in the 1820s devoted to the subject of the apostolic purity of the Church of England and the degeneracy of dissent. In 1825 he insisted that, while dissenting denominations were "scattered, or divided," the Church of England — with a form of government sanctioned by tradition and Christ himself — proceeded "with all the advantages, which union, discipline and order can produce."[33] He also declared that the liturgy of the Church of England was distinguished both for the clarity and elegance with which it expressed the central truths of the Christian faith, and for the effectiveness with which it united all Anglicans in a closely-knit fellowship:

> the form of prayer, which we are bound to use, unites all the congregations of our Church in the principal part of their worship, as if they were only one congregation and assembled in the same temple, and it presents to them with great force simplicity and beauty, the ways, means and appointments of God, to restore our fallen nature to purity, and everlasting life .... [34]

Equally interesting are other sermons preached in the early 1830s. In an 1831 sermon Strachan claimed that all those who adhered to the "doctrine, the worship and Government which Christ and his Apostles established" were members of the visible Church of Christ on earth, and that "sinful men" who tampered with the structure of this church were destroying the unity of the Christian religion, and thus ignoring the admonitions of Christ and his Apostles.[35] In a sermon of 1832 he

In His Name

asserted that salvation could not be obtained outside the catholic and apostolic church.[36] Another sermon of the same year, ironically entitled *Church Fellowship*, warned that the goal of inter-denominational harmony should never be pursued if religious principles were to be diluted in the process. "All attempts to reconcile differences among Christians," Strachan stated, "which involve the smallest sacrifice of truth, or seek in any manner to explain away or compromise it, are altogether inconsistent with the Christian character."[37] While expressing his grief over the internal divisions of the Christian community, Strachan criticized those dissenting preachers who rejected the sacraments and liturgy of one of the most illustrious churches in the world.[38]

Two years later Strachan again attacked that lukewarmness in religious feeling which, under the guise of tolerance, would compromise the doctrinal purity of the Church of England for the sake of a temporary accommodation with dissent. Arguing that Anglicans should regard their church as the true Church of Christ, he emphasized that "religion admits of no coalition between right & wrong — of no compromise between truth & error. As Christians it is our duty to maintain those opinions only which bear the stamp of the Almighty and will be received at the Treasury of heaven in the great day of account." Strachan continued to bemoan the hostile feelings that prevailed between different denominations, but he remained firm in his conviction that religious peace would be obtained only when dissenters repented of their sins and returned to the Church of England. He thus prayed that "it would please God to bring into the way of truth all such as have erred and are deceived."[39]

High Church ideals were also expressed in a pamphlet written in 1832 as a tribute to the late Bishop Hobart. Here Strachan lauded the American bishop for his steadfast support of the institution of episcopacy, his belief in the importance of the liturgy and the sacraments, and his defence of the apostolic character of the Church of England. On the subject of episcopacy, Strachan asserted that this government "had continued without interruption [for] fifteen centuries," and that there was not "in the history of Christianity a single Church which has remained one-third of that time under any other system of government, nor an example of any successful and permanent propagation of the Gospel without the superintendence of Bishops."[40] He also commended Hobart for his refusal to recognize as part of the true church any Christian body that did not subscribe to the doctrines, ordinances and government of the Church of England.[41]

Interestingly enough, High Church theology went hand in hand with a deeply hostile attitude towards inter-denominational organizations. During the immediate post-war period the creation of the Bible and Common Prayer Book Society of Upper Canada, which was open to the members of all religious groups, had been a concrete expression of the Anglican clergy's commitment to inter-denominational harmony. In later years, however, such enterprises fell into disfavour. Strachan along with other Anglicans now argued that the Church of England could best serve its own interests by working through organizations that were under its exclusive control. In part, this attitude reflected the conviction that the Church of England should have nothing to do with those denominations which had shown themselves to be inveterate opponents of the Anglican cause. It also reflected the High Church position — one which was itself directly related to the religious and political conditions of the post-war era — that by cooperating with dissenters in inter-denominational organizations Anglicans were tarnishing the Church of England's image as a branch of the true church.

Strachan's new attitude towards inter-denominational organizations was first made known in late 1820. In the *Christian Recorder* of November 1820 he declared his firm opposition to religious organizations that did not recognize the liturgy and Thirty-Nine Articles of the Church of England as the purest expression of the Christian faith, and which were not based on apostolic principles of church government. He insisted that "to neglect discipline and order is to neglect to lay the foundation stone, for all things must be done decently and in order," adding that "those Societies ... with no form of Church Government, or a form not sanctioned by the primitive times, cannot secure lasting success. Their converts have no bond of union, no common principles of action, no subordination, and consequently can have no permanence as a Christian Society ...."[42] A few months later, at a meeting of the York committee of the SPCK, Strachan declared that "to those who conscientiously differ from us, the utmost charity is due; but in disseminating Christianity among the young, or in reclaiming the careless, we ought most assuredly to inculcate the form prescribed by

In His Name

our own establishment."[43] It was probably at this point that Strachan severed his association with the non-sectarian Bible Society of Upper Canada, an organization he had actively supported in the years just after the war. Henceforth he would support the local branches of the SPCK against all inter-denominational rivals.

Opposition to non-sectarian religious organizations was also a keynote of Strachan's tribute to Bishop Hobart. In this piece Strachan praised Hobart for his hostility towards the inter-denominational British and Foreign Bible Society, remarking that if Anglicans sincerely believed their church to be the true Church of Christ, they could never in good conscience associate "for religious purposes with those who differ from us in many of what we believe to be the most essential articles of our holy faith."[44] He also asserted that bishops and clergymen who served as officers of Bible societies were "traitors to their own church and promoters of division,"[45] and that Anglicans who contributed to the support of dissenting missionary organizations were guilty of "false liberality."[46]

These views were echoed by other Anglicans. As early as May 1819 an anonymous correspondent of the *Christian Recorder* called for the creation of branch committees of the SPCK in order to provide schools for the education of the Anglican poor, to enlarge the supply of Anglican clergymen and to distribute "copies of the Church Liturgy." The Bible and Common Prayer Book Society of Upper Canada could not be relied on to perform these tasks, since "the Dissenters from our Church, whilst they unite with us in the distribution of the Scriptures, are not unmindful of inculcating by every means in their power, their own doctrines and their own practices." Dissenters had their own missionary, school and tract societies, but in this respect they were hardly to be criticized: "On the contrary we ought to go and do likewise."[47]

Similar points were made by other *Recorder* correspondents. In late 1819 and early 1820 one writer, in a lengthy exposition on forms of prayer, emphasized the importance of distributing prayer books as well as Bibles so that the religiously destitute of Upper Canada might be protected against the "delusions of false interpretation, by illiterate preachers."[48] Soon afterwards a correspondent signing himself "C" replied to an earlier letter by "A.K." entitled "On the Increase of the

Christian Spirit." Addressing himself to "A.K."'s argument that the British and Foreign Bible Society was an example of the religious harmony of the age, "C" denounced "that spurious liberality which seeks to soften down and melt away religious distinctions, however important, and to associate all denominations under some specious rule which implies not even a conviction in the peculiar doctrines of the Christian Faith." Such "liberality," he felt, could be more aptly described as a cowardly reluctance to defend the doctrines of the true faith. "The principle from which we can never depart," "C" stressed, "is this, that whatever system of Faith we believe to be true, that system we are bound to maintain, even to death."[49]

"C"'s position was reiterated by "Titus," a Lower Canadian Anglican, in the September 1820 issue of the *Recorder*. Criticizing the paper for its praise of the London Missionary Society, "Titus" attacked all inter-denominational organizations for repudiating the apostolic government of the Church of England and thereby fostering "confusion and anarchy." His letter concluded with a plea that all Anglicans support the SPG and SPCK. The chastened editor of the *Recorder* admitted that "Titus"'s views displayed "much good sense."[50]

In the case of one Anglican clergyman, John Wenham, hostility towards inter-denominational organizations took such a fanatical form that the Church of England's missionary work was directly threatened. A former dissenter who had come to regard the Church of England as a branch of the catholic and apostolic church,[51] Wenham was appointed in 1824 to the parish of Waterloo, where he noted bitterly that the house provided him was "a wretched tenement, perfectly uninhabitable." Transferred to Brockville in 1825, he repeatedly complained about the inadequacy of his stipend, and in 1827 he told the SPG that the large number of "Romanists" and Presbyterians in his parish "precludes any very satisfactory account of the growth of Religion exhibited in a steady attachment to our devotion and worship." Violently critical of dissenters for their opposition to the established status of the Church of England, Wenham was prepared to suspect the worst when the SCCIPGDS dared to employ a Presbyterian agent in the Brockville area. His own views on the man's activities were made clear in a virulent and protracted controversy in the pages of the *Brockville Recorder*. Arguing that the agent's only object was self-aggrandizement, Wenham claimed that the new missionary society

In His Name

was a dissenters' plot to destroy both the SPG and the SPCK. He asserted that religious destitution did not exist in Upper Canada, that churchmen could not "cooperate with those who undervalue the Sacraments & teach men so," and that the Presbyterian agent was an enemy to the Church of England and the state. A redoubtable opponent named "Gulliver" responded to all his charges, and in May 1827 a subdued Wenham noted that his career as a controversialist had made him a "marked man." Complaining of poverty, poor health and the strength of dissent, he resigned the parish of Brockville in 1831. The SPG, no doubt relieved, transferred him to a parish in England and later to Ceylon.[52]

Another clergyman, George Okill Stuart of Kingston, does not seem to have had any problems with inter-denominational organizations. Yet he too, thanks less to theological principles than to an obsession with his church's legal privileges,[53] displayed an attitude that was hardly conducive to religious harmony. In 1824-25 he became involved in a dispute that vividly illustrated the ridiculous extremes to which Anglican intolerance could go. It all began in late 1822, when John Barclay, the Church of Scotland minister in Kingston, asked Stuart for permission to bury the Presbyterian dead in the Anglican cemetery known as the "lower burial ground." Stuart refused, stating that other denominations could use the cemetery only if they followed Anglican burial services. There matters rested until December 1824, when Barclay, determined to press the issue, led a funeral procession to the cemetery. Met by Stuart at the burial ground, Barclay retreated, but only for the time being. After Stuart turned down Barclay's appeal for negotiations — a solution that had been suggested by Attorney General John Beverley Robinson — Barclay led another procession to the cemetery in April 1825. There followed a bizarre confrontation that would have been hilarious had it not been so pathetic. At the burial site Stuart made his stand, reading Anglican prayers over the Presbyterian corpse. Not to be bested, Barclay ordered the grave to be filled as quickly as possible, and so for the remainder of the "service" shovels flew as Stuart spoke.

Stuart described this incident as "indecent, outrageous and profane," and Barclay, for his part, swore that until the dispute was settled, "those who may use force to prevent my Congregation from getting admittance to bury their dead ... must be responsible for all the evil that may result from it." The controversy reached the Executive Council, but that body, with Strachan in attendance, referred the matter to the imperial government while upholding, in the meantime, the right of "dissenters" to be buried in the cemetery on the condition that they accept the Anglican burial service. Barclay, thrown into a fury by the council's categorization of Presbyterians as dissenters, besieged York officialdom with documents supporting his congregation's case and forwarded a petition to the crown. In May 1826 the British government ruled in Stuart's favour, but Barclay was still not prepared to surrender. He responded to the verdict by publishing a pamphlet—described by one Anglican, Robert Stanton, as "dull, dirty & disgusting" — forcefully defending the Church of Scotland's co-established status in Upper Canada and its claim to a share of the clergy reserves. This sally, in turn, led to published rebuttals by two Anglicans, the prominent Tory Christopher Hagerman and the clergyman William Macaulay. The whole sorry business was brought to an end only by Barclay's premature death in September 1826.[54]

* * * * *

Although Strachan's assault on dissent can lay no claim to intellectual originality, it nevertheless occupies an important place in the history of Upper Canadian Anglicanism. It is important because it highlights the intellectual preoccupations of a man who, perched as he was at the upper reaches of the colonial establishment, was well situated to transform his ideas into public policy. It is important, as well, because it underlines both the increasingly angry spirit of the colony's leading Anglican clergyman, and, at a more general level, the extent to which inter-denominational relations had soured since the period from the 1790s to the immediate post-war years. Finally, it is important because it provides a window onto the Anglican community as a whole. The record is admittedly spotty, consisting of letters to the *Christian Recorder* and the curious cases of John Wenham and George Okill Stuart. But there is still every reason to believe that the anti-sectarianism expressed by Strachan, along with the values and assumptions that

In His Name

sustained it, was widely shared among the Anglican clergy. Lending support to this claim is the fact that, after the rebellion of 1837, hostility towards dissent was almost an article of faith for most Anglican clergymen. In sermons, newspapers, pamphlets and private correspondence, clergyman after clergyman poured out his hatred against the apostles of schism. Interestingly, this war against dissent was marked by many of the same arguments, and indeed much of the same language, as Strachan had used in earlier years.

One final point. When Strachan and other Anglicans began shunning inter-denominational organizations, they threw into stark relief the growing introversion of the Upper Canadian church. While Anglican clergymen clung well into the 1830s to the old dream of an Anglican Upper Canada, they were slowly losing their commitment to the salvation of souls outside the fold. This "isolationist" mentality, first evident in the opposition to inter-denominational Bible societies, was to become even more pronounced in the 1840s and 1850s. By the time the clergy reserves were secularized in 1854, many Anglicans took the view that the church should respond to reverses in this world not only by cutting its ties with rival denominations, but also by concentrating on its spiritual mission as a branch of the true church. The times had indeed changed, but the roots of that change lay in a much earlier era — in the strife-ridden, poisoned atmosphere of the 1820s and early 1830s.

NOTES

1. See Chapter One.
2. *Christian Recorder*, November 1820, p. 328.
3. Ibid.
4. Ibid.
5. Ibid., pp. 328-37.
6. Ibid., p. 337.
7. In this connection, see Strachan's letter of 1803 to Dr. Brown, cited later in this chapter. The letter clearly reveals Strachan's tactful attitude towards dissent in these years.
8. See the following sermons in the collection of Strachan Sermons at the AO: "And it shall be said in that day Lo this is our God" (19 Dec. 1824); "We pray you in Christ's stead be reconciled to God" (14 April 1828); "His commandments are not grievous" (13 Aug. 1837); "If thou wilt enter into life keep the commandments" (21 Nov. 1847); "And there was also a strife among them — which of them should be accounted the Greatest" (25 July 1848); "But to sit on my right hand and my left is not mine to give" (15 Dec. 1850).
9. Strachan Sermons, "But to sit on my right hand" (15 Dec. 1850).
10. Ibid., "If thou wilt enter unto life" (21 Nov. 1847).
11. Ibid.
12. Strachan Papers, Strachan to Brown, 27 Oct. 1803.
13. *Kingston Gazette*, "The Reckoner," 19 May 1812.
14. Strachan Sermons, "Let your light so shine before men that they may see your good works" (22 Feb. 1829).
15. Ibid., "Another parable he spake unto them" (1 Feb. 1835). A fine analysis of Strachan's redemption theology, and the critique of "enthusiasm" to which it gave rise, can be found in McDermott, "The Theology of Bishop John Strachan," pp. 170-212.
16. Strachan Papers, Strachan to Brown, 13 July 1806.
17. Strachan Sermons, "We are confident and willing to be absent from the body, and to be present with the Lord" (30 June 1822).
18. Ibid., "All Scripture is given by inspiration of God" (24 June 1804).
19. Strachan, *Sermon on the Death of the Bishop of Quebec*, p. 19.

In His Name

20   Strachan Sermons, "Now when they saw the boldness of Peter and John" (21 Oct. 1832).

21   For early expressions of Strachan's anti-Americanism, see Chapter Five.

22   Strachan, *Sermon on the Death of the Bishop of Quebec*, p. 19.

23   John Strachan, *Canada Church Establishment. Copy of a Letter Addressed to R.J. Wilmot Horton, Esq....dated 16th May, 1827; respecting the State of the Church in that Province* (London, 1827).

24   Strachan, *An Appeal in Behalf of the University of Upper Canada*, p. 10; *Observations on the Provision Made for the Maintenance of a Protestant Clergy*, p. 28.

25   John Strachan, *A Speech ... in the Legislative Council, Thursday Sixth March, 1828; on the Subject of the Clergy Reserves* (York, 1828), pp. 27-28.

26   The majority of the clergymen in the Scottish Episcopal Church in the eighteenth century did not embrace the Hanoverian dynasty until 1778. See William Ferguson, *Scotland: 1689 to the Present* (Edinburgh, 1969).

27   Strachan Sermons, "And the dead in Christ shall rise first" (25 Aug. 1811, "on the death of Dr. Stuart"). Mark McDermott advances a much different interpretation of Strachan's theological development in his thesis, "The Theology of Bishop John Strachan," claiming that Strachan's High Church principles had been formed by 1804 — thanks largely to the guidance of John Stuart — and that these principles were later strengthened by his friendship with Bishop Hobart. While not disputing Hobart's influence on Strachan, this writer finds McDermott's evidence for his other arguments rather thin. Strachan may indeed have been influenced by Stuart, but the fact remains that significant evidence of his High Church views dates only to the 1820s.

28   Hobart may also have sparked Strachan's interest in the idea of synodical government. See Chapter Seven for a discussion of this issue.

29   *Christian Recorder*, November 1820, pp. 321-32.

30   Ibid., February 1821, pp. 410-11.

31   Ibid., p. 416.

32   Ibid., 448.

33   Strachan, *Sermon on the Death of the Bishop of Quebec*, p. 13.

34   Ibid.

35   Strachan Sermons, "But sanctify the Lord in your hearts" (16 Jan. 1831).

36 Ibid., "Except the Lord build the House their labour is but lost that build it" (7 June 1832).

37 John Strachan, *Church Fellowship. A Sermon Preached on Wednesday, September 5, 1832. At the Visitation of the Honourable and Right Rev. Charles James, Bishop of Quebec* (York, 1832), p. 9.

38 Ibid., pp. 3-18, passim.

39 Strachan Sermons, "Earnestly contend for the Faith which was once delivered to the Saints" (9 March 1834).

40 John Strachan, *A Letter to the Rev. Thomas Chalmers, D.D. Professor of Divinity in the University of Edinburgh, on the Life and Character of the Right Reverend Dr. Hobart, Bishop of New York, North America* (New York, 1832), pp. 19-20.

41 Ibid., p. 37.

42 *Christian Recorder*, November 1820, pp. 321-23.

43 Ibid., February 1821, p. 441.

44 John Strachan, *A Letter on the Life and Character of Dr. Hobart*, p. 23.

45 Ibid., p. 26.

46 Ibid., p. 21.

47 *Christian Recorder*, May 1819, pp. 104-6. McDermott, in "The Theology of Bishop John Strachan," claims that articles attributed to correspondents in the *Recorder* and later the *Church* were probably written by Strachan. However, there is insufficient evidence to support this argument in the case of the *Recorder*, and the argument is definitely wrong in the case of the *Church*. Many *Church* correspondents who signed their articles with their initials can be positively identified.

48 *Christian Recorder*, December 1819, pp. 368-71; and January 1820, p. 414.

49 Ibid., March 1820, p. 37.

50 Ibid., September 1820, pp. 249-55.

51 See John Wenham, *A Sermon Preached before the Bishop of Quebec, and the Clergy of Upper Canada, at his Lordship's Primary Visitation, Held in York, on Wednesday, 30th Aug. 1826* (Brockville, 1826).

52 On Wenham's career as an Anglican clergyman, see Millman, *Jacob Mountain*, p. 222; and SPG Letters, Series C, Box IVA/40, no. 460. The latter contains the pertinent clippings from the *Brockville Recorder*.

53 George Okill Stuart could not be described as a profound theological

In His Name

    thinker. To the extent that his theology can be characterized at all, he was a Low Churchman — from the early 1850s he was aligned to the Low Church party within Upper Canadian Anglicanism. See Chapter Eight.

54   This account of the Stuart-Barclay battle is based on Robert Fraser's biography of Barclay in *DCB* VI (Toronto, 1987), pp. 31-33.

CHAPTER FIVE

THE DEFENCE OF THE OLD ORDER

As an ideologue, Strachan was anything but listless in responding to the religious and political developments of the 1820s and 1830s. Besides fighting a no-holds-barred battle with dissenters, he spent much of his time during these years expounding his highly conservative social and political philosophy. And he took every opportunity to defend the Church of England's established status against the attacks of those who were calling for religious equality. Without question, his pronouncements on these subjects reflected his feisty frame of mind as he locked horns with the forces of reform. Yet, at the same time, they could conceal neither his chastened perception of his church's future nor his increasingly sombre view of the state of Upper Canada and the world as a whole. The depth of his gloom was especially evident during the cholera epidemics of the early 1830s and the rebellion of 1837-38. When Strachan attributed such events to the wrath of God — and he was not the only clergyman to do so — he provided further evidence that the days of Anglican utopianism were drawing to an end.

*****

Strachan's vision of the good society, like his critique of "enthusiasm," was anything but original, resting on ideas and values which were commonplace in his time. In fact, the content of his vision was identical to that of the ideology which, according to the historian J.C.D. Clark, defined Britain's response to the French Revolution and long afterwards served as the intellectual foundation of the nation's social and political order.[1] During the conflict with revolutionary and Napoleonic

France, the conservative principles that had long reigned supreme in British culture reached the height of their influence. Proclaimed with greater passion and frequency than ever before, conservative ideology responded to the challenge of revolution by emphasizing the value of social subordination, political obedience and church establishment. With the restoration of peace in 1815, British conservatism remained immensely influential and, in the hands of leading members of the political and religious elite, became the prime ideological rationale for the defence of the existing order in church and state. Over time, however, the conservative cause lost support, and eventually suffered defeat with the achievement of Roman Catholic emancipation, the repeal of the Test and Corporation Acts, and the passage of the Reform Bill of 1832 — measures which, taken together, delivered a decisive blow to Britain's *ancien regime*. Yet throughout the battles of these years, defenders of that regime remained steadfast, refusing to yield on principles which in their mind were crucial to the very fabric of British society.

Strachan was a part of this conservative tradition; he subscribed to its main tenets and shared its unwavering attachment to the existing structure of society. Additionally, as was true of so many conservatives in the early nineteenth century, Strachan's social and political ideology crystallized during the French Revolution and its Napoleonic aftermath. Appalled by the bloodshed and disorder of the revolution, and no less disgusted by the career of Napoleon, Strachan waged an intense ideological campaign against the revolutionary spirit and the Napoleonic tyranny which it had produced. But he did not confine himself to denouncing the forces of darkness. Besides urging Upper Canadians to give their full support to the British cause, Strachan often waxed lyrical on Britain's divinely ordained mission in the struggle against revolutionary madness.

The depth of Strachan's feelings on these subjects was graphically illustrated in a sermon preached on 16 March 1804, "a day of humiliation and prayer on account of the war against Bonaparte." In this sermon Strachan began by portraying the conflict as a divine chastisement of the British people, who, because of economic prosperity, had fallen into habits of "rancorous discontent," "licentiousness," and "ostentatious extravagance." Then, proceeding to less gloomy matters, he confidently predicted that national repentance would inevitably

The Defence of the Old Order

lead to happier times in which the "God of battles" would stand fast with Britain. Proclaiming that "never did we stand up in a more glorious cause," Strachan urged his listeners to do their part in helping the mother country to resist a "sanguinary enemy" who aimed at the destruction of its "glorious constitution."[2]

The intensity of Strachan's conservatism and patriotism was just as evident in his *Discourse on the Character of King George the Third*, published in 1810. In this particularly florid piece of writing, Strachan described George III as a paragon of domestic and public virtues, heaped praise on Britain's constitution and its Upper Canadian copy, and expressed his disgust with the "terrible convulsion"[3] of the French Revolution and with Napoleon — that "betrayer of nations" and "scourge of the human race" whose unquestioned abilities were those of a "demon, always employed in promoting evil."[4] In addition, with Britain's deteriorating relations with the United States very much on his mind, Strachan singled out the American government and people for special abuse. Expressing views of the United States which would be central to the Upper Canadian Tory mind for decades to come,[5] he attributed the American Revolution to a "mania for undefined liberty and licentiousness"[6] and portrayed American society as a mobocracy where immorality, irreligion and political demagoguery reigned supreme.

With the outbreak of the War of 1812, Strachan found himself face to face with the forces of revolution, and his intellectual reaction was a combination of alarm and tenacity. He openly expressed anxiety about the state of the colony in a sermon preached at the start of the war, in which he announced that Upper Canada was threatened not only by the nation to the south but also by "doubtful characters and secret Traitors" within its own borders.[7] During the war he remained deeply concerned about the extent of disaffection in Upper Canada,[8] and as a means of ensuring the colony's survival he urged the local government to adopt the sternest measures, including the suspension of civil law, in dealing with the disloyal.[9] He also continued to attack the revolutionary spirit, particularly its American manifestation, and to express his patriotic message. In a sermon preached on 3 June 1814, another day of "General Thanksgiving," Strachan eulogized Britain's heroic role in resisting a "torrent of anarchy and next a military despotism," and attributed its success on the battlefield to the workings of a "superintending Providence."[10] He then turned on the United States, expressing his astonishment that this nation had, of its own free will, "deserted the cause of humanity, and joined the tyrant" in a campaign against a country that was the "shield of afflicted humanity, and the successful hope of a suffering world."[11] Regarding such behaviour as the result of the diseased nature of the American body politic, Strachan called on Upper Canadians to continue their heroic resistance to the "cruel invaders," assuring them that the "dawn of the happiest times is rising upon us."[12] Already, he stressed, their "glorious career" on the battlefield had won for them a reputation among British subjects that would be "forever precious."[13]

Strachan's anxieties abated somewhat after the war, but the respite was only temporary. With the first stirrings of religious and political discontent in the late 1810s and early 1820s, he became convinced that demagogues were once again at work in Upper Canada, and his conviction grew stronger and stronger in subsequent years. Believing that demands for political reform and the crusade against the established church were additional manifestations of the cancer of revolution, he reacted in a predictable fashion. Throughout the 1820s and 1830s he assailed doctrines which, like the people who advocated them, were subversive of Upper Canada's social and political order. At the same time, as if he were intent on reproving Upper Canadians for their public sins, he set out his own ideological outlook on the world. The main elements of this vision had been present in his sermons and writings during the Napoleonic Wars and the War of 1812; his pronouncements in the post-1820 period dealt with the same themes and in much the same way, underlining the remarkable consistency of his political ideology over several decades. But there was a new feature in Strachan's public expressions of conservative ideology: for the first time, his commitment to the policy of church establishment occupied a central place in his resistance to the spirit of revolution.

Strachan's social and political philosophy, both before and after 1815, posited a view of the natural and social order that had deep roots in Western culture. By the early 1800s it was a basic assumption of Anglican thought that there was an overall design and structure in the natural world, with each of its parts ranked according to its function, and that all of this was the handiwork of an all-seeing and all-powerful God. In addition, extending its analysis to the affairs of human beings,

Anglican theology saw the class divisions of society as a reflection of the structure of the universe as a whole. This view of the natural and social order partly rested on the old Christian perception of the world as a "Great Chain of Being," in which every creature, from the lowliest insect to the angels in heaven, had an assigned place.[14] It also derived its inspiration from the precepts of natural theology. Receiving its initial formulation in the late seventeenth century, natural theology gradually gained a central place in the Anglican imagination. Its view of the universe as a finely crafted mechanism, where all was orderly and everything had a place, reflected the rationalist assumptions of the age. As well, it meshed perfectly with prevailing conservative doctrine, and indeed provided that doctrine with an intellectual justification of great force. For conservatives, it was but a short step from marvelling at the rank and order of creation to perceiving the hierarchical structure of society as the product of a divine intelligence. In this grand system, the poor and weak had their place while the rich and powerful had theirs. The former were obliged to accept their lot in life, respect their social superiors, and obey the laws of the land and the authorities that ruled over them; the latter were duty-bound to carry out their responsibilities conscientiously and to treat their inferiors with kindness and charity. For both groups, the structure of society, like that of the universe of which it formed a part, operated in their best interest.[15]

In Strachan's case, the framework of natural theology had a flexibility that it often lacked in the minds of others. Probably because he himself had risen from a humble background to a position of power and influence, he was sensitive to the need for a certain degree of social mobility,[16] and his opinions on this subject explain why he supported scholarships for intellectually able but financially disadvantaged students in Upper Canada's grammar schools. Even so, Strachan's progressive stance on matters of class should not be exaggerated. Far from being an apostle of egalitarianism, he too saw the hierarchical structure of society as divinely ordained. While he favoured the idea of promoting social mobility for the talented poor, he never went so far as to claim that most of the poor, if given a chance, would be able to climb the social ladder. Quite the opposite. His declarations on the subject of the social structure make clear his essentially pessimistic view of the ability of human beings to improve their lot.

In His Name

In the first decade of the century Strachan frequently defended class divisions as part of the natural order of things. For example, in an 1806 sermon preached before Lieutenant Governor Peter Hunter, he claimed that those who were "obscure in the world of no account or consideration" owed their "low station" to the "will of God."[17] Later, in his 1814 sermon on the day of "General Thanksgiving," he announced that

> ...the present age has demonstrated, that no great and decided amelioration of the lower classes of society can be reasonably expected .... much improved they certainly may be; but that foolish perfectability with which they have been deluded, can never be realized .... In times of tranquility, the people may be better instructed, the laws may be made more equal and just; and many new avenues of enjoyment may be opened, but labour is the lot of man; and no system of policy can render it unnecessary, or relieve the greater proportion of mankind from suffering many privations.[18]

Of course, what constituted "foolish perfectability" for one person meant significant improvement for another. Strachan's belief that even the latter was beyond the reach of most people was revealed in a sermon first preached in 1824 and repeated again in 1825, 1827, 1828 and 1836. The sermon gave explicit expression to his belief that the different ranks of society reflected the structure of the universe:

> in the natural world we see objects differing from one another in all the degrees of Beauty & excellence and a mutual connection and independence pervading the whole. The various classes — and the various parts of the individual — all subsisting by their dependence upon one another .... It is evident that there is a subordination in the Natural World. We may extend the analogy and suppose that it is the intention of nature that the like subordination should prevail in the Moral world. Accordingly we find an infinite diversity in the tempers dispositions and talents of men .... One is

> formed to rule another to obey .... Hence it would appear that they who labour in the inferior departments of life are not on that account the slaves of their Superiors. The Magistrate requires the aid of his people. The Master of his Servant. They are all dependent upon one another, as they subsist by an exchange of good Offices .... The lowest order enjoys its peculiar comforts, and privileges, and contributes equally with the highest to the Support and dignity of Society.

Having tied social divisions to the rank and order evident in creation, Strachan then underlined the need for all human beings to resign themselves to the position which God had assigned them. In a world of order and structure, Strachan argued, "all murmuring at the inferiority of our station is most unreasonable." While not condemning the innate human desire for social advancement, he urged those in humble positions to compare their own happiness with the cares that would inevitably be their lot if they attained greatness, cares "which neither the most delicate repast nor costly apparel nor a multitude of friends and dependents nor all the glories of a crown can alleviate." This consolation was coupled with others grown equally threadbare with age. Strachan emphasized that people would be more contented with their position in life if they reflected on the situation of those who were their inferiors in the social scale. He also declared in his peroration that the earthly sufferings of individuals were divinely ordained for their temporal and spiritual welfare. "The Father whom we serve," he explained, "will never permit anything to happen to his children but what must in the end promote their happiness." His listeners were consequently urged to bear with "patience and submission the dispensations of their Creator," remembering that "to murmur against those events which he permits is to rebel against his Government and to complete our own misery."[19]

Strachan was not the only clergyman to speak in such terms. One of his clerical colleagues, Thomas Phillips, preached in 1826 that sincere Christians had a duty to obey those who were in positions of civil authority and to remain contented in their earthly stations. "The Almighty, who created men for two worlds," he noted, "has decreed ... that there should be different orders and classes in society; the high and the low, the rich and the poor; some who have riches, and others who have none; some to bear rule, and others to obey." Distinctions among people relating to worldly possessions and power, far from being the cause of unhappiness, were "calculated to produce the general enjoyment and welfare" of all his creatures. Poverty enabled the poor to display "honest industry," to "shew forth patience & contentment in difficulties," to display their gratitude to God and their fellow human beings for whatever happiness they did enjoy, and to "fulfill the various useful offices, which it is necessary some of us should perform, in order that the existence, support, and business of society may be maintained." Conversely, the sharing of power among all people would lead to a "universal struggle" in which the most evil and powerful would emerge triumphant, ruling with a "rod of iron" over the weak and virtuous, and depriving both rich and poor of "rights, liberties & property."[20]

In 1835 another clergyman, Adam Burwell of Bytown, was equally categorical in arguing that the the duty of obedience to the "powers that be" was inseparable from the duty of individuals to remain satisfied with their earthly station.[21] In his *Doctrine of the Holy Spirit*, Burwell announced that the lot of all people, be they rulers or subjects, had been determined by God. He emphasized that only those chosen by God could attain lofty heights of power and influence and that "it is not education, but God that makes the gift; and if God has not given it, all the art of man cannot confer it." There then followed the classic defence of a stratified society — the notion that, since God was the author of social divisions in this world, attempts to advance beyond an assigned station would be a rejection of God's will which could result only in profound unhappiness. "Hence the grievous disappointments men experience from human selection to places of trust and importance," he wrote, "and the pain and loss, both of money, care, and future usefulness, from the education of children at random, or from ambition for that profession or calling, to which God never adopted their proper gift."[22]

The rub in all of this was sin: human beings, flawed as they were, showed a deep-seated tendency to ignore God's design for the social and political order. Strachan saw the sinfulness of human nature as the root cause of the world's troubles before 1815, and he saw no reason to change his mind in the years that followed. On the contrary, the notion that human beings were inherently sinful was central to his conservative ideology in the post-1820 period. He declared in a sermon of 1823 that "it is not from without but from within that our greatest enemies arise," and to support his argument he pointed to "our evil passions our inordinate desires our craving apetites [sic] our secret rivalships and jealousies our false estimations of present things."[23] In another sermon preached throughout the 1820s and 1830s he drew attention to the numerous imperfections in body, mind and spirit which men inherited as "created but fallen beings." Those who doubted that the follies of human beings were a matter of serious concern were reminded of the misery resulting from the "extravagant indulgence of our apetites and passions."[24] Yet another sermon, preached one year before the rebellion, contained the following exclamation: "how many sources of wickedness are there within us — do not our will, our reason prove the corruption of our nature ... do we not see vice & wickedness everywhere around us and polluting us by their contamination ...."[25]

This view of human nature had important implications for Strachan's view of the function of society. In his eyes, society, through its laws and regulations, served to guard against the complete collapse of social order that would inevitably occur if human passions were given free rein. According to this perspective, society maintained security in "person and property" and acted as the foundation of "true liberty," while individuals, in return, undertook to fulfill those social obligations on which their earthly happiness and spiritual well-being depended. The other side of the coin was that the abolition of laws would destroy the happiness and prosperity of everyone, even the virtuous. As early as 1810, in reference to the Lockean theory of the social contract, Strachan wrote: "A principle has been adopted by some writers, and held up as indisputable, that in society we surrender part of our natural liberty to secure the rest. This principle is false — we make no such surrender — we gain everything, we lose nothing."[26] He advanced a similar argument in the 1820s. The congregation at St. James's, York, was told in an 1821 sermon that the legal restraints controlling the conduct of "all states and conditions of men" were the "surest foundation of true liberty," for in the absence of such restraints people could not expect to "live happily & securely together and enjoy the comforts of society." The reluctance of so many to accept this truth

In His Name

forced Strachan to warn his flock that the absolute freedom of the individual would lead inevitably to anarchy and widespread suffering. "We are too much disposed to look for the sources of felicity," he announced, "in being free from all restraints — and controlled by no law — limited by no authority & with the full power of doing whatever we please. But were all this granted instead of happiness we should reap misery."[27]

Yet, if only because society's laws and regulations could sometimes be avoided with impunity, they alone were not sufficient to protect society from the consequences of human sinfulness. Religion, as Strachan repeatedly observed, was also indispensable to the cause of maintaining social order. Reflecting the potent blend of religious and secular principles that accounted for much of the power of conservative ideology, Strachan maintained that one of the central functions of religion was to remind the wealthy of their obligations towards the less fortunate, thereby cementing those paternalistic bonds which made the poor more contented with their earthly lot and less bitter towards their social superiors. At the same time, religion had a particularly important role to play in controlling the baser instincts of human nature, especially those "contending passions," wicked "apetites," "malignant desires" and "secret envyings" which Strachan claimed were "ever ready to burst into flame."[28] Religion also performed a critical social function by reminding people, rich and poor alike, of two basic truths: that their temporal sufferings were, to borrow a phrase used by Strachan in 1819, "dispensations of Providence" which were meant as trials of faith and to which all Christians were required to submit in a spirit of "ready acquiescence";[29] and that any act of disrespect or disobedience towards their "betters" and the "powers that be" would lead to misery in the present life and damnation in the next. In an 1819 article in the *Christian Recorder*, Strachan pointed out that the Christian religion, with "its tone of tranquility and peace, its anxiety to inculcate patience, resignation and forebearance, and to give honour to whom honour is due," was the pillar of any stable and civilized society.[30] Many years later, preaching after the death of one of his grandsons, he declared that to banish the terrors of the Last Judgment from the human mind would result in "general confusion and the total destruction of all the blessings of society." "For it is not the

The Defence of the Old Order

power of reason it is not the sense of duty — it is not even obedience to the commands of our Maker that keeps men to their stations — but it is the love of life ... the dread of death and the darkness and gloom which cover the eternal world...."[31]

Strachan's deep attachment to the Church of England was directly related to his views on the role of religion in society. His fervent Anglicanism was primarily motivated not by a spirit of fanaticism or intolerance, but by a passionately held conviction that the Church of England was the denomination best suited to perform the social functions of religion. Throughout his life he maintained that the Church of England, renowned for its historic role as one of the pillars of the British constitution, was the ideal instrument to remind people of the necessity of "due subordination" in the social and political structure. Thus, in an 1824 address to Lieutenant Governor Maitland on behalf of the Clergy Reserves Corporation, he stated that the Anglican clergy were engaged in the diffusion of "those principles of piety, loyalty and obedience for which the Church of England has ever been distinguished."[32] The same ideas were expressed in his 1828 speech to the Legislative Council, in which he clearly implied that the Church of England was the most effective bulwark of the social and political order.[33]

The Church of England was to be prized for another reason as well. It was Strachan's belief that, because of its well-known attachment to Britain and its character as a vital part of the British constitution, the Church of England played a critical role in promoting loyalty to the imperial tie. To him, the point was not insignificant. In the years before 1815, Strachan's view of the supernatural significance of the war with Napoleonic France rested on an intense devotion to Britain — a nation whose religious and moral life was presided over by a branch of the catholic church, whose incomparable constitution reconciled the claims of individual freedom and public security, and whose social and political structure was founded upon the principle of subordination. During the War of 1812 — as his 1814 sermon on the day of "General Thanksgiving" showed — this messianic perception of the British cause underwent a subtle shift in emphasis, becoming linked with a nascent sense of Upper Canadian identity. Seeing that conflict as the inevitable product of the degeneracy of American society,

Strachan reached the conclusion that Upper Canada had an obligation to act as the guardian on the North American continent of the values it had inherited from the parent state. In the years that followed, therefore, Strachan's imperial patriotism, reinforced and accorded a distinctively Upper Canadian tone by the wars against France and the United States, was always reflective of a more fundamental loyalty to certain values which Britain embodied and which Upper Canada had a mission to defend. And it was precisely because of his commitment to these values that he was so passionately attached to the insitution that, more than any other, upheld them: the Church of England.[34]

Strachan's view of the Church of England as a guardian of the imperial tie was revealed in 1824, when he wrote in a letter to the Colonial Office that "the great bond of all attachment between the Colonies and Great Britain depends almost exclusively upon the progress and influence of Church Principles," and that the American Revolution would never have occurred had the Church of England in the Thirteen Colonies been properly supported by the home government.[35] Again, in his 1824 address on behalf of the Clergy Reserves Corporation, he noted that an established church was "an effectual part of our happy Constitution" and that the rejection of this truth would prevent "the Inhabitants of the Province from looking up to the British Empire for the preservation of their religious as well as civil liberty."[36] The same arguments were made in his 1825 sermon on the death of Bishop Mountain, his 1827 pamphlet on the subject of the clergy reserves, his 1827 *Ecclesiastical Chart* and his 1830 *Letter to Thomas Frankland Lewis*.

In relation to this, Strachan's opinions on the value of an Anglican establishment must be seen as part of his overall response to Upper Canada's changing religious and political climate. Before 1820, probably because of his belief that dissenters would re-enter the Anglican fold if care was taken not to arouse their prejudices, Strachan had maintained a discreet silence on questions relating to the political status of the Church of England: only once, in an article for the *Kingston Gazette* in 1812, did he set forth his views on the issue of church establishment, and even then he did not so much defend the Church of England's established position as discuss in general terms the concept of establishment itself.[37] Such restraint seemed both pointless and dangerous in the 1820s, when non-Anglican denominations were displaying a new political self-consciousness and campaigning vigorously for religious equality. Strachan, convinced that the Church of England's interests were intertwined with the interests of Upper Canadian society as a whole, now abandoned his earlier policy of moderation and embarked on a crusade designed to defend the policy of church establishment. The case he presented for this policy drew upon two distinct strands in Anglican thinking. One was the utilitarian view that the established Church of England had a vital role to perform in upholding the social and political order; the other was the organic theory of the essential unity of church and state.

The main tenets of the utilitarian position had been set out by William Warburton in 1748. Instead of basing his defence of church establishment on religious claims concerning the Church of England's doctrinal purity, Warburton argued that the policy of church establishment was grounded in the principle of "public utility." For him, the church needed the assistance of the state in its religious work, while the state needed the services of the church in the promotion of social stability. Accordingly, the two parties had entered into a "politic League and alliance for mutual support and defence."[38] By the terms of this alliance, the church surrendered a measure of authority over its affairs and in exchange acquired financial assistance, laws protecting it from its rivals, and the right to a place in the national legislature; the state, for its part, acquired new obligations in supporting the cause of religion, but also gained the support of an institution that, by means of its promise of eternal rewards and its threat of eternal punishment, exercised unmatched power over human conduct. As for the theoretical question of which church in a given society deserved the status of an establishment, Warburton asserted that on this issue as well the criterion of utility should apply. Since the function of an established church was to preserve social order, the privileges of an establishment should be conferred on the denomination that could best perform that role. In every instance, the denomination with the greatest ability to promote social order would be the one that commanded the loyalty of a majority of the population. If, having received the status of an establishment, it then lost that status, said Warburton, "the alliance becomes void...the state becomes disengaged. And a NEW ALLIANCE is, of course, contracted with the now prevailing church, for the reasons which made the old."[39]

In His Name

In 1783 William Paley restated and modified the utilitarian case. Illustrating the extent to which, by the late eighteenth century, the church-state connection had become an article of faith in British political thought, Paley—unlike Warburton—ignored the theoretical justification for a church establishment. Instead, taking the fact of establishment for granted, he concentrated on the principal features of an established church and the role it performed in society. On the first of these issues, Paley held that an established church had a regular body of clergy involved in its work, that it supported the clergy with revenue derived from the state, and that it was the only denomination to enjoy the state's financial assistance. On the second issue, he too based his analysis on the principle of utility, but his focus was different from Warburton's. Whereas Warburton had dwelt on the role of the established church as an ally of the state and a mainstay of the social order, Paley described its mission in strictly religious terms: its task was the "preservation and communication of religious knowledge,"[40] and nothing more. Like Warburton, however, Paley believed that only a denomination representing a majority of the population was entitled to established status, because only such a denomination could confer religious benefits on society as a whole. If no church enjoyed majority status, said Paley, no church should be established.[41]

By the late eighteenth century the utilitarianism of Warburton and Paley found itself challenged by a much different position. Increasingly popular in religious and political circles, this position was most eloquently expressed in 1790 by Edmund Burke in his *Reflections on the Revolution in France*. According to Burke, the Church of England's established status was not the product of a compact between church and state; nor should it be justified on the grounds of utility. Rather than being just an ally of the state, the church was essential to the state's very nature as a "consecrated" institution permeated by the "sublime principles" of religion.[42] More than this, while he agreed that the Church of England was a mainstay of the social order, he had little use for theories of a church-state alliance because in his mind the two bodies were, and had always been, indivisible. Their unity, moreover, was a reflection of the greater unity of the constitution of which they were parts. For Burke, the church was the state, the state was the church, and both were the constitution. As he put it, Englishmen "do not consider their church establishment as convenient, but as essential

The Defence of the Old Order

to their state; not as a thing heterogeneous and separable; something added for accommodation; what they may either keep or lay aside, according to their temporary ideas of convenience. They consider it as the foundation of their whole constitution, with which, and with every part of which, it holds an indissoluble union."[43]

For Upper Canadian Anglicans like Strachan, neither the utilitarian case for church establishment nor the organic case were completely satisfactory. Utilitarianism, at least of the Warburtonian variety, certainly reinforced claims that the Upper Canadian church was critical to the maintenance of social stability; but on the other hand, its argument that an established church should represent a majority of the population was dangerous, to put it mildly. As for the organic argument, it had the advantage of ignoring the thorny question of popular support, but it could hardly be relied on exclusively when, in Upper Canada, the unity of church and state was under sustained attack. Obviously, more practical arguments were needed as well. For all these reasons, Strachan combined selective elements of the utilitarian position with organic theory. He portrayed the policy of church establishment as crucial to Upper Canada's future as a stable and loyal colony, sidestepping the issue of popular support by arguing that a strong church establishment would in the long run make the Church of England the church of the majority. At the same time, the policy was defended as a public recognition of the unity of church and state that characterized the British constitution and its colonial "image and transcript," the Constitutional Act of 1791. This blend of arguments may have lacked philosophical consistency, but Strachan, never a philosopher, was not concerned with such matters. He was prepared to use any argument that could serve his church's interests.[44]

Strachan's belief in the social and political utility of Upper Canada's Anglican establishment was expressed on numerous occasions in the 1820s and 1830s. In an 1824 letter to the Colonial Office he argued that the "Great William Pitt," being well aware that the establishment of the Church of England in the Thirteen Colonies would have prevented the American Revolution, made provision in the Constitutional Act for the endowment of the Church of England so that "the Canadas might be attached to the Parent State by religious as well as political feelings."[45] In 1824 he announced to Lieutenant Governor Maitland that the form of Christianity taught by the Church of England was "the most compatible with our form of government" and that Anglican clergymen, "if left in the free enjoyment of those rights and privileges embodied in the Constitutional Act," would unite "as a phalanx round the Colonial Administration."[46] The same insistence on the role of the established Church of England in instilling loyalty into the hearts of Upper Canadians can be found in Strachan's sermon on the death of Bishop Mountain, his *Ecclesiastical Chart* and his *Letter to Thomas Frankland Lewis*.[47]

No less frequent were Strachan's defences of church establishment as a reflection of the unity of church and state. In his 1827 *Observations on the Provision Made for the Maintenance of a Protestant Clergy*, he asserted that "by the law of England the church is an integral part of the state."[48] Three years later he announced his intention to remain unyielding in his defence of the "unity of church and state," which was the "brightest ornament of the British constitution."[49] In an 1835 series of Lenten lectures delivered in St. James's Church he denounced the "wickedness, infidelity and guilt of professing Christians, who try to separate Church and State; civil and religious institutions inseparably connected by the appointment of Heaven, and the constitution of human nature."[50] Finally, at a meeting of the archdeaconries of York and Kingston in 1836, he reflected that "Church and State, comprehending the whole Clerical and lay population, should be mixed and blended into one Constitution." He added that this "is precisely the character which Christianity has assumed since it was freely recognized in the world, and which it is now sought to destroy; — but as well may you seek to separate soul and body, as to separate Church and State in a Christian nation."[51]

Strachan's opinions on the subject of church establishment were also revealed in his criticisms of the Church of England's opponents. Throughout the 1820s and 1830s Strachan argued that a decision to share the bounty of the clergy reserves with the "sectaries" would assist their endeavours to spread sedition and fanaticism, thus negating whatever stabilizing influence the Church of England could exert. The same argument, of course, could not be used against the Church of Scotland, that pillar of conservatism which proposed not that all denominations be publicly supported but only that its claim to co-establishment be recognized. But even the Church of Scotland could be criticized for not seeing the implications of its demands. Strachan pointed out in 1824 that the creation of "two rival Establishments" would "infallibly produce" a "Spirit of disunion, competition, and irritation."⁵² A few years later he drew attention to an even more disastrous consequence that would inevitably follow the granting of the Presbyterian request for a portion of the reserves. He quoted from a memorial drawn up in 1823 by the bishop of Quebec and the clergy of Upper Canada, which warned that acceptance of the Kirk's interpretation of the words "Protestant Clergy" in the Constitutional Act would make it morally and legally impossible to resist the demands of the more obscure sects for a share of the Church of England's patrimony. The rejecton of these claims, which were no less valid than those of the Kirk, would "scatter the seeds" of religious controversy and thereby further undermine the strength of the Church of England, one of the "safest bonds" connecting Upper Canada and the parent state.⁵³

This response to the campaign for religious equality was complemented by a narrowly legalistic view of the Church of England's established status. Since the Constitutional Act made provision for the endowment of the Church of England, Strachan was not compelled to defend the policy of church establishment on theoretical grounds; he merely had to point to the clauses of the Upper Canadian constitution which defined the Church of England's status in law. Accordingly, Strachan often refuted voluntarists not by critically examining their various arguments but simply by declaring, with an air of authoritative finality, that the Constitutional Act recognized the unity of church and state and made provision for the endowment of the Church of England. Similarly, the Kirk's campaign for co-establishment status led Strachan to compose minor treatises, such as his 1839 *Letter to Dr. Lee*, designed to establish conclusively that the phrase "Protestant Clergy" referred only to the Church of England.⁵⁴ Not once did it occur to him that the ecclesiastical clauses of the Constitutional Act, having been drawn up by mortal men, might have been misguided. Nor did he ever admit that the religiously pluralistic nature of Upper Canadian society might necessitate a reconsideration, and perhaps even abandonment, of the policy of church establishment set out in the 1791 Act. From his legalistic perspective, the fact that the Church of England was a church of the minority in no way affected its established status. As he wrote in 1829 to another Anglican clergyman, John Bethune, "I contend that were we not half so numerous as we are the reserves are legally ours."⁵⁵

Strachan's inflexibility in this respect can be easily explained. From his standpoint, people who were willing to tamper with the ecclesiastical clauses of the Constitutional Act could be criticized on a number of grounds. They displayed their support of the revolutionary doctrine that constitutions could be altered or discarded whenever demands arose for change. They demonstrated a lack of respect for a constitution which, as a copy of Britain's own, was the embodiment of the wisdom of the ages. Finally, they ignored the fact that the established Church of England was an integral component of the British constitution, and that consequently, Upper Canada's rejection of the policy of church establishment would lead to a drastic alteration of its social and political structure — perhaps even to a severance of the imperial tie. Acutely aware of these errors on the part of his opponents, Strachan adopted an entirely different approach to the issue of church establishment. All of his major published defences of the Church of England's established position rested on the assumption that the Constitutional Act, with its provision for the endowment of the Church of England, enshrined principles which could not be repudiated without unravelling the legal fabric of society.

Strachan was equally inflexible when he responded to those who argued that the Church of England should follow the example of other denominations and derive its support from the voluntary contributions of its own members. The application of the voluntary principle to the Church of England, he believed, would destroy the unity of church and state, thereby depriving the Church of England of the financial resources it needed to perform its social and political duties as well as to spread the principles of sound religion. In addition, as will later be shown in greater detail, Strachan took the position, shared by many of his clerical colleagues, that voluntarism would have insidious effects both on clergymen and on the church's efforts to fulfill its religious responsibilities. With respect to the clergy, Strachan contended that voluntarism would destroy the independence and status of the ministerial calling, transforming clergymen into public wards whose teachings would have to conform to the tastes of their flocks, and undermining the appeal of Christianity in those "respectable" circles that placed great stock on the ministry's social position. As for the church as a whole, Strachan insisted that a Church of England supported by its own flock would not be able to overcome the religious destitution afflicting the Anglican community. Ignoring the fact that a lack of state support had not prevented other denominations from growing at a remarkable rate, Strachan frequently asserted that his church, because of the impoverished condition of Anglican settlers, could not rely exclusively on voluntary contributions if its ministrations were to be made available throughout a colony as immense as Upper Canada.[56]

Strachan's arguments in defence of church establishment were bound together by his vision of the future. In his eyes, a Church of England that retained its established status, and strengthened its position at the same time, would forever guarantee the survival of Upper Canada as a stable and loyal society. It would also be well placed to bring the majority of Upper Canadians into its fold, thus undermining the voluntarist argument that religious equality was the only practical policy in a society as diverse as Upper Canada. This ingenious adaptation of utilitarian theory served to support the Church of England's claims to established status as well as Strachan's plans for improving its fortunes. Yet it was not merely a propaganda tool: until the 1830s Strachan believed with all his heart that, if steps were taken to assist the Church of England, the goal of an Anglican Upper Canada was within reach. In his sermon on the death of Bishop Mountain, Strachan announced that additional British financial assistance to the Church of England establishment would unite the "whole population" in "one holy communion."[57] A couple of years later, in a letter accompanying his *Ecclesiastical Chart*, he asserted that the "tendency of the population is towards the Church of England, and nothing but the want of moderate support prevents her from spreading over the whole Province."[58] And again, in a letter to George Jehoshaphat Mountain, he stressed that "our argument is not what we are but what we shall soon be if left unmolested."[59]

One clergyman, John Leeds of Brockville and Augusta, dissented from this view, claiming that the Church of England's connection with the state was "a main obstacle to its advancement."[60] But it was Leeds, not Strachan, who was unusual. The 1823 memorial of the bishop of Quebec and the Upper Canadian clergy echoed Strachan's belief that "there manifestly appears the fairest prospect that the Church of England, from the favourable disposition that now exists towards it, will be able to collect within its bosom the bulk of the inhabitants of the

In His Name

Province, should no prospect of supporting their Clergy be held out to the various Protestant denominations."[61]

*****

Such confidence could not last forever. As the struggle for religious and political reform gained momentum, Anglican clergymen became increasingly angry and frustrated, and they expressed their feelings in embittered attacks on those responsible for blocking the Church of England's progress. Strachan's charge, for example, that Methodist preachers disseminated fanaticism and republicanism was both an attempt to strengthen his church's exclusive claim to the clergy reserves, and a reflection of his hostility towards the denomination that was leading the crusade against the policy of church establishment. Similarly, his criticism of the Presbyterian demand for co-establishment revolved around the idea that the Kirk was guilty of unprovoked aggression against a church which was entirely innocent of any wrongdoing. In 1827 he complained that Anglican clergymen were "attacked and reviled on all sides" and that the Kirk was filling newspapers with "unmerited and vulgar abuse of the Church of England."[62]

Other Anglican clergymen were equally enraged when they considered the besieged position of their church. Adam Burwell, never one to conceal his strong opinions, wrote in 1831 that "every dissenter is in the train of rebellion" and that the Church of England's opponents "must be attacked as if they were a drove of hogs in mischief."[63] William Bettridge of Woodstock informed the colonial secretary in 1837 that, by responding favourably to the demands of the "enemies of the Church," the imperial government was endangering "not the prosperity or efficiency only, but the very existence of the established Church of England in U.C."[64] Another Anglican clergyman, who preferred to remain anonymous, expressed his regret that the Kirk, which had previously been on friendly terms with the Church of England, had decided to "raise the sudden and angry cry of discontent and hatred, and strike at us with a concealed poignard steeped in the 'gall of Bitterness.'"[65] In 1837 a correspondent to the *Church* denounced those

The Defence of the Old Order

"who, though calling themselves Christians, are seen, in these our days ... leaguing themselves with men whose sole object, under the specious pretext of securing religious liberty and freedom of worship, is to destroy all religion and worship." Warning of "the countless infidel hordes, ready to burst upon the Church," he urged "every true friend of religion ... to brave himself for the glorious toil, the severe struggle, of attempting to achieve the deliverance of the Church from her present desolate and oppressed state."[66]

The anger and frustration of Anglican clergymen were also attributable to developments outside Upper Canada. In the 1820s and 1830s liberalism seemed to be sweeping the Western world. Its progress was marked by the triumph of Jacksonian democracy in the United States and the French Revolution of 1830. Its influence was also evident in Britain; there, the dawning of a new order was symbolized not only by the achievement of religious equality for Roman Catholics and dissenters and by the Reform Bill of 1832, but also by the call for a reduction in imperial commitments, the growing demand for the replacement of imperial tariffs with a system of free trade, and the emergence of working class protest in the form of the Chartist movement. In these circumstances, it was only natural that Anglican clergymen should display a sense of alienation from a world which seemed determined to rush headlong into infidelity and anarchy. It was equally natural that they should regard the turbulence of Upper Canadian society as a manifestation of the same revolutionary ideas which were wreaking such havoc in the United States, Britain and Europe.

John Strachan exemplified alienation in the midst of the revolutionary age, and the tendency to equate the state of Upper Canada with the state of the world. In 1832 he told John Macaulay that "infidel and democratic principles are in unison and are spreading fast & wide"; he noted with respect to the "present deplorable situation" of Britain that "in all probability sad convulsions and many years of darkness are to come — in some of which we must participate." He also asserted that Upper Canada's Alien Bill,[67] which made "rebels equal to Loyalists," and the crusade against the established Church of England were destroying those distinctive rights which Upper Canadians enjoyed as British subjects. From this he concluded that "under such circumstances to talk of attachment to British institutions is quite ridiculous," though he cautioned against despair and emphasized "our duty to persevere to the last in resisting what we believe evil."[68] A year later, in a letter to a British correspondent, he reflected solemnly that a revolution was already in progress in Britain and its colonies, one which might "be quieter or slower in its movements as circumstances fall out," but which would "never rest till the Glorious Fabric of the Constitution is crumpled in the dust."[69] He informed another British correspondent, that "whatever commotions you may have we proceed in your wake. It appears to me that unless a great union of parties now take place & a determined stand be made against further innovation there is no hope and revolution becomes inevitable."[70]

This sort of world view — so indicative of the spirit of conservatism in the first half of the nineteenth century — was shared by A.N. Bethune, the Anglican clergyman in Cobourg, and by Adam Burwell. In 1831 Bethune, reporting from London on the progress of the Reform Bill in Parliament, wrote to Strachan that "it is hard to say what the consequences will be — great confusion I fear. Even now master[s] of a revolutionary spirit show themselves."[71] He was equally apprehensive towards the end of the year, when he told Strachan that "the spirit of revolution was spreading" throughout Europe.[72] In his 1835 pamphlet, *A Voice of Warning and Instruction Concerning the Signs of the Times*, Burwell argued that the French revolution was the first manifestation of that spirit of "Infidel Lawlessness ... which has carried all the revolutionary measures in England from the repeal of the corporation and test acts down to the present hour; which has caused all the difficulties in Lower Canada; which has so much agitated Upper Canada within ten or twelve years past; and ... which bids fair to demolish everything worth preservation."[73] Hysteria and pessimism also featured in Burwell's *Doctrine of the Holy Spirit*, in which the world was attacked for its "infidel radicalism," its separation of church and state, its susceptibility to the "demon of demagoguism," and its attachment to the violence and moral barbarism that characterized "popular elections."[74] All these signs of sinfulness, Burwell claimed, were especially evident in Britain, a nation whose leaders had "apostatized from every principle of the Reformation and in addition to this wickedness, destroyed even the Christian character of the fundamental principles of the constitution."[75] Moreover, Britain's guilt

The Defence of the Old Order

was magnified by the fact that imperial statesmen were partly responsible for the troubles of the Canadas. The fatal mistake of Britain in dealing with Upper and Lower Canada, said Burwell, was in following "that constant course of concession to the clamour and insolence of designing revolutionists, and the sacrifice of the firm supporters of the crown to their malice."[76] Thus, Britain's sinfulness was both the "presage" of its "downfall" and "the cause of the disorders that of late have broken forth throughout the empire."[77]

The events of the 1830s had a profound impact on Strachan's perception of the Church of England's place in Upper Canadian society. Religious and political warfare did not persuade him to renounce his belief that a Church of England which retained its landed endowment would soon attract the allegiance of all Upper Canadians. But as the crusade for religious equality gained increasing support, it gradually became clear to him that the Church of England might in the near future be deprived of its established status and forced to reconcile itself to the denominational pluralism of Upper Canadian life. This prospect, combined with the setbacks experienced by the church on other fronts, eroded Strachan's optimism. The notion that God had ordained the imminent triumph of the Anglican cause was slowly undermined by the conviction that the Church of England was being abandoned by its friends and ruthlessly persecuted by its enemies. His new and more pessimistic frame of mind, evident in his vehement attacks on the church's opponents both in Upper Canada and Britain, was perhaps best expressed in an 1836 sermon which he preached, in his capacity as archdeacon of York, before the assembled clergy of Upper Canada. Though at this time he stressed the necessity of more concerted action on behalf of the Anglican cause, he also spoke almost despairingly of a church that was "separated, in a great measure, from the Mother Church, and deprived, by the pressure of the times, of much of that protection which the Civil Government has hitherto willingly accorded — assailed on every side by enemies whose hostility is openly avowed."[78]

The events of these years also led to a reconsideration of the Church of England's responsibilities. Throughout this period Strachan never doubted that his church was peculiarly fitted to disseminate conservative ideology, to act as the cement of the social order and to

In His Name

ensure the maintenance of the imperial connection. Still, the prospect of disestablishment left him no alternative but to adopt a more narrowly ecclesiastical view of his church's role in the wider community. Recognizing that the clergy reserves might soon be divided among all denominations or even secularized entirely, he was compelled to make a virtue of necessity and to insist upon something that could not be affected by reverses in the world of politics — the Church of England's distinctive spiritual mission. He was also compelled to admit, however grudgingly, that the Church of England might have to abandon its social and political responsibilities and become a sort of spiritual society whose only concern was the salvation of souls. Thus, in a sermon preached in 1837 before the clergy of the archdeaconry of York, a plea for a more aggressive defence of the policy of church establishment was coupled with the assurance that the Church of England, as a primarily spiritual institution, did not depend for its vitality on the constantly shifting policies of governments. "The basis of the Church of Christ," Strachan proclaimed, "is not secular but spiritual, it is not to be considered merely a civil institution — an erection or portion of the State; — nor does it depend upon the breath of Governments or upon the enactments of human law. On the contrary, it is an ordinance of God."[79] Following this repudiation of "Erastianism" — the doctrine that, broadly speaking, emphasized the subservience of church to state — Strachan argued that the Church of England could best respond to disestablishment by concentrating on its religious task and ignoring those secular duties it had traditionally performed as an institution deeply rooted in the outside world. This new vision of the Church of England's role, a vision which contrasted sharply with Strachan's earlier view that the church had an essential part to play in the secular domain of Upper Canadian life, was neatly summed up in the following statement:

> if, therefore, the property of the Church be taken from us by legal oppression, we must receive it as a trial of our faith, and, submitting in all patience, seek consolation in turning with redoubled ardour to our sacred duties. From teaching the Gospel in the purest form to the inhabitants of Upper Canada we cannot be driven. We are a Missionary Church; — in this consists our true character; and as our

organization is Missionary, let us cherish more and more a Missionary Spirit. This can be done amidst the wreck of our temporalities as well as amidst the slander and contumely of our enemies, without affording them a single just cause of irritation. By thus proceeding we shall exhibit the character and principles of the Church in all their attractive beauty, and win far more friends in the day of our adversity than in that of our prosperity.[80]

The course of religious and political life in the post-war era also had a profound impact on the Anglican view of Upper Canada itself. For Strachan and other Anglican clergymen, nothing happened by chance; the design and order characteristic of creation were evidence of a God who was an active presence in human affairs. This perception of the power of the divine lay at the heart of Strachan's pre-1815 belief that God had chosen Britain to humble the forces of revolution. But it could also give rise to ideas that were less flattering to Britain, and to Upper Canada as well. As already noted, during the conflict with Napoleonic France, Strachan's view of Britain's providential mission went side by side with a conviction that the war was divinely ordained as a punishment for British sins. In later years, the same frame of mind was evident as Strachan and his clerical colleagues responded to events in Upper Canadian life. The popular support given a campaign designed to overthrow the social and political order, together with the growing number and increasing militancy of local demagogues, made it obvious to them that Upper Canadians had become a sinful people. They also felt in the marrow of their bones that the failure of Upper Canadians to repent and mend their ways would have terrible consequences.

The Anglican clergy's response to the cholera epidemics of the early 1830s revealed a deep concern about the increasing sinfulness of their society.[81] The "pestilence" was seen as a divine visitation, a scourge sent down from heaven in order to punish sinfulness and awaken all people, including Upper Canadians, to the necessity of immediate repentance. In an 1832 sermon, preached during "a time of Cholera Asiatic Morbus," Strachan emphasized the importance of repentance, declaring that "if we are anxious for the salvation of our Souls ... then ought we to take advantage of God's particular warnings and applications."[82] R.D. Cartwright, describing his exertions during the 1832 epidemic, asserted that "it is God's doing — and blind must they be who do not perceive that it is his work."[83] The following year, on a "day appointed by proclamation for a General Thanksgiving to Almighty God for Having removed the heavy Judgment of the pestilence," every Anglican congregation in the diocese, "under the prevailing apprehension" of a new outbreak of cholera, confessed "with shame and contrition, that, in the pride and hardness of our hearts, we ... have followed our own imaginations instead of Thy holy laws." Having thus acknowledged their sinfulness, they then appealed to their "merciful Father" not to allow his "destroying angel to lift up his hand against us."[84] In 1835, Adam Burwell reflected angrily that Upper Canadians had not yet repented for "those crying political and national sins for which God sent us pestilence & death."[85]

The most forceful statement on the cholera epidemics was made in a sermon by A.N. Bethune on 14 February 1833, another day of "General Thanksgiving." Bethune urged his flock to be thankful for the fact that divine providence had spared Upper Canada the widespread desolation which Europe had experienced as a result of the cholera epidemic. Yet he also stated that Upper Canadians, like people elsewhere, were tainted with sinfulness and their failure to repent might provoke a "severer visitation from heaven."[86] Pointing to the crimes against God and man that were common in both Upper Canada and the world as a whole, Bethune warned that:

> we have sins to deplore and abandon — sins of dye so deep and character so heinous, that the cry of them has gone up into the presence of God and caused Him to 'smite the earth with a curse.' It is emphatically a sinful, a rebellious, an apostate world — treason and crime, infidelity and vice, are pervading characteristics of the times .... That perverse and unhallowed temper, that recklessness of the wholesome restraints, which the laws of God and the wisdom of man has imposed, hidden as it often is under the specious covering of a prostituted liberality — that impatience of rule which is fostered by a spirit of impiety and the instigations of Satan — that dislike of the salutary obligations

which maintain the orders and courses of society within their appointed channels, are sins and evils which the kind and merciful Father of the Universe could never view with complacency.[87]

The 1830s were a difficult time—after the cholera epidemics came the rebellion and the subsequent "patriot" raids from the United States. Both Strachan and Bethune greeted the events of 1837-38 with alarm and astonishment but also with a firm determination to suppress the forces of treason. On 9 December 1837 Bethune, as editor of the *Church*, denounced the rebels for "murdering peaceful inhabitants, burning the houses of the unoffending, and plundering the property of the defenceless," and reminded all loyal Upper Canadians of their duty to "rise at the summons of authority, buckle on his armour for the contest, and march, secure in the protection of the God of battles, to crush rebellion, and bring the traitors to justice."[88] In a sermon of 14 December, "a fast day by public proclamation on account of the rebellion & attacks from the U States," Strachan criticized those "Traitors & Robbers who thirst for our blood & our possessions—bad men, who without religion or principle are deterred from no crime." He urged Upper Canadians "to throw aside all causes of wrath & Strife hatred & ill will and to band together as Brothers for the defence of our country our wives & our children."[89]

Yet, if the rebellion strengthened the resolve of Strachan and Bethune to crush the forces of disorder, it also confirmed their fear that Upper Canadians had become a sinful people. There were, it was true, positive notes about the rebellion: only a handful of Anglicans took part in it,[90] and the victory of the Loyalist cause could be attributed to the intervention of divine providence.[91] Still, it could not be forgotten that many Upper Canadians had risen up in arms against the civil authority; nor could it be forgotten that divine providence had allowed the rebellion to occur. For Strachan and Bethune, the rebellion was primarily to be regarded not as one more instance of God's protection of his chosen people, but as a sign of divine anger intended to punish Upper Canadians for their sinfulness and awaken them to the need for repentance.

This view of the rebellion as a divine visitation was first advanced by Strachan in his sermon of 14 December. Whereas he had earlier been immensely proud of the colony's record in defending "king and constitution" during the War of 1812, he now felt that the failure of Upper Canadians to support the "Church of our Redeemer," combined with Britain's negligence in aiding the cause of religion in the colonies, had led to widespread sinfulness. "Can we therefore wonder," he asked, "that heavy calamity is permitted to afflict us — we are not innocent sufferers but are active partakers in the guilt — nor can the judgments be removed nor the plague stayed but by deep repentance and devout prayer to God."[92] In the same vein, A.N. Bethune wrote in a *Church* editorial that "in sending judgments upon his people, Christians know and confess that He is not chastening them without cause."[93] Soon afterwards in February 1838, on a day of public fasting and humiliation, Bethune preached a sermon in which he urged his parishioners to give thanks to God for having ensured Upper Canada's deliverance during the late rebellion, an event staged by "depraved individuals" who had sought to destroy "our happy institutions" and "to place us under a polity and a domination to which both we and our fathers were strangers." Then, in almost the same breath, he announced that "all troubles & calamities of whatsoever nature ... are evidences of our heavenly Father's displeasure: they are proof that He has been offended by our sins, our carelessness, our negligence; and that correction from his hand is necessary to ensure the humbling of our hearts and the improvements of our lives." Only a determination on the part of each Upper Canadian to "avoid those transgressions which provoke his righteous anger" would guarantee "future exemption from the calamities from which we have so recently escaped."[94]

Later in 1838 Bethune wrote another *Church* editorial in which the cholera epidemics, the rebellion and the patriot raids were discussed in the same context as the "spirit of disobedience and of resistance to constituted authority" that was "among the baneful characteristics of the times." The essence of his argument was that God could punish sinfulness either by "direct manifestations of his wrath" or by "the intermediate agency of his fellow mortals." The cholera epidemics of 1832 and 1834 were an example of the first form of punishment. Unfortunately, these epidemics had not brought about "the change of our hearts or the reformation of our lives." The result was that God had adopted a different strategy, punishing Upper Canadian society through the actions of those "traitors within and plunderers without" who "have conspired to plunge us into civil strife, and convert our peace into confusion, our freedom into anarchy." In this situation it was necessary for Upper Canadians to appeal to God "in the posture of supplicants, with the voice of contrition, and with vows of future obedience."[95]

Another Anglican clergyman, whose identity remains unknown, looked on the rebellion in the same light. According to him, the cholera epidemics had been a divine punishment of Upper Canadian sinfulness. Even these "judgments," however, had not induced Upper Canadians to repent and change their ways. Consequently, Upper Canada had recently been afflicted with rebellion and was now threatened with invasion. In the perilous times that lay ahead, Upper Canadians could count on divine assistance only if they repented and remained loyal towards constituted authorities, thus distinguishing themselves from those individuals whose involvement in the rebellion had violated the Christian doctrine that it was the duty of all people to obey their "rightful Sovereign" and the "powers that be." If, on the other hand, Upper Canadians continued in their sinful ways, the future was uncertain.

> So far God has mercifully averted the threatened blow, and signally appeared in our behalf. But yet a dark cloud seems to be gathering; our political horizon appears tinged with its ominous hue; and *when*, or *how*, or *with* what calamities charged, it may be permitted to burst over our heads, is known only to Him, who holds the destinies of the nations in his hands. We are a sinful people, Brethren, and the Lord has a controversy with us .... He has visited us with awful judgments, but alas! they have left no impression. O, who that witnessed the devastation of that dire pestilence, which afflicted these provinces in 1832 and 1834, can readily forget them? ... Ah! while death stared in the face, the heart appeared humbled; but no sooner was the cause of terror removed, than the good impression vanished, and ... left not a trace behind. Shall not God visit [us] for this forgetfulness of Him? Surely he is not mocked with impunity. And if he is now

In His Name

> about to commission another messenger of vengeance, and to say — 'Sword, go through this land!' are we prepared?[96]

* * * * *

The Anglican preoccupation with Upper Canadian sinfulness underlines the connection between Strachan's conservative ideology and the events of the 1820s and 1830s. Before 1815 Strachan's ideological pronouncements were clearly inspired by his firm belief in the essentially evil nature of the age — an age that, in his view, had lost sight of the principles of religion and of the basic laws and values on which civilization depended. The same seems to have been true after the conclusion of hostilities. Strachan's declarations in this period on such issues as the essential nature of human beings, the structure of society, and the function of government and religion were not made in an vacuum. Rather, whenever Strachan spoke on these subjects, he did so with Upper Canadian conditions in the back of his mind. To claim otherwise is to argue that his ideological statements on the characteristics of the good society were formulated in one compartment of his mind, while his attitudes towards Upper Canada's sins were formulated in another. Such an argument strains credulity. It seems more reasonable to say that Strachan's expounding of conservative ideology was both an expression of ideas he strongly believed in and an attempt to influence the course of Upper Canadian life. More often than not, he was chastening Upper Canadians for the folly of their ways and at the same time pleading with them to return to the paths of righteousness.

All in all, the Anglican mind from the early 1820s to the time of the rebellion, as it was expressed in the statements of Strachan, Bethune and a handful of other clergymen, was marked by an ideological fervour and intransigence that bordered on the fanatical. Yet there was more to the Anglican experience in these decades than an almost mindless clinging to the truths of the past. Even as a clergyman like Strachan was bending every effort to maintain the old older, he was slowly beginning to drift away from the intellectual moorings that had anchored his life for so long. In this respect, his growing acceptance of the religiously pluralistic nature of Upper Canadian society, as well as his evolving conception of the Church of England as a primarily spiritual organization, demonstrated just how far he had travelled intellectually since his arrival in the colony. Another measure of the distance of Strachan's ideological journey was his increasingly strong belief that Upper Canadians had proven themselves unworthy of God's favour and, as a result, had been afflicted with disease, rebellion and invasion. By the late 1830s Strachan, and other clergymen as well, no longer thought of Upper Canada as a land set apart for some special purpose. On the contrary, they now spent much of their time agonizing over how much additional suffering was in store for Upper Canada before an angry God was placated. F.L. Osler put it well in November 1838 as he contemplated the possibility of a patriot invasion: "My trust is in the Lord God, He reigneth over all, yet He may yet see fit to punish us for our sins—and cause the enemy to triumph over us."[97] The brave new world of the early 1800s — a world in which Upper Canada was an earthly agent in a divinely ordained plan — was long forgotten.

In His Name

NOTES

1 Clark, *English Society, 1688-1832*, passim. Another fine study of Anglicanism and conservative ideology during this era is Soloway's *Prelates and People*.

2 Strachan Sermons, "Now no chastening for the present seemeth to be joyous but grievous" (16 March 1804). For a perceptive analysis of providential messianism in British North America in the early nineteenth century, see S.F. Wise's article "God's Peculiar Peoples."

3 *A Discourse on the Character of King George the Third. Addressed to the Inhabitants of British America. By the Rev. John Strachan. Rector of Cornwall, Upper Canada* (Montreal, 1810), p. 32.

4 Ibid., p. 66.

5 On anti-Americanism and the Tory mind, see Jane Errington, *The Lion, the Eagle, and Upper Canada: A Developing Colonial Ideology* (Kingston and Montreal, 1987); and S.F. Wise and R.C. Brown, *Canada Views the United States: Nineteenth Century Political Attitudes* (Toronto, 1967).

6 John Strachan, *A Discourse on the Character of King George the Third*, p. 31.

7 John Strachan, *A Sermon Preached at York before the Legislative Council and House of Assembly, August 2nd, 1812* (York, 1812).

8 The problem of wartime disaffection, and the response of the Upper Canadian elite to that problem, is explored in W.M. Weeks, "The War of 1812: Civil Authority and Martial Law in Upper Canada," *OH*, XLVIII (Summer, 1956), pp. 147-61; Ernest A. Cruikshank, "John Beverley Robinson and the Trials for Treason in 1814," *OHSPR*, XXV (1929), pp. 191-219; and Robert L. Fraser, "Jacob Overholser," *DCB* V, pp. 642-45.

9 Strachan to Francis de Rottenburg, 14 Aug. 1813. Included in William Wood, ed., *Select British Documents of the Canadian War of 1812*, 3 vols. (Toronto, 1920-28), II, p. 200.

10 *A Sermon Preached at York, Upper Canada, on the Third of June, Being the Day Appointed for a General Thanksgiving. By the Revd. John Strachan, D.D.* (Montreal, 1814), pp. 5-6.

11 Ibid., pp. 17 and 24.

12 Ibid., pp. 37-38.

13 Ibid., pp. 34 and 37-38. For other expressions of Strachan's social and political thought before 1815 see two sermons: "But if our gospel be hid it is hid to them that are lost" (30 March 1806); and "Arise and get thee to Zarep" (4 May 1806). Also of interest are *The Christian Religion Recommended in a Letter to his Pupils, Andrew Stuart and James Cartwright*

(Montreal, 1807); and the *Kingston Gazette*, "The Reckoner," 16 July and 19 Nov. 1811. Strachan would restate his criticisms of the United States just after the war in a tribute to Richard Cartwright. See *A Sermon on the Death of the Honourable Richard Cartwright. With a Short Account of His Life. Preached at Kingston, on the 3rd of September, 1815. By John Strachan, D.D. Rector of York, Upper Canada* (Montreal, 1816).

14   See Arthur O. Lovejoy, *The Great Chain of Being: A Study of the History of an Idea* (Cambridge, Mass., 1942).

15   A leading exponent of natural theology was William Paley, whose book *Natural Theology, or Evidences of the Existence and Attributes of the Deity Collected from the Appearances of Nature* appeared in 1802. For the impact of natural theology on Upper Canadian thought, see Westfall, *Two Worlds*, pp. 30-33; Carl Berger, *Science, God and Nature in Victorian Canada*, pp. 32-35; and A.B. McKillop, *A Disciplined Intelligence: Critical Inquiry and Canadian Thought in the Victorian Era* (Montreal, 1979), pp. 59-61.

16   In 1832 Strachan told a Select Committee of the House of Assembly that "the whole expence [of education] in a free country like this should be defrayed by the public that promising boys giving indication of high talent tho' poor might have an opportunity of cultivating their faculties & if able taking a lead in the Community." See Spragge, "Elementary Education in Upper Canada," p. 116.

17   Strachan Sermons, "Whether therefore ye eat or drink, or whatsoever ye do — do all to the Glory of God" (3 Aug. 1806).

18   John Strachan, *A Sermon Preached at York, Upper Canada, on the Third of June* [1814], pp. 27-30.

19   Strachan Sermons, "Godliness with contentment is great gain" (7 Sept. 1824, 24 April 1825, 28 Oct. 1827, 27 Dec. 1829, 13 Nov. 1836). See also the following sermons: "In keeping of them (i.e. thy Statutes) there is great reward" (21 Nov. 1824); "Let your light so shine before men that they may see your good works" (22 Feb. 1829); "Yea ye yourselves know that these hands have ministered unto my necessities" (13 April 1834); "So then, after the Lord had spoken unto them he was received up into heaven" (23 May 1819).

20   Thomas Phillips, *The Canadian Remembrancer. A Loyal Sermon. Preached on St. George's Day, April 23, 1826; at the Episcopal Church in York* (York, 1826), pp. 15-18.

21   Burwell, admittedly, was not a typical Anglican clergyman. His *Doctrine of the Holy Spirit* and his other 1835 pamphlet, *A Voice of Warning and Instruction Concerning the Signs of the Times*, contained lengthy defences of the Irvingite sect and particularly its practice of "speaking in tongues,"

as well as harsh criticisms of the Church of England's blindness to the role of the Holy Spirit in the affairs of this world. So fervent were Burwell's feelings on these subjects that in 1836 he left the Church of England and became an Irvingite preacher. Still, his social and political philosophy was shared by Strachan. Proof of this was provided in 1831, when Burwell, admitting that he was the author of the rabidly conservative "One of the People" articles in the *Kingston Chronicle*, obtained Strachan's support for his proposal to establish a counter-revolutionary journal. The new journal never went into operation, for Burwell, despite his conviction (the result of a recent dream) that he was destined for literary greatness, soon concluded that the scheme was impractical. Nevertheless, Strachan thought that Burwell would have made a fine editor of the journal; he believed, on the whole, that Burwell's essays were "good" and "very clever," and was critical merely of his verbose writing style and his tendency to dwell upon the "more difficult doctrines of Theology." See *Kingston Chronicle*, 28 May 1831-18 Feb. 1832; and AO, Macaulay Papers, assorted letters from 13 Aug.-24 Oct. 1831.

22 Adam Burwell, *Doctrine of the Holy Spirit: and its Applications to the Wants and Interests of Corporate Man under the Providence and Moral Government of God, Stated and Defended from Holy Writ and the Practice of the Apostles of our Lord and Saviour Jesus Christ; and in these days Revived in Britain by the Rev. Edward Irving; Exhibiting the Sole Means of National Reformation and Preservation* (Toronto, 1835), pp. 92-93.

23 Strachan Sermons, "And Noah did according unto all that the Lord Commanded him" (9 Nov. 1823).

24 Ibid., "I pray not that thou shouldest take them out of the world but that thou shouldest keep them from evil" (8 May and 25 Sept. 1825, 16 July 1826, 16 Sept. 1827, 22 Sept. 1833, 3 June 1837, 18 March 1838).

25 Ibid., "Weeping may endure for a night, but joy cometh in the morning" (14 Aug. 1836).

26 Strachan, *A Discourse on the Character of King George the Third*, p. 20-21.

27 Ibid., "Now the Lord is that Spirit and where the Spirit of the Lord is there is liberty" (4 Feb. 1821).

28 Ibid., "Thus saith the Lord stand ye in the ways and see and ask for the old paths" (2 Oct. 1825).

29 *Christian Recorder*, September 1819, "The Late Duke of Richmond," p. 252.

30 Ibid., p. 266.

The Defence of the Old Order

31 Strachan Sermons, "Weeping may endure for a night, but joy cometh in the morning." See also the following sermons: "Now the Lord is that Spirit and where the Spirit of the Lord is there is liberty" (4 Feb. 1821); "Except the Lord build the House their labour is but lost that built it" (7 June 1832).

32 Strachan Papers, 1824.

33 Strachan, *A Speech in the Legislative Council on the Subject of the Clergy Reserves*, pp. 27-28.

34 A solid analysis of the values symbolized by the imperial tie can be found in David Mills, *The Idea of Loyalty in Upper Canada, 1784-1850* (Kingston and Montreal, 1988).

35 Strachan Papers, Strachan to Horton, 5 June 1824.

36 Ibid., 1824.

37 *Kingston Gazette*, "The Reckoner," 21 April 1812.

38 William Warburton, *The Alliance between Church and State; or the Necessity of an Established Religion and a Test Law Demonstrated* (London, 1811), p. 88.

39 Ibid., pp. 243-47.

40 *Moral and Political Philosophy, in Paley's Works: Consisting of Evidences of Christianity, Moral and Political Philosophy, Natural Theology, and Hora Paulinae. Complete in One Volume* (London, 1835), Book VI, "Elements of Political Knowledge," p. 169.

41 Ibid., pp. 168-79.

42 Edmund Burke, *Reflections on the Revolution in France and on the Proceedings in Certain Societies in London Relative to that Event* (Penguin edition, Conor Cruise O'Brien, ed., 1969), pp. 189 and 194.

43 Ibid., pp. 197-98.

44 For a discussion of the same themes with a slightly different emphasis, see William Westfall's *Two Worlds*, pp. 91-97.

45 Strachan Papers, Strachan to Horton, 5 June 1824.

46 Ibid., Address of Clergy Reserves Corporation, 1824.

47 Strachan, *A Sermon Preached on the Death of the Bishop of Quebec*, pp. 25-27; Strachan Papers, 16 May 1827 (Ecclesiastical Chart); *Letter to Thomas Frankland Lewis*, p. 19.

48 See p. 3 of this pamphlet.

49 Strachan, *A Letter to Thomas Frankland Lewis*, p. 3.

In His Name

50   Strachan Papers, Syllabus of lectures to be delivered at St. James' Church weekly during Lent, 1835.

51   John Strachan, *The Church of the Redeemed. A Sermon Preached on Wednesday, 5th October, 1836, at a Meeting of the Clergy of the Established Church of Upper Canada. Under their Archdeacons Assembled* (Toronto, 1836), p. 52.

52   Strachan Papers, Address of the Clergy Reserves Corporation, 1824.

53   Strachan, *Observations on the Maintenance of a Protestant Clergy*, pp. 14-17.

54   *A Letter from the Hon. and Venerable Dr. Strachan, Archdeacon of York, U.C. to Dr. Lee, D.D. Convener of a Committee of the General Assembly of the Church of Scotland* (Kingston, 1829).

55   Strachan Letter Book, 1827-39, Strachan to Bethune, 26 Jan. 1829.

56   See Chapter Seven.

57   Strachan, *Sermon on the Death of the Bishop of Quebec*, p. 30.

58   Strachan Papers, "Canada Church Establishment," Strachan to Horton, 16 May 1827.

59   Strachan Letter Book, 1827-39, Strachan to Archdeacon of Quebec, n.d.

60   SPG Letters, Series C, Box IVA/39, no. 451, 5 Feb. 1828.

61   Strachan, *Observations on the Maintenance of a Protestant Clergy*, pp. 39-40.

62   Strachan Letter Book, 1827-39, Strachan to Stewart, 5 Nov. 1827.

63   Macaulay Papers, Burwell to Macaulay, 13 Aug. 1831.

64   Strachan Papers, Bettridge to Glenelg, 25 Sept. 1837.

65   *An Apology for the Church of England in the Canadas, in Answer to a letter to the Earl of Liverpool, Relative to the Rights of the Church of Scotland. By a Protestant of the Established Church of England* (Kingston, 1826), p. 4.

66   The *Church*, 3 Sept. 1837.

67   The Alien Bill of 1827 granted American-born residents of Upper Canada "all the privileges of British birth," thereby ending a controversy that had bedevilled political life in the colony since the early 1820s. The clearest analysis of this complex issue is provided in Errington, *The Lion, the Eagle and Upper Canada*.

68   Macaulay Papers, Strachan to John Macaulay, 16 Feb. 1832.

69   Strachan Letter Book, 1827-39, Strachan to Oliver Hargrave, 18 March 1833.

70 Ibid., Strachan to George Baillie, 18 March 1833.

71 Strachan Papers, Bethune to Strachan, 4 Oct. 1831.

72 Ibid., Bethune to Strachan, 14 Dec. 1831.

73 A.H. Burwell, *A Voice of Warning and Instruction Concerning the Signs of the Times, and the Coming of the Son of Man, to Judge the Nations, and Restore all Things* (Kingston, 1835), p. 35.

74 A.H. Burwell, *Doctrine of the Holy Spirit*, passim.

75 Ibid., p. 97.

76 Ibid., pp. 95-96.

77 Ibid., p. 97.

78 *The Church of the Redeemed*, p. 28.

79 John Strachan, *Address to the Clergy of the Archdeaconry of York. By the Honorable and Venerable The Archdeacon of York. Delivered at Toronto on Wednesday the 13th September, 1837* (n.p., n.d.), p. 9.

80 Ibid., p. 11. Mark McDermott again sees matters differently. In his thesis "The Theology of Bishop John Strachan" (pp. 115-16 and 193) he argues that Strachan always saw the Church of England as a primarily spiritual institution; and that his expressions of that view in the 1830s and 1840s, far from signalling a retreat from the world, were designed to strengthen the Church of England's claims to the status of an establishment. Such arguments, however, misread Strachan's statements while also ignoring declarations made by other clergymen and the Anglican press. The Anglican clergy's changing conception of the nature of their church is traced in greater detail in Chapters Six, Seven and Eight.

81 John Bethune, an Anglican clergyman stationed in Lower Canada, delivered two of the more interesting sermons on the subject of the cholera epidemics. See *A Sermon Preached in Christ's Church, Montreal, on Friday, the 9th of May, 1832, Being the Day Appointed for a Public Fast, Occasioned by the Apprehension of Being Visited by the Pestilence which is Scourging the Nations of Europe* (Montreal, 1832); and *A Sermon Preached on Wednesday, February 6, 1833, Being the Day Appointed by Proclamation for a General Thanksgiving to Almighty God for Having Removed the Heavy Judgment of the Pestilence* (Montreal, 1833). Both these sermons took the view that the cholera epidemics were a divine punishment of human sinfulness.

82 Strachan Sermons, "Wherefore the Holy Ghost saith today if you will hear his voice harden not your hearts" (8 July 1832).

83 AO, Cartwright Papers, Cartwright to Rev. James Hitchings, 27 Oct. 1832.

84 For the text of this prayer, see John Bethune's 1833 sermon, cited above.

85 Burwell, *Doctrine of the Holy Spirit*, pp. 108-9.

86 A.N. Bethune, *A Sermon, Preached in Saint Peter's Church, Cobourg; U.C. on Thursday, the 14th, February, 1833. Being the Day Appointed for a General Thanksgiving to Almighty God, for Having Removed the Heavy Judgments with which these Provinces Have Recently Been Afflicted* (Cobourg, 1833), passim.

87 Ibid., pp. 16-17.

88 The *Church*, 9 Dec. 1837.

89 Strachan Sermons, "And thy judgments are as the light that goeth forth" (14 Dec. 1837).

90 Ronald Stagg has estimated that only 19 of 216 people involved in the Yonge Street rebellion were Anglican, and that 12 of these came from one church — St John's, York Mills. As for the western rebellion, another scholar, Colin Read, was not able to find a single Anglican among the 200 people connected with the Duncombe rising. See Ronald John Stagg, "The Yonge Street Rebellion of 1837: An Examination of the Social Background and a Re-assessment of the Events," Ph.D. thesis, University of Toronto, 1976, pp. 185, 205-6 and 227-28; and Colin Read, *The Rising in Western Upper Canada, 1837-8: The Duncombe Revolt and After* (Toronto, 1982), appendix 1.

91 For this point of view, see the *Church*, 16 and 30 Dec. 1837; and 20 Jan., 3 Feb., 10 Feb. and 17 Feb. 1838. See also AO, Osler Papers — Diaries and Journals, Series II-I, "Sketch of my life, p. 69; and Series II-I, vol. 2, Osler to Proctor, 29 March 1838. Bethune went so far as to claim that the weather conditions during the rebellion had been the most striking illustration of God's support of the Loyalist cause. On 16 Dec. 1837 he wrote in a *Church* editorial: "It cannot fail to be remarked — and we do so with unfeigned thankfulness — how singularly the devices of these atrocious individuals have been baffled by a gracious and merciful Providence ... it mercifully happened that the weather, during the period of the temporary ferment, was such that, contrary to the experience of almost any former year, Steam Boats were enabled to traverse the lake in safety, and convey succours of men and the munitions of war with a speed that served at once to disconcert and ruin their iniquitous designs."

92 Strachan Sermons, "And thy judgments are as the light that goeth forth" (14 Dec. 1837).

93 The *Church*, 20 Jan. 1838.

94 Ibid., 17 Feb. 1838.
95 Ibid., 24 Nov. 1838.
96 Ibid., 3 Feb. 1838, extracts from a sermon.
97 Osler Papers, Series I-1, vol. 2, Osler to Proctor, 5 Nov. 1838.

Episcopal dignity: Jacob Mountain, first bishop of the diocese of Quebec
(J. Ross Robertson Collection, Metropolitan Toronto Library, T16087).

John Stuart, eulogized by John Strachan as the "Father of the Episcopal Church" in Upper Canada (Courtesy National Archives of Canada, C11057).

"A miserable scratch of a thing" was how artist George William Allan described the first St. James' Church, York, 1816 (Courtesy Metropolitan Toronto Library, T30854). It was built over the years 1803-7, enlarged in 1818-19, and replaced by a new building in 1831.

Charles James Stewart, bishop of Quebec from 1826 until his death in 1837 (J. Ross Robertson Collection, Metropolitan Toronto Library, T16088).

Poised for power: John Strachan, *circa* 1820 (Archives of Ontario, Acc. 3077, S2328).

Thomas Young's sketch of King Street East, York, 1835, showing St. James' Church. (J. Ross Robertson Collection, Metropolitan Toronto Library, T10248). Destroyed by fire in 1839, this church was succeeded by the first St. James' Cathedral, which in turn burnt in 1849. The present-day St. James' Cathedral opened in 1853 but was not finished until 1874.

George Okill Stuart, archdeacon of Kingston, 1830s (Courtesy Metropolitan Toronto Library, T30839).

The first issue of the *Church*, May 6, 1837. Politically, the paper was to speak for the church as a whole. Theologically, it was less inclusive, representing the high church party (Courtesy Metropolitan Toronto Library).

The original Trinity College, located off Queen Street West, Toronto. The college remained on this site until 1925, when it moved to its present location on Hoskin Avenue. The Queen Street building was used by the Kiwanis Boys Club until its demolition in 1956. (Courtesy Metropolitan Toronto Library, T13049).

Strachan's protégé — A.N. Bethune, archdeacon of York from 1847 and the second bishop of Toronto (Courtesy Metropolitan Toronto Library, T13653).

Benjamin Cronyn, one of Upper Canada's leading low churchmen and first bishop of the diocese of Huron (J. Ross Robertson Collection, Metropolitan Toronto Library, T33848).

CHAPTER SIX

DEFEAT

If the 1830s were a bad dream for Anglican clergymen, the 1840s and 1850s were a nightmare. For Strachan, who became the first bishop of the diocese of Toronto in 1839, and indeed for the entire Anglican clergy, the union of the Canadas and the inauguration of responsible government spelled the end of the loyal and conservative Upper Canada they had always known. On top of this, with the transformation of King's College into the completely secular University of Toronto and the secularization of the clergy reserves, Anglican clergymen were forced to admit defeat in the long, tempestuous struggle to maintain the policy of church establishment. In their response to these developments in the religious and political spheres, Anglican clergymen gave no quarter, denouncing the apostles of liberalism and clinging to the values of the past as to life itself. Yet, predictably enough, the clergy's failure to have a significant impact on the course of events led to deteriorating morale, profound pessimism about the future of Upper Canada, and — as disestablishment became a reality — serious rethinking of the relationship between church and state. In more ways than one, therefore, the post-rebellion period was of decisive importance in the evolution of Upper Canadian Anglicanism.

*****

Within the Church of England, the emergence of a new political order in the post-rebellion period triggered a flurry of statements expressing the Anglican vision of what a truly civilized society should be like. There was nothing new in this vision — all of its main elements had been present in Strachan's pronouncements in earlier years. Nor did it

In His Name

serve a new purpose. Before the rebellion, Strachan's conservative ideology had allowed him to make sense of his world, revealing to him the role of human sinfulness in human affairs from the 1790s on, and had also strengthened his determination to resist demands for change. After the rebellion, conservative ideology performed the same function. It provided Anglican clergymen with a frame of reference that explained to them the events of their time, and gave them a sense of mission as they stood their ground in battles with their ideological enemies.

The events of this period heightened fears among the Anglican clergy that Upper Canada had been contaminated by republican ideology — an ideology committed, it was felt, to an egalitarian social structure and the untrammelled freedom of the individual. In dealing with this state of affairs, Anglican clergymen partly relied on the old idea that social and political subordination was a central feature of God's plan for the world. As he had done prior to the rebellion, Strachan repeatedly emphasized in these years that the structure of society was divinely ordained, and that all citizens had an obligation to respect their superiors, obey those in authority, and accept the sufferings of the present life as a trial of faith, shortly to be followed for true Christians by the eternal bliss of the world to come.[1] Others agreed. The *Church* argued in 1840 that the "miseries of the present life would indeed be greatly alleviated, were we to discard a foolish aspiration after things beyond our reach, and learn, with the Apostle of Christ, in whatsoever state we may be placed, therewith to be content."[2] Henry Scadding was just as forthright in a sermon of 1844. Christianity, he asserted,

> so far from having a tendency to undermine the institutions of civil society ... is peculiarly calculated to uphold those distinctions among men which have been wisely ordered in the good providence of God, which are essentially requisite to man's happiness as a social being. The Gospel clearly points out the duties which attach to that sphere of life in which every individual is placed...it unequivocally condemns that turbulent spirit which renders a man discontented with his lot....

Scadding concluded that the true Christian is one who, "while he gratefully enjoys the unmerited blessings mingled in his earthly arp, & sedulously attends to the duties of that sphere in which he has been placed, his affections are plainly set on things above."[3]

This commitment to social and political subordination was one example of the Anglican debt to contemporary conservative ideology, but it was not the only one. Another example, which was related to the doctrine of subordination, was the firm rejection of the Lockean theory that justified the right of resistance to government when the latter infringed the terms of the "social contract." After the mid-eighteenth century Lockean political theory had gradually fallen into disrepute in Britain. Taking its place at the heart of British political thought was a new, highly conservative view which stressed the divine origins of government and ruled out the legitimacy of resistance in all except the most extreme circumstances. This ideological framework, essentially a modified version of the doctrine of the divine right of kings, was a key element in the conservative response to the French Revolution and Napoleon, and after 1815 it remained central to the conservative defence of civil authority.[4] The extent of its influence is graphically revealed by the support it enjoyed as late as the 1840s among Upper Canadian Anglicans.

The earliest record of anti-Lockean thinking in Upper Canada is Strachan's *Discourse on the Character of King George the Third*, in which criticisms of the doctrine of the social contract were coupled with dismissive references to the Lockean view that a "state of nature" had preceded the formation of society.[5] Two other clergymen, John Hudson and Adam Burwell, later followed Strachan's lead. In a sermon of 1827 Hudson, chaplain to the York garrison, argued that the "Christian Religion sanctions and upholds the authority of Kings, and of all others who lawfully bear rule over us" and that the abuse of power by those in "exalted stations" should be checked not by experiments in political reform but by the preaching of the Gospel.[6] Burwell took the same line in his *Doctrine of the Holy Spirit*. He too believed that rulers were ordained by God and that their subjects were morally obliged to respect their authority and obey their will. Operating from this perspective, he flatly denied that rebellion was legitimate in the face of misrule. God, he claimed, has made it awfully penal for a subject to resist 'the power,' and lift his hand against the Lord's annointed. And he makes no exception whether 'the power' is in holy or wicked hands ... Resistance is the devil's doctrine, and the practice of his children .... It is the subjects' duty to suffer under oppression, but not to resist; to entreat, but not to revile; to remonstrate if need be, but not to threaten and 'agitate'; to pray to God for deliverance his own way; but not to take his cause into his own hands. Especially he should pray that God would convert wicked rulers and put his Spirit upon them ... [7]

The rebellions of 1837-38 reinforced extreme views on the relationship between rulers and subjects, and in so doing accentuated the Anglican community's isolation from the liberal currents of the time. The *Church* first addressed itself to the subject of political obedience in a November 1838 article, in which a threatened patriot invasion prompted the assertion that "by the Divine will `kings reign and princes decree justice,' and to their rule we are obedient as to the ordinances of God, for `they that resist shall receive to themselves damnation.'"[8] A similar point of view was advanced one month later, when it was announced in the "Saturday Preacher" column that monarchical government was divinely ordained to restrain man's evil instincts, that even a tyrant had the right to demand the unconditional allegiance of his subjects, and that those who rebelled against constituted authority would be punished by God.[9] The most categorical rejection of the Lockean defence of rebellion appeared in 1840, when the *Church* stated in an editorial that sovereigns, including those who treated "the advocates of a pure and hearty loyalty" with "coldness or discouragement," could never be disobeyed, for men had an obligation as Christians and as members of society to remain loyal to a form of government that was divinely sanctioned. Criticizing the view that "the sovereign power is legitimately lodged in the people, and that, with this persuasion, they are at liberty to adopt what seems to comport with their present interests, or to accord with their present states," the *Church* went on to argue that the subjects of a monarchy could not, "without impiety, — not to speak of the criminal violation of human law, — undertake to destroy the authority of the sovereign, or do ought that would wrest it from his hands." Loyalty was not a duty that could be "yielded or withheld, as our interests serve or our inclinations may direct." On the contrary, "the sovereign, by a divine as well as human law, claims our obedience; and on the immutable principle of a moral and Christian duty, we are bound to yield it." Furthermore, it could not be said that "the fact of encouragement, — of good or ill requital for the faithful performance of this obligation, diminish in the slightest degree its force." The *Church* emphasized that

> what we unequivocally condemn is, that, if a man happens to receive no such return for his valuable and faithful services, he is at liberty to express his complaints in condemnation of his sovereign, or is justified in the threat ... that he will transfer his allegiance to a quarter where it will be more highly rewarded! ... Our attainment of every wish is, in this world, impossible, and the disappointment of reasonable expectations is no excuse for seeking to overturn what the Divine wisdom itself has established, and human experience, during a long series of ages, has pronounced best adapted to social and individual interests and to the welfare of the world.[10]

These arguments were echoed in letters to the *Church*. One correspondent, using the pseudonym "An Anglo-Catholic," wrote in 1850 that a sovereign, exercising his powers by divine right, could not be overthrown without defying the will of God. He claimed that sovereigns ruled "by virtue of the authority granted them by God Himself, and which right man can neither give nor take away," adding significantly that "when he commands his subject to any thing contrary to God's word, he must be disobeyed, but not deposed," since "they who are deposers of such monarchs are guilty of sin."[11] Another correspondent, one "Erieus," wrote two letters to the *Church* in 1844 entitled "On the Origin of Human Society and Government." According to his analysis, Locke's theory of a state of nature and a social contract ignored the fact that the abilities necessary to form a society had to be developed within society itself, that the human race in its "natural state" would probably have lacked any desire to raise itself to a more

In His Name

civilized existence, and that man was incapable of restraining his animal passions and preventing his own destruction without "an external power watching over, controlling, and enforcing him at every moment of his life." It therefore followed that the government under which society exists was "not the effect and result of an instinct or any such thing, nor of a mere mutual agreement between two parties," but the ordinance and institution of God. Thus, any political philosophy based on the doctrine of popular sovereignty was "the most fearful blasphemy that man can utter," for "all government ought to be considered as parental ... (because from GOD THE FATHER it comes forth), while subjects stand in the relation of children, whom God hath commanded to honour and reverence and obey their fathers, who are His representatives."[12]

The same political philosophy inspired A.N. Bethune's *The Duty of Loyalty*, a sermon preached in the midst of the annexation crisis of 1849. The central argument in this sermon was that the "obligation of loyalty" could not be regulated by "what personal and most commonplace interests may dictate."[13] Supporters of annexation to the United States might argue that "the sacred bond of allegiance, and the awful solemnity of an oath" were "only binding so long as it is agreeable to, or subserves, worldly interest, convenience, or caprice."[14] But such an argument was denounced by Bethune on two counts: it was a blasphemous repudiation of the divine injunction, found in numerous passages of scripture, to obey "constituted authority"; and it ignored the fact, which also rested on scriptural foundations, that the monarchical form of government had been ordained by God. Bethune, appalled by the "proneness to change" that drove people "to the sin of severing the dearest ties, breaking the most solemn bonds, and overturning the most sacred religious obligations,"[15] declared that "the question of reverence for those that are in authority, respect for the laws, and submission to to the government, is not a mere question of expediency or self, but a duty which ranks high amongst Christian ordinances ... it is something for the neglect or slight of which we shall one day give an account at the general judgment of the world."[16] He also declared that "God has been pleased to ordain it as our lot to live under that form of government which is nearest allied to the examples and ordinances furnished in his own Scriptures." Upper Canadians, he announced in his stirring peroration, should remember these truths, and shun those

Defeat

"who would rate their loyalty by a standard of gain, and shift their allegiance with the alterations of commerce," and confront the "reckless and godless cry" of treason "with the blunt and honest opposition which so audacious a wickedness deserves."[17]

Imperial patriotism was another key component of Anglican ideology in these years. Before 1837 it had been Strachan's belief that the imperial connection provided Upper Canada with a distinct sense of identity, committing it to a set of values which had been inherited from Britain and which now had to be defended on the North American continent. The same belief was held after 1837 by Anglican clergymen, including Strachan. In the post-rebellion period the Anglican clergy remained firm in the conviction that Upper Canada had a duty to remain closely tied to the parent state and to maintain its character as a "Little England," a society where the Church of England was dominant in religious life, where an "image and transcript" of the British constitution avoided the extremes of democracy and despotism, and where all men fulfilled their obligation to respect their superiors and obey constituted authorities. It was this very conviction, in fact, that underlay the *Church*'s response to the patriot raids. For the *Church*, which delighted in contrasting the anarchy of life in the American republic with the blessings Upper Canada enjoyed as a British colony, a patriot victory would lead to a severance of the imperial tie. That development, in turn, would rob Upper Canada of the stability that was its lot under British rule and transform it into a northern extension of the United States, a country characterized by anarchy and corruption.

The *Church*'s attitude towards the patriot raids was revealed on several occasions. In November 1838, for example, it argued that those "born and bred" under a monarchy would never consent to live under a form of government which had "no other sanction than the will of the people," and emphasized its determination to "cling to, and contend for the integrity of our glorious Constitution, because with religion as its basis and perfect freedom as its superstructure, we consider that it yields to us that enlightened, stable, and good government which it is impossible that a republic from its clumsy, complicated, and unscriptural machinery can ever afford."[18] The following month another article reminded Upper Canadians of their duty to remain loyal to their monarch and also lavished praise on the British constitution,

In His Name

"which throws the shield of protection over more than 125 millions; which has stood the united shock of the whole civilized world in arms; which is the workmanship of time, from materials gathered from the evidence of all ages." It then compared Britain's constitution to the constitution of a society where "government was incompetent to protect virtue, or restrain vice," and where a "loud and annually repeated `Declaration' of `the inalienable rights' of man" was heard "at the same moment with the lash of a Slave-driving President, or the groans of the down-trodden aborigines."[19]

The equation of the imperial connection with the basic values of conservative ideology determined the Anglican response to Lord Durham's *Report on the Affairs of British North America*. Throughout his six-month stay in the Canadas, Durham enjoyed the support of Strachan and A.N. Bethune, the former arguing privately in his correspondence and the latter publicly in the pages of the *Church* that the new governor general should have been given an opportunity to fulfill the purpose of his mission before being forced to return to England because of the machinations of his critics.[20] With the publication of the *Report*, however, it became impossible to regard Durham as an ally of the conservative cause. He was now denounced by the *Church* as a dangerous revolutionary and an enemy of the Church of England, who "adopted as his text-book the volumes of grievances with which, for the last ten years, our pseudo-reformers have been encumbering the world."[21] He was also accused of being a traitor, thanks to his recommendation of responsible government. The *Church* contended that responsible government was incompatible with the maintenance of the imperial tie and would inevitably lead to independence and the repudiation of those values which Upper Canada had inherited from Britain. The sequel to this development, it claimed, would be absorption into the United States, since an independent Upper Canada, militarily weak and lacking a sense of identity as a conservative society, would be unable to defend itself against either an American armed invasion or the infiltration of republican ideology.[22]

The *Church* was equally enraged with the reaction of the imperial government to the Durham *Report*. True, colonial responsible government had been rejected as impractical and expedient, a political innovation that could result only in a dissolution of the imperial tie. But

Defeat

Durham's recommendation that a union of the Canadas would restore political stability and bring about the assimilation of the French Canadians was accepted by the imperial government, and an act creating the United Province of Canada became law in early 1841. The *Church* predicted that the union would weaken the conservative cause by allowing Upper Canadian Reformers to join forces with their more numerous Lower Canadian counterparts,[23] and its prediction was proven accurate by political developments under successive governors general in the 1840s. Sydenham's implementation of his concept of coalition government in 1841; Bagot's appointment of Robert Baldwin and Louis-Hippolyte Lafontaine to the executive council in 1842; the failure of Metcalfe to fashion a stable conservative ministry in the period from 1843 to 1845; and Elgin's inauguration of responsible government in 1849—all of these developments confirmed the *Church*'s fear that the union of 1841 could lead only to the political dominance of the "rebellion faction" and to the separation of the Canadas from the parent state.

In 1843, shortly after the death of Bagot, the *Church* declared angrily that "the cause of truth and loyalty" had recently been "paralyzed by the elevation of the agitator and the traitor to offices of honour and emolument, and by suffering the pardoned, but impenitent rebel to mingle, upon equal terms, and with equal privileges, amongst those who fought and bled for the supremacy of the Crown."[24] Its hostility to the new political order was even greater in 1849, when it asserted that the annexation movement was the result of the oppressive policies of the Baldwin-Lafontaine government, policies which had driven the "best men" to propose, "in an emotion of despair," an extreme solution "as a remedy to our troubles." It continued: "the arbitrary proceedings of the radical faction are sweeping away one after another all the safeguards of the British Constitution in this Province ... the powers of Government are now possessed by a democracy of the worst description — a democracy as thoroughly selfish and remorseless as any that the world has ever seen."[25]

The bitterness evident in the *Church*'s response to the political events of the 1840s was also apparent in Anglican fulminations against the colonial policy of the imperial government. A.T. Townley, a former Wesleyan Methodist who had become an Anglican minister in 1841, wrote a letter to the *Church* in August 1849 entitled "Why We Cannot

In His Name

Annex?" In this letter Townley criticized the unscriptural nature of republicanism and insisted upon the duty of Christians to remain loyal to their sovereign, but he also asserted that Upper Canada would be justified in requesting a dissolution of the imperial tie, for Britain was anxious to rid itself of its colonial responsibilities and the British constitution had been overturned by the doctrine of popular sovereignty.[26] Another Anglican clergymen, W.S. Darling, attacked the "obstinate incredulity and suicidal policy of the Colonial Office" in his 1849 novel, *Sketches of Colonial Life*. Lamenting that "radicalism, which was but a puny infant even in '37 has been so skillfully papped and nursed by the Colonial Office, that it has attained its present alarming growth," he wrote that rebels "have returned or been recalled and appointed to offices of honour and emolument, while those who shed their blood for the cause of British institutions have been unrewarded and forgotten." Was it any wonder, he asked, "that cold indifference should have taken the place of ardent loyalty?"[27]

Anglican bitterness was based on a unique perception of the political events of the 1840s. Because the imperial connection held such a central place in the Anglican mind, its apparent dissolution in the late 1840s, as a result of the repeal of preferential duties on colonial grain and timber and the achievement of responsible government, made it difficult for Anglican clergymen to be optimistic about Upper Canada's future. It now seemed clear that the values symbolized by the imperial tie had been repudiated, that Upper Canada was destined to be absorbed by the United States, and that a distinctive vision of the good society had been abandoned in favour of the radical ideology of the revolutionary age.

This view of the deeper meaning of the events of the 1840s explains the lukewarm loyalty displayed by the *Church* when it heard of the violent reaction of Montreal Tories to the Rebellion Losses Bill. Though the *Church* deplored the burning of the parliament buildings and the ensuing riot in the streets of Montreal, it refused to come to the defence of a governor general who had championed the cause of the "rebellion faction" and had presided over the destruction of Upper Canada's character as a loyal and conservative society. The paper's anger and bitterness were reflected in its curt statement that "men with true British hearts" could not "testify that sympathy in the deep

Defeat

humiliation of Her Majesty's Representative...because that representative... has used his freedom to sanction oppression. He has placed his untrammelled responsibility at the beck and service of legislative tyranny."[28] The *Church*, it is true, firmly opposed the annexation movement in the months ahead, declaring in numerous editorials that it was the duty of Upper Canadians to remain loyal to the "powers that be."[29] But its imperial patriotism was henceforth tempered by a feeling of betrayal. The lesson it drew from the constitutional and economic changes of the 1840s was that British statesmen and colonial governors were guilty of propelling Upper Canada along a road which led directly into the outstretched arms of the American republic.

* * * * *

Compounding the Anglican clergy's concern as they followed the constitutional developments of the 1840s was a series of reverses in the realm of church-state relations. On the educational front, the school system established after the War of 1812 was replaced during this period with a new system which, besides accepting the principle of local assessment and replacing all appointed trustees with locally elected ones, actively discouraged denominational teaching. Under the direction of Egerton Ryerson, who was appointed general superintendent of education in 1844, this non-sectarian common school system experienced uninterrupted growth and consolidation, though provision was made in the 1850s for the creation of Roman Catholic separate schools. The Church of England waged a prolonged campaign for the right to establish Anglican separate schools, but its efforts met with the unyielding opposition of successive governments.[30]

Even more damaging for the Church of England was the loss of its favoured position in the field of university education. In 1843 Governor Bagot successfully arranged the long delayed opening of King's College. Strachan fully expected that his beloved college, having been stripped of its exclusively Anglican council by the 1837 amendments to its charter, would no longer be an object of voluntarist wrath, but he proved to be mistaken. The college's principal and the majority of its professors, including its professor of divinity, were Anglicans, and the possession by such a "sectarian" institution of a lavish public endowment aroused widespread resentment both among denominations desiring support for their own colleges and among those voluntarists calling for a state-supported but non-denominational system of university education. Pressure exerted by the Church of Scotland and the Methodist Conference led to the introduction of university bills in 1843, 1845 and 1847. The Baldwin bill of 1843 and the Draper bill of 1845 proposed to transform King's College into a non-sectarian arts college and to divide its endowment among the denominational colleges that decided to affiliate. The Macdonald bill of 1847, much to the disgust of the voluntarists, proposed to allow the Church of England to remain in exclusive control of King's College and suggested that its endowment be divided among totally independent denominational colleges. The failure of these three bills to attract sufficient support either in the Assembly or in the colony at large forced Robert Baldwin to introduce a second university bill in 1849. Under the terms of this bill, King's College was transformed into the secular and non-denominational University of Toronto; religious tests and theological teaching were abolished; clergymen were ineligible for the offices of chancellor and president; and divinity halls wishing to affiliate with the new university were warned that they could expect nothing from its endowment. The bill, which provided for a more thorough secularization of university education than had ever been suggested before, received the enthusiastic support of the voluntarists and was passed by the legislature. The rout of the Church of England in the field of higher education was complete.[31]

The most serious reverse suffered by the Church of England in this period was the loss of its landed endowment. In 1840 Governor Sydenham, determined to settle a controversy that Durham had seen as one of the major causes of the rebellion, ignored the outraged protests of Anglican clergymen and persuaded the Assembly to agree to a bill which stated that one-half of the proceeds of the clergy reserves were to be divided in equal proportions between the Church of England and the Church of Scotland, leaving the remainder to be shared among all denominations. Although this settlement represented a recognition of the religiously pluralistic nature of Upper

Defeat

Canadian society, the creation of such a multi-headed establishment failed to satisfy those denominations pledged to the separation of church and state. By the early 1850s the secularization of the reserves was being demanded by politicians in all political camps and by a broad, informal alliance of religious groups. The reform ministry of Francis Hincks and A.N. Morin, officially pledged to secularization by the Price Resolutions of 1850, was reluctant to grapple with such a contentious issue as the clergy reserves, and its policy of procrastination in the face of the broadly based and immensely influential voluntarist movement seriously undermined its position in Upper Canada.

The secularization of the clergy reserves was finally achieved in 1854. In an election held that summer the Hincks-Morin ministry, still reluctant to deal with the reserves issue even though the necessary enabling legislation had been recently passed by the imperial government, found itself beset on all sides by forces committed to the cause of secularization. When the legislature reopened in the fall, the government was defeated on a question of privilege and replaced by a coalition of Upper Canadian Conservatives and Lower Canadian Reformers. The new ministry, led by A.N. Morin and Allan MacNab, introduced a clergy reserves measure immediately after assuming office. Under it, the proceeds from the sales of clergy reserve lands were to be transferred to the Municipalities Funds of Upper and Lower Canada; provision was made for the payment of existing stipends during the lifetimes of the present incumbents; and, as a concession to the supporters of the 1840 settlement, the recipients of stipends were to be allowed to cede their life claims to their respective churches, which in turn could commute the total sum of these claims with an annual interest rate of six percent. The voluntarists, predictably, attacked the commutation scheme as a shameful exercise in denominational favouritism, but their opposition proved futile in the face of a widespread desire to settle a controversy that had poisoned religious and political life for the past three decades. In mid-December the clergy reserves bill, after winning overwhelming support in the House of Assembly, received the assent of the governor general and became law.[32]

In reacting to all these developments, the Anglican clergy showed no awareness of the need to come to some sort of compromise with

In His Name

their church's opponents. On the contrary, as the voluntarist crusade went from victory to victory, Anglican clergymen remained convinced that they were right and their critics wrong. At the same time, however, the Anglican defence of church establishment underwent a subtle shift in emphasis. For one thing, in a society where the state seemed more interested in disentangling itself from religion than in supporting it, arguments concerning the unity of church and state were no longer relevant. They still could be heard, it is true, but on the whole utilitarianism now prevailed. Just as significant, the idea of church establishment was no longer linked to a vision of a Christian polity founded upon the unity of church and society. In the 1830s the argument that a strong established church would be able to create an Anglican Upper Canada had increasingly inspired more lip-service than fervent belief, but not until the post-rebellion period was it buried once and for all. The clergy of the 1840s and 1850s, accepting Upper Canada's religious pluralism as a permanent condition, concentrated exclusively on arguments which enabled them to defend the policy of church establishment even though the Church of England was and would remain only one denomination among many. Ignoring the question of whether or not the Church of England possessed sufficient popular support to justify its established status, they were content to reiterate that the church's establishment in the British Isles was a valid reason for its establishment in Upper Canada, that the principle of establishment was enshrined in constitutional enactments which could not be altered, and that the establishment of the Church of England was vital if Upper Canada was to remain socially stable and firmly attached to the parent state.

As was true of Strachan in earlier years, the Anglican clergy's thinking on church-state relations revolved around a conservative view of the role of religion in society. The Christian religion, with its emphasis on the rewards and punishments of the afterlife, was seen as the bulwark of the social order, controlling the baser passions of human nature and providing men with a powerful incentive to cultivate those virtues, such as charity towards the less fortunate, on which the existence of a stable and civilized society depended. It was also seen — Henry Scadding's 1844 sermon is instructive in this regard — as a philosophy of life which taught men to obey constituted authority and to remain contented in their assigned position in the social scale.

Defeat

The Anglican perception of Christianity as an agency of social control inspired the Church of England's opposition to the nonsectarian common school system established in the 1840s. Throughout the post-rebellion period The *Church* attacked the common schools as "hotbeds of sedition and nurseries of rebellion" which, because of their exclusion of denominational religious teaching, threatened to undermine the entire social and political order.[33] Similarly, H.C. Cooper, the Anglican clergyman at Etobicoke, criticized the irreligious nature of the Common School Act of 1844 and demanded that the Church of England be allowed to establish separate schools, a right that had already been recognized in the case of Roman Catholics.[34] Another clergyman, Adam Townley, denounced the government for its refusal to authorize the creation of Anglican separate schools[35] and railed against the "insidiously irreligious"[36] nature of the Common School Acts of the 1840s, acts that would "eventually raise up a large body of ill-informed sceptics, puffed up with the miserable cant of a maudlin rationalism."[37]

The same belief in the close connection between religion and social stability provided the intellectual rationale for church establishment. Anglican clergymen frequently stated that the happiness, prosperity and stability of society depended on the existence of a church establishment, the implication being that the moral influence and financial resources of such an establishment enabled it to propagate the conservative teachings of Christianity with an efficiency which other denominations could never rival. Conversely, they were equally insistent that a society deprived of a church establishment would soon disintegrate, for the Christian religion could exert its influence as a bastion of the social order only when it was supported and "cherished" by the state. The *Church* editorialized in 1838 that "for the moral and spiritual, yes and the political advancement of any Christian country, an Established Church is an essential and ought to be an integral appendage." It asserted that "for internal quiet, for social peace, and national unity, the best, and it will be found the only guarantee is that universal prevalence of the Christian Religion and of Christian influences which an Established Church can alone ensure.[38]

R.J. MacGeorge, the Anglican clergyman in Streetsville, reiterated these arguments in an 1846 sermon. In his view, the campaign for disestablishment was sinful in its intent, for the separation of church and state would allow the baser passions of human nature to assert their dominance and would eventually lead to the collapse of society. MacGeorge argued that, because of Adam's rebellion in the Garden of Eden, we "come into this world with the chains of bondage rivetted to our limbs ... the enslaved subjects of the Prince of Darkness, without strength to break his yoke, and, what is worse, without inclination to disobey his commands."[39] Such a sinful race could never expect to enjoy true liberty in the present life, let alone eternal bliss in the next, were it not for the Christian religion, which reconciled individual freedom and the interests of the community. Asserting that "liberty at no time has permanently flourished when divorced from religion," and that "every political or social system which is not based upon the rock of God's most holy word" should be regarded with "suspicion and distrust,"[40] he pointed to Britain as an example of a country whose recognition of the inseparable nature of religion and liberty had made it "great in power, great in commerce, great in solid and substantial freedom, equally removed from monarchical despotism, and from the more degraded tyranny of a licentious democracy."[41] But he also admitted sadly that in recent years Britain's "matchless constitution" had been "marred ... by reckless hands," and that "wily demagogues," a phrase clearly intended to apply also to Upper Canada, had attempted to sever completely the ties between church and state, ignoring the fact that kings and queens had been commanded by God to be "nursing fathers" and "nursing mothers" of the church.[42] If these assaults upon the constitution continued, religion would be banished from the state and the sinful instincts of human nature would have free rein. Britain, and by inference its colonies as well, would then share the fate of revolutionary France, where "an experiment in government without religion" changed "all the histories of the preceeding sufferings of mankind into idle tales."[43]

Of course, Anglican clergymen were not content to explain the conservative function of a church establishment *per se*; their principal object was to defend the position of the Church of England in Upper Canada. And for them, justifying the presence of an Anglican establishment in their society was as natural as breathing. In their eyes, the Church of England was a branch of the catholic and apostolic church, a church whose purity of doctrine and beautiful liturgy were admired throughout the world. It was also a pillar of the British constitution, the foundation of a social structure which recognized the need of "due

Defeat

subordination," and the guardian of the imperial connection and of all those conservative values which that connection symbolized. Holding such views, they naturally concluded that the Church of England's claims to established status were legitimate, since its ability to diffuse "true religion," promote social and political stability, and defend the imperial tie could not be matched by other denominations. In sum, it was clear to them that the Church of England was ideally suited to perform those conservative tasks which were the very *raison d'être* of a church establishment.

This conviction was expressed in Strachan's 1840 petition to the House of Commons on the subject of the Sydenham reserves settlement, in the Reverend William Bettridge's *Brief History of the Church in Upper Canada*, and in an 1845 letter from William Herchmer, a clergyman stationed in Kingston, to the SPG.[44] It was also expressed in several *Church* editorials. Throughout the post-rebellion years the paper constantly declared that the established Church of England in Upper Canada was the safeguard of "rational" religion, social and political stability, monarchical institutions and the imperial connection.[45] Typical was an editorial of August 1838, which stated that a flourishing Church of England establishment was essential "for the propagation of sound Christianity in the land, for the best welfare of the country, for the maintenance of order, good government and peace, for the preservation of our connexion with the crown of Great Britain."[46] The *Church* also argued that the effective establishment of the Church of England would have prevented the rebellion of 1837, substantiating this claim by referring to the conspicuous absence of Anglicans from the rebel force.[47]

A strong belief in the social and political importance of an Anglican establishment was also evident in the annual reports of the Upper Canadian Travelling Missionary Fund. According to the line of reasoning that runs like a unifying thread through these reports, the Church of England taught Upper Canadians to obey constituted authorities and to cherish the imperial connection. Unfortunately, the church was crippled financially, neglected by a British government that had withdrawn its annual grant to the SPG, and persecuted by demagogues who desired to rob it of its landed endowment. This combination of neglect and persecution was having terrible results, for

In His Name

hordes of recently arrived Anglican immigrants, deprived of the services of their own church, were turning in desperation to the sects, religious groups characterized by their love of emotional hysteria in religious worship and by their determination to subvert the social and political structure. The end result was the rampant disloyalty and insubordination that had led to the rebellion of 1837. In brief, it was now clear that Upper Canada's future hinged upon the willingness of political authorities, both locally and in Britain, to fulfill their responsibilities to the Church of England, an institution that would always strive to promote the best interests of Upper Canada and the empire as a whole.[48]

An intense commitment to the importance of the Church of England establishment in Upper Canadian society was the motivating factor behind the violent Anglican reaction to the Baldwin and Draper university bills. The *Church* denounced the Baldwin bill of 1843 as evidence of the "anti-monarchical and anti-British" intentions of the Reform ministry, which was determined to transform Upper Canada into an "independent democracy."[49] As for the Draper bill of 1845, the *Church* asserted that it would force the Church of England to "strip herself of her distinctive character as a Church of Christ, and reduce herself to the level, — nay place herself under the control in her own educational seminaries, — of every wild and conflicting sect and denomination which has started into existence within the last three hundred years."[50] Using much the same language, an angry Strachan described the Baldwin bill as revolutionary in scope and tyrannical in nature, a shocking violation of property rights, a repudiation of the principles of the British constitution, a threat to "the safety of the Colony and its dependence on the Crown," and an atheistic attempt to set the catholic and apostolic teachings of the Church of England on an equal footing with the errors of countless sects — an attempt which, if successful, would "utterly destroy all that is pure and holy in morals and religion and would lead to greater corruption than any thing adopted during the madness of the French Revolution."[51] Two years later he insisted that the Draper bill, a measure "even worse than Mr. Baldwin's," was "subversive of all those principles upon which the security of property rest and the order of Society is maintained," and would "compromise and surrender the dignity of our Church," bringing "her authority indirectly at least under the cognizance and control of her avowed enemies" and submitting "her teaching to the interference & even dictation of those who are oppugners of her doctrines & hostile to her communion."[52]

Anglican clergymen were not hostile to the Macdonald University bill of 1847; they probably shared the *Church*'s view that the bill, which allowed King's College to remain under the control of the Church of England and divided its endowments among denominational colleges, should be supported for the sake of peace.[53] The Baldwin bill of 1849, however, was another matter. This measure not only destroyed one of the main institutional props of the established Church of England but also signalled the total exclusion of religion from an institution of higher learning, thus ignoring the Anglican belief that education should always have a religious basis. Consequently, it was only to be expected that Anglican clergymen would have difficulty in controlling their rage when such a "godless" and "subversive" piece of legislation passed the Assembly and became law.

The Anglican reaction to the Baldwin bill of 1849 was swift. Strachan declared that the bill was designed to "crush the National Church, and peril her existence,"[54] and he later criticized the government for repudiating the "undeniable truth that there was an Established religion in the country and giving countenance to the new and unreasonable assumption that all forms of religion and all varieties of doctrine, whether true or false, rational or absurd, were equally entitled not only to their protection but to their actual encouragement and support."[55] Convinced that "to separate religion from education is the suggestion of the Evil One," he emphasized that the Church of England would have nothing to do with the "anti-Christian" University of Toronto and announced plans to establish a seminary where secular and religious instruction would be provided "according to the principles" of the Anglican faith — plans which were crowned with success when Trinity College was founded in 1851.[56] The *Church* was just as hostile to the University of Toronto, describing it as "godless"[57] and the product of "the jealousy felt by those who envy the Church her prosperity,"[58] and insisting that Anglican involvement in such an institution would inflict irreparable damage on the catholic and apostolic character of the Church of England.[59]

In His Name

The prevalence in Anglican circles of these views on the Baldwin bill, and of the philosophical assumptions underlying the idea of religious education and the policy of church establishment, is shown by the number of Anglican clergymen who enthusiastically supported the cause of a new "church university." Both F.J. Lundy and J. Flood, clergymen in Niagara and Richmond respectively, were critics of the "infidel" University of Toronto and champions of Trinity College.[60] Henry Scadding, Walter Stennett, J.G.D. Mackenzie and Stephen Lett, four clergymen stationed in Toronto, joined their congregations in early 1850 in presenting addresses to Strachan on the eve of his departure for England, where at the age of seventy-two he was to spend an exhausting six months soliciting funds for Trinity College; in these addresses the Baldwin bill was pilloried as unchristian and the hope was expressed that Strachan's efforts in England would prove successful.[61] Thirteen clergymen signed a petition in 1851 protesting against the Baldwin bill,[62] while Strachan's pastoral letter of the same year revealed that fifty-two Anglican clergymen had made financial contributions to the endowment fund of Trinity College.[63] In 1852 A.N. Bethune, enraged that the Church of England had been "so unfeelingly robbed ... and so ruthlessly cast overboard,"[64] went to England to continue Strachan's work in drumming up support for Trinity College.[65] The same task was undertaken in Upper Canada by T.B. Fuller and Saltern Givins, and in the United States by William McMurray.[66]

Understanding this utilitarian conception of the function of the Church of England establishment also helps to explain the Anglican clergy's almost hysterical reaction to the reserves settlement of 1840. Since the established Church of England was regarded as the guardian of religious truth, social stability and the imperial connection, Anglican clergymen inevitably concluded that the campaign against the clergy reserves was designed to destroy the very fabric of Upper Canadian society. Strachan charged in an 1840 speech to the Legislative Council that the Sydenham reserves bill, "such a tissue of injustice, cruelty, and absurdity, as was never before concocted by any Legislature," would sever the union of church and state, overthrow the British constitution and foster sectarianism.[67] The *Church* argued in a series of editorials in early 1840 that the bill "held out a premium ... not only to the propagators of religious errors but in many cases to the disseminators of sedition and republicanism," was destructive to the fundamental principles of the constitution, and would lead to independence and the transformation of Upper Canada into a democracy.[68]

Even more virulent was the Anglican response to the secularization of the reserves in 1854, an event that sounded the death-knell of the policy of church establishment. In a letter to A.N. Morin printed in the *Church* in late October, Strachan denounced the clergy reserves agitation as the product of "unprincipled office hunting, and a desire for reckless innovation," described the reserves measure itself as "the most atrocious specimen of oppressive legislation that has appeared since the days of the French Convention," and warned that the bill would lead to the destruction of the Roman Catholic Church's "magnificent" endowments in Lower Canada.[69] The *Church* itself displayed a similar attitude. An editorial of October 1854 stated that "we cannot conceive how any one maintaining a respectable position in the world, would propose to rob a church, a corporation or an individual of property of which they are in actual possession, and their undoubted right to which cannot be denied."[70] Equally uncompromising was a letter to the *Church* in late December from a certain "J.M.", who wrote that,

> demoralizing as the present unholy agitation eviently proves our religious world to be, the awful impiety of the public robbery of God must yet, when witnessed in all its ramifying evil consequences, open the eyes of the blindest and wickedest to the fearfulness of its character. It will then be but a poor consolation to the spoliators to look on the the other side of the account and to behold the 'field of blood' which they have gained as the equivalent for which they have sold and pulled down the altars of God and devastated his holy temples.[71]

The notion that the Church of England was suffering unjust persecution, a notion first glimpsed in its embryonic stages in the years just before the rebellion, became even more pronounced in the post-rebellion period. At a meeting of the Eastern Clerical Association in Bytown in 1839, attended by George Archbold, E.J. Boswell, S.W. Harper, Joseph Harris, J.G.B. Lindsay, James Padfield, Henry Patton, R.V. Rogers, S.S. Strong and W.W. Wait, one of the subjects discussed was "the cruel and unjust system of persecution to which the Church

In His Name

in this Province is at present exposed."[72] This preoccupation with the trials and tribulations of the Church of England was also evident in the case of Strachan. In 1850, at a meeting of the SPG in Liverpool, Strachan buttressed his appeal for contributions to the endowment fund of Trinity College by noting that,"notwithstanding her wonderful progress, the Church in Canada has been since 1840 a persecuted and suffering church."[73]

The Church of England had one consolation in the midst of its sufferings: the conviction that nothing transpired in the present world without being known to, or directly sanctioned by, God. This belief in an omniscient God and a structured universe performed a dual function for Anglican clergymen. It enabled them to think that the church's earthly sufferings had been ordained by God either as a trial of faith or as a punishment for transgressions on the part of its own members — thus could Bethune declare, in a sermon preached in 1841 at Strachan's first visitation as bishop of Toronto, that the recent reserves bill was "one of the chastisements which Almighty God, from time to time, is pleased to send upon his church, whether ... to try our patience for the example of others, and that our faith may be found in the day of the Lord laudable, glorious, and honourable or else to correct and amend in us whatsoever doth offend the eyes of our heavenly Father."[74] It also provided them with the assurance that God watched over the church even as he chastised it, allowing it to experience a certain dgreee of suffering for its own spiritual good, but always protecting it from fatal blows at the hands of its enemies and promising it the glory of ultimate triumph if it remained faithful. Strachan explained in 1840 that "the evils which at present threaten this portion of our Lord's Vineyard will only be permitted to proceed so far as is good for us and that out of darkness our Saviour can bring marvellous light."[75] This viewpoint was also expressed in a sermon preached by Strachan in July 1853, in a *Church* editorial of 1843, in an address drawn up in 1851 by seventeen members of the Midland Clerical Association, and in sermons preached by William Macaulay and Arthur Palmer.[76]

Associated with this reliance on divine protection was the conviction that those responsible for the persecution of the Church of England would be sternly dealt with by God. The *Church* announced in 1846 that the secularization of the clergy reserves would provoke "God's judgments,"[77] and in 1849 the Reverend James Beaven warned the House of Assembly that Upper Canada would suffer the consequences of divine wrath if the Baldwin university bill became law.[78] Similar warnings were issued by other clergymen — for example, J.G.D. Mackenzie and A.N. Bethune in 1850, R.G. Cox in 1851, and Adam Townley in 1853 — and also by the Church Union, a lay organization established in 1851 for the purpose of defending the Anglican share of the reserves.[79] R.G. Cox was especially forceful in the expression of his views, declaring that "if the Clergy Reserves be seized ... the country will have committed a blunder and a crime which shall entail upon it the withering curse of an avenging God, through successive generations ... a blighted commerce, unfruitful seasons, and unyielding fields, trouble, perplexity, distress and death, will evidence that no nation can insult heaven by flagrant wrong, and pass unscathed."[80]

The secularization of the reserves in 1854 provoked more statements on the subject of divine retribution. One correspondent to the *Church* expressed the hope that the "spoliators" of the clergy reserves would, "before the night of eternal sleep falls upon them, receive grace sufficient to open their eyes to the heinousness of their crime — that their consciences may be smitten with the pangs of saving remorse, so that finally they may receive pardon at the hands of Him against whom while it was in their power they fought on the earth; and that mercy which they unfeelingly denied to his people."[81] Other Anglicans were seriously concerned that the secularization of the reserves would prompt God to punish not merely the Church of England's opponents but Upper Canada as a whole. At the visitation of clergy and lay delegates held in October 1854, a committee composed of two clergymen, Arthur Palmer and Stephen Lett, and two laymen, G.J. Boulton and G.W. Allan, declared that the reserves bill had to be considered by "every right-minded person as a sin in the sight of Almighty God, both on the part of the individuals by whose influence it is effected, and on the part of the country at large, by whom it was permitted." That being so, the committee was certain that such a sinful measure was "calculated to call down upon this people and land the judgments which the principles of the Divine government have ever attributed to the perpetuation of iniquity, whether by individuals or nations."[82]

Yet, if Anglican clergymen were confident that God would protect the Church of England and punish its enemies, they also began to

In His Name

reconsider the relationship of church and state in Upper Canadian society. Their new frame of mind was reflected both in their growing hostility towards the state connection, and in their increasing impatience with the Erastian philosophy that saw the church as a subservient tool of the state. In an editorial published in November 1854, the *Church* criticized the "secularization agitators" for attempting "to make it appear that the Church was the mere creature of the state," and confidently predicted that Upper Canadians would "soon learn that the Church takes much higher ground."[83] The same line of reasoning was pursued by one "W.S." in a letter to the *Church* in October of the same year. After first explaining that "I am not one of those who look upon the secularization of the reserves as an unmitigated evil," he expressed the hope that, with the loss of the church's landed endowment, the "bitter and unjust taunt of `State-paid Clergy' would no longer be heard," and clergymen and laymen would acquire a "consciousness of strength to throw off all dependence upon the State, and seek in trusting in their Divine Head alone a remedy for existing evils."[84]

As "W.S."'s statements suggest, the Anglican clergy's mounting hostility towards the church-state connection went hand in hand with the view, advanced initially by Strachan in the 1830s, that the Church of England was a primarily spiritual organization. On a number of occasions in this period the argument was put forward that the Church of England could easily survive disestablishment since its authority was derived not from its connection with the state, but from its character as a channel of grace and an instrument of salvation. The *Church* claimed in 1850 that "whether the law recognizes or does not recognize an established Church in these Provinces is a matter of secondary moment ... the United Church of England and Ireland is `established' and on a much firmer basis than any human law. It is established on the Word of God."[85] H.C. Cooper declared in a series of speeches in the 1840s that the influence of the Church of England depended upon the esteem in which it was held by its own members, rather than upon "her connexion with the State, and upon her position as `the established church.'" He also argued that disestablishment would awaken the "energy and zeal" of Anglicans and, in so doing, actually strengthen the Church of England.[86]

Defeat

Similar statements were made by Strachan. In his 1847 charge to the clergy of the diocese he emphasized that the principle of church establishment was divinely sanctioned,[87] but he also denied that the abandonment of this principle would lead to the Church of England's destruction. Insisting that the Church of England was not "an institution of earth, an instrument or creature of the state,"[88] he made it clear that a church commissioned by God to preach the Gospel would not be seriously affected by a change in worldly fortunes. "For some time past," he stated, "our Church hath been taught, by dear bought experience, to depend less upon the state and more upon herself, and to perceive ... the necessity of coming out in all the holiness of her teaching, as a true branch of the Church of God."[89] Four years later he reiterated, in another charge, that attempts to secularize the reserves are "indeed the less to be dreaded, because they are chiefly of a temporal, and therefore of a transient character; but even should they multiply and become more gloomy, what are they but trials for our good, so long as we possess God's holy Word, his blessed sacraments in all their pureness and integrity, the Book of Common Prayer, and full liberty to meet for divine worship."[90]

Clearly, the idea that the Church of England would react to disestablishment by becoming a primarily spiritual organization was at odds with the claim that God would protect the interests of the established church and punish the advocates of religious equality. Though the contradiction was never entirely resolved, the setbacks experienced by the Anglican cause slowly gave rise to the belief that the Church of England would triumph only in the sense of meeting its religious responsibilities, that its ultimate vindication would take place not in this world but in the next, and that in the meantime it should console itself with the reflection that its earthly sufferings would soon be followed by the glory of the life to come. As early as 1840, the year of the Sydenham reserves settlement, the *Church* urged Anglicans to "resist the contemplated overthrow of all that they hold dear in our civil institutions, and prize in our religious heritage; that when all are swept away ... this with our eyes directed to a land which clouds never darken nor troubles distract, may be our hearty language, `Arise let us be going — this is not our rest.'"[91]

This belief in the essentially other-worldly nature of the Church of England's mission was also revealed in an 1845 letter from Strachan to

In His Name

Ernest Hawkins, Secretary of the SPG, and in an 1851 letter from the Reverend W.S. Darling to the *Church*. Strachan wrote that "the Church has been a suffering Church from the beginning it has ever been her lot to struggle with the powers of evil and ever will be ... but we ought neither to complain or be cast down for she may suffer in our time and appear sorely pressed she will yet triumph for Christ is with her & *she is his Kingdom tho' not of this world*."[92] Darling was more oblique, declaring that the Church of England would triumph only after it was "made perfect" through a long period of suffering, a period in which it would remain "a faithful witness for God ... in the very bed of the torrent of ungodliness ... learning from her Master to dwell more alone upon the mountain top, in prayer, and fasting, and the discipline of a lowly heart."[93]

* * * * *

A review of Anglican ideology in the years after the rebellion highlights the extent to which the Upper Canadian church was immersed in the conservative ideology of the age. Whatever the issue — the structure of society, the responsibilities of subjects, the value of the imperial tie, or the function of a church establishment — Anglican clergymen invariably defended a conservative point of view. Further, even those who left no record of their political philosophy — and they are the majority — revealed the values that governed their lives in the way they responded to such events as the destruction of King's College and the secularization of the clergy reserves. Their actions, combined with the public statements of a number of their colleagues and *Church* editorials, make it abundantly clear that Strachan was merely the most prominent and active spokesman for a philosophical perspective that pervaded the entire clerical body. In terms of its vision of the good society, the church operated as an ideological monolith.

The Anglican clergy's conservatism had serious implications. In the 1840s and early 1850s, Conservatives in the political arena were beginning to adopt a moderate approach to the issues of the day, and one reflection of their new attitude was a growing acceptance of the

Defeat

Reform vision of the meaning of loyalty — a vision that was far more flexible and accommodating than the traditional Tory view.[94] This developing consensus in the world of politics embraced most Upper Canadians, but not the clergy of the Church of England. For them, loyalty to the imperial tie still entailed a commitment to a wide range of specific values, and could not be reconciled with such new-fangled notions as responsible government. Their position had the virtue of consistency, but it also placed them on the periphery of Upper Canada's political culture.

The Church of England's defeats in the post-rebellion period left the world of Anglican clergymen in tatters. Reeling in confusion and rage, they lashed back by rallying around the ideals of the past. Yet in so doing they revealed a frame of mind that had little in common with the aggressive attitude displayed by Strachan in earlier years. When Strachan in the 1820s and 1830s had defended the policy of church establishment and set out his vision of the good society, he made it clear that his main objective was to halt the spread of radicalism in Upper Canadian society. In the post-rebellion period, however, this crusading spirit quickly gave way to a far more chastened and pessimistic mood. For most Anglican clergymen, including Strachan, there now seemed every reason to believe that Upper Canada had fallen victim to the spirit of the revolutionary age and would never again be characterized by its devotion to the ways of righteousness. Accordingly, when they defended their church's privileged position and expounded their conservative views, they succeeded only in betraying their own sense of isolation and helplessness. Their major concern, it seemed, was not to crush the forces of radicalism but rather to let it be known that in a world gone mad they themselves, if no one else, remained faithful to principles that Upper Canada had long since renounced.

Of course, while remaining true to the past was not without its consolations, it was also futile. What made it especially pointless was the undeniable reality that even the Church of England was deeply affected by the winds of change. By the early 1850s it was becoming increasingly apparent that Anglican clergymen, notwithstanding the forcefulness of their ideological pronouncements, were slowly coming to accept the inevitability of disestablishment, thus resigning themselves to the dissolution of a union of church and state which, for the last fifty years, had provided them with a social and political *raison d'être*

In His Name

that the clergy of other denominations lacked. Even as they were defending the policy of church establishment, reverses on a number of fronts were forcing them to see their church as an essentially spiritual organization, concerned primarily with the religious welfare of its own flock and destined to triumph not in this world but in the kingdom of heaven. This intellectual revolution, the single most important development in the history of the Church of England in the post-rebellion period, was also evident in the church's attempts to make itself more financially self-supporting and to fashion an organizational structure that was better suited to the era of disestablishment.

Defeat

NOTES

1 See Strachan Sermons, "And he came to Nazareth where he had been brought up" (27 Oct. 1847); "O that they were wise that they understand this that they would consider their latter end" (9 April 1839); "I am he that liveth and was dead" (8 May 1840); "And as Jesus passed forth from thence he saw a man named Matthew" (22 Oct. 1848); "And he made his grave with the wicked" (1 Aug. 1849); "Every man that striveth for the mastery is temperate in all things" (5 March 1851).

2 The *Church*, 29 Aug. 1840. The *Church* — edited by A.N. Bethune from 1837 to 1841 and from 1843 to 1847, by the layman John Kent from 1841 to 1843, and by a series of anonymous clergymen from 1847 to 1854 — operated as the *Canadian Churchman* from 5 Aug. 1852 to 23 June 1853. For the sake of clarity and simplification, the name *Church* has been used throughout this book.

3 BRMTL, Scadding Sermons, vol. A11, "That they may adorn the doctrine of God our Saviour in all things" (10 March 1844).

4 Clark, *English Society, 1688-1832*, passim.

5 Strachan, *A Discourse on the Character of King George the Third*, pp. 18-19.

6 John Hudson, *A Sermon on the Death of His Late Royal Highness the Duke of York, Commander in Chief of His Majesty's Forces. Preached in the Episcopal Church of York, Upper Canada, at the Garrison Service, on Sunday Morning, March 11, 1827* (York, 1827), pp. 5-8.

7 Burwell, *Doctrine of the Holy Spirit*, p.107

8 The *Church*, 17 Nov. 1838.

9 Ibid., 22 Dec. 1838.

10 Ibid., 19 Sept. 1840.

11 Ibid., 5 Dec. 1850.

12 Ibid., 26 April and 17 May 1844. John Kent, the English immigrant who edited the *Church* from 1841 to 1843, wrote an article in 1838 in which he revealed his belief in the theory of the social contract and in the legitimacy of rebellion. Still, he made a point of emphasizing that rebellion was justifiable only when misgovernment had been notorious and after constitutional means of redress had first been exhausted. Furthermore, in the case of Upper Canada, a stable and prosperous society, Kent was convinced that rebellion would never be justifiable. See the *Church*, 22 Sept. 1838, "The English Layman," no. XVII.

13 A.N. Bethune, *The Duty of Loyalty. A Sermon, Preached in Saint Peter's Church, Cobourg, on Sunday, XXI, October, M.DCCC.XLIX* (Cobourg, 1849), p. 7.

In His Name

14. Ibid.
15. Ibid., p. 15.
16. Ibid., p. 7-8.
17. Ibid., p. 16.
18. The *Church*, 17 Nov. 1838.
19. Ibid., 22 Dec. 1838. On the relationship between imperial patriotism and conservative ideology, see also an 1838 sermon by Palmer which was published in the *Church* on 24 Nov. 1838; Bethune, *The Duty of Loyalty*, p. 14; and F.J. Lundy's letter to the *Church* on 10 Jan. 1850.
20. For Strachan's early attitude towards Lord Durham, see the following letters in the Strachan Letter Book, 1827-31: Strachan to Buller, 20 Sept. 1838; Strachan to ?, 8 Oct. 1838; Strachan to Bond Head, 13 Oct. 1838. The *Church* expressed some apprehensions when it first heard of Durham's mission (see 24 March 1838), but changed its mind in the course of the year. See the *Church*, 11 Aug. and 8 Dec. 1838.
21. The *Church*, 13 April 1839. Also: 22 June, 10 and 24 Aug. 1839.
22. For the *Church's* views on Durham's recommendation of responsible government, see the same editorials cited in note 21 and the full-page, five-column editorial on 31 Aug. 1839.
23. See the *Church*, 7 and 21 Dec. 1839, 21 March 1840, 30 Jan. 1841.
24. Ibid., 6 Oct. 1843.
25. Ibid., 29 March 1849.
26. Ibid., 9 Aug. 1849.
27. W.S. Darling, *Sketches of Canadian Life, Lay and Ecclesiastical, Illustrative of Canada and the Canadian Church* (London, 1849), p. 195.
28. The *Church*, 3 May 1849.
29. Ibid., 29 March, 12 July, 27 Sept., 18 and 25 Oct., and 1 Nov. 1849.
30. For a discussion of the Anglican response to the emergence of a non-sectarian common school system, see Moir, *Church and State in Canada West*, pp. 139-80; and Houston and Prentice, *Schooling and Scholars*, pp. 112 and 276-78.
31. The university question is dealt with exhaustively in Moir, *Church and State in Canada West*, pp. 82-128.
32. For a discussion of the clergy reserves question after the union of 1841, see Moir, *Church and State in Canada West*, pp. 27-81; and Wilson, *The Clergy Reserves*, chapters ten to fourteen.

Defeat

33 See, for example, the *Church*, 30 Oct. 1851 and 12 Feb. 1852.
34 Ibid., 2 and 16 Oct. 1846; 29 Jan., 2 and 30 July 1847.
35 *Seven Letters on the Non-Religious Common School System of Canada and the United States. By Adam Townley, Presbyter of the Diocese of Toronto* (Toronto, 1853).
36 Ibid., p. 54.
37 Ibid., p. 39.
38 The *Church*, 17 Feb. 1838. Also: Adam Townley, *Ten Letters on the Church and Church Establishments in Answer to Certain Letters of the Rev. Egerton Ryerson, by an Anglo-Canadian* (Toronto, 1839), pp. 65-66; "Religious Instruction," an excerpt from what is clearly Strachan's "Letters on a General Union of the British North American Provinces" (the *Church*, 25 May 1839); TDA, Manuscript Lecture Notes of A.N. Bethune (Lectures XX11-111, "On the Lawfulness and Benefits of Church Establishments").
39 *The Perfect Law of Liberty: A Sermon, Preached at Trinity Church, Streetsville on Sunday, XII July, M.DCCC.XLVI* (Toronto, 1846), pp. 3-4.
40 Ibid., p. 5.
41 Ibid., pp. 5-6.
42 Ibid.
43 Ibid., pp. 6-7.
44 Strachan Papers, n.d., form of petition to House of Commons; Bettridge, *Brief History of the Church in Upper Canada*; SPG Letters, Series C, Box. VI/46, no.544, 3 March 1845.
45 The *Church*, 24 Feb., 17 and 31 March, 14 April and 4 Aug. 1838; 4 May 1839; 25 Jan., 1, 8, 29 Feb., and 4 April 1840; 22 Jan. 1842; 29 Jan. 1847; 8 Sept. 1853.
46 Ibid., 4 Aug. 1838.
47 Ibid., 10 March 1838, 2 Nov. 1839, 4 April 1840. On this theme, see also a speech by the Reverend S.B. Ardagh that was published in the *Church* on 8 March 1849; and *The Claims of the Church Society, A Sermon Preached Before the Parochial Association of Belleville, in connexion with the Incorporated Church Society of the Diocese of Toronto, in the Parish Church of St. Thomas, on Thursday, 1st day of May, 1845. By the Rev. Job Deacon, Rector of Adolphustown* (printed in the *Church*, 25 July and 1 Aug. 1845).
48 Upper Canada Travelling Missionary Fund reports, passim.
49 The *Church*, 17 Nov. 1843.
50 Ibid., 7 March 1845.

In His Name

51 See Strachan's petition to the Legislative Council, printed in the *Church*, 10 Nov. 1843; Strachan Letter Book, 1839-43, Strachan to John Cartwright, 10 Oct. 1843; Strachan Papers, Strachan to Metcalfe, 2 Nov. 1843.

52 Strachan Letter Book, 1844-49, Strachan to William Boulton, 17 Feb. 1845; Strachan to William Robinson, 23 Feb. 1845; Strachan to A.G. Sherwood, Edward Murney and A.H. Meyers, 5 March 1845. Also of interest in this regard is John McCaul, *The University Question Considered: By a Graduate* (Toronto, 1845).

53 The *Church*, 23 July 1847.

54 John Strachan, *A Letter from the Lord Bishop of Toronto, to the Rev. T.B. Murray M.A., Secretary of the Society for Promoting Christian Knowledge, on the Subject of Establishing a Church University in Upper Canada* (London, 1850), p. 6.

55 Strachan Papers, Memorandum, 1851.

56 See Strachan's speech at the meeting of the SPG in Liverpool in 1850 (printed in the *Church*, 10 Oct. 1850); and Strachan Papers, Strachan to Elgin, 9 Nov. 1849).

57 The *Church*, 19 April 1849.

58 Ibid., 9 May 1850.

59 Ibid., 18 July 1850.

60 AO, F.J. Lundy Diaries, 1849-67, 5 and 26 Feb. 1850; the *Church*, 13 Feb. 1851.

61 Strachan Papers, 1850, addresses of the Church of the Holy Trinity, St. George's Church and St. Paul's Church.

62 Strachan Papers, 5 June 1851.

63 John Strachan, *Church University of Upper Canada. Pastoral Letter from the Lord Bishop of Toronto. Proceedings of the Church University Board. List of Subscribers, &c.* (Toronto, 1851), pp. 52-64.

64 Strachan Papers, Bethune to Strachan, 10 April 1850.

65 The *Church*, 20 May 1852.

66 Ibid., 15 April and 10 June, 1850; William McMurray, *An Appeal to the Members of the Protestant Episcopal Church in the United States, in Behalf of Trinity College, Toronto, Canada West* (New York, 1852). The above analysis is not meant to suggest that all clergymen were supporters of Trinity College. For the attitude of Evangelicals towards Trinity College, see Chapter Eight.

67 The speech was printed in the *Church*, 9 Feb. 1840.

Defeat

68   The *Church*, 11 Jan., 1, 8 and 24 Feb. 1840. Also: Strachan Papers, C.C. Brough to Strachan, 24 March 1840.

69   The *Church*, 26 Oct. 1854.

70   Ibid., 19 Oct. 1854.

71   Ibid., 21 Dec. 1854.

72   Ibid., 26 Jan. 1839.

73   Ibid., 10 Oct. 1850.

74   A.N. Bethune, *The Church of God. A Sermon preached in the Cathedral Church of St. James, Toronto, on Thursday, Sept. 9, 1841, at the Primary Visitation of the Lord Bishop of the Diocese* (printed in the *Church*, 18 Sept. 1841).

75   Strachan Letter Book, 1839-66, Strachan to A.M. Campbell, 28 April 1840. Also: Strachan Sermons, "And he spoke a parable unto them to this end" (24 July 1853).

76   Strachan Sermons, "And he spoke a parable unto them to this end"; the *Church*, 30 June 1843 and 16 Oct. 1851; *A Sermon Preached in the Cathedral Church of St. James, Toronto, on Thursday, June 6th, 1844, on Occasion of the Visitation of the Lord Bishop of the Diocese, by the Rev. William Macaulay* (printed in the *Church*, 28 June 1844); *On the Difficulties and Encouragements of the Christian Ministry, with Some References to the Past and Present Condition of the Church in Western Canada. A Sermon Preached in the Cathedral Church of St. James, Toronto, June 3rd, 1847. On the Occasion of the Triennial Visitation of the Lord Bishop of the Diocese, by the Rev. Arthur Palmer, A.B. Rector of Guelph* (printed in the *Church*, 16 July 1847).

77   The *Church*, 27 March 1846.

78   See Beaven's petition to the House of Assembly in the *Church*, 17 May and 7 June 1849.

79   See ibid., 31 Jan. and 23 May 1850, 3 April and 8 May 1851, and 8 Sept. 1853.

80   Ibid., 3 April 1851.

81   Ibid., 21 Dec. 1854.

82   *Proceedings of the Synod of the United Church of England and Ireland in the Diocese of Toronto, Held October 25, 26, & 27* (Toronto, 1854), p. 27.

83   The *Church*, 30 Nov. 1854.

84   Ibid., 5 Oct. 1854.

85   Ibid., 26 Sept. 1850.

86 *Characteristic Principles of the Church of England: Three Speeches of the Rev. H.C. Cooper, B.A., at the Annual Meetings of the London and Huron Branch Association of the Church Society of the Diocese of Toronto, in 1845, 1846, and 1847* (Toronto, 1847), pp. 16-18.

87 John Strachan, *A Charge Delivered to the Clergy of the Diocese of Toronto at the Visitation in June MDCCCXLVII by John Lord Bishop of Toronto* (Toronto, 1847), pp. 20-21.

88 Ibid., p. 34.

89 Ibid., p. 43.

90 John Strachan, *A Charge Delivered to the Clergy of the Diocese of Toronto, in May, MDCCCLI. By John, Lord Bishop of Toronto* (Toronto, 1851), p. 4.

91 The *Church*, 4 Jan. 1840.

92 Strachan Letter Book, 1839-66, Strachan to Hawkins, 17 March 1845. My italics.

93 The *Church*, 24 April 1851.

94 See David Mills, *The Idea of Loyalty in Upper Canada.*

CHAPTER SEVEN

THE SEEDS OF INDEPENDENCE

The Anglican experience after 1837 had its share of paradox. In the same period in which Anglican clergymen were affirming their belief in the tenets of conservative ideology and in the policy of church establishment, important strides were being made in the transformation of the Church of England into a self-governing, self-supporting and democratic institution. This transformation — highlighted by the campaign to establish a church synod with elected lay representatives, and by the efforts of an organization known as the Church Society to render the church more self-sufficient financially — was on the verge of completion by the time the clergy reserves were secularized in 1854.

It is tempting to see both the cause of synodical government and the Church Society as evidence of the Church of England's acceptance of the democratic and pluralistic nature of Upper Canada. The reality, however, was more complex. The institutional evolution of the Church of England from 1837 to 1854 was driven not by a democratic awakening, but by two conflicting ideas. One of these ideas held that only a more self-reliant and self-governing church would be able to defend the policy of church establishment. The other — the one that seemed to be gaining the upper hand by the early 1850s — linked state persecution of the Church of England with a more inward-looking vision of the church's role. According to this view, the creation of a self-reliant and self-governing Church of England was not a matter of coming to terms with a democratic society, but of accepting the inevitability of disestablishment and concentrating on the church's duties as a spiritual organization.

* * * * *

In His Name

While definite conclusions are impossible because of a lack of evidence, it is probable that the cause of synodical government in Upper Canada drew its inspiration from south of the border: in contrast to the situation in Britain, where the Church of England was without a convocation from 1717 until 1867, synods composed of both clergy and lay delegates were a regular occurrence in the United States from the founding of the Episcopal Church in the late 1780s.[1] Yet, while waging their battle for a church synod, Anglican clergymen in Upper Canada never once acknowledged their debt to American episcopalianism. Their silence in this regard was striking but not surprising. At a time when Anglican clergymen were embroiled in a tooth-and-claw struggle with what they regarded as the forces of infidel republicanism, they would have found it awkward to admit that their campaign for a new form of church government rested on an American precedent.

The idea of synodical government was first advanced by Strachan in the early 1830s. In two letters to Bishop Stewart in the spring of 1831, Strachan expressed his opinion that the creation of a church convocation was made necessary by the nature of the times; he noted that "had the Church of England annual meetings it would have retained much stronger hold of the population than it has at present ... many of the evils now complained of would have been prevented, lessened or removed."[2] Although Stewart ignored this proposal, Strachan's belief in the importance of establishing a new form of church government remained as firm as ever. In June of the same year he wrote to R.D. Cartwright, another believer in the value of synodical government,[3] declaring that "regular annual convocations" were imperative if clergymen themselves were to become more steadfast in their support of the Anglican cause and the policy of church establishment, if the church was to possess the judicial machinery it needed to regulate its own internal affairs, and if a degree of control was to be exerted over the actions of a bishop who had been neither zealous nor vigilant in his defence of the church's interests.[4] A few months later, in a letter to John Macaulay, he again denounced Stewart's apathy and laziness, and asserted that the creation of a church convocation, a goal he was still determined to achieve, would have a vital bearing on the church's attempts to defend itself against its opponents.[5]

The year 1832 marked a significant turning-point in Strachan's

The Seeds of Independence

efforts to provide the church with a new institutional structure. Until then Strachan had called only for the convening of an annual convocation of clergy, never once suggesting that such a convocation should include lay representation. In early 1832, however, with the benefit of advice from William and John Macaulay, A.N. Bethune, R.D. Cartwright and G.O. Stuart, he drew up a constitution for a church convocation which made provision for the election of two lay delegates from each congregation. Admittedly, the power of these lay delegates was to be curtailed by the stipulation that they were to vote not individually but by congregation, thereby ensuring that the voting strength of clergymen and laymen would be evenly balanced.[6] Yet that being said, the mere fact that Strachan was willing to include lay representation in a church synod was an indication both of the bold nature of his thoughts on the subject of church government, and of the lengths he was prepared to go in order to establish a firm basis of popular support for an Anglican convocation in Upper Canada. It was also a reflection of his belief that the church would have to rely more and more on the laity if it was to improve its financial position and retain its established status.

Strachan forwarded a copy of his constitution to Bishop Stewart in March 1832,[7] even though he was still convinced that the apathy of his diocesan superior, a man he described as "paralyzed & weak as water,"[8] had made him totally oblivious to the need for fundamental reforms in the government of the church. His pessimism regarding the probable fate of his constitutional proposals was well expressed in a letter to John Macaulay. "I am not sanguine that the Bishop will consent," he wrote. "I have however considered it my duty to tell his Lordship that it cannot be long delayed & that it will be forced upon us if we do not anticipate the wish of our people." He then told Macaulay that Stewart might be prodded into action if each congregation petitioned for the transformation of Upper Canada into a separate diocese, a tactic, incidentally, that coincided nicely with his own ambition to be elevated to the episcopacy. No other approach, he concluded, was likely to produce results, for Stewart had become a tool of Archdeacon George Jehoshaphat Mountain, "a compound of timidity selfishness & cant with some eloquence & talent" who had "governed the Church absolutely since the death of his Father and made everything in this Province subservient to the Lower." Further, Stewart himself was showing signs of "imbecility," a trait that had been painfully evident on his recent visit to England, when "instead of vindicating the rights of the Church he went ... about societies & private Lotteries getting praise for his piety & Lord Goderich laughed at him and listened to Ryerson."[9]

Strachan's comments about Stewart may have been unfair, but his forecast regarding the reception his constitutional proposals would receive in Quebec City proved to be accurate. Seriously ill and harassed by financial worries, Stewart remained deaf to all appeals for a church convocation, and Strachan's constitution, with its startling provision for lay representation, did not induce him to change his mind.[10] Strachan, not easily discouraged, made one last effort to overcome episcopal indifference to the idea of synodical government, explaining in a sermon at Stewart's 1832 visitation in York that the withdrawal of the SPG's parliamentary grant would make it necessary "for us in the future to depend more and more upon our resources and exertions than has been hitherto required," and that only a self-governing Church of England could be expected to survive the financial difficulties that lay ahead.[11] When even this argument left Stewart unmoved, it was apparent that the cause of institutional reform had run into an insuperable obstacle. Finally ready to admit defeat, Strachan abandoned his idea of forcing the issue of synodical government through the organization of a campaign for a separate diocese. The idea of synodical government was not proposed again, by Strachan or anyone else, until the mid-1830s, when the realization that Stewart's life was drawing to an end sparked a renewed interest in the institutional structure of Upper Canadian Anglicanism.

One sign of this renewed interest in the subject of church government was the publication in 1836 of Thomas Fuller's pamphlet, *Thoughts on the Present State and Future Prospects of the Church of England in Canada*. Fuller, a clergymen stationed in Chatham, argued that the withdrawal of the SPG's grant would accentuate the church's already serious problems in Upper Canadian society, depriving it of the resources it needed to build up a larger body of clergy and to minister more effectively to a religiously starved immigrant population. As a way of dealing with this crisis, Fuller called for the creation of a church synod with lay representation, asserting that such a body, besides acting as a safeguard of doctrinal uniformity, would strengthen the church by making it more independent financially and so ensuring its prosperity even in the event of disestablishment. To those who were critical of the idea of lay representation, Fuller simply replied that as long as ecclesiastical government was monopolized by the clergy, it was unreasonable to expect the laity to contribute to the church's support. "The laity alone have in their hands what can supply our wants," he wrote. "Before we can avail ourselves of it, we must allow them to have some voice in its disbursement. This is human nature." If the church refused to accept this fact and ignored the importance of establishing a new form of government, it would undoubtedly suffer severe consequences. For as Fuller concluded, any delay in the implementation of desperately required institutional reforms would fatally weaken the church in its efforts to protect its own flock against the forces of "popery," infidelity and dissent.[12]

Fuller's commitment to the idea of synodical government was shared by other Anglican clergymen. In November 1835 the Western Clerical Society, meeting in William Bettridge's rectory in Woodstock, proposed the calling of a general meeting of the clergy to discuss the need for a church synod and a separate Upper Canadian diocese. Archdeacons Strachan and G.O. Stuart accepted this proposal, and shortly afterwards, in February 1836, the Western Clerical Society not only gave its approval to Strachan's constitution for an Anglican synod — by now the document was apparently circulating among the clergy — but also began sending circulars to clergymen throughout the province inviting them to discuss the subject of Anglican self-government at the approaching archdiaconal assembly.[13]

This meeting of the Upper Canadian clergy took place in October 1836, a mere month after Stewart's deteriorating health had led to his return to England and to the appointment of G.J. Mountain as suffragan bishop of the diocese. In his address to the assembled clergy Strachan contended that the Upper Canadian church, deprived of the SPG's financial assistance and threatened with a loss of its "vested rights," was "in a manner cast off & left to herself."[14] As a result, he said, significant alterations in the structure of ecclesiastical government were needed immediately. Anxious to resolve any doubts which might hinder the church's evolution into a self-governing institution, Strachan noted that English history provided numerous examples of church synods, that the principle of lay representation had been accepted by the apostolic church, and that the church in Upper Canada was legally empowered to act on its own and establish a diocesan synod. He also emphasized that the creation of a synod with lay representation was necessary if the church was to be able to exist on its own financial resources, minister to the needs of a growing flock, and defend its privileges in an increasingly turbulent political climate.[15] On this last point, he made it very clear that the project of synodical government was inseparable from the church's struggle against the forces of voluntarism. He declared that "it is quite evident that a greater degree of union is necessary among us than has hitherto prevailed," and that the church would have to act in "one compact body" if it hoped to surmount its present "dangers, troubles and anxieties":

> a season of emergency has evidently arrived.... Are we to wait for a season still more perilous? Attempts are making to deprive us of our most valuable privileges, and to degrade and vilify our religious institutions in public estimation. — And are such difficulties to be overcome by shutting our eyes? It has been my full persuasion for many years, that the obstacles in the way of the progress of the Church are only to be conquered by organized meetings of the Clergy, assisted by the Laity; and that had such been instituted when suggested much evil would have been prevented.[16]

The actual proceedings of the archdiaconal meeting of 1836 remain a mystery. Many years later William Bettridge stated in a letter to the *Church* that the 1836 meeting had given its unanimous support to a resolution advocating the creation of a church synod with lay representation.[17] This view, however, was contradicted by another clergymen, E.J. Boswell. Besides claiming that the movement for the revival of church convocations was a conspiracy on the part of the Low Church party, Boswell noted that at the 1836 meeting some clergymen — he did not specify how many — objected to the proposal for a synod with lay representation. He also asserted that "when the clergy met in Toronto, they were not forgetful of what too many appear willing to forget now, that this branch of Christ's Church is not independent and consequently that there are persons in authority at Home, who have to be consulted."[18]

The Seeds of Independence

Whatever this meeting agreed on, it did not lead to action on the issue of synodical government. When Stewart died in July 1837, the imperial government failed to take advantage of the event to reconstruct the church's ecclesiastical government: Upper Canada was not transformed into a separate diocese — G.J. Mountain, to Strachan's bitter disappointment,[19] succeeded to the post of bishop of Quebec, with jurisdiction over the two Canadas, and no church convocation was created. Then, soon after Mountain's elevation to the episcopacy, the rebellion broke out, diverting the Anglican clergy's attention from the comparatively less pressing question of institutional reform.

Strachan did finally achieve his cherished ambition of becoming Upper Canada's first Anglican bishop in 1839, but much time was to pass before he used the power and prestige of his position to advance the cause of synodical government. In fact, in his 1841 episcopal charge, he dismissed the idea of a diocesan synod as impractical because of the opposition of imperial authorities. He also contradicted his earlier position and announced that he was opposed to the inclusion of lay representatives in a church body, an astounding intellectual reversal that is difficult, if not impossible, to explain. This deviation from an otherwise consistent stance — he would never again question the wisdom of including lay representatives in a church synod — was summed up in his statement that the election of laymen to the conventions of the American Episcopal Church was "a most dangerous innovation on her Constitution, and likely to lead in time to the most deplorable consequences."[20]

The cause of synodical government emerged from its state of suspension when the struggle for the separation of church and state reached a new level of intensity in the middle and late 1840s. In 1846 a *Church* editorial asserted that "the combinations of events in recent times have created the conviction ... in the minds of most men really attached to the Church that her power of self-government should be increased rather than diminished."[21] Two years later another *Church* editorial claimed that the Church of England in the British Isles needed a convocation to protect itself against state oppression, a claim that was obviously meant to be applicable to the Upper Canadian church as well.[22] More revealing still, a layman using the signature "Y.Z." emphasized in an 1849 letter to the *Church* that the creation of a diocesan synod would allow the Church of England, now dependent on an

In His Name

inadequate landed endowment, to become more self-supporting financially. "Y.Z." explained that "if the Church in this Province at least held her regular convocations, the laity would be early taught to know their duty, and quickly become acquainted with her temporal wants; as it is, most of us labour under a vague idea that she possesses some secret El Dorado from which she is upheld."[23]

Ironically, the individual primarily responsible for rekindling interest in the idea of synodical government was regarded by many clergymen as a traitor to the Anglican cause. Peter Boyle de Blaquière, a prominent Anglican layman, a member of the Legislative Council, and, to his lasting discredit in the eyes of many of his co-religionists, first chancellor of the "godless" University of Toronto, had two major concerns as a public figure in the early 1850s: defending a non-sectarian system of university education against Strachan's attempts to establish an exclusively Anglican "church university"; and increasing the influence of the laity in the Church of England's internal affairs.[24] The latter concern, which probably reflected a desire to liberalize the church's political position by vesting greater authority in the hands of a more flexible laity, was the motivating factor behind de Blaquière's decision to give his support to the cause of synodical government. In a letter to the *Church* in February 1850 de Blaquière unveiled a plan for a diocesan synod which he intended to submit to the legislature in the form of a comprehensive church government bill. This plan — which was apparently based on the assumption (a curious assumption for a liberal like de Blaquière) that the legislature could alter the government of a church that was still, at least in theory, the established church of the colony — resembled Strachan's earlier proposals in its acceptance of the idea of lay representation. But in another respect, it signified an important step forward from Strachan's plan since its most distinctive provision gave the proposed synod the power to elect bishops, a power that was without precedent in the history of Anglicanism in the British Empire.[25]

This plan unleashed a storm of controversy, its critics focusing both on its democratic features and on its idea that the local rather than the British government should take the lead in remodelling the church's affairs. The *Church* denounced de Blaquière for his ignorance of the principles of church government, and announced its determination to

The Seeds of Independence

"protect both the Laity and Clergy from the results of an undue preponderance of Lay influence," which had already reached alarming proportions because of the laity's possession of the "power of the purse."[26] William Macaulay and the vestry committee of St. Mary's Church, Picton, claimed that de Blaquière's scheme would vest control over "the important subjects connected with the Church" in the unskillful hands" of the laity.[27]   H.C. Cooper attacked de Blaquière's "republican proposition," emphasizing that such a proposal, besides "upsetting the entire fabric of the polity of the church," would eventually bring spiritual doctrines "within the scope of popular jurisdiction" and undermine "the prerogative of the Sovereign in whom the appointment of Bishops has been vested for many centuries, thus severing another link of the union of our Province with the Crown." He also expressed his indignation that the promise of increased power in ecclesiastical government was being used as a bribe in order to encourage the laity to contribute financially to the church's support.[28]

Yet, while the *Church*, Macaulay and Cooper were violently critical of de Blaquière's proposals, the reaction of church authorities was more cautious and conciliatory. A.N. Bethune, who had succeeded Strachan as archdeacon of York in 1847, and George Okill Stuart, the archdeacon of Kingston, were in charge of the church during the period of Strachan's mission to England on behalf of Trinity College, and in June 1850 they persuaded de Blaquière to delay the introduction of his church government bill until the opinions of the bishop and clergy could be ascertained.[29] An equally tactful approach was adopted by Strachan upon his return to Upper Canada that fall. In a letter to de Blaquière that was later published in the *Church*, Strachan expressed his regret that a plan for a diocesan synod had been introduced in his absence, but he also noted that he and de Blaquière were in full agreement on the pressing need to overhaul the church's institutional structure. Although he ignored de Blaquière's proposal that a church synod should have the power to elect bishops, and although he pointed out that the idea of lay representation presented certain difficulties and that the permission of the crown would have to be obtained before the Upper Canadian church could establish a synod, he promised to give the question of synodical government his careful consideration and to discuss it in the near future both with his own clergy and with his fellow bishops in Lower Canada.[30] That these were not empty promises became apparent in early 1851, when Strachan attended a meeting of the British North American bishops in Quebec City. Resolutions agreed upon at this meeting called for the creation of diocesan synods with lay representation and the appointment of a provincial metropolitan.[31]

Strachan's letter to de Blaquière and his support of the Quebec City resolutions clearly revealed that, since the time of his 1841 charge, he had grown less wary of the idea of lay representation and less pessimistic about the prospects of the cause of synodical government. To prove that this change in attitude was sparked by a heightened awareness of the relationship between synodical government and the maintenance of the policy of church establishment, it is sufficient to examine Strachan's justification for a decision he made just after his return from Quebec City, a decision that was to be of vital importance to the future of the church. In a pastoral letter of 3 April 1851, surely the most significant of his entire episcopate, Strachan declared that "many of the most pious and respectable members of our communion, both lay and clerical," had come to the conclusion that "the church ... ought to express her opinion as a body, on the posture of her secular affairs, when an attempt is again [in the] making by her enemies to despoil her of the small remainder of her property ... and that it is not only her duty to protest against such a manifest breach of public faith, but to take such steps as may seem just and reasonable to avert the same." Since Strachan himself agreed with the view that the entire church would have to act in unison if it was to resist the attacks of its opponents and retain its landed endowment, his letter instructed the regular communicants of each congregation to elect two lay delegates to a visitation that was to be held on 1 and 2 May in the Church of the Holy Trinity, Toronto.[32] This visitation, a synod in fact if not in name, was to have a threefold purpose: it was to set a precedent for lay representation in a church body; it was to convince the imperial government that a diocesan synod was desired by an overwhelming majority of Upper Canadian Anglicans; and it was to provide the church with the foundations of the institutional structure it so urgently required if it was to respond more effectively to the threat of disestablishment.

Unexpected in its timing and portentous in its implications, Strachan's letter naturally produced, as one layman reported at a

The Seeds of Independence

meeting of a Toronto branch of the Church Society, a feeling of "nervous distress" in some quarters of the church.[33] But it also renewed the hope of many clergymen and laymen that the creation of a synod was within the realm of possibility. The Reverend James Beaven, for instance, speaking at the same meeting of the Church Society, asserted with an air of exultation that the approaching visitation would be an epochal event in the history of Upper Canadian Anglicanism, providing the movement for synodical government with an important historical precedent and a popular base of support, and initiating the process by which a miserly Anglican laity was to be instructed in its financial obligations to the church.[34]

Beaven's confident, aggressive tone was a foretaste of the spirit of militancy that was to prevail during the visitation. In his opening charge to the enormous gathering of clergy and laity, Strachan declared that "our meeting and proceedings will begin a new era in the history of the Colonial Church, and may be the prelude, not only of diocesan Synods, but of the ultimate union of all the British North American Bishoprics, to convene at stated times in general Synods or convocations."[35] He also underlined the point that the demand for a synod was directly related to the church's efforts to defend its established status. After denouncing the agitation for the secularization of the clergy reserves as a manifestation of "the torrent of infidelity and radical licentiousness which is threatening pure and undefiled religion, and all the foundations of social peace and order,"[36] he urged the assembled clergy and laity to forward petitions to the colonial legislature and imperial government protesting against the proposed secularization of the clergy reserves, demanding the right to establish Anglican separate schools, and requesting permission to create a diocesan synod with lay representation, a form of government that would allow the church to act as a united body in defence of its "temporalities."[37] This stirring appeal did not go unanswered. With the unanimous consent of all present, resolutions were passed attacking the voluntarist crusade, defending the Anglican claim to separate schools, and calling on imperial authorities to sanction the formation of a church synod in Upper Canada.[38] Committees were established to draft the necessary petitions to the two levels of government, and shortly after the visitation one of these committees sent a petition on

In His Name

the subject of a church synod to the Queen. Accompanying this petition were addresses from Strachan on the same subject to the colonial secretary and the Archbishop of Canterbury.[39]

In the period immediately after the 1851 visitation, the cause of synodical government was still seen as an essential part of the church's strategy to survive the current campaign for disestablishment. The *Church*, no longer fearful of the influence of the laity, argued in an 1853 editorial that the purpose of an "ecclesiastical parliament" was to ward off the impending blow against the clergy reserves.[40] Strachan insisted in his *Letter to the Right Hon. Lord John Russell on the Present State of the Church in Canada* that imperial authorities, having severed the union of church and state, could no longer withhold the right of self-government from the Church of England, and that the creation of a synod in Upper Canada would allow the church to defend itself against "a host of enemies from every quarter ... agreeing in no one thing but their wish to destroy the only true branch of the Catholic Church which is able to stem the torrent of irreligion, fanaticism, and presumption, which is threatening to overwhelm the civilization of the world."[41] A similar statement on the relationship between synodical government and the church's struggle against the forces of evil was made in January 1852, when Strachan told a group of Anglican laymen that the church was now compelled "to present herself in action as a determined and united body, and thus to protect herself from the daily aggressions of the many bitter enemies with which she is environed."[42] He then added that

> were the Church to meet annually in synod, she not only would be able to defend her own just rights but feel herself, with God's blessing, in a position to arrest the torrent of socialism and infidelity, which has made so frightful progress among our secularly educated population during the last four years as to threaten us with total anarchy, and the destruction of every thing valuable in this splendid country.[43]

Even the forcefulness of Strachan's arguments, however, could not camouflage the ambiguity that was now apparent in the ultimate objectives of the movement for synodical government. As already

The Seeds of Independence

noted, the Anglican defence of the policy of church establishment in the 1840s and 1850s was coupled with an evolving conception of the Church of England as an institution that was independent of the state and more narrowly religious in the range of its concerns. This contradiction, a revealing indication of the Anglican clergy's confusion as they came face to face with the prospect of disestablishment, was also visible in the case for synodical government after the visitation of 1851. A diocesan synod was now defended not only as an instrument of self-defence that would be of great assistance in the church's efforts to maintain its established status, but also as a form of government that would allow the church to throw off the yoke of an oppressive state connection.

This latter view, which rested on a firm rejection of Erastian notions of the subservience of church to state, provided additional evidence that Anglican clergymen were beginning to reconsider the place of their church in Upper Canadian society. According to the line of thought on which it rested, synodical government had become necessary for several reasons. Political authorities in both England and Upper Canada, it was thought, were anxious to dissolve the union of church and state. Recently, moreover, the Church of England's close ties with the government had resulted in its own persecution. Given all of this, if the church was to protect itself against future persecution and escape from its humiliating dependence on a hostile government, it would have to accept the painful truth that the separation of church and state was inevitable, and become an independent, self-governing institution — an institution responsible for the management of its own affairs and free to pursue its religious activities unfettered by political interference.

The anti-Erastian sentiments underlying demands for a church synod came to the surface in a *Church* editorial of August 1851, in which it was declared that the demand for "synodical action" was a natural response to the desire of politicians "to treat the church as a mere state machine, of human invention and of human foundation."[44] The same argument was presented in a series of editorials on church organization published in the summer of 1852. The unifying theme of these editorials was that the church's present plight, both in England and Upper Canada, was the direct result of its subordination to the state. Convinced that the "Erastian system of government" had enabled the

In His Name

state to persecute the church with impunity, interfere in its internal affairs, and deprive it of the organizational structure it needed to meet its religious responsibilities and defend itself against the attacks of rival denominations, the *Church* announced in a spirit of icy determination that the time had come to free the Anglican cause from the "thraldom" of the "civil arm." Pointing to the situation in Upper Canada in particular, it noted that "in this Province legislation has discarded the Church, and placed her, so far as it has the power, in the position of a purely Missionary Church .... Fewer branches of the Church have been more sorely tried ... and none has more cruelly suffered the yoke of oppression ... while her enemies have had complete and wild freedom, she has been chained by absolute laws to the State, a mark for the arrows of her foes." If the Church of England was to improve its position in Upper Canadian society, the *Church* concluded, if it was to be able to resist its opponents and spread the gospel to the religiously deprived, a synod would have to be created. In taking this stand, the Upper Canadian church was demanding "her inheritance — the inheritance of Christian Englishmen — Freedom!"[45]

The stage was set for another outburst of anti-Erastianism when, in the fall of 1853, the Colonial Church Regulation Bill, designed to enable Anglican churches in the colonies to establish synods, failed to pass the British House of Commons and was temporarily shelved. Shortly after this latest setback to the campaign for synodical government, a second visitation of clergy and laity was held in Toronto. In the episcopal charge delivered on the opening day of the visitation, Strachan referred to the "dark and threatening" position of the Anglican cause and expressed the hope that the passage of a bill designed to "emancipate" the church would not be delayed much longer.[46] The clergy and laity were no less alarmed by the church's plight, and resolutions protesting against the clergy reserves agitation and demanding the right to establish Anglican separate schools were passed unanimously. On the subject of synodical government, a momentous step was taken when the delegates gave their overwhelming support to resolutions calling not only for the creation of dioceses in eastern and western Upper Canada, but also for the election by synod of the new bishops. The call for the synodical election of bishops — which previously only one Anglican, de Blaquière, had dared to utter — was a striking illustration of how far the church had come in its thinking on

The Seeds of Independence

the subject of ecclesiastical government. It also underlined the depth of the church's alienation from the state connection that had once sustained it.[47]

Yet all was not harmony at the 1853 visitation. When it came to the precise means by which the church was to achieve its goal of self-government, some delegates expressed such a violent brand of anti-Erastianism that others, more cautious, drew back. The layman James Bovell, venting the anger and impatience that by now had reached fever pitch in the Anglican community, declared that the church was entitled to take synodical action "without any permission, and that it would be an act of the grossest and most oppressive tyranny to throw any obstacle in our way." He then moved a resolution announcing the intention of Upper Canadian Anglicans to assert their "right to meet as a Synod, refusing to admit the right of interference from any quarter." This resolution was seconded by the Reverend Benjamin Cronyn and supported by the Reverend Arthur Palmer and a layman, Captain Baker; but it was opposed by Strachan and James Beaven on the grounds that it ignored the legal impediments which would have to be overcome before a synod could be established.[48]

Eventually a committee composed of both clergymen and laymen prepared the way for an acceptable compromise. The committee suggested a resolution protesting against the deferral of the Colonial Church Regulation Bill, and also drew up a petition stating that the imperial government, "having in its wisdom thought it right to withdraw from the Church that protection in regard to its property which it had hitherto enjoyed," could not in fairness maintain "the restrictions hitherto imposed on the free action of the Church in reference to the holding of Diocesan Synods, while it is entirely deprived of the advantages of an Establishment."[49] In the ensuing debate H.C. Cooper introduced an amendment stating that "all further discussions ... or any memorial or remonstrances" relating to the defunct Colonial Church Regulation Bill were "utterly unnecessary and derogatory to this synod." His principal argument in defence of the amendment was that the church in Upper Canada, having been stripped of its privileges, should not have to recognize the supremacy of an "infidel" parliament.[50] Although Cooper's anti-Erastian speech, as it was later said in the report of the visitation, "elicited much applause,"[51] the somewhat reckless nature of his proposal was viewed with a good deal of alarm. Several clergymen and laymen spoke out in opposition to the Cooper amendment, and Arthur Palmer went so far as to accuse Cooper himself of "hoisting the flag of Canadian independence."[52] In the end, Cooper's amendment attracted only two votes, and the committee's resolution on the Colonial Church Regulation Bill, together with the accompanying petition to the same effect, passed in its original form."[53]

Notwithstanding the fate of Cooper's amendment, hostility towards the state connection remained strong after the conclusion of the 1853 visitation. In December 1853 the *Church* carried an overtly anti-Erastian letter from James Bovell that was addressed to all Upper Canadian Anglicans. It was Bovell's belief that the dissolution of the union of church and state destroyed the basis of all objections to the idea of a self-governing Church of England, and that recourse should be had to the colonial legislature if the imperial government remained obdurate and continued to reject Anglican appeals for a diocesan synod. After stressing that "the time has come, the hour has arrived at which we are forced to act, our enemies are mighty, we have no arm of flesh to lean on now," he issued a proclamation that contrasted strangely with the ringing declarations in support of the unity of church and state which had resounded in Anglican circles a scant decade earlier:

> we are not striving to free ourselves from our mother Church, but we are determined to be freed from unjust State persecution, and as England's Crown has been removed from beneath the altar of the Colonial branch of the Anglican Church then is that Church bound to emancipate itself from the hands of the Crown .... Let the Church in this Diocese, acting as if endowed with life, cease to cringe at the feet of a Colonial Secretary or an Archbishop thrust upon us, not by any Ecclesiastical law but by the illegal intrusion of the Crown ....[54]

Significantly, once the campaign for the secularization of the clergy reserves entered its final phase in 1854, the *Church* and Strachan began echoing the call for unilateral synodical action. The *Church* argued in May 1854 that the dissolution of the church-state connection made it incumbent on civil authorities to extend the right of self-government to the Upper Canadian church;[55] and later in the year it declared in an editorial that, since the imperial government was blind to the needs of the colonial church, the Anglican community should act independently in asserting its right to manage its own affairs.[56] Strachan shared this point of view, writing in early June to the bishop of Nova Soctia that, "threatened with the loss of the small remainder of our Church property & with diminished Assistance from the two great Church Societies [the SPG and the SPCK] Synods or Convocations are necessary to our vitality." This statement was coupled with the suggestion that "so soon as we have established Synods in our Several Dioceses we must unite as an Ecclesiastical Province & have a general Synod of the British North American Dioceses under a Metropolitan with a House of Bishops."[57] Soon afterwards, at a meeting of a committee formed at the last visitation, Strachan announced that if the Colonial Church Regulation Bill was not passed during the current parliametary session, the Upper Canadian Church would be justified in establishing a synod without the approval of the imperial government.[58] This determination to circumvent the dilatory tactics of the imperial government was again evident at the visitation held in Toronto in late October 1854. There Strachan claimed that, although the Colonial Church Regulation Bill had not yet been passed by the British government, the church would have no legal impediments to overcome if it decided to move unilaterally and transform its visitations of clergy and lay delegates into *de jure* synods.[59]

As it happened, the imperial government continued to delay, and the Upper Canadian church did not move unilaterally. Yet, at length, Britain acted, passing a bill in 1857 which recognized the right of the Canadian church both to administer its own affairs through synods and to elect its bishops in the same bodies. In June of that year the first synod in the history of Upper Canadian Anglicanism, a synod including both clergy and elected lay delegates, met in Toronto. The occasion was without doubt an historic one; but a decision taken at the same time to create the diocese of Huron, comprising thirteen counties in the western part of Upper Canada, led over the next few weeks to an unseemly fight between the Evangelical and High Church wings of the Anglican community. Revolving around the choice of a head for the

In His Name

new see, the contest between the two factions eventually ended in a clear-cut victory for the Evangelicals: at a meeting of clerical delegates from the western parishes, called to elect a bishop for the new diocese, the episcopal prize went to the Low Churchman, Benjamin Cronyn, rather than to the High Church candidate, A.N. Bethune. For Strachan, who had strongly supported Bethune's candidacy, the events of 1857 must have aroused mixed feelings. The synod he had worked so hard to establish was finally a reality, but instead of uniting the church it had served to bring its internal divisions into public view. He could not have missed the irony.

* * * * *

At the same time as they were worrying about the state of the Church of England's institutional structure, Anglican clergymen were also wrestling with another, and equally difficult, problem—their church's inadequate financial resources. Addressing this problem meant overcoming attitudes that were deeply rooted among clergy and laity.

For the first two decades after the foundation of the see of Quebec in 1793, the Church of England in the Canadas was supported partly by the SPG and partly by the local government. This situation changed substantially after 1815, when the SPG, aided by an annual grant from the imperial government, assumed a greater degree of responsibility for the maintenance of the colonial church.[60] Over the next two decades the SPG acted as the parent of the church in the colonies, and without its assistance the child probably could not have survived. In addition to supplying the church with missionaries, the SPG payed the salaries of all clergymen while also helping to build churches and endow them with land. It also eliminated variations in clerical salaries. Prior to 1815, these salaries had ranged from £100 to over £200 annually. Afterwards, the SPG was able to provide each clergyman with an annual stipend of £200.

The other side of this picture was that after 1815 the fortunes of the colonial church were directly tied to the fortunes of the SPG. The dangers implicit in such a relationship became apparent when in 1831 the British government announced that the parliamentary grant to the SPG, which then amounted to just over £15,000, was to be reduced to £12,000 in 1832, £8,000 in 1833 and £4,000 in 1834, and that after 1835 the SPG was to receive no parliamentary grant whatsoever. The SPG, dependent upon its parliamentary grant for roughly £7,000 of the £10,000 it spent annually on the church in the Canadas, immediately protested against the government's decision, pointing out in particular that a shortage of funds would now force it to betray those clergymen who had gone to the colonies before 1831 on the understanding that they would receive a stipend of £200. Eventually, in 1834, the government agreed to a compromise whereby the Society was to receive, for a limited period of time, an annual grant of about £4,000 to enable it to pay the salaries of clergymen then resident in the colonies. But even this concession could not alter the fact that the SPG would have to reduce drastically the amount of its financial assistance to the Canadian church. In terms of clerical salaries alone, a revised salary schedule adopted by the SPG meant that clergymen appointed before 1833 were to receive 85 percent of their current stipends, or approximately £170 annually, as long as they lived, while clergymen appointed after 1833 were to receive stipends of only £100, exactly 50 percent less than the salaries previously enjoyed by SPG missionaries.[61]

In the 1840s the SPG strengthened its hand in the Canadas. By redirecting some of its resources, it was able to support roughly fifty missionaries and spend about £47,000 in the Diocese of Toronto over the years 1841 to 1847.[62] Yet, while the SPG's generosity was considerable, it could not keep pace with the mounting needs of the Upper Canadian church. What is more, the salary schedule adopted in the 1830s remained in place during the following decade. Dissatisfaction with the level of clerical salaries became public at the end of the 1840s when the local government announced that a surplus was available in the clergy reserve fund. At that time no fewer than seventeen clergymen from the Eastern District argued that the SPG, which had control over reserve revenues under the Act of 1840, should raise the salaries of clergymen appointed before 1833 to the £200 level. Strachan, enraged by this display of "insubordination and selfishness," quelled the controversy by persuading the SPG to agree to a plan whereby clergymen of twelve years' service would receive stipends of £150, and those of nine years' service £125. Shortly afterwards, however, the SPG decided to make major changes in its relationship with the colonial church. Anxious to shift its expenditures to parts of the world that had a greater need for its help, it replaced the system of fixed stipends with a policy of matching grants. Under the new regulations, the SPG matched funds raised by local congregations to a maximum level of £100, with the proviso that such matching grants would be withdrawn from the more settled parishes as they fell vacant.[63]

The reduction in SPG stipends in the 1830s, followed by the loss of a large portion of the clergy reserves in 1840 and changes to the SPG's financial policies, underlined the need for the Upper Canadian church to become more self-reliant. The main obstacle in the church's way as it tried to achieve that goal had been identified by Stuart, Addison and Langhorn in the 1790s — the unwillingness of many Anglicans to contribute to their church's support. This failing on the part of the Anglican faithful was commented upon by F.L. Osler in the 1830s, by C. Wade in a sermon in 1840, by the *Church* in editorials of 1841, 1843, 1845 and 1848, and by Strachan in numerous letters to various clergymen and laymen in the 1840s.[64] Of special interest was a letter of 1843 in which Strachan responded to the complaint of one layman about the extent of religious destitution in his township. "I am grieved to say," Strachan wrote,

> that in the different townships our people are very ready to complain but they will give little or nothing to the service of God — they speak of their poverty when you ask them to assist the Church & yet they blame the Bishop because he does not send Missionaries whom they refuse to support. Now our people are not poorer than other denominations ... yet other denominations pay for the support of their ministers — if our people were to do their duty as Gods people we should very soon have Clergymen in all quarters but until they feel & are convinced that it is their bounden duty to give of their substance to sustain the worship of God we shall continue to have many waste places .... were you & others instead of talking of neglect & dissatisfaction & making unjust complaints to bestir yourselves to join together as the Friends of our

Saviour ought to do in binding yourself to support a Clergyman & build a Church in your own locality we should have the happiness to see a Church & Clergyman in every township.[65]

As already indicated, the Anglican laity's niggardliness had a number of causes, not the least of which was the widespread belief that the clergy reserves provided the Church of England with abundant financial resources. This belief, which seems to have gained popularity when the reserves became more profitable in the 1830s and 1840s, was frequently commented upon by Anglican clergymen. James Magrath told the SPG in 1834 that, although he was experiencing severe financial difficulties as a result of the reduction in his stipend, many of his parishioners refused to contribute to his support, maintaining that his salary should be paid out of the clergy reserves fund.[66] George Mortimer, rector of Thornhill, declared that his congregation, when asked to support the church financially, had "that admirable loop-hole for escape — the clergy reserves, which seemed to promise every thing, but have done scarcely any thing; a broken reed which is perpetually piercing those who lean on it with sorrow; but which affords our people so ready an excuse for refusing to come to our aid."[67]

In addition to the laity's parsimonious habits, one other problem stood in the way of the church's achievement of self-reliance. This was the belief of clergymen themselves that the voluntary system — by which religious groups were required to depend exclusively on the voluntary contributions of their own members — was both impractical and a threat to their "respectability." Regarding the impracticality of the voluntary system, the Anglican position was straightforward, if unconvincing. Ignoring the fact that other denominations, notably the Methodists, had flourished without the benefit of state support, Anglican clergymen argued that the laity was too impoverished to provide the church with the funds it needed. They also argued that voluntarism was inherently illogical, for the church would have to possess sufficient financial resources to spread the Christian message before naturally sinful people could be expected to see the light and assist the cause of religion with their worldly "substance." And finally, they argued that a church supported solely by the contributions of its members would never be able to minister effectively to a society where a rapidly growing population was scattered over an immense distance, and where religious deprivation had reached staggering proportions. These three arguments appeared again and again in *Church* editorials, reports of clergymen to the Upper Canadian Travelling Missionary Fund, and the writings of Strachan.[68]

The clergy's belief that voluntarism threatened their "respectability" was more complex. On this score, a few comments should be made concerning the Church of England's class position in Upper Canadian society. Although the nature of the extant sources rules out an attempt to analyze the class composition of any denomination, it does seem clear that the Church of England — certain scholarly arguments notwithstanding[69] — was a socially inclusive institution. Bearing out this claim are the reports of clergymen to missionary organizations; from their numerous references to the religious deprivation of impoverished Anglicans, it is apparent that the Church of England's members came not only from the colonial but from every class elite and group imaginable, including that rapidly growing body of recently arrived immigrants who were dispersed through the backwoods.[70] If additional proof of the broad base of support enjoyed by the Anglican cause is desired, recall that the census of 1841 showed the Church of England to be the single largest denomination in Upper Canada. Such a level of numerical strength would never have been attained had the Church of England been mainly an institution of the colonial gentility.[71]

Then there is the matter of the social standing of Anglican clergymen. Ever since the Henrician reformation of the sixteenth century, the Church of England's status as the established church of the realm and one of the main institutional props of the secular order had provided its clergymen with a position of some distinction in English society. The inevitable result was that Anglican clergymen, though usually no wealthier and often considerably poorer than the flocks they served, adopted a lofty view of their social importance, regarding themselves as a class of "gentlemen" whose educational qualifications and commission from a catholic and apostolic church clearly set them apart from the mass of their fellow mortals. Naturally, the same class consciousness was noticeable in the branch of the Church of England planted in Upper Canada.

The Seeds of Independence

The clergymen who served in Upper Canada after 1791 were not uniformly upper class in their socio-economic backgrounds. Nor can they be described as upper class in terms of their financial situation: while the salary of £200 provided by the SPG in the period 1815 to 1831 must have been a respectable sum in a society where cash was scarce and many economic activities were still conducted by barter, the reduction of stipends after 1834 made life extremely difficult for Anglican clergymen, with the exception only of those few individuals like Strachan, R.D. Cartwright, William Macaulay and William Herchmer who were independently wealthy.[72] At the same time, however, Anglican clergymen in Upper Canada, like clergymen in the mother country, did have a high opinion of their social status, an opinion that was based on their church's established position and on their own perception of themselves as representatives of a branch of the catholic and apostolic church. Furthermore, their sense of social superiority had some justification. Although Anglican clergymen, as a group, were hardly wealthy enough to emulate the lifestyle of the larger landowners and the more prosperous business and professional people, they were still influential figures in Upper Canadian society. As was the case with the clergy of other denominations, the average Anglican clergyman was a member of that tiny minority in a pioneer society who could boast of a higher education.[73] Equally important, he was often the pivot around which the life of the community revolved, the respected pastor whose advice was eagerly sought, whose ministrations were much appreciated by isolated and religiously deprived settlers, and whose values and opinions, as expressed in sermons, exercised an enormous influence on his flock. In sum, on the basis of his educational training and social importance, the Anglican clergyman's claim to membership in the colonial elite was perfectly legitimate.

The Anglican clergy's view of their class position was revealed, in an indirect fashion, in their boast that large numbers of socially distinguished individuals were members of the Church of England, a boast which was clear evidence of their tendency to identify themselves not with the lower orders but with the elite. The *Church* noted with pride on several occasions that the Church of England possessed great influence among the colony's "better classes." For instance, in 1838 it stated that Anglicans comprised "a great proportion of the

In His Name

wealth, the education, and the virtue of Upper Canada."[74] A few years later, in 1841, the paper announced that the Church of England identified itself with "that large body of Conservatives in the province, embracing individuals of the most prominent standing, the greatest stake, and the highest talents in the country."[75] An even more interesting declaration was made in 1844, when the *Church*, describing a service that Strachan held in the course of his pastoral visitation, reported that "here the Bishop was much gratified at meeting several of the principal inhabitants of the neighbourhood, many of whom had moved in the best society, both in England and in India, and all of whom appeared to evince a most friendly feeling to the Church."[76]

The Anglican clergy's class consciousness was also revealed in their growing preoccupation with their financial position. In a memorial sent to the colonial secretary in the early 1830s concerning the reduction in SPG stipends, sixty-four Anglican clergymen claimed bitterly that they would never have come to Upper Canada if they had realized their livelihood was to be so precarious. They also warned that the new financial arrangements would destroy their "respectability" by causing them "positive and severe embarrassment and distress," by forcing them to dismiss the servants who until now had performed the "menial offices of the house," and by making them dependent on the laity, which was barely able to support itself.[77] This fear that a loss of income would have serious consequences for the clergy's social status was still strong at the end of the decade. In 1839 the *Church* asserted that an impoverished Anglican clergy would be of little use among either the upper or lower class. Insisting that, "if there was a time when Gospel preachers had to toil as fishermen, or labour at tent-making for their subsistence, it was because a better provision for their wants was not practicable," it declared its opposition to the policy of reducing the salaries of clergymen, which

> in worldly condition would place them almost upon an equality with the day labourer ... while such lowliness of earthly state would too often exclude from all companionship with, and all influence upon, the higher orders of society, there are very many of its humblest grades who would be amongst the foremost to regard with indifference or contempt an office so apparently degraded.[78]

The Seeds of Independence

The clergy's argument that their financial position was of crucial importance to their social status was far from novel. As early as 1801 Bishop Mountain had told the SPG that a clergyman's financial needs ought to be considered in the light of "the rank of the society with which he ought to mix" and of "the appearance he should maintain."[79] Similarly, Strachan, in his 1830 *Letter to Thomas Frankland Lewis*, noted that over several years there had been "a progress in the circumstances of the Clergy, towards obscurity and degradation, — let this be suffered to continue for a few years to come and their usefulness is annihilated, and their respectability is gone forever," a prospect that was all the more dreadful to contemplate when it was remembered that "religion will lose its estimation the moment that Ministers lose their influence & respectability."[80]

Yet, if the argument was familiar, it was certainly advanced with special intensity after the announcement in 1834 of the new salary schedules for SPG missionaries. With a mounting sense of urgency it was now repeatedly explained that Anglican clergymen had to have an adequate income if they were to preserve their respectability as a class and their influence among all levels of Upper Canadian society. Typical, perhaps, was a *Church* editorial of 1841, which remarked that an annual salary of £100 was hardly sufficient "to maintain the appearance of a gentleman," and that an Anglican clergyman would have to possess sufficient financial resources if he was "to be all things to all men" — the implication again being that a poverty-stricken clergy would accomplish little among the prosperous.[81] The same emphasis on the relationship between the clergy's income and their social status was apparent in a *Church* editorial of 1848, which insisted that clergymen should have enough money to live lives of "comfort and respectabilty."[82] It was also apparent in George Okill Stuart's 1846 charge to the archdeaconry of Kingston, in an anonymous individual's speech of the same year at a meeting of the Thornhill branch of the Church Society, and in an 1847 letter to the *Church* from John Dawson, an Anglican churchwarden.[83] The last two pieces of evidence are particularly interesting, for their common concern was the fact that a clergyman, who, as Dawson put it, was expected "to live like a gentleman," earned the same salary as a "mechanic" or "labourer."[84]

It was this class consciousness, rather than actual class status, that prevented the Anglican clergy from embracing the voluntary system.

From their viewpoint, the most decisive argument in favour of the policy of church establishment was that the voluntary system was incapable of providing them with the income they needed if they were to live like "gentlemen." They also felt that such a method of church financing, if applied to the Church of England, would undermine their independence by transforming them into public wards who, in order to eke out a miserable livelihood, would have to tailor their teachings to suit the tastes and whims of their congregations.

This position on the subject of the voluntary system, first advanced by Strachan in an 1812 article for the *Kingston Gazette*,[85] became a common refrain in the 1830s and 1840s, when the reduction of SPG stipends and the success of the campaign for disestablishment made it clear that at some time in the near future the Church of England might be thrown on its own resources. R.D. Cartwright wrote in 1836 that "a minister paid by his congregation & dependent upon them for his support must in nine cases out of ten preach to please ... God preserve his Ministers from such a state of dependence."[86] A.N. Bethune expressed identical sentiments in his lectures at the Cobourg Theological Institute, informing his students that voluntarism turned a clergyman into a beggar, a prisoner of a "capricious multitude" who adapted his preaching to suit popular fancies.[87] Equally categorical were a number of statements in the *Church*. In 1846 it claimed that the voluntary system made the clergyman "subservient to the will and caprice of the richer and poorer portion of his flock at least, if he would maintain his living,"[88] and two years later it pointed to the sad state of the church in England, where an Anglican clergyman in a rural area was generally a "half-starved menial" who was frequently tempted to "flatter" the "foibles" of his "capricious, much exacting, miserly pay-masters."[89]

Still, if there was strong resistance in the Church of England to an exclusive reliance on the "voluntary principle," the Anglican clergy never denied that their church should supplement its state support with the voluntary contributions of its members. This commitment to a limited form of voluntarism became especially strong when the political developments and SPG cutbacks of the 1830s cast a pall over the church's financial future. One tangible result of the church's desire to make itself more self-reliant was the founding in 1830 of the SCCIPGDS, the objective of which was to encourage the laity to contribute financially to the cause of missionary expansion. Another

The Seeds of Independence

was the launching of the campaign for synodical government, a campaign which, as already shown, was inspired by the conviction that laymen would be more generous in their support of the church as soon as they were given a voice in the management of its affairs.

Although Bishop Stewart failed to lend his support to the demand for an Anglican synod, he was aware of the need to make the church less dependent on the assistance of the state. Soon after learning in May 1832 of the imperial government's decision to cut its ties with the SPG, he set out on an episcopal tour of his diocese, holding visitations in Montreal, Kingston and York. In the charge delivered on these occasions he expressed his regret that the SPG's parliamentay grant had been withdrawn, and urged his clergy to "represent to His Majesty's Government, the claims of the Church on their bounty and justice, especially considering the means for her support which are in their power." He also announced his intention "to issue a circular to the Clergy of this Diocese, directing them to point out to their congregations their obligations to honour the Lord with their substance, in giving a part of it towards the support of the services of the sanctuary and those who perform them."[90]

In the late 1830s and early 1840s Anglican efforts to make the church more financially independent gained momentum. The *Church* argued in editorials of 1838, 1839 and 1840 that Anglican laymen were obliged to devote a portion of their worldly resources to the maintenance of their ministers and to the support of the church as a whole.[91] This argument was echoed in resolutions passed by the Eastern Clerical Association in 1840,[92] and in a sermon by Saltern Givins in St. Peter's Church, Cobourg, in 1841.[93] It also received concrete expression in Strachan's actions as bishop. Immediately after his elevation to the episcopacy in 1839, Strachan made it clear that in the future a clergyman would not be assigned to a parish until the congregation of that parish had agreed to build a parsonage, to set aside four to six acres for a church site and cemetery, and to supplement the basic SPG stipend of £100 with at least £50 in voluntary contributions.[94] A couple of years later, in 1842, Strachan was instrumental in the creation of the Church Society, which absorbed the SCCIPGDS and henceforth played a crucial role in the church's struggle to become more self-supporting.

The Church Society was established in a mood of euphoria at a

In His Name

meeting of clergy and lay representatives in Toronto's City Hall on 28 April 1842. According to its constitution, its main objectives were the creation of an endowment for the bishopric of Toronto, the provision of salaries for archdeacons and clergymen, the building of a parsonage and a stone or brick church in every township, the establishment of Sunday schools, and the accumulation of the funds that were necessary to appoint additional resident clergymen and travelling missionaries. It also declared its intention to distribute religious books and tracts, and to furnish financial assistance to young men studying for the ministry, clergymen incapacitated by age or illness, and the widows and orphans of deceased clergymen.[95]

Obviously, such a broad range of goals would be achieved only if the Church Society was able to encourage the laity to contribute financially to its support. It was therefore no accident that laymen were allowed to occupy a dominant position at every level of the Church Society's organizational structure. Under Strachan, who as bishop of the diocese was president of the Church Society, were approximately fifty vice-presidents, well over half of whom were laymen, and a central board of management composed of roughly fourteen clergymen and thirty-seven laymen.[96] Control over the actual operation of the Church Society was vested neither in the vice-presidents, who appear to have been mere figureheads, nor in the Central Board, but in a separate committee composed of nineteen laymen and known, appropriately enough, as the Lay Committee. Membership in the Church Society was open to any Anglican who was willing to pay a fee of 15s per annum or £12 10s for life. The payment of this fee enabled an individual to become a member of a parochial branch of the Church Society, a body whose affairs were conducted by a committee consisting of the local clergyman and churchwardens. It also made that person a member of one of the Church Society's district associations, which were managed by the clergymen of the district and one or two laymen from each parish or mission. The clergymen and laymen on these district boards attended the general meeting of the Church Society that was held in June of each year. At this time the work of the parent organization was reviewed and the Central Board of Management was elected.[97]

Just as significant as the dominance of the laity in this elaborate and democratic structure was the system adopted in the management of the Church Society's funds. Rather than place these funds at the disposal of the parochial branches of the Church Society, the founders of the organization took care to ensure that the expenditure of all Church Society revenue was made the responsibility not of the parochial branches but of the district associations and of the central body.[98] The advantages of these arrangements, from the standpoint of the Anglican clergy, were considerable. Under the voluntary system a clergyman was dependent for his livelihood on the generosity of his congregation, which could decide at any time to reduce the amount of his salary. In contrast, the system adopted by the Church of England in the 1840s meant that locally raised money, which supplemented SPG stipends and eventually replaced them, was channelled to clergymen through an institutional intermediary beyond the reach of individual congregations. This system was designed both to encourage the laity to contribute to the church's support, and to use these contributions in such a way as to provide clergymen with a stable and adequate income, thus protecting their "independence" and their status in the community at large. Its significance lay in the fact that it was an attempt to reap the benefits of the "voluntary system" while simultaneously avoiding the consequences which so often ensued when individual congregations were directly responsible for the maintenance of their ministers.

The laity's duty to assist the Anglican cause financially was frequently emphasized in the decade following the foundation of the Church Society. It was one of the subjects addressed in Strachan's charges of 1844, 1847, 1851 and 1854, and it was discussed at length in the Church Society's annual reports, *Church* editorials, Stuart's 1848 charge to the archdeaconry of York, and sermons preached by A.N. Bethune, Job Deacon and Henry Patton.[99] As a review of the Church Society's record indicates, however, appeals to Anglican laymen to do their share in the maintenance of the church met with mixed results. On the positive side, the Church Society, unlike the SCCIPGDS, attracted its support not only from the Toronto elite but from all classes and regions: in 1854 the Church Society had approximately 4,000 subscribers, the vast majority of whom lived outside of Toronto and made annual contributions of less than £1. Furthermore, whereas the funds of the SCCIPGDS never amounted to more than a few hundred pounds annually, the Church Society's financial resources were not inconsiderable. Thanks to the generosity of its members, whose donations came

In His Name

in the form of both money and land, the central body's funds increased from £1,836 in 1843 to £5,419 in 1854, while its landed endowment, which stood at 12,124 acres in 1843, reached 27,976 acres in 1854.[100] The district branches, especially those in the western part of the province, showed a comparable increase in funds. By 1851 the total funds of the various district associations were as follows: Newcastle and Colborne District, £195; Midland District, £195; Niagara District, £305; Gore and Wellington District, £890; London, Huron and Western District, £2,083.[101] Finally, the Church Society's fairly secure financial position enabled it to achieve some of the goals that had been set out in the 1842 constitution. Funds were established for the endowment of the bishopric of Toronto, and for the assistance of divinity students and the widows and orphans of deceased clergymen. More impressive still, the Church Society and its district associations were able to support a total of twenty-two travelling missionaries in the period from 1842 to 1854.[102]

The negative side was equally obvious. In 1848 one clergyman rightly noted in a letter to the *Church* that the Church Society's total of 2,800 subscribers was nothing to boast about in a society where 32,101 people attended Anglican worship, and that in the past year only 67 of 190 churches and 102 of 210 stations had bothered to make collections in aid of the Church Society.[103] A few years later the Church Society itself presented an analysis of its popular support. A select committee consisting of one layman, de Blaquière, and four clergymen, Stephen Lett, Dominick Blake, W.S. Darling and T.S. Kennedy, reported in 1853 that the Church Society's subscription list, which then had 4,000 names, had to be regarded as highly satisfactory when it was recalled that the Upper Canadian church possessed roughly 200,000 members, 40,000 of whom regularly attended Anglican services. It also reported the following facts: 60 missions had not established parochial branches; only 44 of 129 missions had made all of the appointed collections on behalf of the Church Society; 37 of 81 parochial branches had not fulfilled their obligation to direct one-quarter of their funds to the central body of the Church Society; and 67 of 138 clergymen had failed to pay their annual fee of 15s to the Widows and Orphans Fund.[104] This lack of zeal on the part of clergy and laity meant that the Church Society was unable to accomplish its objective of providing Anglican clergyman with adequate incomes. Strachan had stated in 1842 that the Church Society should aim to raise clerical salaries to roughly £250 annually,[105] but by 1853 most clergymen still earned incomes ranging from £100 to £150.

The laity's half-hearted response to the Church Society is not surprising, given its long-standing reluctance to help the church financially. But the attitude of the clergy was another matter and deserves a few words of explanation. Anglican clergymen, without exception, were solidly behind the Church Society's efforts to make the Church of England more self-reliant by convincing the laity of its financial obligations to the cause of religion. The problem seems to have been not a lack of support for the idea of a financially independent Church of England, but a certain amount of dissatisfaction with the management of the Church Society's central body. In part, this dissatisfaction was due to an occurrence in 1851, when Thomas Champion, assistant secretary of the Church Society, defaulted with £700.[106] But it also had more subjective causes — specifically, opposition to certain Church Society policies, and dislike of the Church Society's theological complexion.

The first of these factors was evident in a memorial sent by the Reverend John Flood to the SPG in 1851. Here Flood expressed the opinion that "the Clergy Reserves Fund, instead of being applied as far as practicable in supporting ministers in poor settlements ... seems to be expended in satisfying the demands of individuals who are in wealthy parishes & who have been receiving a large amount from their congregation." He added that "under such circumstances" he would not use his considerable political influence in Carleton County to return members to the House of Assembly who would protect the church's landed endowment.[107] Two other individuals highlighted the role of theological differences in undermining support for the Church Society. In a letter to the *Echo and Protestant Episcopal Recorder*, an Evangelical newspaper established in Port Hope in 1851, a correspondent using the signature "X.Y.Z." drew attention to the possibility that the Tract and Book Depository of the Church Society was distributing works of a "romanizing tendency."[108] A more indirect assault on the Church Society's theological orientation was made by John Grier, a clergyman stationed in Belleville, in an 1849 letter to the SPG, in which he complained angrily about a recent Church Society decision to appropriate a portion of the Widows and Orphans Fund for the payment of salaries to the bishop and the archdeacon of York and for

In His Name

the support of the Cobourg Theological Institute. His thinly veiled message was that the Church Society's decision had antagonized Evangelical clergymen by raising the spectre of an opulent hierarchy and by endowing an institution whose principal, A.N. Bethune, was widely suspected of "puseyism" — the High Church brand of theology espoused by the Oxford movement of the 1830s and 1840s.[109] Grier praised his fellow clerics in the western section of the province, where Evangelical sentiment was strongest, for their opposition to the Church Society's "fraud," and warned that "such a wrong will lessen our exertions for the various objects of the Church Society & drive some of us out of it altogether."[110]

To a considerable extent the campaign to lay the foundations of a self-supporting Church of England was a reflection of the Anglican clergy's growing acceptance of the inevitability of disestablishment. On first glance, admittedly, it might seem as though the Church Society was formed to assist the Church of England in its struggle to maintain its established status. This conclusion, indeed, has much to recommend it, since reports of the Church Society, at both the central and local levels, are replete with proclamations denouncing politicians for their oppression of the church and calling on the Anglican community to exert itself to the utmost to preserve its educational privileges and its share of the clergy reserves.[111] But to view such proclamations as an example of the Anglican clergy's inability to adapt to a new religious and political order is to ignore other evidence which, in the long run, is far more significant. In this regard the most interesting evidence, paradoxically enough, was the work of the Church Society itself, for no organization would have been founded to render the Anglican cause more independent financially if the clergy and a large number of laymen had not been convinced that the Church of England could no longer depend upon state support.

The Church Society's reports offer further confirmation of the relationship between Anglican efforts to become less dependent on state assistance and the church's gradual acceptance of the inevitability of disestablishment. Throughout the reports of the Church Society's central body, defences of the policy of church establishment were coupled with the view that the Church of England should pride itself not on its political position but on its mission to preach the Gospel to a religiously destitute society and on its character as a branch of the catholic and apostolic church. This changing perspective on the church's place in Upper Canadian society, with its underlying implication that some sectors of the Anglican community were coming to regard the separation of church and state as unavoidable, was also evident in the 1847 report of the Gore and Wellington District Association of the Church Society. In this report it was argued that the Church of England, "instead of having been supported and encouraged, has been abandoned by the state, and ... thrown upon her own resources, viz., the zeal, devotion, and liberality of her members."[112]

Even more instructive were declarations on the same theme made by private individuals. At the 1849 meeting of a parochial branch of the Church Society in St. George's Church, Toronto, a certain Mr. Cooper emphasized that the Church of England should reconcile itself to disestablishment and concentrate on its religious responsibilities. Announcing that "the civil power throws us off, in one country as well as in the other" and that "it has pleased the ALMIGHTY to place us in this position," he proclaimed that "if each one will do his duty, then, with the blessing of Providence, although the Church of England in Canada may not stand as an Establishment — may not have the state for its patron, its protector or its friend, that Church may occupy a more Holy eminence still, it will be, among Christian communities, the foremost, in doing good."[113] The following year, at a meeting in Toronto of the St. Paul's parochial branch of the Church Society, another layman, also named Cooper, stated that the Upper Canadian church depended for its prosperity "not on state favour, or state endowments or political aid ... but on the dutiful conduct of her children and the blessing of God thereon."[114]

* * * * *

The movement for synodical government and the Church Society were an immense boost to the fortunes of the Church of England. True, neither was a complete success by the time church and state were severed in 1854 — the advocates of a diocesan synod still had to overcome the lethargy of imperial authorities, the Anglican laity

In His Name

remained reluctant to contribute to the church's support, and the progress of the Church Society was hindered by internal dissension. Nonetheless, by the early 1850s the first steps had been taken to provide the laity with a more influential role in the organizational structure of the church, and to turn the church itself into a self-governing and self-supporting institution.

There were important similarities between the Church Society and the campaign for a diocesan synod. Both were inspired by the belief that laymen would be more willing to assist the Anglican cause with their worldly resources if they were given a voice in the management of church affairs, and that the laity's financial support was indispensable if clergymen were to have an income befitting their status as "gentlemen" and leading figures in the community. Further, all attempts to enhance the church's economic and political independence shared a common perspective on the position of the church in Upper Canadian society. The idea of synodical government, which was initially a reflection of the church's determination to defend its established status, became increasingly intertwined with hostility towards the state connection and with a growing awareness of the inevitability of disestablishment. Similarly, the driving force behind the Church Society was the conviction that the church should accept disestablishment as a virtual *fait accompli*, turn its back on an oppressive state, and confine its energies to those religious tasks which were beyond the reach of political interference. Underlying this conviction was the image of the church as, to cite a phrase used in the 1847 report of the Church Society, "a city on a hill"[115] — a religious organization whose greatness was based not on its influence in the world of politics but on its divine commission to save souls and to act as a witness to the true faith.

The Seeds of Independence

NOTES

1 See Norman Sykes, *Church and State in England in the Eighteenth Century*; and James Thayer Addison, *The Episcopal Church in the United States, 1789-1931* (New York, 1951).

2 Strachan Papers, Strachan to Stewart, 16 March and 21 May, 1831.

3 Cartwright expressed his support for the idea of a church synod in a letter to Strachan in April 1831. See Cartwright Papers, Cartwright to Strachan, 16 April 1831.

4 Strachan Letter Book, 1827-39, Strachan to Cartwright, 27 June 1831.

5 Macaulay Papers, Strachan to Macaulay, 24 Oct. 1831.

6 Strachan commented upon this constitution and mentioned the people he had drawn on for advice in two letters to Macaulay in 1832 (Macaulay Papers, 12 and 23 March 1832).

7 Ibid., Strachan to Macaulay, 23 March 1832.

8 Ibid., Strachan to Macaulay, 16 Feb 1832.

9 Ibid., Strachan to Macaulay, 24 March 1832.

10 It is T.R. Millman who has suggested that Stewart's failure to lend his support to demands for a church synod was caused by his ill health and his preoccupation with financial problems. See Millman, *Life of Stewart*, p. 123.

11 Strachan, *Church Fellowship*, pp. 21-22.

12 T.B. Fuller, *Thoughts on the Present State and Future Prospects of the Church of England in Canada, with Hints for Some Improvements in her Ecclesiastical Arrangements; Humbly Addressed to the Rt. Rev. the Lord Bishop and the Rev. Clergy* (1836), passim.

13 See William Bettridge's letter to the *Church*, 27 June 1850; and T.R. Millman, "Beginnings of the synodical movement in colonial Anglican churches, with special reference to Canada," *JCCHS*, XXI (1979), p. 5.

14 Strachan, *Church of the Redeemer*, p. 27.

15 The above section is based on ibid., pp. 27-40.

16 Ibid., p. 40.

17 The *Church*, 27 June and 25 July 1850.

18 Ibid., 27 June and 8 Aug. 1850.

19 Strachan's attitude towards Mountain's appointment was revealed in his correspondence with Mahlon Burwell in 1836 and in his address at

In His Name

      the opening of Burwell's church in Port Talbot in the same year (Strachan Papers, 12 April 1836).

20   Strachan, *A Charge Delivered on the 2nd September, 1841*, pp. 32-34.

21   The *Church*, 25 Sept. 1846.

22   Ibid., 7 Jan. 1848.

23   Ibid., 12 April 1849.

24   Comments on de Blaquière's career can be found in Moir, *Church and State in Canada West*, pp. 24, 42, 109, 120 and 131.

25   The *Church*, 14 Feb. 1850. It should be noted that bishops of the Episcopal Church in the United States, from the time of their church's founding just after the conclusion of the American Revolution, were elected by synods of clergy and elected lay representatives.

26   The *Church*, 21 Feb. and 22 Aug. 1850.

27   Ibid., 12 April 1850.

28   Ibid., 14 and 21 March, and 11 April 1850. Also of importance was a letter to the *Church* from "A Rector" on 21 Feb. 1850. Interestingly enough, Francis Evans, a leading Evangelical clergyman, expressed his support of de Blaquière's scheme in a letter to the *Church* on 11 April 1850, a fact which would seem to point to a connection between "Low Church" Anglicanism and demands for greater lay influence in church affairs. This question is explored in Chapter Eight.

29   The *Church*, 6 June 1850.

30   Ibid., 21 Nov. 1850.

31   The Quebec City meeting is discussed in Armine W. Mountain, *A Memoir of George Jehosaphat Mountain* (Montreal, 1866), pp. 290-99.

32   The pastoral letter can be found in *Proceedings of Synod, Diocese of Toronto*, 1851, pp. 1-2.

33   This meeting was held in St. George's Church. See the *Church*, 24 April 1851.

34   Ibid.

35   Strachan, *A Charge Delivered in May, MDCCCLI*, p. 47.

36   Ibid., p. 26.

37   *Proceedings of Synod*, 1851, pp. 6-7.

38   Ibid., pp. 10-12.

39   The petition of the synod and Strachan's addresses were published in the *Church*, 17 July 1851.

40 The *Church*, 22 Sept. 1853.

41 Strachan, *A Letter to Lord John Russell*, pp. 20-25.

42 The *Church*, 16 Jan. 1852.

43 Ibid.

44 Ibid., 21 Aug. 1851.

45 Ibid., 29 June, 1 and 8 July 1852.

46 Strachan, *A Charge Delivered on Oct. 12, 1853*, pp. 43 and 46.

47 For the various resolutions passed at the visitation, see *Proceedings of Synod*, 1853, pp. 10-17.

48 Ibid., pp. 6-7.

49 Ibid., p. 9.

50 Ibid., pp. 11-13. See also Cooper's letter to the *Church*, 27 Oct. 1853.

51 *Proceedings of Synod*, 1853, p. 11.

52 For the debate on Cooper's amendment, see ibid., pp. 11-13; for Palmer's speech, see ibid., p. 12.

53 Ibid., p. 13.

54 Ibid., 22 Dec. 1853.

55 Ibid., 4 May 1854.

56 Ibid., 27 July 1854.

57 Strachan Letter Book, 1854-62, Strachan to the bishop of Nova Scotia, 2 June 1854.

58 The *Church*, 15 June 1854.

59 *Proceedings of the Synod of the United Church of England and Ireland in the Diocese of Toronto, Held October 25, 26 & 27, 1854* (Toronto, 1854), pp. 3-4.

60 In Lower Canada the imperial government continued to be responsible for a number of expenses relating to the colonial church, including the salary of the bishop (Millman, *Life of Stewart*, p. 114).

61 Much of the above section is drawn from Millman, *Life of Stewart*, pp. 114-23; and Westfall, *Two Worlds*, p. 102-05.

62 Westfall, *Two Worlds*, p. 102.

63 See Westfall, *Two Worlds*, pp. 102-05; and SPG Letters, Series C, Box V/43, no. 516, memorial from clergy of the Eastern District, 5 July 1849. Also: John Strachan, *The Secular State of the Church, in the Diocese of*

In His Name

Toronto, Canada West (Toronto, 1849); Strachan Letter Book, 1844-49, Strachan to A.N. Bethune, 17 Nov. 1848, Strachan to Arthur Palmer, 5 Dec. 1848, Strachan to the bishop of Montreal, 20 Dec. 1848, Strachan to clergy, 2 March 1849, Strachan to anonymous clergyman, 8 May 1849; ADO, Stuart Papers, G.O. Stuart to A.N. Bethune, 1848 (?); F.J. Lundy Diaries, 1849-67, 29 Jan. 1849; AO, Bishop Strachan Letters, Strachan to A.N. Bethune, 7 March 1849, R.G. Cox to A.N. Bethune, 18 April 1849, Strachan to A.N. Bethune, 8 Oct. 1849; SPG Letters, Series C, Box V/46, no. 547, F.J. Lundy, 15 Jan. 1849; SPG Letters, "D," 14, vols. 8-9, Edward Denroche, 16 Feb. 1850, and Job Deacon, 9 Feb. 1850; the *Church*, 9 Nov. 1848, 18 Jan. 1849 and 8 Aug. 1850 (letter from Edward Denroche).

64 Osler Papers (Series I-1, vo. 21, Osler to Procter, 26 Oct. 1837; SPG Letters, Series C, Box IV/41, no. 492, F.L. Osler, 3 Nov. 1837; the *Church*, 30 Jan. 1841, 18 Aug. 1843, 24 Oct. 1845, 20 March 1848; Strachan Letter Book, 1839-43, Strachan to Wilson, 3 Jan. 1843, Strachan to S.S. Strong, 4 Dec. 1843, Strachan to W. Wood, 5 Dec. 1843; Strachan Letter Book, 1844-49, Strachan to Joseph Biddle and George R. Johnston, churchwardens, Trinity Church, Moore Township, 7 Aug. 1846, Strachan to Thomas Coleman and John Smith (?), Oct. 1846, Strachan's reply to petition from Maryburgh, (? Oct.) 1847; Wade's sermon was published by the *Church* on 5 Sept. 1840.

65 Strachan Letter Book, 1839-43, Strachan to John Wilson, 3 Jan. 1843.

66 SPG Letters, Series C, Box IVA/40, no. 467, James Magrath, 25 June 1834.

67 *The Life and Letters of the Rev. George Mortimer, M.A. Rector of Thornhill, in the Diocese of Toronto, Canada West, Compiled and Prepared by the Rev. John Armstrong* (London, 1847), pp. 209-11.

68 See especially: Strachan, *Letter to Thomas Frankland Lewis*, pp. 108-9; Strachan Letter Book, 1844-49, Strachan to Waddilove, 30 April 1840; the *Church*, 8 May 1841; Upper Canadian Travelling Missionary Fund reports, 1838-40 (Thomas Green's 13th, 16th and 17th letters; extract from a Toronto clergyman's letter, n.d. — included in 1838 report; 2nd, 4th and 7th letters from George Petrie); *A Charge Delivered at Visitations of the Clergy and Churchwardens of the Archdeaconry of York, Held at Thornhill, on Tuesday, April 22; at Hamilton, on Tuesday, April 27; and at London, on Thursday, April 29, 1852, by the Ven. A.N. Bethune, D.D. Archdeacon of York* (Toronto, 1852), pp. 5-7.

69 S.D. Clark, *Church and Sect in Canada*, pp. 125-29.

70 This is particularly true of the Upper Canadian Travelling Missionary Fund reports.

The Seeds of Independence

71   J.W. Grant claims in *A Profusion of Spires* (p. 159) that by the 1870s the Church of England was no longer "predominantly a church of the privileged and instead catered mainly to first- and second-generation immigrants from Ireland and England. In Hamilton by mid-century its members were less affluent, on the average, than either long-settled Wesleyan Methodists or aggressive Free Church Presbyterians. Proportionately, Anglicans were most numerous in the cities and towns, though not to the extent they had once been or would be again." No evidence is given to support these claims, but if they are correct they support the view that the Church of England drew its membership from a broad range of classes and groups.

72   Strachan's salary as rector of York and then as archdeacon, combined with his wife's dowry, enabled him to build a house, known as the "Palace," that was regarded as the "finest house in the town." It also allowed him to give entertainments that outshone those of the lieutenant governor (Eric Arthur, *Toronto: No Mean City* [Toronto, 1964], p. 37). Similarly, William Herchmer was wealthy enough to donate £1,000 to St. George's Church, Kingston (the *Church*, 1 Jan. 1842); William Macaulay was able to contribute £12,000 to the building of his church and parsonage in Picton (ibid., 11 Oct. 1844); R.D. Cartwright in 1842 had savings of £1,500 and was willing to pay a clergyman £100 annually to act as his assistant in Kingston (Cartwright Papers, Cartwright to ?, 24 Oct. 1842 and 3 March 1843).

73   The importance of the clergy's superior education was first pointed out by Professor S.F. Wise in his article "Sermon Literature and Canadian Intellectual History," p. 6.

74   The *Church*, 13 Oct. 1838.

75   Ibid., 10 April 1841.

76   Ibid., 16 Aug. 1844. On this subject see also a *Church* editorial of 25 Sept. 1841, and a letter to the *Church* on 5 April 1849 from "One of the Laity."

77   SPG Letters, Series C, Box IVA/41, memorial to Lord Stanley.

78   The *Church*, 3 Jan. 1839.

79   SPG Journals, vol. 28, Jacob Mountain, 18 Dec. 1801.

80   Strachan, *Letter to Thomas Frankland Lewis*, pp. 104-5.

81   The *Church*, 17 July 1841.

82   Ibid., 21 Jan. 1848.

83   Stuart's charge and the speech at the Thornhill branch of the Church Society were published in the *Church* on 24 July 1846. The letter from

In His Name

Dawson appeared in the *Church* on 14 July 1847. The Anglican clergy's belief that their meagre incomes prevented them from living like gentlemen can also be seen in the following: Upper Canadian Travelling Missionary Fund reports, 1838-40 (9th and 24th letters from Thomas Green, and 2nd letter from George Petrie); SPG Letters, Series C, Box IVA/41, no. 489, Richard D'Olier, March 1835. In some cases this belief was well founded. James Coughlan was forced to resign his parish of Port Hope after the reduction in his SPG stipend had led to his imprisonment for debt (SPG Letters, Series C, Box IVA/40, no. 478, 1 Sept. 1834, 1 July 1837 and 27 Feb. 1838).

84   The *Church*, 24 July 1846 and 14 July 1847.

85   *Kingston Gazette*, "The Reckoner," 21 April 1812.

86   Cartwright Papers, Cartwright to Conway Dobbs, 21 July 1836.

87   Bethune's Manuscript Lecture Notes, Lectures XXII-III, "On the Lawfulness & Benefits of a Church Establishment."

88   The *Church*, 26 June 1846.

89   Ibid., 26 Oct. 1848.

90   Charles James Stewart, *A Charge to the Clergy of the Diocese of Quebec Delivered at the Visitation in Montreal, Lower Canada, 9th August, Kingston, Upper Canada, 23rd August, York, Upper Canada, 5th September. In the year 1832* (Quebec, 1834), pp. 16-20.

91   The *Church*, 24 March 1838, 13 July 1839 (editorial on a book by Henry Caswall entitled *America and the American Church*), and 11 Jan. 1840.

92   The *Church*, 29 Feb. 1840.

93   Ibid., 13 March 1841.

94   Strachan announced these pre-conditions for the appointment of clergymen to parishes in a report to the SPG in 1840 (SPG *Report*, 1841, p. lxiv) and in a letter of 1840 (Strachan Letter Book, 1839-43, Strachan to Andrew Geddes, 20 Feb. 1840).

95   *The Constitution and Objects of the Church Society of the Diocese of Toronto. Established 28 April, 1842* (Toronto, 1842), pp. 6-10.

96   It is impossible to give exact figures when analyzing the composition of the upper echelons of the Church Society, since the chairmen of the district associations, who could be either clergymen or laymen, were also vice-presidents and members of the Central Board of Management.

97   The above information can be found in *The Constitution and Objects of the Church Society*, pp. iii-10.

The Seeds of Independence

98   Ibid., pp. 6-10.

99   The *Church* editorials in question appeared on 24 and 31 Oct. 1850; Stuart's and Bethune's charges can be found in ibid. (28 Dec. 1848 and 1 Nov. 1849); for the sermons of Bethune and Deacon, see ibid., 7 Feb., 25 June and 1 Aug. 1845; finally, the need for contributions to the support of the church was emphasized in *Attachment to the Church of God. A Sermon Preached in the Cathedral Church of St. James's, Toronto, on Wednesday, October 12th, 1853, at the Visitation of the Right Reverend the Lord Bishop of the Diocese of Toronto. By the Reverend Henry Patton, Rural Dean and Rector of Cornwall* (Toronto, 1853), pp. 20-21.

100 See Church Society reports, 1842-54.

101 *The Ninth Annual Report of the Church Society of the Diocese of Toronto, for the year ending on the 31st March, 1851* (Cobourg, 1851), pp.60-61.

102 This figure is based on a study of Church Society reports.

103 The *Church*, 10 March 1848.

104 *Report of a Select Committee of the Church Society. Presented on Wednesday, February 2nd, 1853* (Toronto, 1853), pp. 1-9.

105 *The Constitution and Objects of the Church Society*, p. 12.

106 This *cause célèbre* was mentioned in the *Eleventh Annual Report of the Church Society of the Diocese of Toronto, for the year ending on the 31st March, 1853* (Cobourg, 1853), pp. 12-15. See also Thomas Fuller's letter to the SPG in SPG Letters, "D," 14, vols. 8-9, 11 March 1852.

107 SPG Letters, "D," 14, vols. 8-9, memorial of John Flood, 6 Aug. 1851.

108 The *Echo and Protestant Episcopal Recorder* (hereafter referred to as the *Echo*), 18 Nov. 1851.

109 The Oxford movement and the High Church-Low Church battles to which it gave rise in Upper Canada are explored in detail in Chapter Eight.

110 SPG Letters, Series C, Box V/43, no. 509, John Grier, 26 March 1849.

111 See *The Constitution and Objects of the Church Society*, pp. 22-26 and 47; *The Twelfth Annual Report of the Church Society of the Diocese of Toronto, for the year ending on the 31st March, 1854* (Cobourg, 1854), p. 18; *The Thirteenth Annual Report of the Church Society of the Diocese of Toronto, for the year ending on the 30th April, 1855* (Cobourg, 1855), pp. 11-12; *St George's Parochial Branch of the Church Society of the Diocese of Toronto. Report and Proceedings of the Annual Meeting Held in St. George's Church, on the 17th April, 1851* (Toronto, 1851), p. 10.

In His Name

112 The *Church*, 19 Feb. 1847.
113 Ibid., 22 March 1849.
114 Ibid., 7 March 1850.
115 *The Fifth Annual Report of the Church Society of the Diocese of Toronto, for the year ending on the 31st March, 1847* (Cobourg, 1847), p.28.

CHAPTER EIGHT

A HOUSE DIVIDED

From the late 1830s on, in the wake of the resurgence of High Anglicanism triggered by the Oxford movement in England, the Church of England in Upper Canada was deeply split along theological lines. While the *Church* and a large number of clergymen, including Strachan, were deeply influenced by Tractarianism — as the ideas of the Oxford movement were known — there was also a formidable group of clergy who denounced the Oxford theology as a form of "popery" and upheld the Evangelical vision of the church's nature and mission. This confrontation between High Churchmen and Evangelicals was serious enough when it took the form of vitriolic debates on theological subjects and open hostility towards the doctrinal position of the *Church*. It became even more serious when the two groups engaged in quarrels relating to the management of the church's internal affairs, and when theological controversy cast a shadow over the church's work in the political arena. By the early 1850s almost fifteen years of internal strife had seriously weakened the Church of England's position in secular affairs and, at the same time, clouded its future as a spiritual society.

*****

The Oxford movement originated in 1833. At Oxford on July 14 of that year John Keble declared in a sermon, later published under the title of *National Apostasy*, that the government's recent decision to suppress several Irish bishoprics was an act of intolerable oppression and that Anglicans everywhere should rally to their church's defence. Shortly afterwards, a small group of Oxford divines led by John Henry

In His Name

Newman and Richard Hurrell Froude began publication of the *Tracts for the Times*, a series of pamphlets on theological issues designed to strengthen the church's intellectual and spiritual foundations. The first tract, written by Newman himself, appeared on 9 September 1833, and roughly twenty others had followed by the end of the year. Contributors to the series included John Keble and Edward Pusey, an Oxford professor of divinity and one of the church's leading intellectual figures.

Yet the Tractarian movement was not to experience uninterrupted progress. Soon after the launching of the tracts the suspicion arose that the proponents of the Oxford theology were sympathetic to "romanism," a suspicion that was confirmed by various Tractarian publications in the late 1830s. The turning-point for the movement came with the publication in 1841 of Tract 90, in which Newman's growing uncertainty about the tenability of the Anglican theological position was indirectly revealed in his claim that the church's Thirty-Nine Articles were perfectly compatible with Roman Catholic doctrine. University authorities promptly condemned this latest Tractarian heresy, and Newman, by now the acknowledged leader of the Oxford movement, was forced to agree to the demand of his diocesan that publication of the tracts be discontinued. Two years later, after Pusey had been temporarily suspended from university preaching, Newman left Oxford and became a virtual recluse in his "monastery" at Littlemore. When in October 1845 he eventually decided, along with a few of his closest disciples, to be received into the Roman Catholic Church, the Tractarian movement at Oxford entered a period of irreversible decline, although its central theological principles gained increasing support in the nation at large.

At the basis of the Oxford theology was a High Church or "Anglo-Catholic" view of the Church of England's religious character which was both intellectually sophisticated and emotionally compelling, qualities that were noticeably lacking in the brand of Anglicanism espoused by most clerics in the early decades of the nineteenth century. Throughout the 1830s it was maintained in the *Tracts for the Times*, as it had been maintained by Anglo-Catholics in centuries past, that the Church of England had all the marks of a branch of the catholic and apostolic Church of Christ — its doctrinal position upheld the pure

Christianity of the apostolic age, its episcopal government was sanctioned by ecclesiastical tradition, and its bishops stood in a line of direct succession from the twelve apostles. Other Anglo-Catholic doctrines expounded in the tracts dealt with the church's authority as an institution, an authority that was embodied in its role as an intermediary between God and man in the salvation of souls; the responsibility of the church to act as a guide to the individual conscience in the interpretation of scriptures; the nature of the sacraments not as mere as symbols but as instruments of divine grace; the spiritually enriching effects of the Anglican liturgy and ritual; and the need for the church to insist upon a strict observance of its fasts and festivals and an equally strict adherence to the rubrics — regulations governing Anglican liturgical life — found in the Book of Common Prayer and the Thirty-Nine Articles.

Linked to this Anglo-Catholic view of the church's religious character was an anti-Erastian attitude towards the state connection, an attitude which marked a sharp break from previous Anglican political theory. According to the Tractarians, the most disturbing feature of the times was the civil government's policy of undermining the church's position as the established church of the realm while simultaneously depriving it of control over the management of its internal affairs. In these circumstances, they argued, the church had to grow less dependent on a sinful government if it was to protect itself against state oppression. It also had to emphasize, both to its own members and to the entire nation, that its authority was derived not from its alliance with the state but from its divine commission to uphold the pure and unadulterated Christianity of the apostolic age.[1]

The profound influence of Tractarianism on the Church of England in Upper Canada was well illustrated in the case of Strachan. Not surprisingly, given his High Church perspective during the 1830s,[2] Strachan was an enthusiastic supporter of the Oxford movement in its early days. In an 1839 letter to Newman, written in London while he was awaiting his consecration as bishop, Strachan requested assistance "in making me personally known to yourself and your associates in your invaluable labours to protect the Church from Popery on the one hand & dissent on the other," adding that "it will be to me a source of permanent delight while travelling in the silent & primeval forests of my Diocese to have spent a single day nay even an hour with men whom I already love and admire for the inestimable services they have done to our beloved Church." He also revealed that the Tractarians' teachings had served not to inspire him with a view of the church with which he had previously been unfamiliar, but to strengthen his commitment to the High Church principles he had embraced in the 1820s. Admitting that "when I went to Canada about forty years ago my notions respecting the Church — her Government, the efficacy of the blessed Sacraments etc .... were crude & unsatisfactory," he noted that "it pleased God by reflexion rather than books of which I had few to improve my views on all these points," and expressed his joy at discovering in the tracts "the results at which I had slowly and laboriously arrived carried still further and a flood of light let in upon them which I trust in God will never be extinguished."[3]

Although Strachan was unable to meet Newman or any of the other Tractarians during his stay in England in 1839, he continued to lavish praise on the Oxford movement after his return to Upper Canada. In a second letter to Newman in 1840 he indicated that he had read tracts one to eighty, expressed "the high opinion which I cherish for you & your Friends and of the vast benefit which your labours are conferring upon the church we love," and stated his approval, with a few reservations, of Froude's *Remains*, a work that in England had been harshly attacked for its Roman Catholic leanings.[4] One year later, in his first episcopal charge, Strachan announced that the Tractarians, while sometimes guilty of doctrinal errors, "have been instrumental in reviving most important and essential truths, and in awakening the members of the Church to a higher estimate of her distinctive principles."[5]

After the publication of Tract 90 in 1841, Strachan's attitude towards the Oxford movement underwent a gradual change. In another letter to Newman in 1842 Strachan reiterated his belief that the "earlier Numbers [of the tracts] wrought wonders for our Church and revived with a force never I trust to be diminished that Spirit of reverence for primitive truth & order which in many places seemed to be entirely forgotten." Yet he also emphasized that he could not "accord with severe Strictures on our early reformers — or with the tone not always dutiful to my Mother Church of England — or with some palliations as they seem to me of the Church of Rome."[6] These reservations about certain aspects of the Oxford theology were not as evident in a sermon of 1843, in which Strachan declared that the "discordant materials" of the current religious awakening "will be gradually purged away or combined & harmonised so as to favour through the influence of the Holy Spirit the movement heavenward which has been so happily begun."[7] But the following year in an episcopal charge he again stated that, while the Tractarian movement deserved to be praised for its revival of Anglo-Catholic doctrines, it also had to be strongly condemned for "indulging a leaning towards Rome" and attempting "to gloss over or palliate" some of "her numerous and deadly corruptions."[8] When Newman converted to Roman Catholicism in 1845, Strachan told a fellow Anglican clergyman, Henry Patton, that the positive achievements of the Tractarian movement did "not excuse the insidious proceedings of Mr. Newman & his Party — whose conduct appears to be a sort of insanity — we are well rid of such men they have proved themselves totally unequal to the crisis and unworthy of confidence."[9] The same point of view was expressed in 1847, when Strachan reflected bitterly in his third episcopal charge that individuals whom the church

> had treated as her favoured children ... have turned against her with a simulation almost without parallel in the history of delusion. They continued within her pale, sapping her foundations and undermining her influence; and when concealment was no longer practicable, they deserted to her most powerful enemy against which they had so frequently protested.[10]

Yet, if Strachan became increasingly hostile towards the "romanizing" tendencies of the Oxford movement and eventually repudiated Newman as a traitor to the Anglican cause, he never left any doubt that the basic tenets of Tractarian theology were identical to his own High Church principles. In his charges of 1841, 1844, 1847 and 1851, and also in innumerable sermons preached both before and after Newman's defection, Strachan vigorously maintained that the church's claim to greatness rested on its character as a witness to the true faith. Underlying this argument was a set of ideas which, though long central to Strachan's theological perspective, had been reinforced by the Oxford movement's revival of the church's Anglo-Catholic heritage. For Strachan, the Church of England was a branch of that catholic and apostolic church established in the first few centuries of the Christian era, when the message of the gospel had not been contaminated by Roman Catholic novelties and superstitions. Its doctrinal principles, inherited from the apostolic age and restored to their original purity during the Reformation, adhered to the celebrated *via media* — a middle position equally removed from the errors of Roman Catholicism on the one side, and Lutheranism and Calvinism on the other. Its bishops were descendants of the apostles and transmitted their authority to the clergy through the rite of ordination, thereby enabling the church as a whole to pride itself upon its apostolic succession. Its sacraments, instituted by Christ himself, acted as a channel of grace between God and man. And finally, its knowledge of ecclesiastical tradition enabled it to play a key role in the interpretation of scriptures.[11]

Besides accepting the fundamental ideas of Tractarian theology, Strachan made it clear that the Oxford movement had influenced him in two basic ways. First, by expounding his High Church principles on a more frequent basis than ever before, Strachan demonstrated conclusively that Tractarianism had strengthened his determination to provide Upper Canadian Anglicans with a more coherent, comprehensive and sophisticated view of the distinguishing characteristics of their own denomination. Secondly, after his appointment as bishop of Toronto in 1841, Strachan revealed his intellectual debt to the Oxford movement by stressing the need for a rigorous observance of the church's rubrics, a subject he had largely ignored in earlier years. This new concern about religious "externals" was evident in Strachan's belief, expressed only privately, that the offertory prayer and the prayer for the church militant should again be used in Anglican worship.[12] It also received concrete expression in his support of the idea that the surplice rather than the gown should be worn in the pulpit, though he was careful to point out that this practice would not be insisted upon.[13] Even more significant were his instructions to the clergy in his episcopal charges to maintain proper standards of clerical dress, conduct morning prayer services whenever possible, administer communion on a monthly basis, celebrate religious holidays and saints' days, and perform baptisms and churchings during public worship rather than in private homes.[14]

The Oxford movement's enormous influence was also apparent in the case of the *Church*. In August 1839 the *Church*'s editor, A.N. Bethune, wrote that he had just begun to read the *Tracts for the Times*. He then stated that "the champions of the Oxford theology," though open to criticism for displaying a "tendency" to "erroneous" doctrines and resorting to "expressions and sentiments" which were "inexpedient" and "of questionable lawfulness," should be applauded for restoring "many a half-buried and forgotten truth to a prominence and importance, to which they have long been strangers."[15] This position on the subject of Tractarianism, advanced again in an editorial of October 1839,[16] was not shaken even by the publication of Tract 90. In 1841 the *Church*, still under Bethune's editorship, criticized Tract 90 but at the same time acknowledged that Anglicans should be deeply grateful to the Oxford theologians for "rescuing from oblivion, and revealing to the religious inquirer many points in the Christian government, discipline, and usages of the early ages, which are of the highest value."[17] Early the following year the paper's new editor, John Kent, who shortly before had coupled an attack on Tract 90 with the admission that his knowledge of the tracts as a whole was confined to three or four of the initial issues,[18] stated his opinion that the principles known collectively as "Puseyism" were in accord with the fundamental doctrines of the church.[19] He returned to the same theme in March 1843, when he again professed his ignorance of the tracts, defended Puseyism against its critics, and said of the objectionable features of the Oxford theology that "some imperfections, and some extravagances & excesses" were naturally to be expected in the great "work of restoration and reformation" which the church was currently undergoing.[20]

As Newman moved inexorably forward on the journey that would eventually lead to Roman Catholicism, the *Church* repeatedly argued that the Tractarian movement's achievements could not be obscured by the doctrinal errors of a single individual. In an April 1843 editorial, Kent declared angrily that "the sooner the church is rid of such wavering Protestants as Mr. Newman, the sooner will her peace be restored." But he also expressed his confidence that "the same principles which, carried to excess, are luring Mr. Newman into Romanism, have, in the exercise of their legitimate and scriptural influence, restored thousands to the arms of the Church, and will, we firmly believe, still more promote the cause of unity and Apostolic

In His Name

order."[21] Bethune was even more generous in his praise of the Oxford movement after his return as editor in July 1843. That August he stated in an editorial that the Tractarians, the "overwhelming majority" of whom were "sound and steadfast in the faith," had transformed the church from an institution which was "trampled upon, insulted and reviled" into one which raises "her head in majesty and strength."[22] Later, when Newman was admitted into the Roman Catholic Church, Bethune went so far as to intimate in another *Church* editorial that the "sin and peril of his calamity," a calamity occasioned by serious mental instability, could possibly have been avoided had worldly-minded elements not offered factious opposition to the Tractarian movement.[23] Even in 1847 Bethune could assert that "the good that has been effected by this movement is now a matter of history: the contingent evils by which it has been attended, however deeply to be deplored, are as nothing in comparison with the benefits that have been achieved."[24]

As was true of Strachan, moreover, the *Church*'s expressions of support for the Oxford movement were inseparable from its wholehearted acceptance of the basic theological principles of Tractarianism. Dozens of *Church* editorials from the late 1830s to the early 1850s were detailed and lengthy disquisitions on the importance of the church's apostolic succession and episcopal government in setting it apart as a guardian of the true faith, and in providing its clergy with a spiritual authority that other denominations lacked.[25] Countless other editorials, also revealing the influence of Tractarian theology and the entire Anglo-Catholic tradition, emphasized the role of the sacraments in the communication of grace, the significance of the liturgy in the religious life of the faithful, the church's duty to provide direction in the interpretation of scriptures, and the *via media* of Anglican doctrines between the fallacies of dissent and the "corruption" of Roman Catholicism.[26]

The *Church*'s theological viewpoint was revealed in an equally striking fashion in editorials relating to the question of religious "externals." Like Strachan, the *Church* strongly believed in the importance of upholding Anglican rubrics. Besides echoing Strachan's position on the practice of wearing the surplice while preaching, the *Church* called on clergymen to provide daily religious services whenever possible, observe all religious fasts and festivals, administer baptism during public worship, use the offertory prayer and the prayer for the church militant, and celebrate the Holy Eucharist on a weekly basis.[27] It also argued that the church's "catholic" character could be strengthened by placing altars in the east end of churches and by using the word "altar" instead of the expression "holy table."[28]

Nor was the Oxford movement's influence confined to Strachan and the *Church*. Although it is impossible to calculate the exact number of High Churchmen in Upper Canada,[29] there is no mistaking the enormous popularity of Anglo-Catholic principles among the Anglican clergy — a popularity that was almost certainly due to the work of the Oxford movement. F.L. Osler, a leading Evangelical, admitted the strength of the High Church faction in a letter of 1846, in which he wrote that "a large portion of our Clergy if not literally Puseyites are yet very ultra."[30] But there is other evidence too. From the late 1830s to the early 1850s, no fewer than seventeen sermons preached by eleven different clergymen dealt with themes that were central to Tractarian theology and the High Church tradition, notably the importance of apostolic succession and episcopal government as marks of the true church, the role of the sacraments in the communication of grace, and the Church of England's responsibility to exert its authority as a spiritual institution in matters of doctrine and in the interpretation of the Bible.[31] One of the most thoughtful of these sermons was delivered by Henry Patton at Strachan's 1853 visitation. According to Patton, the Church of England was "the church of the living God, the pillar and the ground of truth," the "divinely constituted instrument for the salvation of immortal souls," and the "most scriptural and perfect Branch" of the "Catholick and Apostolical Church." To substantiate his argument, he pointed both to the "evangelical purity of Anglican doctrines," which were founded on the word of God, and to the church's willingness to draw upon the wisdom of the apostolic age in the interpretation of scriptures. He also drew attention to the efficacy of the sacraments of baptism and the Lord's Supper in the transmission of divine grace, described the Anglican liturgy as an "unrivalled" work of art, and asserted that the church's three-tiered ministry of bishops, priests and deacons dated to the time of the apostles.[32]

This Anglo-Catholic conception of the church's nature as a religious organization was also evident in the writings of James Beaven, in an 1844 pamphlet by Thomas Fuller, and in letters to the *Church*.

In His Name

Beaven advanced High Church opinions on a number of subjects, including the function of the sacraments as channels of grace and the church's authority in doctrinal questions and in the interpretation of scriptures. These views were set forth in his *Help to Catechising* and *Catechism on the Thirty-Nine Articles*, and again at greater length in his *Life and Writings of Saint Irenaeus* — a work which also revealed a strong belief in the value of patristic studies and in the importance of ecclesiastical tradition as the basis of the church's doctrinal position.[33] Fuller showed less intellectual sophistication in his 1844 pamphlet, *The Roman Catholic Church Not the Mother Church of England*, but he too displayed an essentially High Church theological perspective in his argument that the Church of England at the time of the Reformation, already in possession of "the orders of the ministry established by Christ and his Apostles," "reformed herself and returned to the independence and the purity which she possessed before she had any connexion with Rome," thus "resuming her rank as an independent branch of the Church Catholic."[34] Similar views on the church's religious character were expressed in letters to the *Church* from Adam Townley, one "H.C." of Brockville, and Joseph Flanagan, a former Methodist who had become an Anglican clergyman.[35] Townley's letter was the most interesting of the three, stressing as it did "the necessity of Episcopacy and of an Apostolic succession in order to constitute a comple[te] and valid ministry," "the sacramental character of the Church as the Body and Bride of Christ," and the church's role as "the only Divinely appointed keeper and interpreter of Holy Writ ... the voucher of its authenticity and genuineness, the interpreter of its doctrinal mysteries, and the authorized dispenser of its promised salvation and blessings."[36]

Perhaps the most impressive testimony to the Oxford movement's influence in Upper Canada was the large number of Anglican clergymen who, like Strachan and the *Church*, revealed a growing interest in the question of church rubrics. In 1842 a *Church* correspondent signing himself "A Presbyter of the Diocese of Toronto" expressed his unqualified agreement with the rubrical principles laid down in Strachan's recent episcopal charge, explaining that he had long been "deeply convinced of the great disadvantage under which the Church labours from the want of due attention to the *Rubrics*, and consequently of uniformity in the performance of her public services."[37] This point of view, also put forward in letters to the *Church* in the early 1840s from "A Catholic Presbyter," "Prester Ergenia," and "You know who,"[38] underlay the attempts of many individuals in the post-rebellion period to revive liturgical practices that had fallen by the wayside. In 1841, for example, at a meeting of the Eastern Clerical Association, seven clergymen discussed the obligation of Anglicans to observe the appointed fasts and festivals of the church,[39] a subject later expounded in an 1843 sermon delivered by T.S. Kennedy before the Midland District Clerical Association and in Henry Patton's 1851 pamphlet, *Questions on the Chief Festivals and Holy Days*.[40] Two other clergymen, G.M. Armstrong of Louth and William Shaw of Emily, together with a few *Church* correspondents who concealed their identity with pseudonyms, gave their support to the idea of a distinctive form of clerical dress and to such practices as daily religious services, wearing the surplice while preaching, the celebration of the Eucharist on a weekly basis, the churching of women, and the performance of baptisms and marriages in churches rather than in private homes.[41]

Related to this preoccupation with church rubrics was a tendency on the part of many Anglicans to place increased emphasis on the role of ritual in religious worship. While Strachan and the *Church* largely ignored the ritualist movement that had arisen in England as part and parcel of the Anglo-Catholic revival, several clergymen were joined by a large number of *Church* correspondents in calling for a variety of alterations in the format of religious worship and in the architectural design of churches. These alterations, some of which were borrowed from Roman Catholicism, were designed to enhance the beauty and mysticism of Anglican religion, thereby strengthening the church's ability to act as a channel of communication between God and man. With this end in view, eleven of the twelve clergymen assembled at a meeting of the Western Clerical Association in 1838 gave their approval to the "ancient and edifying practice" of bowing at the name of Jesus during the recitation of the Apostles' Creed,[42] and in an 1852 letter to the *Church* a correspondent with the pseudonym "Anglo-Catholic" suggested that an Anglican minister should conduct religious services with his back to the congregation.[43] Other changes in the church's religious "style" that were recommended, and in some cases implemented,

In His Name

in the post-rebellion period included the presence of baptismal fonts inside the entrances of churches, the use of crosses both in the interior of churches and on the tops of steeples, the placing of candlesticks on altars, the erection of rood screens to separate minister and congregation during public worship, and the decoration of churches with images and sculptures.[44]

In order to explain the impact of Tractarianism on the Upper Canadian church, several points must be made. One of the most basic concerns the relationship of Tractarian theology to the Anglican critique of dissent. In the 1820s and 1830s Strachan had repeatedly denounced the "sectaries" as promoters of "enthusiasm" and as schismatics from a branch of the catholic and apostolic church, a church whose episcopal government, doctrinal purity and edifying liturgy marked it out as God's chosen instrument in the salvation of souls. This High Church attitude towards dissenting denominations remained a significant feature of Strachan's ideological make-up after the emergence of the Oxford movement. In the post-rebellion years, Strachan made it clear that the Anglo-Catholic revival had strengthened his determination to discredit the theological position of the Church of England's sectarian rivals: in three sermons preached throughout the 1840s and 1850s, Strachan emphasized that secession from the Church of England was a sinful act, that "sectarianism" had transformed the Christian church into a collection of warring fragments, and that dissenters would have to face the consequences of divine wrath if they continued in their evil ways.[45] Even more important, these various expressions of religious intolerance highlighted one of the main reasons why Strachan had embraced the Oxford movement so enthusiastically: its central tenets confirmed his own objections to the theological basis of dissent.

The connection between Tractarian theology and Anglican intolerance was not typified solely by Strachan. After the birth of the Oxford movement, Strachan's campaign against dissent was assisted by other clergymen and by the *Church* newspaper. The idea that dissenters were sinful schismatics was advanced in countless *Church* editorials and in sermons and pamphlets published by James Clarke, William Macaulay, Adam Elliott, J.A. Mulock, Henry Scadding, Arthur Palmer and A.N. Bethune.[46] Further, as was true in the case of Strachan, these declarations on the subject of dissent underlined the intimate relationship between Tractarian theology and the Anglican attitude towards "sectarianism." In one sense, these editorials, sermons and pamphlets indicated that the Tractarian revival of Anglo-Catholic principles had had the effect of encouraging clergymen to speak out publicly on the theological fallacies of dissent. In another sense, the same writings made it plain that Tractarianism gained broad appeal in Upper Canada because it confirmed traditional Anglican prejudices towards dissenting denominations, while at the same time providing some clergymen with a distinctive view of their church's religious character.[47]

A second reason for the Oxford movement's influence on the Upper Canadian church was the fact that certain Tractarian doctrines meshed perfectly with the conservative ideology of Anglican clergymen. This was particularly true of two intimately related Tractarian arguments — that Anglican bishops and clergymen traced their authority to the apostles, and that the church's hierarchical structure was sanctioned by ecclesiastical tradition. From the standpoint of a conservative-minded Anglican clergyman, the theory of apostolic succession was based on the principle that secular and spiritual leaders owed their position not to the multitude but to the will of God; A.N. Bethune could thus declare in an 1838 sermon, later published as *The Christian Shepherd*, that both kings and Church of England ministers obtained their "commission" from the "same heavenly source" rather than from the voice of the people.[48] Similarly, in the eyes of Upper Canadian High Churchmen, the Tractarian commitment to the church's three-tiered government of bishops, priests and deacons had a double significance: it emphasized that the Church of England's hierarchical structure was a reflection of the graded social order in which it operated; and it underlined the basic truth that a church which accepted the "episcopal principle" also accepted class distinctions as the work of God. On the latter point, an article published in an 1838 issue of the *Church* was especially illuminating. In this article, entitled "The Want of a Bishop in Upper Canada," John Kent drew a direct connection between episcopacy and what he saw as the hierarchical structure of the universe. He put it this way:

> Were there no social inequalities in the world, men would quickly forget their allegiance to God, and seeing no one in their pilgrimage below up-lifted beyond their own level, would rebel in their hearts against the majesty of heaven. Thus, in civil polity, men may be considered as a monarchical, — and, in ecclesiastical government, as an episcopal, — being .... In Episcopacy ... we not only conform to the rule of Scripture, and the apostolical practice, but we act in accordance with the laws of nature herself. We admit, in effect, what none will deny in the abstract, that there is a diversity of gifts among men, — that some are born to command, and others to obey; that as, in the scale of creation, there is a descending link from man to the most sagacious and semi-human of the irrational tribes, and from thence downwards to the scarcely animated zoophyte, so among men, even in a state of refined civilization, there exist a variety of intellectual gifts which can only be brought into full and beneficial operation by a corresponding diversity of situations, each ranking below the other.[49]

The most important reason for the popularity of Tractarianism in Upper Canada was intertwined with the church's perception of its position *vis-à-vis* the state. The Oxford movement's view that the Church of England should become less dependent on an apostate civil government, as well as its belief that the church's authority was based not on its ties with the state but on its character as a branch of the catholic and apostolic church, could not have been more suited to the needs of Upper Canadian Anglicanism. Without a doubt, the Tractarians' anti-Erastian attitude struck a responsive chord in the hearts of those Upper Canadian Anglicans who were displaying growing hostility to the state connection. Equally important, the Tractarian claim that the church's relationship with the state had no bearing whatsoever on its greatness as a religious institution was a source of much consolation to the Upper Canadian clergy. When it became increasingly clear in the late 1840s and early 1850s that disestablishment was only a matter of time, an Anglican High Churchman could find solace in the Tractarian argument that the church's loss of its temporal privileges would have little effect on its ability to act as a witness to the true faith. Accordingly, the *Church* could announce in 1846 that, although "the state, in its liberality, has well nigh stripped us of all the adventitious advantages connected with the implied alliance," it should not be forgotten that "no earthly power, much less an earthly opposition or railing, can divest the church" of "her holy character and spiritual pre-eminence—it is hers by gift of her Divine head."[50]

All this raises an interesting question concerning the connection between Tractarianism and the growing introversion of the Upper Canadian church. Essentially, it appears that Tractarianism gained considerable support in Upper Canada partly because it provided many clergymen with a sense of religious mission, something that was indispensable if the church as a whole was to react to disestablishment by turning its back on the state and concentrating on its duties as a primarily spiritual organization. The importance of this sense of mission was particularly evident in Strachan's 1837 address to the archdeaconry of York. While reflecting on the threats to the policy of church establishment, Strachan made it obvious that he could never have looked forward with confidence to the Church of England's future as a "Missionary Church" had the Oxford movement not inspired him with a compelling view of the Anglican mission.[51] After announcing that it was through the Church of England that Upper Canadians could "transform this beautiful country to a moral garden," he went on to state that

> our Apostolical church seems to stand alone, as a beacon on a hill, emitting a clear and steady light, for the direction of the world; and her wisdom in adhering, through good report and evil report, to the doctrines and principles of the primitive age will yet appear in this growing Province, and be fully admitted by many who now consider such adherence to be little else than the extreme of bigotry and folly.[52]

* * * * *

In His Name

The rift that developed between High Churchmen and Evangelicals was rooted in the theological ambiguity of the Anglican *via media*. In the sixteenth century the Elizabethan settlement had provided the Church of England with a doctrinal position that was a delicate balance of Roman Catholic, Lutheran and Calvinist ideas. Although this compromise was certainly ingenious, its lack of intellectual precision meant that the Anglican message could be interpreted in a variety of ways. The inevitable result was that, from the Reformation on, the Church of England was internally divided along theological lines. These internal divisions were particularly noticeable after the emergence of the Oxford movement. At that time the church was split into three groups. There was a small and increasingly isolated "Broad Church" faction that adhered to the ideas of eighteenth-century latitudinarianism. There was a High Church party — itself divided between the supporters of Tractarianism and a more conservative wing — which espoused the "catholic" principles of Richard Hooker, principal apologist for the Elizabethan settlement, the Caroline divines of the seventeenth century, and the non-jurors of the late seventeenth and early eighteenth centuries. Finally, there was a large and influential body of Low Churchmen who stressed the Protestant heritage of the Anglican faith, and who traced their intellectual ancestry to the puritanism of the sixteenth and seventeenth centuries and to the Evangelical movement of the late eighteenth century.

The theological differences between Low Church and High Church Anglicans were numerous. Low Churchmen placed far more emphasis on the "reformed" nature of the Anglican faith than on the Church of England's character as a branch of the catholic and apostolic church. They were primarily concerned with the spiritual welfare of the individual rather than with the religious life of the entire body of faithful. The central tenet of their theology, the doctrine of justification through faith alone, went hand in hand with a tendency to downplay the importance of the visible church as an intermediary between God and man in the process of salvation. Lastly, the Low Church position on several specific theological points was firmly grounded in the doctrinal principles of the Reformation. According to the Low Church tradition, episcopacy was not a mark of the true church but a matter of administrative convenience; Christians had the right to exercise their private judgment in theological questions and in the interpretation of scriptures without being restrained by the authority of the church; sacraments were commemorative symbols rather than channels of divine grace; ritualism and ceremonialism in religious worship savoured of "popish corruption" and should be avoided at all costs; and the sermon was the centrepiece of Anglican liturgy.[53]

In Upper Canada, the cause of Low Church Anglicanism had definite regional and ethnic characteristics. After the early 1830s Upper Canada, and in particular the area between Toronto and the Thames River, became the home of a large number of clergymen who had been born and educated in Ireland, a country whose brand of Anglicanism had always been noted for its intense antipathy towards Roman Catholicism and its Low Church theological orientation.[54] It was therefore hardly surprising that Evangelical ideas were especially prevalent in the western part of the province and among those clergymen of Irish origin. In the post-rebellion period, there were thirty-three clergymen who could certainly be described as Evangelicals.[55] Of this group, four (G.O. Stuart, R.D. Cartwright, Saltern Givins and William Herchmer) had long associations with Upper Canada — a fact which serves as a reminder that Low Church Anglicanism, like the "High Churchism" espoused by Strachan, pre-dated the birth of the Oxford movement. Fifteen resided west of Toronto, four were stationed in the Kingston area and the remainder were scattered throughout the province.[56] Twelve had been born in Ireland, and eleven of these had received their theological education at Trinity College, Dublin, a bastion of Low Church Anglicanism.[57]

The strength of the Low Church party in western Upper Canada was convincingly demonstrated in 1857, when, in the episcopal election in the new diocese of Huron, about half of the clergy present voted for the Evangelical candidate, Benjamin Cronyn.[58] As for the Irish origins of many Low Church ministers, consider a letter written by Strachan in 1834 to the archbishop of Dublin. Here Strachan complained that "with the exception of one or two clerical Gentlemen introduced to me by your Grace the Clergymen who come to this country from Ireland are strongly Calvinistic in their sermons & go much farther than those who are called Evangelicals in England." He then asserted that "these persons are so wild in their doctrines & unguarded in their statements that I am really afraid to allowing [sic] them to preach for they seem

In His Name

never to have known the distinctive principles of the Church of England or to have thrown them away on the voyage."[59]

Another interesting feature of the theological climate of the post-rebellion period was the strength of Evangelicalism among the Anglican laity. One scholar has estimated that, from the 1850s to the 1870s, the overwhelming majority of laymen active in church politics were Evangelicals[60] — a state of affairs attributable both to fears of the High Church emphasis on the distinctiveness of the clerical calling, and to the violent hostility towards Roman Catholicism that pervaded Upper Canadian society in the second half of the nineteenth century. The evidence for earlier years is not as conclusive, but on the whole it appears that the laity of that period also inclined to Evangelicalism. Certainly, before the secularization of the clergy reserves, Evangelical clergymen themselves believed the laity to be sympathetic to their cause. The Evangelical campaign for a more democratic form of ecclesiastical government was based partly on the belief that the influence of Tractarianism could be checked only if the laity, or rather those middle-class laymen likely to be interested in such matters, were given a larger voice in the church's internal affairs. The accuracy of their analysis of the religious sentiments of the Anglican faithful was proven with Cronyn's election as bishop of Huron. In that election, with Bethune and Cronyn having almost equal numbers of clerical supporters, it was the laity's votes that proved decisive. Twenty-three laymen voted for Cronyn, while only ten voted for Bethune.[61]

Part of the conflict between High and Low Churchmen revolved around the Church of England's relations with inter-denominational organizations. While the High Church party frequently made known its view that Anglicans should remain aloof from all organizations which were open to rival denominations,[62] Evangelical clergymen tended to adopt a more tolerant attitude. Ignoring the criticisms of Strachan and the *Church*,[63] Evangelicals took the position that, since the Church of England was an essentially "protestant" denomination, Anglicans should be encouraged to cooperate with Presbyterians and dissenters in ventures that would prove beneficial both to the cause of religion and to the welfare of society.[64] Consequently, the Low Church party supported temperance societies and Sunday School Unions, and such organizations as the British and Foreign Bible Society, the Religious Tract Society, the Evangelical Alliance, the Scripture Readers

Association, the Irish Church Missions and the Anti-Slavery Association. The clergymen involved in these various organizations included Joseph Harris, R.V. Rogers, T.E. Welby, Alexander Sanson, John Grieg, E.C. Bower, William David, J.A. Mulock, Benjamin Cronyn, Hannibal Mulkins, Jonathan Shortt, S.B. Ardagh, F.A. O'Meara, Edmund Baldwin, Francis Evans and B.C. Hill.[65]

High and Low Churchmen also came into conflict over a number of theological issues. For example, Evangelical clergymen alienated themselves from their Anglo-Catholic brethren by performing baptisms in private homes and by altering many aspects of the Anglican form of worship.[66] Although frequently attacked by Strachan and the *Church* for these liturgical irregularities,[67] Low Churchmen remained tactfully silent. On one occasion, however, the different positions of High and Low Churchmen on this highly contentious subject were publicly set out in the pages of the *Church*. In December 1842 a Lower Canadian clergyman calling himself "Philahosmos" wrote a letter to the paper in which he attacked his clerical colleagues in the diocese of Quebec for ignoring many of the church's rubrics.[68] Early in the new year "A.B." replied to these charges by explaining that some rubrical practices were simply impractical in a society where clergymen had to "supply on a Sunday two or three congregations at remote distances from each other."[69] This position was in turn condemned by "E.," an Anglo-Catholic. After remarking that he had been able to observe the rubrics even though he lived in the "back-woods" and was responsible for three congregations, "E." declared that "to follow the rule of A.B. would be to open the door to every kind of novelty" — such as "shortening," "altering," and "mutilating" the services, "which in England and Ireland, and I believe in this Province, has been done in the Baptismal Service." His letter concluded with an excerpt from a pamphlet dealing with the Church of England in Britain which, in his view, was equally applicable to the state of Upper Canadian Anglicanism. Its central theme was that many clergymen were showing their contempt for the Book of Common Prayer by neglecting to observe the church's fasts and festivals, ignoring the offertory prayer and the prayer for the church militant, and baptizing children "in their father's dining-room" rather that "at the font during Divine Service."[70]

This exchange was restrained in tone compared to other theological debates of the post-rebellion period. In letters to the *Church*

In His Name

throughout these years, representatives of the church's opposing factions aired their differences not only on the controversial practices of preaching without notes, wearing the surplice in the pulpit, and using the word "altar" rather than the expression "holy table," but also on such thorny matters as the nature of the sacraments, the place of ritual and ceremony in religious worship, and the role of the church in the interpretation of scriptures.[71] One of the most violent of these debates was waged in 1848 between "H." and "B.C." (probably Benjamin Cronyn), who traded *ad hominem* attacks in the course of an argument on the pros and cons of "extempore preaching." The debate began calmly enough when "B.C.," in a letter to the *Church* in September, defended the practice of extempore preaching against criticisms advanced by "H." But shortly afterwards an enraged "H." denounced "B.C." for being addicted to that "irreverent and uncertain mode of address from his pulpit, which I have deprecated and condemned," for "attempting to push his opinions and practices down my throat," and for displaying in his writings the same "cumulative, blundering inconclusiveness ... which generally characterize extempore preachers in their public prelections." This hysterical tirade prompted "B.C." to repeat his arguments in favour of extempore preaching, and to remark contemptuously that "H." was hardly to fit to criticize another's writing style when his own letters to the *Church* made it evident that "he is not qualified to instruct even boys of ten years old in the first elements of English composition."[72]

Less vitriolic, but more revealing of the theological chasm separating High and Low Churchmen, was an 1847 debate between "A Catholic" and "H.C.C." (probably H.C. Cooper) on the respective roles of private judgment and the authority of the church in the interpretation of scriptures. In the opening stages of this debate, which lasted from May until September, "A Catholic" argued that "the Church is the Divinely appointed interpreter of Holy Scripture" and that reliance on the individual's judgment in this matter led to the proliferation of schismatic sects and the corruption of biblical truth. He also declared that his objective was "to save His blessed Word from the dangerous corruptions necessarily consequent in a greater or less degree, upon the weak, fallible, or wilful interpretations of individuals, and to place it in the hands of that Universal Church which He who cannot lie, has promised ever to be with." In response, H.C.C. declared angrily that his fellow correspondent's "manner of viewing the Church has been the very process by which some minds of late years have been most egregiously misled," warning that "the belief ... of an infallible power of interpretation existing in the Church ... conducts ... to the principles on which the Papal usurpation, with all its concomitant heresies, is grounded." To these attacks on his position, "A Catholic" replied by reiterating his view that "the decision of the church catholic" was "infallible," and by expressing his indifference to the abuse he was receiving from "a self-idolizing section of the church."[73]

One principal cause of division between Evangelicals and High Churchmen was the *Church* newspaper itself. Throughout the post-rebellion period the paper published editorials criticizing specific aspects of Evangelical Anglicanism, such as the practice of extempore preaching, and attacking Evangelicals for hindering the progress of the Anglican revival.[74] Predictably, these editorials, combined with frequent expositions on the doctrines of Anglo-Catholic theology and sympathetic reviews of the work of the Oxford movement, enraged the church's Evangelical wing. In November 1843, F.L. Osler wrote to a clerical friend in England that the *Church* was continually excusing "the errors of the Oxford heresy." He also stated that "a large body of the most influential clergymen" was "strongly opposed to the principles advocated by the paper," and that some had "already refused to take it unless a great change is soon made ... most of us will enter a protest." He added, "this will be the more awkward to do as the Bp is a personal friend of the Editor and holds the same views."[75] Strachan was not oblivious to these feelings of dissatisfaction with the *Church*'s doctrinal position. Writing to Bethune in January 1844, he noted that Osler and Francis Evans, the Anglican clergyman in Simcoe, were among the "Promoters" of the current agitation against the paper. To deal with the problems posed by this agitation, Strachan counselled that, while "the persons who object are of morbid temperaments and miserable judges — yet as they can do mischief we must yield a little in taking selections now & then from their own School when it can be done without any compromise of principles."[76] Two years later he declared in a letter to the bishop of Nova Scotia that "complaints are made by the Low Church that it [the *Church*] does not pay sufficient respect to their views & are not therefore zealous in its favour."[77]

In His Name

The *Church*'s unpopularity among Evangelical clergymen was reflected in the statements made by some of its correspondents. In a series of letters in 1847, "B.C." attacked the paper for claiming that ecclesiastical tradition was infallible and of equal authority with scripture, a principle which had recently brought about defections from the Church of England to Roman Catholicism and which every loyal clergyman "must repudiate with horror."[78] Two other churchmen were even harsher in their criticisms. In March 1847, C.C. Brough, the Anglican clergyman in Cavan, stated that "the character of many of the articles, found from time to time in the Church newspaper, has awakened an apprehension in the minds of many, at home and in this country, that our orthodoxy is unsound," and that were he not actually "upon the spot to see, and believe, and hope otherwise," he too would come to the conclusion after reading the *Church* that "there existed in Canada an approximation to the system which has of late plunged so many of our communion into the abyss of Romanism."[79] A couple of years later, a *Church* editorial praising the creation of Anglican convents and monasteries in England moved "Lucius" to exclaim that such views "are pregnant with danger to our venerable Church establishment, and were your design to undermine her foundations, and to pull down her walls and battlements, a more effectual path could not be chosen."[80]

This belief that the paper was subverting the Church of England's doctrinal position prompted many Evangelical clergymen to give their support to rival Anglican journals. In the 1840s the *Berean*, a Low Church newspaper published in Quebec City, was supported by several Upper Canadian Evangelicals, including H.J. Grasett, the curate of St. James's Cathedral and Strachan's personal secretary and chaplain, A.F. Atkinson, R.V. Rogers and S.B. Ardagh, the latter two clergymen even acting as the paper's agents in their respective parishes of Kingston and Barrie.[81] When the *Berean* folded in 1849, Upper Canada's Evangelicals lost little time in starting a journal of their own. *The Echo and Protestant Episcopal Recorder*, under the editorship of the Anglican minister Jonathan Shortt, began publication in Port Hope in 1851, and within one year had established its reputation as the organ of the Low Church party in Upper Canada. Heading the *Echo*'s list of roughly one thousand subscribers was the layman P.B. de Blaquière and a large group of twenty-three Evangelical clergymen, prominent among whom were

G.O. Stuart, Benjamin Cronyn and John McCaul, the former principal of King's College. Four of these clerical subscribers — Cronyn, R.V. Rogers, Alexander Sanson and S.B. Ardagh — as well as the editor Jonathan Shortt were on the *Echo*'s Trustees and Managing Committee, and Sanson and Rogers also served as the paper's travelling agents.[82]

A divided press, of course, was a severe handicap to a church that was struggling to redefine its role in the religious life of Upper Canada. Yet, when the *Church* called on the Anglican press to submerge its differences, the *Echo* retorted that it would never agree to compromise its fundamental principles. In September 1854 the *Church*, while referring to the "fallacies and shortcomings" of its "quasi-church rival," emphasized that "we long for unity; we abhor controversy" and proposed the replacement of itself and the *Echo* with a non-partisan church gazette. The *Echo* dismissed this idea with the curt statement that neutrality was out of the question when the church was "threatened with great innovations from within both of doctrine and of practice."[83] The same position was advanced in a December editorial, in which the *Echo* argued that "surely this is no time for peace; when professed clergymen of the Church of England are inculcating, directly or indirectly, some of the most subtle, insidious, and dangerous of the Romish doctrines."[84]

Another bone of contention between High and Low Churchmen was the teaching provided by A.N. Bethune at the Diocesan Theological Institute in Cobourg, an Anglican seminary which operated from 1842 until the opening of Trinity College in 1852.[85] As principal and, for some years, the only professor at the institute, the learned and gentle Bethune was highly respected by most, though not all, of his students. Those who disliked him, unsurprisingly, took exception to his High Church theology. The first sign of hostility to Bethune's teaching appeared after the arrival in Cobourg in 1844 of Edward Ellis, later described by Strachan as "a sort of religious adventurer." Admitted into the school on a trial basis, Ellis soon made his presence felt by criticizing Bethune's High Church views, distributing Evangelical tracts throughout the parish of Cobourg, and attending the religious services of dissenters. Bethune was about to report these antics to Strachan and to recommend Ellis' dismissal from the institute when he was forced to turn his attention to another matter. In September 1845 two of Ellis' fellow students, a certain Marsh and Isaac Hellmuth, later Cronyn's successor as bishop of Huron, were so offended by a Bethune lecture that they left Cobourg and made their way to Montreal. Soon afterwards the exiles wrote a letter to an English Evangelical journal, the *Record*, describing the Cobourg institute as a "fearful hotbed of Tractarianism," and on the basis of this report the *Record*'s editor, W. Carus Wilson, published a series of articles attacking the school and accusing Bethune and Strachan of having Tractarian sympathies.[86] Strachan responded to these charges in a letter to Wilson in January 1846 by denying that either he or Bethune were Tractarians, denouncing the malcontents who had caused so much trouble in Cobourg, and expressing his deep regret that Wilson himself had become associated with "a Party of which it is painful to observe that some of its Leaders are more prominent in efforts to disturb the peace and order of the Church than to promote truth of doctrine, unity of sentiment & holiness of life."[87]

In the year after Strachan's reply to Wilson, the town of Cobourg was in turmoil. Edward Ellis, informed by Strachan that he would never be ordained in the diocese of Toronto,[88] remained in Cobourg and, in the words of one witness, imitated "the conduct of the turbulent and factious politician who, other measures failing, invariably has recourse to agitation, exciting discord, where before was harmony."[89] His efforts in this direction were checked when, in May, seventeen former pupils of the institute signed an address to Bethune in which they expressed their firm conviction that "the standard of Divinity which you have adopted is built upon the testimony of the Holy Scripture, and the authentic exposition set forth by the Church of England in her Articles and Formularies."[90] But even such a glowing tribute to Bethune's theological orthodoxy could not calm the troubled waters of religious controversy. This became evident when Robert Shanklin, a student who had refused to sign the May address, began announcing publicly in the streets of Cobourg that Strachan and Bethune were Tractarians.[91] By now Strachan had lost all patience with the troublemakers in Cobourg, and he promptly informed Shanklin that he was no longer considered a suitable candidate for the ministry.[92] When A.F. Atkinson, the Anglican clergyman in St. Catharines, dared to defend Shanklin as a victim of persecution and to assert not only that the Cobourg Institute was infected with Tractarianism but that ministerial candidates in Upper Canada were subjected to unlawful tests,[93] Strachan expressed his fury in a September 1846 letter to Bethune, noting that "I am roused against this set of ungrateful heartless men, who under the cloak of religion sacrifice for party everything truly just & honourable."[94] He regained his composure only the following month, when Shanklin agreed to retract his charges, setting an example that would later be followed by Atkinson. Strachan was now prepared to forget the past, and on 16 October he reversed an earlier decision and admitted Shanklin into the ministry.[95]

There was another High Church-Low Church battle in which Bethune again found himself in the eye of the storm. This battle originated in 1853, when Upper Canadian Anglicans began hearing rumours — incorrect ones, as it turned out — that the imperial government was about to establish a diocese in the Kingston area. In response, clergymen John Wilson and William McMurray distributed circulars promoting Bethune, their superior as archdeacon of York, for the bishopric of the new diocese.[96] The Low Church party's reaction to these tactics was immediate. George Okill Stuart — probably inspired both by a dislike of Bethune's High Church views and by a belief that he, as archdeacon of Kingston, should have first claim on the bishopric — asked each of the clergymen under his jurisdiction for their opinion of Bethune's qualifications, and also planned a clerical meeting to discuss the proposed see. As it happened, Stuart decided to cancel the meeting when Strachan warned that such an action would be both illegal and a threat to the church's unity.[97] Yet matters did not rest there. A number of laymen from the Kingston area, with Stuart's active support, sent a delegate to London to block the appointment,[98] while several Low Churchmen wrote letters to the *Echo* from December 1853 to the summer of 1854 attempting to arouse opposition to Bethune's candidacy by attacking his Tractarian views and reviving accusations that had been levelled during the Cobourg affair. Benjamin Cronyn fulminated against the "partizanship" and "secret proceedings" of McMurray and Wilson, and asserted that Bethune's selection would be "a measure fraught with danger to the Church in this country."[99] R.V. Rogers urged that a memorial be sent to the archbishop of Canterbury "praying that no such affliction be suffered to fall on our struggling church" in Upper Canada as the choice of "one so distasteful to those that are without, and possessing so little of the confidence of those within our communion." He added that "the appointment, not only of Dr. Bethune, but of any man of his extreme views would greatly paralyze, if not destroy our Church."[100] "A Layman" stated in equally categorical language that

> we do not want a Bishop to avow and teach the pernicious and Romanizing doctrines of Dr. Pusey, that traitor within the Church; we want not a man who will, in a most unwarrantable manner, press his views upon Divinity students as a *sine qua non* to their ordination .... what, may I ask, is to be expected if, under Bishop Bethune, the novelty of a white surplice should be uplifted in the Pulpit as a badge or standard of a party, and other novelties introduced where they have not yet appeared? .... Instead, then, of the Archdeacon of York being the man 'of all others the best qualified,' he is, of the clergy in this diocese, the most unfit to preside over the new See of Kingston .... Far better that we should have no Bishop at all, and that we should remain as we are, than that Dr. Bethune should be appointed over us.[101]

These statements did not go unanswered. While emphasizing in a letter to the *Echo* in December 1853 that he had no designs on the Kingston bishopric, and that the action of his supporters in resorting to an episcopal "canvas" had set a "vicious precedent," Bethune challenged his critics to prove "that I have taught or preached any doctrine not in accordance with the tenets of the Church of England; or that, as a conscientious member of that Church, I entertain or advocate 'extreme views of doctrine.'"[102] Other Anglicans were no less indignant. "A Presbyter," writing to the *Church*, defended Bethune's theological orthodoxy and chastized R.V. Rogers for displaying "morbid sensitiveness," noting that "the task is onerous enough of counteracting the effects of division around us, without engendering strife amongst ourselves."[103] Adam Townley, though deprecating the practice of episcopal canvassing, urged all Anglicans to refrain from patronizing the *Echo*, a journal intent on "sowing schism," and warned that "the unhappy violence of a meagre faction was bringing disgrace upon the Upper Canadian church."[104] John Wilson defended Bethune's conduct in the Cobourg affair, and criticized the *Echo* for being blinded "by the spirit of party" and for "fomenting strife and envy, and heartburning, amongst brethren."[105]

The dispute between High and Low Churchmen over the see of Kingston — which, incidentally, was not established until 1862 — was closely related to the more general issue of how future bishops were to be chosen. When rumours of the impending creation of the diocese of Kingston first began to circulate, the *Echo* suggested that the new bishop should either be appointed by the archbishop of Canterbury from among the ranks of the English clergy, or elected by a synod composed of clergymen and lay delegates.[106] That the latter suggestion had wide appeal became apparent at Strachan's third visitation of clergy and laity, which, as already recounted, gave its almost unanimous support to the idea that bishops of the new dioceses it hoped to establish in eastern and western Upper Canada should be elected by synods. There were dissenters — Adam Townley argued, both at the 1853 visitation and one month later in a letter to the *Church*, that bishops should be appointed by the crown as long as the Church of England in Upper Canada relied on the SPG for financial support,[107] while the *Church* took the position in late 1854 that the laity should not have any say in the selection of bishops.[108] Yet, these exceptions aside, the concept of electing bishops in synods composed of both clergy and laity was one of the few issues on which High and Low Churchmen were able to agree. The reasons why the two factions supported this idea were never made explicit, but they seem obvious enough. On the subject of church government, theological differences were irrelevant — all Anglicans were one in believing that a more democratic and broadly based system of ecclesiastical government was essential if the church was to become financially self-supporting. As well, since the laity tended to adhere to the Low Church theological line, the Evangelical party had every reason to uphold the right of laymen to play a part in the election of bishops. To put the case simply, its episcopal candidates would stand a better chance of election if they could draw on lay votes.[109]

The 1853 visitation should have settled the matter of how future

In His Name

Upper Canadian bishops were to be chosen, but it did not. The problem was that the visitation had sown the seeds of future difficulties by altogether ignoring the question of whether the bishops of the new sees were to be elected by local synods established for that purpose or by the synod of the Upper Canadian church as a whole. Its failure to deal with such a basic issue led directly to the dispute over the Kingston bishopric, when clergymen from the archdeaconry of York intervened in the religious affairs of the eastern region. It also led to some astonishing developments in western Upper Canada, the stronghold of Anglican Evangelicalism. At a meeting of the London District Branch of the Church Society in February 1854, Benjamin Cronyn, in his capacity as chairman, emphasized that future bishops should be drawn from those clergymen who were "perfectly independent" of Strachan. Similarly, no doubt with the Kingston dispute much on their minds, the clergy and laity who were present passed a resolution stating that contributions to the episcopal endowment fund in Upper Canada — the creation of such funds had been authorized by the 1853 visitation — should "be solicited on the express condition that the clerical and lay delegates from the several congregations *within the limits of each diocese respectively shall be permitted to elect their own bishop.*"[110] Although the purpose of this resolution was clearly to ensure that the High Church clergy of central and eastern Upper Canada would be barred in voting in an episcopal election in the western part of the province, Strachan responded by publicly expressing his support of the principle of local synodical elections.[111] Cronyn, who seemed to be everywhere soliciting contributions to the western endowment fund, relayed Strachan's message to meetings of clergy in Hamilton and Simcoe.[112] Interestingly enough, however, not even Strachan's conciliatory stance could prevent the Simcoe meeting, as well as a meeting held at an unspecified location in the Home District, from passing resolutions identical to the one that had recently been passed in London.[113]

As if all this in-fighting was not enough, High Churchmen and Evangelicals tangled over the issue of rectory patronage. During the summer of 1852 the local legislature passed an act vesting in the Church Society the patronage of forty-four rectories established by Lieutenant Governor Sir John Colborne in 1836, which essentially meant that individuals appointed to these charges would now be nominated not by the governor general in consultation with the bishop, as had previously been the case, but by an organization representing the clergy and laity of the entire church.[114] This piece of news triggered a lengthy debate in the *Church*. In August 1852 an editorial dealing with the government's action suggested that, whenever a rectory became vacant, the bishop should appoint one of three candidates nominated beforehand by members of the Church Society.[115] When a correspondent named "D.C.L." criticized this suggestion and recommended instead that the bishop have exclusive control over all clerical appointments,[116] the whole subject of rectory patronage became charged with emotion. Another correspondent, "A Well-Wisher of the Church Society," noted that the *Church*'s plan would vest excessive power in a Toronto group which had already shown its incompetence in allowing the Church Society's secretary to default with more than £1,000, whereas the acceptance of "D.C.L."'s proposal might enable Strachan's successors as bishop to place "over parishes men of the orthodoxy of whose opinions the Church is not satisfied."[117] In response, "D.C.L." warned against the dangers of according the laity a greater voice in church affairs,[118] a warning echoed by Adam Townley.[119] Other churchmen, however, were more sympathetic to the idea that the bishop's power over rectory appointments should be shared with the clergy and laity. "A Presbyter of the Diocese of Toronto" and "A Rector," viewing parish clergymen as the individuals most intimately acquainted with religious conditions at the local level, proposed that the bishop make rectory appointments with the advice and consent of special clerical councils in the area concerned and the churchwardens of the vacant rectory.[120]

It was not long before the controversy over rectory patronage developed into a serious confrontation between Strachan and the Low Church party. At a meeting of the Church Society in November 1852, Strachan attacked the rectory bill as another instance of state oppression and stressed that "it shall never be said that the first Bishop of Toronto permitted, without decided remonstrance, the curtailment of privileges which our Prelates in Canada have always exercised, because from a false delicacy he was ashamed to defend them."[121] This declaration, together with certain resolutions stating that rectory patronage should be administered by Strachan and his successors as bishop, aroused the hostility of four Evangelical clergymen—Benjamin

Cronyn, S.B. Ardagh, C.C. Brough and Dominick Blake — all of whom took the position that the church could hardly expect to prosper if the laity were forever to be excluded from the management of ecclesiastical affairs. Eventually, after a long and often stormy debate, the meeting passed a compromise resolution indicating that rectory patronage was to be vested in Strachan merely for the remainder of his incumbency, and a committee was formed to draft the necessary amendments to the Church Society's constitution.[122]

Strachan was quite satisfied with the results of this meeting, and in a letter to the SPG in late November he claimed sole credit for quashing a revolt against his authority and predicted that the Church Society committee would recommend the ceding, in perpetuity, of rectory patronage to the episcopacy.[123] But as it turned out, his optimism was premature. In the first week of December the committee, ignoring the terms of the resolution already agreed on, published a report which echoed Strachan's argument that rectory appointments should always come under episcopal jurisdiction, but which also stated that all such appointments should be subject to the veto of the Church Society's lay and clerical members.[124] These controversial proposals would undoubtedly have sparked another bout of internal feuding had Strachan not decided to assume the role of conciliator. At the Church Society's annual meeting in June 1853 he was able to avoid a confrontation by suggesting that further debate on the rectory question be postponed pending the outcome of current discussions regarding the division of the diocese of Toronto. Although this cautious approach was criticized by E.J. Boswell, a High Churchman, Strachan's influence proved decisive. The meeting passed a resolution stating that the debate on the rectory question was to be temporarily halted.[125]

The Low Church position in this controversy was not based on any philosophical commitment to the rights of the laity: when the diocese of Huron was created in 1857, one of the first acts of the new synod was to give Benjamin Cronyn exclusive control over rectory patronage.[126] Yet, even so, the Low Church party's stance on rectory patronage was closely intertwined with its approach to the question of church government. For Evangelicals, a greater lay presence in ecclesiastical government would help to ensure the theological orthodoxy of Upper Canadian Anglicanism, not only by paving the way for the election of Low Church episcopal candidates but also by strengthening the forces of "sound" religion at every level of the church. Consequently, when they demanded that the Church Society be given a role in the administration of rectory patronage, they were essentially proposing a system by which clergymen and laymen of their own theological camp could oversee many of the clerical appointments of Strachan and his successors. They were also publicizing their belief that the Anglican communion in Upper Canada would no longer be plagued by Tractarianism if the laity, with its strong commitment to the Evangelical doctrinal position, was able to exert its rightful influence in the church.

The Evangelicals' conviction that a greater lay voice in church affairs would combat the influence of Tractarianism was expressed in a couple of *Echo* editorials. Declaring in October 1852 that "no Convocation can do the work assigned to it, or be otherwise than injurious to the Church, unless each order in the Church be fully and fairly represented," the *Echo* quoted an article from an English journal which stressed that lay representation in an Anglican synod would check the spread of "semi-Romanism."[127] Later the same month an *Echo* editorial on the rectory dispute argued that, since Strachan's authority as bishop was already excessive, the patronage in question should be vested in the parochial committees of the Church Society. It then quoted the claim of another paper that "Colonial Bishops now have in their hands the power which enables them to repress independent thought, and to mould the opinion of their dependents to their own views."[128] Considering the *Echo*'s anxiety about the influence of Tractarianism in Upper Canada, the implication of this second editorial was clearly that the presence of the laity in a more democratic form of church government would serve as an effective counterweight to the ability of a High Church bishop such as Strachan to impose his doctrinal principles on his clerical subordinates.

Despite all this wrangling between High and Low Churchmen, the two groups had a similar view of their church's status in Upper Canada. From the time of the union of 1841 to the secularization of the clergy reserves, only one Evangelical clergyman, C.B. Gribble of Dunnville, came out in opposition to the policy of church establishment.[129] All other members of the Low Church party stood side by side with their High Church colleagues in defending the Church of Eng-

In His Name

land's share of the clergy reserves and in opposing the voluntarist crusade for the complete separation of church and state. Their loyalty to the Anglican "party line" was revealed at the visitations held in 1851, 1853 and 1854, when resolutions protesting against the clergy reserves agitation were passed with the unanimous consent of all present.[130] It was also revealed in a number of statements, made by such Evangelicals as Benjamin Cronyn, C.C. Brough, William Herchmer, William Bleasdell and S.B. Ardagh, on the issue of church-state relations.[131] Typical of these statements were the ones by Cronyn and Bleasdell. At the 1851 visitation Cronyn supported the policy of church establishment by insisting that, in countries entirely dependent upon the voluntary system, religion "is uniformly found, among the great mass of people, to degenerate and decline ... religious division and animosity increase — erroneous tenets gain strength and prevalence — and infidelity itself spreads to an unwanted extent."[132] Even stronger language was used by Bleasdell in an 1850 speech at a parish meeting in Port Trent, in which he declared that the legislature's recent resolutions on the clergy reserves — resolutions calling for complete secularization — were "a factious pandering to that insatiable spirit of democracy which will never be contented until every Institution essentially British is swept from our Land."[133]

Yet, if Evangelicals and High Churchmen shared a common perspective on church-state relations, they also had serious differences over the tactics to be adopted in defending the church's interests and privileges. A good case in point was the church's response to the clergy reserves agitation of the early 1850s. In the charge delivered at the visitation of 1853, Strachan suggested that Anglican representatives in the House of Assembly should cooperate with their Roman Catholic counterparts from Lower Canada in protecting the endowments of their respective churches.[134] Barely one month had passed after the delivery of this charge before a correspondent of the *Echo*, "A Frontier Synodian Layman," made it known that Strachan's suggestion had "given rise to much excitement among all those who, strong in the faith and in determined Protestant abhorence of Popery in every shape, repudiate all idea of union ... with their bitterest and most malignant foe, even to save their own property from the common spoliator!"[135] The *Echo* commended these remarks and also gave its approval to an article published in the Chatham *Planet*, which asked pointedly if Upper

Canadian Anglicans were not appalled to see their church "crouching at the feet of Catholicism, and imploring, through her highest dignitaries, the aid of her oldest and greatest enemy, to guard her in the continued enjoyment of her temporalities."[136]

The divergent positions of the two factions on the issue of the reserves again became apparent in early 1854, when the *Echo* coupled an attack on the plans of the "secularizationists" with the suggestion that the reserves be shared among all denominations in proportion to their numerical strength."[137] These differences grew even sharper when, on the eve of the 1854 election, the *Echo* declared that Anglicans should rely not "on men or measures, but on Him to whom the earth belongs," and that the clergy reserves question was far less important than the task of spreading the Christian message and maintaining inter-denominational harmony.[138] While there is no evidence that the *Echo*'s combination of liberalism and apathy on the reserves question had support among Evangelical clergymen, its attitude did represent a serious problem to the church since dissent on a matter as fundamental as the reserves could have profoundly damaging effects if it were allowed to spread. Determined to crush the virus in its initial stages, the *Church* lashed out at the *Echo*'s "lukewarmness" and asserted that Anglicans who failed to do their "utmost to avert the curse which inevitably attends the crime of sacrilege, from blighting this flourishing land" was neither a true churchman nor an Upper Canadian patriot.[139]

Another controversy over the church's strategy in the era of disestablishment was directly related to developments in the field of education. In the post-rebellion period the Low Church and High Church parties were united in their opposition to the common schools system: resolutions attacking the system and demanding the right to establish separate schools were passed unanimously at the visitations of the early 1850s.[140] In addition, since not a single dissenting voice was heard when the Baldwin university bill of 1849 was greeted with a chorus of denunciation in Anglican circles, it would appear that Evangelical and High Church clergymen were then fully agreed both on the value of King's College and on the dangers posed by the secular University of Toronto. At the same time, however, the clergy's fragmentation along theological lines was a serious hindrance to the church's efforts to respond in an aggressive and effective fashion to the

In His Name

"godless" nature of the new educational order. Just how serious it was became apparent in the early 1850s, when the loss of King's College prompted Strachan to establish the exclusively Anglican Trinity College. As early as October 1850, "A Clergyman of the Church of England" wrote a letter to the *Church* declaring that, "as I fear Oxford and her influences in England, so do *I fear the new (to be) Episcopal University in Canada.*"[141]

This conviction that Trinity College would be a bastion of High Anglicanism imperilled the future of the "church university." At the 1851 visitation ten clergymen refused to sign a petition on behalf of Trinity College,[142] and according to P.B. de Blaquière, who had been appointed first chancellor of the University of Toronto, several other clergymen would have joined their rebellious colleagues had they not been afraid of incurring episcopal displeasure.[143] Later the same year the publication of a list of subscribers to Trinity's endowment fund showed that, while the new institution enjoyed the support of nine Evangelicals, it was conspicuously weak in western Upper Canada, where the Low Church party was strongest; indeed, the list, besides disclosing that Cronyn's parish of London had contributed nothing to the endowment fund, made no mention either of Cronyn himself or of seven of his fellow Evangelicals in the western region, namely Francis Evans, Richard Flood, Thomas Green, A. St. George Caulfield, Michael Boomer, F.A. O'Meara and B.C. Hill.[144] Still more revealing of the opposition of western Evangelicals to Trinity College was a statement made by Strachan in a June 1851 letter to the SPG: Strachan attacked "the restless faction of the west" for "plotting to get the Revd. Mr. Cronyn appointed Bishop for their division," and accused Cronyn himself, a "very low Churchman" who was "better calculated for a political agitator than a Bishop," of being "the focus of all the agitations against the Society's plans & me for supporting peace & order among the Clergy of that Section." He then declared that Cronyn "did all he could to oppose Trinity College and to bolster up Toronto University & prevented those over whom he had any influence from subscribing to its Funds."[145]

When all these disputes are taken together, it becomes easy to understand why both the *Church* and individual clergymen called for greater unity within the Anglican fold. In June 1853 the *Church* argued, in one of the many editorials of the late 1840s and early 1850s addressed to the problem of Anglican factionalism, that, since "the spirit of party is utterly at variance with, nay most injurious to, the best interests of religion," members of the Church of England should "rest in agreement ... upon the many and great principles in which we are all one, rather than array ourselves against each other on the few points of which our minds take different views."[146] Similar sentiments were expressed by two High Churchmen. In an 1848 letter to the *Church*, W.S. Darling emphasized that theological differences should never be allowed to "lead those who are bound by the same vows ... to regard each other with feelings of unkindliness, or sentiments of ungenerous suspicion," and that such differences could be submerged if clergymen concentrated on the performance of their pastoral duties.[147] A few years later, in a sermon delivered at the 1853 visitation, Henry Patton declared that,

> if differences of opinion there must be, let us at least exercise mutual charity, and forebearance. If we cannot agree on all other points, we may at least agree to love one another, and to respect each other's conscientious opinions or convictions. Let us avoid all reviling and bitterness, all bandying of names and titles of reproach. Let us shun the shibboleths of mere party .... let us carefully avoid every thing that may tend to exasperate existing differences, and let us gladly embrace every opportunity of drawing more closely the bonds of brotherly affection.[148]

Patton's advice was wise, but few people were listening. Instead of subsiding, the hostility between High Churchmen and Evangelicals was to grow steadily through the 1850s and 1860s, with each side gloating after its victories and nursing grudges after its defeats. In the episcopal election of 1862 in the new diocese of Ontario — the long-delayed see of Kingston — A.N. Bethune withdrew from the race when he realized that the Evangelical candidate, John Travers Lewis, could not be beaten. Four years later Bethune finally won an episcopal election, this one for the post of Strachan's coadjutor bishop in the diocese of Toronto. Yet he must soon have wondered whether the prize had been worth the trouble. From the time he succeeded Strachan as bishop in 1867, Bethune watched helplessly as High Churchmen and

In His Name

Evangelicals fought tooth and claw, principally over the place of ritual in Anglican religious worship. To compound his problems, while most of the clergy in his diocese were High Churchmen, their influence was offset by an increasingly vocal and powerful laity. The Low Church party's greatest triumph occurred in 1879, after Bethune's death, with the election of the moderate Evangelical Arthur Sweatman as bishop of Toronto. When the new bishop stated that divisions in the church were "inevitable and allowable," he provided dramatic proof of how entrenched Anglican factionalism had become.[149]

* * * * *

The constant bickering of the High Church and Low Church parties had severe consequences. One result of Anglican disunity before 1854 was that the Church of England was threatened with internal disintegration at the very moment when it was struggling to ward off the blows of rival denominations and Reform politicians. Another was that the church's efforts to defend its interests in a politically difficult period were seriously jeopardized. A church that was bitterly divided over Trinity College and the strategy to be employed in guarding the clergy reserves was hardly in a strong position to protect itself against its opponents. Moreover, internal feuding over Trinity College and the clergy reserves left the impression that the movement for the separation of church and state had the support of some segments of the Anglican community, an impression that could only encourage the voluntarist forces in their campaign against the Upper Canadian church. Strachan said, in an 1851 address on the subject of Trinity College, that "it is indeed to be lamented that we should have any among ourselves indifferent or hostile to our attainment of justice, for though insignificant in number, they are seized upon by our enemies as a pretence for continuing their oppressions, under the assumption that we are not unanimous." This statement was coupled with the warning that the church would soon take action "so that such rotten branches may be cut off and banished from her fold."[150]

Anglican in-fighting also highlighted one of the most ironic aspects of the Church of England's experience in Upper Canada. By the time Patton issued his appeal for church unity in 1853, Tractarian theology had provided some clergymen with a strong sense of identity while at the same time playing an important part in the church's evolution into a "spiritual society." Yet Tractarianism had also weakened the Anglican cause by triggering debates that, in the end, turned the church into two warring camps. This would have been a serious problem for any denomination, but for the Church of England it was especially so. From the late 1830s on, the Church of England, faced with the impending destruction of the policy of church establishment, had begun to turn increasingly inwards, looking forward to the day when it could shun the entanglements of the temporal world and devote itself exclusively to its pastoral duties. Redefining itself in this way, however, ignored reality. By 1854 the factionalism of the Church of England's own clergy and laity had left it without a clear view of its religious character, the very thing it needed most if it was to withdraw from its alliance with the state and confine its energies to the salvation of souls. With its sense of political purpose undermined by its opponents, the Church of England was faced with the task of concentrating on its religious mission when its own people could not agree on what that mission was.

In His Name

NOTES

1. The above section on the history and ideas of the Oxford movement is based on the following: Yngve Brilioth, *The Anglican Revival: Studies in the Oxford Movement* (London, 1933); R.W. Church, *The Oxford Movement, Twelve Years, 1833-1845* (London, 1891); Geoffrey Faber, *Oxford Apostles: A Character Study of the Oxford Movement* (London, 1933); and John Henry Newman, *Apologia Pro Vita Sua* (London, 1888).
2. See Chapter Four.
3. Strachan Papers, Strachan to Newman, 13 Aug. 1839.
4. Strachan Letter Book, 1839-43, Strachan to Newman, 22 May 1840.
5. Strachan, *A Charge Delivered on the 9th September, 1841*, pp. 17-18.
6. Strachan Letter Book, 1839-43, Strachan to Bethune, 21 May 1842.
7. Strachan Sermons, "Through the tender Mercy of our God; whereby the day spring from on high hath visited us" (25 Dec. 1843).
8. Strachan, *A Charge Delivered on the 10th June, 1844*, pp. 53-54.
9. Strachan Letter Book, 1844-49, Strachan to Patton, 19 Nov. 1845.
10. Strachan, *A Charge Delivered in June MDCCCXLVII*, p. 35.
11. See Strachan, *A Charge Delivered on the 9th September, 1841*, pp. 13-18; *A Charge Delivered on the 6th June, 1844*, pp. 20-23 and 54-57; *A Charge Delivered in June MDCCCXLVII*, pp. 38-45; *A Charge Delivered in May MDCCCLI*, pp. 12-13. Also, the following sermons in the collection of Strachan Sermons at the AO: "Earnestly contend for the faith which was once delivered to the saints" (9 March 1834); "When the fulness of time was come God sent forth his Son made of a woman" (25 Dec. 1835); "Lo I am with you always even to the end of the world" (10 Oct. 1838); "That in the dispensation of the fulness of time, he might gather together in one, all things in Christ" (25 Dec. 1838); "And they continued steadfastly in breaking of bread and in prayers" (24 March 1839); "Ye are our Epistle written in our hearts known and read of all men" (22 Dec. 1839, first sermon as bishop); "The Lord added daily to the Church such as should be saved" (28 May 1840); "Whereas there is among you Envying and Strife and Divisions are ye not Carnal and walk as men?" (11 July 1840, "something from Newman"); "And Jesus came and spoke unto them saying all power is given unto me in heaven and in earth" (20 April 1841); "For I say unto you among those that are born of women there is not a greater Prophet than John the Baptist" (24 June 1841); "But I say unto you, I will not drink henceforth of this fruit of the vine" (Dec. 1843); "But I speak concerning Christ and his Church" (10 Aug. 1845); "Thy

Kingdom come" (12 June 1844); "Now when David knew that the writing was signed he went into his house" (Feb. 1845); "Hold fast the form of sound works" (15 May 1845); "Blessed be the Lord who daily loadeth us with benefits even the God of our Salvation" (25 Sept. 1845); "Choose you this day whom ye will serve" (17 Oct. 1847); "And the Lord said unto the Servant Go out into the highways and hedges and compel them to come in" (12 Dec. 1847); "But continue them in the things which thou has learned and been assured of — knowing of whom thou hast learned them" (30 July 1848); "So we being many are one Body in Christ" (22 Oct. 1848).

12 Strachan Letter Book, 1844-49, Strachan to Bethune, ? Nov. 1845.

13 Strachan, *A Charge Delivered on the 6th June, 1844*, p. 30; Strachan Letter Book, 1844-49, Strachan to the bishop of Montreal, 7 May 1845, and Strachan to John Fletcher, 27 Nov. 1848. Even this attitude of flexibility had its limits, however. When H.J. Grasett, an Evangelical, refused to wear the surplice while preaching at the opening of St. George's Church, Toronto, Strachan did not bother to conceal his annoyance. See Strachan Letter Book, 1844-49, Strachan to Grasett, 4 Sept. 1845; Strachan to Bethune, 7 Oct. 1845; and Strachan to William Boulton, 14 Oct. 1845.

14 Strachan, *A Charge Delivered on the 9th September, 1841*, pp. 23-24; *A Charge Delivered on the 6th June, 1844*, pp. 24-41; *A Charge Delivered in June MDCCCXLVII*, pp. 62-64.

15 The *Church*, 24 Aug. 1839. Even as late as 1846 Bethune could still announce that he had read little of the *Tracts for the Times* and that his religious opinions had been formed before the birth of the Oxford movement (the *Church*, 18 Sept. 1846).

16 Ibid., 19 Oct. 1839.

17 Ibid., 15 May 1841.

18 Ibid., 26 Feb. 1842.

19 Ibid., 4 April 1842.

20 Ibid., 10 and 17 March 1843.

21 Ibid., 28 April 1843.

22 Ibid., 4 Aug. 1843.

23 Ibid., 14 Nov. 1845.

24 Ibid., 5 March 1847.

25 See especially the *Church*, 24 June, 15 July, 5 and 26 Aug. 1837; 3 Feb. 1838; 16 Feb., 27 April, 8 June, and 19 Oct. 1839; 28 March and 30 May 1840; 18 Sept., 31 Oct., 13 Nov. and 27 Nov. 1841; 1 Jan. and 2 Sept. 1842; 16 June 1843.

In His Name

26 Ibid., 24 June, 5 and 19 Aug., and 28 Oct. 1837 ("The English Layman"); 29 July and 9 Nov. 1839; 23 Jan., 24 Oct., and 28 Nov. 1840 ("The English Layman"); 20 Feb., 29 May, 5 June and 24 July 1843; 6 Dec. 1844; 28 March, 30 May and 31 Oct. 1845; 20 Feb., 6 and 27 Nov. 1846.

27 Ibid., 6 March 1841; 4 April and 2 Dec. 1842; 7 April and 26 May 1843; 4 April, 14 June and 27 Nov. 1844; 7 Feb. and 19 Sept. 1845; 17 April 1846; 11 Feb. 1848.

28 Ibid., 21 Aug. 1841 and 10 Oct. 1845.

29 For later decades, it is easier to arrive at precise figures because the holding of regular synods led to repeated votes in which Low and High Churchmen broke into their separate camps. One scholar, Harry E. Turner, has estimated that by 1879 four-fifths of the clergy in the diocese of Toronto were High Church in their theological orientation. See Turner's "The Evangelical Movement in the Church of England in the Diocese of Toronto, 1839-1879," M.A. Thesis, University of Toronto, 1959, p. 10.

30 Osler Papers, Series I-1, vol. 2, Osler to Procter, 22 June 1846.

31 See the following: Arthur Palmer, "On the Nature and Extent of Christian Unity" (sermon preached at meeting of the Western Clerical Association; published in the *Church*, 25 Aug. 1838); "The Christian Shepherd: An ordination sermon, preached in Christ Church, Montreal, on Sunday the 12th of August, and in St. James's Church, Toronto, on Sunday the 7th October, by the Rev. A.N. Bethune, Rector of Cobourg" (published in the *Church*, 10 Nov. 1838); sermon preached by James Padfield at meeting of the Eastern Clerical Association (published in the *Church*, 13 April 1839); sermon preached by William Leeming at meeting of Niagara Clerical Association (referred to in the *Church*, 9 Nov. 1839); sermon preached by John Grier at meeting of the Midland Clerical Association (referred to in the *Church*, 29 Feb. 1840); A.E. Elliott, "A Sermon, Preached in Christ Church, Hamilton, on the 13th May, 1840, before the Western Clerical Society, and published at their request" (the *Church*, 25 July 1840); "The Church of God. A Sermon preached in the Cathedral Church of St. James, Toronto, on Thursday, Sept. 9, 1841, at the primary Visitation of the Lord Bishop of the Diocese, by the Rev. A.N. Bethune, Rector of Cobourg and Chaplain to the Lord Bishop" (published in the *Church*, 18 Sept. 1841); *Ask for the Old Paths. A Sermon Preached at the Opening of the New Church of St. James, at Dundas, in Upper Canada, on Sunday, December 31st, 1843: by James Beaven* (Cobourg, 1843); "A Sermon, Preached in the Cathedral Church of St. James, Toronto, on Thursday, June 6th, 1844, on Occasion of the Visitation of the Lord Bishop of the Diocese by the Rev. William Macaulay" (published in the

Church, 28 June 1844); Arthur Palmer, "On the Difficulties and Encouragements of the Christian Ministry" (published in the *Church*, 16 and 23 July 1847); A.N. Bethune, *A Charge Delivered on April 29, 1852*; Henry Patton, *Attachment to the Church of God*; Scadding Sermons, A 108, "And suddenly there was with the angel a multitude of the heavenly host" (25 Dec. 1848); ibid., A 106, "And it came to pass a long time after that the Lord had given rest unto Israel from all their enemies round about" (n.d.); ibid., A 107, "The lip of Truth shall be established for ever" (n.d.); ibid., A 107, "Surely in vain the net is spread in the sight of any bird" (21 Oct. 1850).

32 Patton, *Attachment to the Church of God*, pp. 5-14.

33 James Beaven, *A Catechism on the Thirty-Nine Articles of the Church of England* (New York, 1853); *A Help to Catechising for the Use of Clergymen, Schools, and Private Families* (New York, 1843); *An Account of the Life and Writings of S. Irenaeus, Bishop of Lyons and Martyr* (London, 1841), pp. ix-x, xiv-xvi, 74-87, 147, 172-76.

34 T.B. Fuller, *The Roman Catholic Church Not the Mother Church of England; or the Church of England, the Church Originally Planted in England* (1844), pp. 10-12.

35 The *Church*, 3 July 1851, 6 April 1839, 28 March 1840.

36 Ibid., 3 July 1851. For yet another exposition of High Church doctrines, see *A Memorial of the Reverend William Honeywood Ripley ... Being the sermon preached in Trinity Church ... Oct. the 28th, 1849. By Henry Scadding* (Toronto, 1849).

37 The *Church*, 2 Dec. 1842.

38 Ibid., 26 March 1842, 13 Jan. and 24 Feb. 1843.

39 Ibid., 20 March 1841.

40 A reference to Kennedy's sermon can be found in the 10 March issue of the *Church*; *Questions on the Chief Festivals and Holy Days ... By the Rev. Henry Patton* (Toronto, 1851).

41 See SPG Letters, Series C, Box IV/45, no. 552, William Shaw, 13 April 1841; and Box IV/43, no. 517, G.M. Armstrong, 20 April 1841; also letters to the *Church*, 26 March and 25 Nov. 1842, and 13 Jan. 1843 from "A Catholic Presbyter," "Prester Ergenia," and "Anglicanus."

42 The *Church*, 18 Aug. 1838.

43 Ibid., 11 April 1852.

44 Ibid., 13 April 1839 (sermon preached by James Padfield at meeting of

the Eastern Clerical Association), 23 Nov. 1839 (letter from Henry Scadding), 24 Jan. 1850 (letter from a layman), 22 Feb. 1849 (letter from "A.B."); Scadding Sermons, A 106, "And David built there an Altar unto the Lord" (n.d.). In some cases, innovations in Anglican ritual led to conflicts between clergymen and their congregations. See the F.J. Lundy diaries, 11 June and 9 July 1850, at the AO.

45 Strachan Sermons, "The Lord added daily to the Church such as should be saved" (throughout 1840 and 1842); "Whereas there is among you Envying and Strife and Division are ye not Carnal and walk as men" (15 July 1840; 6 June, 3 Aug. 1841; September 1842; 23 and 30 Sept. 1842; 3 Aug. 1851); "And the Lord said unto the Servant Go out into the highways and hedges and compel them to come in" (throughout 1847 and 1849).

46 The *Church*, 8 June 1839; 30 May and 31 Oct. 1840; 13 March and 18 Sept. 1841; 1 Jan. and 26 March 1842; 22 Sept. and 6 Oct. 1843; 1 March 1844; 6 June, 15 Aug. and 12 Sept. 1845. Also: a sermon preached by Arthur Palmer at a meeting of the Western Clerical Association (the *Church*, 25 Aug. 1838); a sermon preached by A.E. Elliott at a meeting of the Western Clerical Association (the *Church*, 25 July 1840); A.N. Bethune, "The Church of God" (the *Church*, 18 Sept. 1841); *Address to a Large and Respectable Body of Freemasons, on their laying the Corner Stone of St. George's Lodge, no. 15, and of Several Other Lodges* (St. Catherine's, U.C., 1835); *A Sermon, Preached by the Rev. W. Macaulay, Rector of St. Mary Magdalene, Picton, Upper Canada, on Monday, March 20th, 1837, on occasion of the funeral of Mrs. Catherine Wright* (Picton, 1837); Scadding Sermons, A 107, "Behold the days come, saith the Lord" (1844); ibid., A 106, "All the abominations that were spread in the Land of Judah" (n.d.); ibid., A 107, "The lip of truth shall be established for ever" (n.d.); ibid., A 106, "And it came to pass a long time after that the Lord had given rest unto Israel from all their enemies round about" (n.d.); ibid., A 107, "Surely in vain the net is spread in the sight of any bird" (21 Oct. 1850); ibid., A 107, "Lease ye from man whose breath is in his nostrils, for wherein is he to be accounted of" (1 Dec. 1850). Finally, see *Methodism unmasked, in a Review of "A Vindication of the Methodist Church" (so called). "In a Pastoral Address." By Benjamin Nankevill, Wesleyan Minister. By J.A. Mulock, Presbyter of the Church of England* (Carleton Place; Ogdensburgh, N.Y., 1850).

47 The last two points are well illustrated in Arthur Palmer's sermon, cited above.

48 The *Church.*, 10 Nov. 1838.

49 Ibid., 19 May 1838 ("The English Layman").

50 Ibid., 20 Nov. 1846.

51 See Chapter Four for another reference to this address.

52 Strachan, *Address to the Clergy of the Archdeaconry of York*, pp. 9-11.

53 On Anglican Evangelicalism, see: L.E. Elliott-Binns, *The Evangelical Movement in the English Church* (London, 1928); G.R. Balleine, *History of the Evangelical Party in the Church of England* (London, 1909); Charles J. Abbey and John H. Overton, *The English Church in the Eighteenth Century* (London, 1902), pp. 313-403; F.W. Cornish, *The English Church in the Nineteenth Century*, 2 vols. (London, 1910), I, 1-34; S.C. Carpenter, *Eighteenth Century Church and People* (London, 1959), pp. 17-36; and Horton Davies, *Worship and Theology in England: From Watts and Wesley to Maurice, 1690-1850* (Princeton, N.J., 1961), pp. 210-40.

54 Walter Alison Phillips, ed., *History of the Church of Ireland*, vol. III: *The Modern Church* (London, 1933), pp. 325-59 and 381.

55 The following litmus test was used in determining which clergymen were Evangelicals: all clergymen who either expressed open hostility to Tractarianism or took the Low Church side in the religious controversies of the 1840s and 1850s (or did both) have been placed within the Evangelical camp. Using this rule of thumb, I have identified thirty-three clergymen as Evangelicals: Samuel Armour, A.F. Atkinson, R.D. Cartwright, Benjamin Cronyn, H.J. Grasett, Francis Evans, Richard Flood, Thomas Green, R.V. Rogers, George Mortimer, Saltern Givins, Jonathan Shortt, William Herchmer, A. St. George Caulfield, Michael Boomer, E.C. Elwood, William Bleasdell, F.A. O'Meara, C.C. Brough, S.B. Ardagh, F.L. Osler, H.C. Cooper, B.C. Hill, C.B. Gribble, Alexander Sanson, R. [?] Revell, Hannibal Mulkins, E.C. Bower, G.O. Stuart, F.W. Sandys, John Fletcher, T.W. Marsh and Alexander Pyne. For profiles of five Evangelical clergymen, see Osler Papers (Series I-1, vol. 2), Diaries and Journals ("Sketch of my Life"); *Reminiscences of Colonial Life and Missionary Adventure in both Hemispheres. By the Rev. Alex. Pyne, A.M.* (London, 1875); *The Life and Letters of the Rev. George Mortimer*; SPG Letters, "G mss," vol. 3, Journals of the Upper Canada Clergy Society, Journal of B.C. Hill; and Rev. S.J. Boddy, *A Brief Memoir of the Rev. Samuel B. Ardagh* (Toronto, 1874).

56 The fifteen clergymen stationed west of Toronto were: A.F. Atkinson (St. Catharines), Benjamin Cronyn (London), Francis Evans (Simcoe), Richard Flood (Thames River), Thomas Green (London District), A. St. George Caulfield (St. Thomas), Michael Boomer (Galt), E.C. Elwood (Goderich), F.A. O'Meara (Lake Huron), B.C. Hill (Niagara), C.B. Gribble (Dunnville), F.W. Sandys (Chatham), John Fletcher (Mono), T.W. Marsh (Elora), and Alexander Pyne (Lake St. Clair). The four

In His Name

Evangelicals in the Kingston area were R.D. Cartwright, R.V. Rogers, William Herchmer and G.O. Stuart.

57 Those born in Ireland were: Samuel Armour, A.F. Atkinson, Benjamin Cronyn, Francis Evans, Thomas Green, A. St. George Caulfield, Michael Boomer, E.C. Elwood, F.A. O'Meara, C.C. Brough, S.B. Ardagh and Alexander Pyne. Armour received his educational training at the University of Glasgow.

58 See S.W. Horall, "The Clergy and the Election of Bishop Cronyn," *OH*, LVIII (December 1966), pp. 205-20; and Christopher Headon, "The Influence of the Oxford Movement upon the Church of England in Eastern and Central Canada, 1840-1900," Diss., Religious Studies, McGill University, 1974, p. 190. Horrall claims that twenty clergymen voted for Bethune, while Headon has increased this total to twenty-three.

59 Strachan Letter Book, 1827-39, Strachan to the archbishop of Dublin, 28 April 1834. The "Irishness" of the Upper Canadian church is noted in Donald Harman Akenson, *The Irish in Ontario: A Study in Rural History* (Kingston and Montreal, 1984), pp. 263-67.

60 Turner, "The Evangelical Movement in the Church of England in the Diocese of Toronto," p. 17.

61 Horall, "The Clergy and the Election of Bishop Cronyn."

62 The *Church*, 13 Feb. 1841 (report of the Midland Clerical Association); Strachan Letter Book, 1839-43, Strachan to G.J. Mountain, 6 July 1841; the *Church*, 25 Nov. 1842 (reference to the Rev. A. Williams's refusal to join inter-denominational societies); ibid., 24 Jan. 1845 (letter from J. Wilson); Strachan, *A Charge Delivered on the 9th September, 1841*, pp. 29-31; the *Church*, 21 May 1842 (letter from "E"); ibid., 26 Aug. 1842 and 31 March 1843.

63 See Strachan Letter Book, 1839-43, Strachan to Wade, 27 Jan. 1841; the *Church*, 16 Sept. 1842 and 10 Feb. 1843; Strachan Letter Book, 1844-49, Strachan to R.V. Rogers, 12 April 1845; ibid., Strachan to R. Shanklin, 18 Nov. 1848.

64 See Joseph Harris, *A Letter to the Hon. & Ven. Archdeacon Strachan in Reply to Some Passages in his "Letter to Dr. Chalmers on the Life and Character of Bishop Hobart," Respecting the Principles and Effects of the Bible Society* (York, 1833); the *Church*, 30 April 1842 (letter from T.E. Welby); ibid., 31 March 1843 (letter from "Candidus").

65 For information regarding Evangelical participation in these various organizations, see Osler Papers (Series I-1, vol. 2), F.L. Osler to Henry

Osler, 30 Aug. 1837, and Osler to Proctor, 13 June 1839; SPG Letters, "G mss," vol. 3, Journals of Upper Canada Clergy Society, Journal of B.C. Hill, 12 Dec. 1838, and Journals of Alexander Pyne, 16 Jan. 1842; the *Church*, 2 Oct. 1846, 7 July, 24 Nov. and 15 Dec. 1853; the *Echo*, 19 Oct. and 24 Nov. 1853, and 30 June and 3 Nov. 1854; Joseph Harris, *A Letter to the Hon. & Ven. Archdeacon Strachan*; and the *Life and Letters of the Rev. George Mortimer*, p. 290. For the *Echo*'s attitude towards inter-denominational organizations, see the following issues of that journal: 9 Dec. 1851, 14 July and 20 Oct. 1852. If the ministry of B.C. Hill was any indication, Low Church tolerance of inter-denominational organizations also entailed a highly cooperative attitude towards dissenters in all areas of religious life. See SPG Letters, "G mss," vol. 3, Journal of B.C. Hill; and ibid., Series C, Box IVB/42 and Box IV/42, no. 502, letters of Hill to Upper Canada Clergy Society.

66 See Osler Papers, Diaries and Journals (Series II-I), "Sketch of My Life"; Strachan Letter Book, 1844-49, Strachan to T.H.M. Bartlett, 8 Jan. 1845; Strachan to John Pope, 8 Jan. 1845; Strachan to R.V. Rogers, 5 May 1845; Strachan to F.W. Sandys, 24 June 1848; and the *Church*, 29 Jan. and 30 Dec. 1842 (letter from clergyman).

67 See Strachan letters cited above and the *Church*, 29 Jan. 1842.

68 The *Church*, 16 Dec. 1842.

69 Ibid., 6 Jan. 1843.

70 Ibid., 3 Feb. 1843. See also letter of "Prester Ergenia" on 13 Jan. 1843 relating to this controversy.

71 Ibid., 12 Feb., 5 March, 16 and 23 Dec. 1842; 12 and 19 Feb., 21 May, 4 and 11 June, 7 and 20 Aug., 3, 10 and 17 Sept. 1847; 4 Feb., 9 June, 28 Sept., 19 Oct., 16, 23 and 30 Nov. 1848; 1 Feb. and 21 Dec. 1848; 15 March, 5 and 12 April, 3 and 17 May, 7, 14 and 21 June, 2 and 23 August 1848; 3 Dec. 1849; 3, 10 and 31 Oct. 1850; and 3 Feb. and 30 June 1853.

72 Ibid., 31 Aug., 28 Sept., 19 Oct., 16, 23 and 30 Nov. 1848. Preaching without notes seems to have been quite common. See the following: Strachan Letter Book, 1852-66, Strachan to W. Tucker, 5 Nov. 1853; Osler Papers (Series II-1, vol. 2), Osler to Procter, 12 July 1837; F.L. Osler to Henry Osler, 30 Aug. 1837 and 15 Jan. 1838; Osler to Procter, 26 Oct. 1837; the *Church*, 25 March 1852 (letter from "Anglo-Catholic"); Scadding Papers (Diaries), 2 May 1847, 8 Oct. 1848.

73 The *Church*, 21 May, 4 and 11 June, 7 and 20 Aug., 3, 10 and 17 Sept. 1847. Cooper, later an editor of the *Echo*, also revealed his Low Church opinions in the 1847 pamphlet, *Characteristic Principles of the Church of England*.

In His Name

74 The *Church*, 29 May, 5 June and 24 July 1841; 12 Aug. 1842; 20 Oct. 1843; 22 Aug. 1845; 2 Oct. 1846; 5 Feb. and 26 March 1847; 31 Aug. 1848; 6 Sept. 1849; 3 Feb. and 18 Aug. 1853.

75 Osler Papers (Series I-1, vol. 2), Osler to Proctor, 13 Nov. 1843.

76 Strachan Letter Book, 1844-49, Strachan to Bethune, 29 Jan. 1844.

77 Ibid., Strachan to the bishop of Nova Scotia, 15 May 1846.

78 The *Church*, 15 Jan., 12 and 26 Feb., 12 March and 9 April 1847.

79 Ibid., 19 March 1847.

80 Ibid., 25 April and 24 May 1849.

81 Strachan criticized Atkinson and Grasett for supporting the *Berean* in a letter of 1845 (Strachan Letter Book, 1844-49, Strachan to Atkinson, 20 Oct. 1845). The *Berean* listed Rogers and Ardagh as its agents throughout the period of its publication; it also had agents in Toronto, Ancaster, Niagara, Dunnville and London.

82 The figure of 1,000 subscribers is taken from the 20 Oct. 1852 issue of the *Echo*. In addition to Cronyn, Stuart and McCaul, the *Echo*'s clerical supporters were: A. Jamieson, D.E. Blake, H.J. Grasett, Hannibal Mulkins, E. Baldwin, Francis Evans, A. St. George Caulfield, Thomas Greene, T.W. Marsh, J.W. Marsh, C.C. Brough, [?] Allen, [?] Alexander, Michael Boomer, [?] Hepden, George Mortimer, R.V. Rogers, Alexander Sanson, E. Grasett, and S.B. Ardagh; all these individuals were listed as supporters in the pages of the *Echo* itself. See the 24 Nov. 1853 issue for the members of the Board of Management, and the issues of 13 and 19 Oct. 1853 for references to Sanson and Rogers as the paper's agents.

83 The *Church*, 21 Sept. 1854, and the *Echo*, 29 Sept. 1854.

84 The *Echo*, 8 Dec. 1854.

85 J.D. Purdy, "John Strachan and the Diocesan Theological Institute at Cobourg, 1842-1852," *OH*, vol. LXV (June 1973), pp. 113-23.

86 This account of the Cobourg affair is based on: Strachan Letter Book, 1844-49, Strachan to Bethune, 29 Sept. 1845; Strachan to Ellis, 7 Oct. 1845; Strachan to W. Carus Wilson, 19 Jan. 1846; Strachan to Rev. F.S. Bevan, 20 Jan. 1846; Bishop Strachan Letters, Strachan to Bethune, 29 Dec. 1845; the *Church*, 23 Jan. 1846; SPG Letters, Series C, Box V/45, Robert Harding, October 1846.

87 Strachan Letter Book, 1844-49, Strachan to Wilson, 19 Jan. 1846.

88 Ibid., Strachan to Ellis, 7 Oct. 1845.

89 SPG Letters, Series C, Box V/45, Robert Harding, October 1845.

90   The *Church*, 22 May 1846.

91   Strachan Letter Book, 1844-49, "Narrative of a dispute with a Mr. Shanklin and Rev. A.F. Atkinson, *circa* 1846."

92   Ibid.

93   Ibid.

94   Bishop Strachan Letters, Strachan to Bethune, 23 Sept. 1846.

95   Strachan Letter Book, 1844-49, 9 and 16 Oct. 1846. For other material relating to the Cobourg affair, see the *Church*, 28 Aug. 1846 (letter from "A Proctor"), 4 Sept. 1846 (letter from "A Presbyter"), 11 Sept. 1846 (address presented to Strachan by the Anglican parishioners of Cobourg), and 18 Dec. 1846 (letter from T.S. Kennedy). The dispute is also dealt with in Purdy, "John Strachan and the Diocesan Theological Institute at Cobourg."

96   For the first reference to the plan to create a Kingston bishopric, see the *Church*, 12 May 1853.

97   Ibid., 16 March 1854 (letter of Alexander Pyne) and 6 April 1854 (letter of G.O. Stuart); Strachan Letter Book, 1852-66, Strachan to Stuart, 19 Dec. 1853; Bishop Strachan Letters, Strachan to Bethune, 28 Dec. 1853 and 4 Jan. 1854; SPG Letters, "D" 14, vols. 8-9, William Herchmer, 13 Feb. 1854.

98   The *Church*, 6 April and 16 May 1854.

99   *Published Correspondence and Papers Called Forth By a Canvas Among a Section of the Clergy of the Province of Toronto, Having in View the Recommendation of the Venerable the Archdeacon of York, in Said Diocese, as the Incumbent of the Proposed New Bishopric of Kingston, Canada West* (1854), pp. 32-36.

100 Ibid., p. 6.

101 Ibid., pp. 17-19.

102 Ibid., p. 7.

103 The *Church*, 26 Jan. 1854.

104 Ibid., 5 Jan. 1854.

105 *Published Correspondence and Papers*, pp. 21-25.

106 The *Echo*, 11 May 1853.

107 *Published Correspondence and Papers*, p. 3, and the *Church*, 5 Jan. 1854.

108 The *Church*, 16 Nov. 1854.

In His Name

109   J.W. Grant's claim in *A Profusion of Spires* (pp. 128 and 136) that Evangelicals tended to oppose the idea of synodical government is incorrect. The evidence clearly reveals a High Church-Low Church consensus on the subject of church government.

110   The *Church*, 23 March and 6 April 1854. The italics are those of the *Church*.

111   Ibid., 30 March 1854.

112   Ibid., 23 March 1854.

113   Ibid., 23 March and 13 May 1854.

114   The method of appointment previously followed was described by Strachan in his speech to a special meeting of the Church Society in 1852. See *Report of the Special General Meeting of the Church Society of the Diocese of Toronto, Held on Wednesday, 10 Nov., 1852, To Take into consideration the future disposal of the Patronage of the Rectories* (Toronto, 1852), p. 10.

115   The *Church*, 19 Aug. 1852.

116   Ibid., 2 Sept. 1852.

117   Ibid., 16 Sept. 1852.

118   Ibid., 23 Sept. 1852.

119   Ibid., 21 Oct. 1852.

120   Ibid., 4 Nov. 1852.

121   *Report of the Special General Meeting of the Church Society*, pp. 11-12.

122   Ibid., passim. The above account has been simplified somewhat in the interests of brevity and clarity. F.L. Osler broke from his fellow Evangelicals and supported Strachan's position; Dominick Blake has been classified as a Low Churchman because of his support of the *Echo*; and Thomas Fuller and William Bettridge, two moderate High Churchmen who often found themselves on the Evangelical side in religious controversies (the former was elected bishop of Niagara in 1875 with Evangelical support, and the latter voted for Cronyn in the 1857 episcopal election in the diocese of Huron), echoed the Low Church demand for a lay voice in rectory appointments.

123   SPG Letters, "D" 14, vols. 8-9, Strachan, 23 Nov. 1852.

124   The *Church*, 2 Dec. 1852. See also the letter from "An Incorporated Member of the Church Society" in ibid., 26 May 1853.

125   The proceedings of the meeting were reported in the *Church*, 16 June 1853.

126 Turner, "The Evangelical Movement in the Church of England in the Diocese of Toronto," pp. 194-95.
127 The *Echo*, 13 Oct. 1852.
128 Ibid., 27 Oct. 1852. See also ibid., 3 Nov. 1852.
129 SPG Letters, Series C, Box V/45, C.B. Gribble, 1 April 1841. Gribble's case is interesting in more ways than one. While he expressed Low Church views on several subjects, he also took the unorthodox step of refusing to administer the Eucharist to any individual who had violated church discipline. When this action led to Gribble's dismissal, his congregation sent a memorial of protest to Strachan, and Gribble himself published an apologia in the Niagara *Chronicle* and attacked Bethune in the London *Record*. See SPG Letters, Series C, Box V/45, C.B. Gribble, 6 July and 3 Dec. 1841; and Strachan's reply to Gribble's congregation, April 1843. Also: the *Church*, 2 June, 14 July and 22 Dec. 1843; and Strachan Papers, February 1843.
130 *Proceedings of Synod*, 1851, pp. 10-11; *Proceedings of Synod*, 1853, pp. 9-11 and 13-14; and *Proceedings of Synod*, 1854, p. 27.
131 *Proceedings of Synod*, 1851, speech of Benjamin Cronyn, p. 11; Strachan Papers, C.C. Brough to Strachan, 24 March 1841; SPG Letters, Series C, Box V/46, no. 544, William Herchmer, 3 March 1845; the *Church*, 1 Aug. 1850 (letter from William Bleasdell), and 8 March 1849 (speech by Ardagh at meeting of local branch of Church Society).
132 *Proceedings of Synod*, 1851, p. 11.
133 The *Church*, 1 Aug. 1850.
134 Strachan, *A Charge Delivered on Wednesday, Oct. 12, 1853*, pp. 48-49.
135 The *Echo*, 24 Nov. 1853.
136 Ibid.
137 Ibid., 30 March 1854.
138 Ibid., 30 June 1854.
139 The *Church*, 20 July 1854.
140 *Proceedings of Synod*, 1851, p. 12; *Proceedings of Synod*, 1853, pp. 14-15; *Proceedings of Synod*, 1854, p. 28.
141 The *Church*, 3 Oct. 1850.
142 This fact was disclosed by the *Church* itself on 10 July 1851 in the course of an attack on de Blaquière.
143 Ibid. De Blaquière also made a charge which appears groundless: he asserted that a majority of the clergy and laity were opposed to

In His Name

        Strachan's efforts to gain a charter for Trinity College.

144   The list was published as an appendix to Strachan's pastoral letter *Church University of Upper Canada* (pp. 52-64).

145   Strachan Letter Book, 1839-66, Strachan to Hawkins, 6 June 1851. Alan Hayes, in "The Struggle for the Rights of Laity in the Diocese of Toronto, 1850-79," CCHS *Journal*, 26 (April 1984), pp. 5-17, claims that early Evangelical opposition to Trinity College resulted from a belief that that education should be "free of clerical or denominational control." This is incorrect; evangelicals opposed the college because they feared it would be under High Church influence. As for the High Church party itself, the only High Churchman who opposed Trinity College was William Bettridge; in letters to the *Church* on 25 July 1850 and 23 Jan. 1851 Bettridge came out in favour of an inter-denominational University of Toronto, and expressed the opinion that the proposed charter for Trinity College would vest despotic power in the bishop. Another High Churchman, William Macaulay, criticized Strachan for the manner in which he solicited funds for Trinity College (Macaulay Papers, William Macaulay to John Macaulay, 2 Dec. 1851).

146   The *Church*, 16 June 1853.

147   Ibid., 17 March 1848.

148   Patton, *Attachment to the Church of God*, p. 20.

149   For the period after 1854, the best account of Low Church-High Church battles in the diocese of Toronto is Turner, "The Evangelical Movement in the Church of England in the Diocese of Toronto." Sweatman's statement can be found in ibid., p. 328.

150   The *Church*, 16 Oct. 1851.

CONCLUSION

The Anglican experience in Upper Canada was extraordinarily rich and varied, encompassing everything from missionary labours to political battles, from the campaign for synodical government to theological wrangling. An awareness of that richness and variety guards against simplistic characterizations either of the men who served the Church of England, or of the work of the church itself. Like other churches in the colony, the Church of England included among its clergy all kinds of men: the simple and the sophisticated, the incompetent and the immensely skilled. Similarly, its record, like that of all denominations, was mixed. Neither a success nor a failure, the Church of England in pre-Confederation Upper Canada was a bit of both, doing well in some areas and badly in others. Accordingly, its remarkable history, so intertwined with the history of the colony as a whole, should be portrayed not in black and white but in shades of grey.

As a religious institution, the Church of England might have performed better, particularly if the laity had been more generous in its support and if its own clergy had not been so suspicious of the "voluntary principle." All the same, its record was creditable. Its status by 1840 as the single largest denomination in the colony was convincing proof of its success as a religious force, and in itself demolishes the argument that "church types" floundered on the Upper Canadian frontier. Furthermore, its growth in popular support over the years was the result not merely of the arrival of boatload after boatload of Anglican immigrants, but also of its own efforts at keeping these newcomers within the fold. Related to its record in this regard was the flexibility it displayed in adapting its institutional structure to meet the colony's changing needs. From the 1820s on, the church was inspired by a missionary impulse that was revealed in the expansion of extra-parochial work on the part of the resident clergy, the appointment of travelling missionaries, and the creation of the SCCIPGDS and the Church Society. As well, it showed a growing awareness in the 1840s and 1850s, despite its fervent defence of the policy of church establishment, of the necessity of becoming more self-reliant. Evidence of its

In His Name

commitment to that goal was provided by the Church Society and the movement for synodical government, both of which had made significant strides by 1854. In conclusion, the church's achievements may have fallen short of its clergy's dreams, but they were nonetheless considerable. In terms of its institutional growth at least, the Church of England had succeeded by the mid-nineteenth century in laying solid foundations for the future.

In the world of politics, the picture was not as bright. For the first three decades of Upper Canada's history, the Church of England had gone about its work quietly, untouched by political controversy. But all this began to change in the 1820s, partly because of rising political consciousness but also because of Strachan's very public efforts to improve his church's fortunes by increasing the profitability of the clergy reserves and creating an Anglican-controlled university. As it turned out, his plans backfired badly, provoking rival denominations and the colony's nascent Reform movement to launch a campaign against what were seen as the Church of England's schemes for self-aggrandizement and, more generally, the entire policy of church establishment enshrined in the Constitutional Act of 1791. Year by year the campaign gained steadily in momentum, and by the 1840s revolved increasingly around voluntarist demands for the separation of church and state. The voluntarist cause achieved its first victory in 1849, when Strachan's beloved King's College was transformed into the secular University of Toronto. Five years later, the legislature secularized the clergy reserves, lands which had always been the cornerstone of Strachan's design for the religious development of Upper Canada. The Anglican establishment lay in ruins.

In defending its interests in the first half of the nineteenth century, the Church of England was certainly determined, resisting its opponents with every ounce of its strength. In a sense, its determination was a tribute to its vitality as an institution — no one could have accused Anglican clergymen of political weakness — but it also reflected a stubborn streak that in the end impeded rather than furthered the Anglican cause. From the 1820s on Anglican clergymen, far from showing an inclination to reach an accommodation with their church's critics, rejected out of hand the possibility of compromise. Thus, when the policy of church establishment first came under fire in

Conclusion

the 1820s and 1830s, Strachan responded by denouncing the proponents of religious equality and stoutly defending Anglican privileges. Later, in the post-union period, the clergy as a whole took an equally intransigent stance on all issues of church-state relations. The common schools were repeatedly described as a "godless" creation which threatened to destroy the foundations of the social order. Fierce opposition was offered to successive pieces of legislation on the thorny issue of the university, and when the "infidel" Baldwin bill of 1849 became law steps were immediately taken to establish a university under Anglican control. As for the clergy reserves, every attempt to deal with the question, whether by dividing the proceeds among all denominations or by adopting the principle of complete secularization, was characterized as nothing short of robbery.

To some extent, the Church of England's inflexibility on church-state issues reflected the strengths and weaknesses of one clergyman in particular — John Strachan. Extraordinarily able, with a will of iron and almost demonic energy, Strachan was one of the leading Upper Canadians of his generation. Besides being at the centre of virtually all of the political controversies that rocked the colony in the 1820s and 1830s, he was without equal among Anglican clergymen, and until his death in 1867 he played a crucial role in directing the course of the church's evolution in Upper Canadian society. That said, however, certain elements of Strachan's character proved extremely damaging to the Anglican cause. Driven by an unfaltering sense of the validity of his own views, Strachan had little patience with those who dared to criticize his plans for Upper Canada. Whenever his vision of the good society came under attack, he instinctively rushed headlong into the fray, intent not on reasoning with his opponents but on bludgeoning them into submission. In adopting such a combative stance, of course, he was merely displaying one of his most distinctive, and in some ways, admirable, characteristics: his fervent determination to remain unyielding on issues of principle. But, even so, his refusal to consider the possibility of compromise with the Church of England's opponents contributed significantly to the acrimony and polarization of Upper Canadian political life, and at the same time reinforced the church's isolation from the society in which it functioned.

Yet in the end, the Church of England's stance on church-state

In His Name

relations cannot be tied to the limitations of a single individual; Strachan merely reflected attitudes that were generally shared among the Anglican clergy. It must rather be related to the larger religious and political context of the times. The campaign for the separation of church and state in Upper Canada mirrored identical developments in Britain. There, too, the church-state connection came under sustained attack from the 1820s on, with much the same results as occurred in Upper Canada. And in Britain as well, defenders of the old order in church and state refused to give an inch, holding fast to principles which in their view were vital to the survival of the nation. Underlying their intransigence was the firm belief that the unity of church and state was the foundation of the entire social and political order. This belief — an axiom of British political thought since the mid-eighteenth century — led to the entirely logical conclusion that the Church of England could not be deprived of its established status without unravelling the fabric of British society. The Anglican establishment, it was felt, was a public reflection of the unity of church and state, and an indispensable tool in the maintenance of social stability and the authority of the state. If it fell, so would Britain's "glorious" constitution and the society and government that constitution upheld.

The Anglican clergymen of Upper Canada, including Strachan, viewed the world in the same light. Immersed in the assumptions of the late eighteenth century, they saw church establishment not as a strange innovation but rather as part of the natural order of things. Just as important, like apologists of the church-state connection in Britain, Anglican clergymen were inspired by the conviction that the policy of church establishment was crucial to the survival of Upper Canada as a stable society. In their mind, that policy was designed both to serve as a visible reminder of the essential unity of church and state, and to accomplish a wide range of religious and secular objectives. An established Church of England, they maintained, protected the purity of the Christian message against the infection of religious "error," particularly of the "sectarian" variety, promoted social and political stability, and acted as a guardian of the imperial tie. At the same time, there was a belief in Anglican circles until the late 1830s — best expressed by Strachan — that maintaining and strengthening the Church of England's established position would enable it to attract the allegiance of a majority of the population. In doing so, the church would further not only its own interests but the interests of the colony as a whole, for an Anglican Upper Canada by its very nature would be stable, prosperous and contented.

This perspective on the principle of church establishment undoubtedly provided Anglican clergymen with an emotionally powerful, even inspiring, view of their church's importance in Upper Canada. Yet it also locked them into an ideological strait-jacket which blinded them to the realities of the colony's religious life. Although complete religious equality was the only practical policy in a society as pluralistic as Upper Canada, Anglican clergymen persisted in believing that a close connection existed between the Church of England's favoured status and their society's survival as a bastion of stability and British patriotism. Consequently, even when it became apparent that disestablishment was inevitable, Strachan and every other Anglican clergymen saw no choice but to continue clutching the privileges which, in their mind, were essential to the Church of England's mission in Upper Canada. Given their assumptions, it would have been odd if they had acted differently.

The Anglican commitment to the principle of church establishment also accounts for some of the more curious features of Anglican political discourse in the pre-Confederation era. In the case of the leading Anglican clergyman in the colony, S.F. Wise has written that "Strachan's mind was rather like a megalithic monument: strong, crude and simple. It moved in straight lines, was impatient of subtleties and qualifications ... and was unleavened by what might be variously described as realism, a sense of proportion or merely as a sense of the absurd."[1] The same could be said of the Anglican mind in general. Throughout the first half of the nineteenth century Anglican clergymen inhabited a world that was closed to people of other faiths and political persuasions. Convinced that the policy of church establishment had been sanctioned by God, they tended to see the Church of England as an institution which, as a witness to the divine will, was engaged in an endless struggle with the forces of darkness. At no time did they stand back and critically examine the underlying assumptions of their own position on the issue of church establishment; nor did they pay much attention to what was being said by their opponents. When the point was made that no church in a religiously diverse society should receive preferential treatment, Anglican clergymen

In His Name

replied either by dwelling on the established church's role as a mainstay of the social order and the imperial tie, or by insisting with tiresome repetitiveness that the Church of England was legally established under the Constitutional Act. These arguments admittedly possessed an internal logic of their own, but they hardly came to terms with the central issue of the debate: the impracticality of the policy of church establishment in a society where the Church of England was only one denomination among many.

Ironically, the inflexibility of the Anglican mind led Church of England clergymen to underestimate, if not ignore entirely, the fundamental conservatism of their own society. It has long been recognized, thanks, once again, to the work of S.F. Wise, that most Upper Canadian Tories and Reformers shared a common body of assumptions and values, notably a deep-seated suspicion of the United States, a commitment to the imperial connection and all the things which that connection symbolized, and a belief in the desirability of an ordered, class-structured society.[2] This conservative consensus, needless to say, embraced the clergy of the Church of England; indeed, one of the most striking aspects of the Church of England's experience in Upper Canada was the Anglican clergy's profoundly conservative position on a wide range of social and political issues. Still, while they shared the conservative values of their society, Anglican clergymen saw a lot to dislike as they followed the course of political life in the pre-Confederation era, and during these years they frequently accused other denominations and Reform politicians of undermining the fabric of Upper Canadian society. In taking this attitude, they failed to realize that the Church of England and the forces of Reform were divided not over basic values and ultimate goals, but only over the strategy to be adopted in moulding the colony along lines that were favoured by the majority of Upper Canadians. Contrary to Anglican charges, for example, most critics of Upper Canada's system of oligarchical rule, far from aiming at the creation of an independent republic, were inspired by the conviction that responsible government would strengthen the colony's ties with the mother country. Similarly, most opponents of the Church of England's privileged position agreed with the basic tenets of the Anglican vision of the good society; they differed from Anglican clergymen only in believing that the policy of church establishment was a blatant injustice which should be repudiated in the best interests

Conclusion

of the colony as a whole. But Anglican clergymen could see none of this. Since they regarded their church's favoured status not as an impediment to Upper Canada's progress but as an indispensable safeguard of social peace, they inevitably concluded that the voluntarist campaign for the separation of church and state threatened the colony's conservative character. They could not have been more mistaken.

Perhaps the most interesting facet of the Anglican experience in Upper Canada was the church's response to defeats in the political arena. As the events of the 1840s and 1850s unfolded, some Anglican clergymen and laymen began to redefine their church's place in the wider community. While remaining committed to the idea of church establishment, they argued that the Church of England had no choice but to resign itself to the inevitability of disestablishment, free itself from the clutches of an evil state, and devote itself exclusively to its duties as a religious organization. This anti-Erastian view of the church's role stood in marked contrast to the Anglican clergy's earlier belief that the connection between the state and the church was the linchpin of the social and political order. It also signalled a sharp break from the idea, hitherto unquestioned in Anglican circles, that the Church of England's social and religious responsibilities embraced the entire colony. Essentially, the new notion of an Anglican "spiritual society" rested on the conviction that, even in the religious realm, the time had come for the church to turn its back on a community which had grown morally corrupt. More often than not, when Anglicans in the post-union period spoke grandiloquently of their church's mission as a witness to the true faith, the implication was that the Church of England would henceforth concentrate on tending the spiritual welfare of its own members rather than on saving the souls of those unfortunates outside the fold.

An increasing introversion was evident even in one of the church's greatest accomplishments — its gradual evolution into a self-governing and self-supporting institution. During the politically turbulent 1830s Anglican clergymen became convinced of the need to strengthen the church's institutional foundations, and in subsequent years this conviction led to the founding of the Church Society and to the holding of visitations in 1851, 1853 and 1854 which were the precursors of the Anglican synod established in 1857. While these twin developments were testimony to a growing spirit of self-reliance in the

In His Name

Anglican community, they were also inspired by a paradoxical view of the Church of England's position in Upper Canadian society. Again and again Anglican clergymen and laymen argued that only a self-supporting and self-governing church would be able to act as a united body in fending off the attacks of its enemies. Yet, strangely enough, they also let it be known that the Church Society and an Anglican synod should be seen as symbols of the church's independence from a sinful state. These conflicting ideas co-existed in the Anglican mind throughout the 1840s and early 1850s, but when disestablishment became a reality towards the end of that period anti-Erastian tendencies became more pronounced. By the time the clergy reserves were secularized in 1854, it almost seemed that calls for a self-governing and self-supporting Church of England were based on a vision of the day when the church would stand alone, isolated not only from the influence of an oppressive state but also from the moral rot afflicting the entire Upper Canadian community.

Turning inwards, however, was no more practical a response to the threat of disestablishment than a desperate clinging to the old order. For what the vision of an Anglican spiritual society ignored was the undeniable fact that the Church of England, largely because of the theological divisions spawned by the Oxford movement, lacked a clear sense of its nature as a religious institution. From the beginning, Tractarianism provided many clergymen and laymen both with a sophisticated and compelling interpretation of the Anglican religious message, and with an equally inspiring view of the Church of England's role in relation to the state. Yet it also produced a rift between High Churchmen and Evangelicals, a rift that was evident in bitter exchanges on points of theology and in disputes over a variety of issues touching on the church's internal organization and political position. In addition to hindering the church in its struggle to defend its established status, this conflict between High and Low Churchmen made it clear that the Church of England was becoming confused about its spiritual mission at precisely the moment when developments elsewhere were undermining its sense of purpose as a political force. What is more, the internecine battles of these years raised serious questions about the Church of England's future in Upper Canadian religious life. When Anglicans talked of their church's nature as a spiritual society, they were assuming that all clergymen and laymen subscribed to the same

Conclusion

interpretation of the meaning of the Anglican faith. In reality, however, feuding between High Churchmen and Evangelicals made it clear that a shared religious vision was exactly what the Church of England lacked. Other than a mutual commitment to social and political conservatism, the only thing Low Church and High Church Anglicans had in common was an unwillingness to tolerate rival definitions of the *via media*.

None of this is meant to suggest that the Church of England in 1854 was backed into an intellectual cul-de-sac from which it never escaped. Following the secularization of the clergy reserves, the Church of England adapted remarkably well to the realities of disestablishment. Not only did it expand its popular support, add new dioceses and become financially self-reliant, but it also became part of a Protestant consensus that aimed at the moral reformation of an increasingly urbanized, industrialized and materialistic society.[3] Still, it would be a mistake to describe the Church of England as a full partner in the Protestant culture of the late nineteenth century. After 1854 hostility between the Church of England and rival Protestant denominations persisted, Anglicans lagged far behind other Protestants in such interdenominational enterprises as the temperance movement, and the ongoing battles of High Churchmen and Evangelicals distracted the the church's attention from political matters.[4] In sum, while Anglican introversion appears to have waned as the wounds of the 1840s and 1850s began to heal, other features of the Church of England's history before 1854 — a suspicion of other Protestants, and internal strife — continued to divide the Church of England from the society it served.

The Church of England, then, had far more popular support than is generally conceded, proved highly flexible in meeting the religious needs of a rapidly growing society, and made significant progress in the post-rebellion period in transforming itself into a self-supporting and self-governing institution. On the other side of the ledger, the church's failures were just as apparent. The long struggle to defend the policy of church establishment ended in complete defeat, and the energies poured into that struggle would have been better devoted to other causes. In addition, over the course of the 1840s and early 1850s, the Church of England was thrown into intellectual disarray. With every victory for the voluntarist campaign, Anglican clergymen had increasingly come to realize that the Church of England could no

In His Name

longer hope to act as the guardian of the social and political order. Unfortunately, the alternative vision put forward by some Anglicans — a vision of an independent church primarily concerned not with guiding the course of political life but with meeting the needs of its own members — ignored the problem of disunity within the fold. By 1854 even the most optimistic Anglican must have understood that the church would have difficulty evolving into a spiritual society as long as its own clergy and laity were divided along theological lines.

When the clergy reserves bill closed a chapter in the history of Upper Canadian Anglicanism, the Church of England, with more than 200,000 members (roughly twenty-five percent of the total population) and about 140 clergymen, had come a long way from its beginnings in the 1790s. Yet, notwithstanding its strength in numbers, the church was a deeply troubled institution in 1854. Abandoned by the state that had long been its closest ally, beset by divisions among its own members, the Church of England did not have a clear idea of what it stood for or where it was going. In the years ahead, the church would continue to grow in popular support and clerical manpower, but it would also continue to be plagued by intellectual confusion. The precious asset it had once enjoyed — a sense of purpose in serving both God and humanity — had become nothing more than a distant memory.

Conclusion

NOTES

1 Wise, "Sermon Literature and Canadian Intellectual History," p. 14.

2 See particularly Wise's article "Upper Canada and the Conservative Tradition." Jane Errington has challenged Wise's arguments in *The Lion, the Eagle, and Upper Canada*. To my mind, however, the evidence she advances serves only to prove that Upper Canadians admired the American economic model but were critical of American society and politics.

3 The content of this Protestant culture is incisively explored in Westfall's *Two Worlds*.

4 These points have been made by J.W. Grant in a review of *Two Worlds*. See *CHR*, LXX (December 1989), pp. 580-82.

BIBLIOGRAPHY

I. Archives and Manuscript Sources

Archives of the Diocese of Ontario (Kingston) (ADO)

    John Stuart Papers

Archives of Ontario (Toronto) (AO)

    A.N. Bethune Papers
    William Bettridge Papers
    Robert Blakey Parish Registers
    Cartwright Family Papers
    Solomon Jones Papers
    F.J. Lundy Diaries
    Macaulay Family Papers
    James Magrath Papers
    Nelles Family Papers
    Osler Family Papers. Letters, Diaries and Journals of F.L. Osler
    William Ritchie Diaries
    John Beverley Robinson, Letters from Dr. Stuart
    Bishop Strachan Letters
    John Strachan Papers and Letter Books
    John Strachan Sermons
    John Stuart Papers

Baldwin Room, Metropolitan Toronto Library (BRMTL)

    Henry Scadding Diaries
    Henry Scadding Sermons
    Strachan Papers, Scadding Collection

National Archives of Canada (Ottawa) (NAC)

    MG 17, B1, Series G, Journals of missionaries of the Upper Canada Clergy Society
    MG 17, B1, Society for the Propagation of the Gospel in Foreign Parts, Journals

In His Name

MG 17, B1, Series C and D, Society for the Propagation of the Gospel in Foreign Parts, Letters

Toronto Diocesan Archives, St. James's Cathedral (TDA)

A.N. Bethune, Manuscript Lecture Notes on Old Testament and Ecclesiastical History

II. Newspapers

Berean, 1844-49.

Christian Recorder, 1819-21.

Christian Sentinel, 1830-31.

Christian Sentinel and Anglo-Canadian Churchman's Magazine, 1827-30.

Church, 1837-54.

Echo and Protestant Episcopal Recorder, 1851-54 (only scattered copies extant).

Kingston Gazette, 1811-12.

III. Reports

Church Society of the Diocese of Toronto, *Reports*, 1842-54.

The Parliamentary History of England, from the Earliest Period to the Year 1803 (Hansard), XXVIII (1789-91).

Proceedings of Synod, Diocese of Toronto, 1851, 1853 and 1854.

Report of a Select Committee of the Church Society. Presented on Wednesday, February 2nd, 1853. Toronto, 1853.

Report of the Special General Meeting of the Church Society of the Diocese of Toronto, Held on Wednesday, 10 Nov. 1852. To take into consideration the future disposal of the Patronage of the Rectories. Toronto, 1852.

St. George's Parochial Branch of the Church Society of the Diocese of Toronto. Report and Proceedings of the Annual Meeting Held in St. George's Church, on the 17th of April, 1851. Toronto, 1851.

Society for Converting and Civilizing the Indians, and Propagating the Gospel among Destitute Settlers in Upper Canada, *Reports*, 1831-38.

Society for the Propagation of the Gospel in Foreign Parts, *Reports*, 1785-1854.

Upper Canada Clergy Society, *Report*, 1838.

Upper Canada Clergy Society, *Report*, 1840.

Upper Canadian Travelling Missionary Fund, reports, 1838-47 (photocopies at GSA).

IV. Contemporary Works

Abbott, Joseph. *Philip Musgrave: or Memoirs of a Church of England Missionary in the North American Colonies*. London, 1846.

Adamson, W.A. *A Sermon, Preached in St. George's Church, Kingston, the 26th September, 1841, on the Death of Lord Sydenham*. Kingston, 1841.

— *A Sermon ... Preached in the Cathedral, Quebec, on Wednesday, 26th April, 1854*. Quebec, 1854.

Addison, Robert. "An Old Time Sermon." *Niagara Historical Society Transactions* (1899), 1-7.

Alexander, James Lynne. *Ontario's Oldest Poem: A Day at Niagara in the Year 1825 by the Revd. James Lynne Alexander, Anglican Vicar, Revived, Revised and Annotated by his Great-Grandson, Richard Lanton Denison*. N.p., n.d.

Anonymous. *An Apology for the Church of England in the Canadas, in Answer to a Letter to the Earl of Liverpool, Relative to the Rights of the Church of Scotland, &c. by a Protestant of the Church of Scotland. By a Protestant of the Established Church of England*. N.p., n.d.

— *The Call to the Sacred Ministry. A Discourse Addressed to Members of the Church of England. By a Clergyman*. N.p., n.d.

— A Sermon preached in early 1838. Sent to the *Church* by "Verus" and printed in that journal 3 Feb. 1838.

— *Recollections of a Beloved Pastor: By C.M.M.* Kingston, 1845.

In His Name

Armstrong, John. *The Life and Letters of the Rev. George Mortimer, M.A. Rector of Thornhill, in the Diocese of Toronto, Canada West.* London, 1847.

Atkinson, A.F. *The Leading Doctrines of the Gospel. A Valedictory Sermon Delivered in Christ's Church, Montreal, on Sunday, May 15, 1836, on Occasion of his Departure from that Parish.* Montreal, 1836.

Beaven, James. *An Account of the Life and Writings of S. Irenaeus, Bishop of Lyons and Martyr.* London, 1841.

— *A Help to Catechising for the Use of Clergymen, Schools, and Private Families.* New York, 1843.

— *Ask for the Old Paths. A Sermon Preached at the Opening of the New Church of St. James, at Dundas, in Upper Canada, on Sunday, December 31st, 1843.* Cobourg, 1843.

— *Recreations of a Long Vacation; or a Visit to Indian Missions in Upper Canada.* London, 1846.

— *Elements of Natural Theology.* London, 1850.

— *A Catechism on the Thirty-Nine Articles of the Church of England.* New York, 1853.

Bethune, A.N. *Sermons, on the Liturgy of the Church of England; with Introductory Discourses on Public Worship and Forms of Prayer, Originally Preached in St. Peter's Church, Cobourg.* York, U.C., 1829.

— *A Sermon, Preached in Saint Peter's Church, Cobourg, U.C. on Thursday, the 14th, February 1833. Being the Day Appointed for a General Thanksgiving to Almighty God, for Having Removed the Heavy Judgments with which these Provinces Have Recently Been Afflicted.* Cobourg, 1833.

— *A Memoir of the Late Mr. William Ruttan, Son of Henry Ruttan .... To which is Prefixed a Sermon, Preached at the Reinterment of the Deceased.* Cobourg, 1837.

— "Public Thanksgiving." A sermon preached in St. Peter's Church, Cobourg, 6 Feb. 1838. The *Church*, 17 Feb. 1838.

— "The Christian Shepherd. An Ordination Sermon, preached in Christ Church, Montreal, on Sunday the 12th of August, and in St. James's Church, Toronto, on Sunday the 7th October." The *Church*, 10 Nov. 1838.

Bibliography

— *A Sermon Preached in St. Peter's Church, Cobourg, on Sunday the 14th October, 1838, on Occasion of the Death of Mrs. Boulton, Wife of George Strange Boulton.* Cobourg, 1838.

— "Christ the Only Saviour. A Sermon on the Eighteenth Article of the Church of England, preached at the Carrying-Place, Murray, on Wednesday Oct. 16, 1839, before the Midland Clerical Association." The *Church*, 23 Nov. 1839.

— "The Church of God. A Sermon preached in the Cathedral Church of St. James, Toronto, on Thursday, Sept. 9, 1841, at the primary visitation of the Lord Bishop of the Diocese." The *Church*, 18 Sept. 1841.

— *Reports of Archidiaconal Visitations, 1847-50 .... Transcribed ... by Alison Sheppard.* N.p., 1957.

— *The Shulamite and her Son. A Sermon, Preached in Saint Peter's Church, Cobourg, on Sunday, XXVI. September, M.DCCC.XLVII.* Toronto, 1847.

— "A Charge Addressed to the Clergy of the Archdeaconry at York, at Visitations of the Clergy and Churchwardens of that Archdeaconry, held at Newmarket on Thursday, Sept. 6th; at Chippawa, Wednesday, Sept. 12th; at Hamilton, Friday, Sept. 14th; at Woodstock, Tuesday, Sept. 18th; at London, Thursday, Sept. 20th, and at Chatham, Tuesday, Sept. 25th, 1849." The *Church*, 1 Nov. 1849.

— *The Duty of Loyalty. A Sermon, Preached in Saint Peter's Church, Cobourg, on Sunday, XXI, October, M.DCCC.XLIX.* Cobourg, 1849.

— A public letter to Robert Baldwin on the subject of the clergy reserves. The *Church*, 4 July 1850.

— Address to the clergy on the subject of the clergy reserves. The *Church*, 18 July 1850.

— *Four Sermons on the Holy Sacrament of the Lord's Supper; Preached in St. Peter's Church, Cobourg, During the Season of Advent, 1850.* Toronto, 1852.

— *A Charge Delivered at Visitations of the Clergy and Churchwardens of the Archdeaconry of York, Held at Thornhill, on Thursday, April 22; at Hamilton, on Tuesday, April 27; and at London, on Thursday, April 29, 1852.* Toronto, 1852.

— *The Clergy Reserve Question in Canada.* London, 1853.

In His Name

— *Memoir of the Right Reverend John Strachan, D.D., LL.D., First Bishop of Toronto.* Toronto and London, 1870.

Bethune, John. *A Sermon Preached in Christ's Church, Montreal, on Friday, the 4th May, 1832, Being the Day Appointed for a Public Fast, Occasioned by the Apprehension of being Visited by the Pestilence which is Scourging the Nations of Europe.* Montreal, 1832.

— *A Sermon Preached on Wednesday, February 6, 1833, Being the Day Appointed by Proclamation for a General Thanksgiving to Almighty God for Having Removed the Heavy Judgment of the Pestilence.* Montreal, 1833.

— *Address Delivered by the Principal of McGill College, on the Occasion of the Opening of that Institution, on the Sixth September, 1843.* Montreal, 1843.

— *Christian Love, Unity and Peace. A Sermon Preached in Christ's Church, Montreal, on the 17th June, 1849.* Montreal, 1849.

— *A Sermon Preached in Christ Church Cathedral, 21st January, 1852 ... on the Occasion of the Primary Visitation of the Right Reverend Francis Fulford, D.D., Lord Bishop of Montreal.* Montreal, 1852.

Bettridge, William. *Confirmation: A Sermon.* Woodstock, n.d.

— *A Brief History of the Church in Upper Canada.* London, 1838.

— "The Claims of the Church." Excerpt from a pamphlet entitled "The Presbyter of Woodstock to his Flock." The *Church*, 7 March 1840.

Boddy, Samuel J. *A Brief Memoir of the Rev. Samuel B. Ardagh.* Toronto, 1874.

Boswell, E.J. "A Sermon, Preached in Cornwall, 7th December, 1845, on the Death of the Rev. J.G.B. Lindsay, the Rector; and in Williamsburg, His Late Mission, 14th December." The *Church*, 2 Jan. 1846.

Burke, Edmund. *Reflections on the Revolution in France and on the Proceedings in Certain Societies in London Relative to That Event* (Conor Cruise O'Brien, ed., Penguin edition, 1969).

Burwell, A.H. *A Voice of Warning and Instruction Concerning the Signs of the Times, and the Coming of the Son of Man, to Judge the Nations, and Restore all Things.* Kingston, 1835.

Bibliography

— *Doctrine of the Holy Spirit; and its Application to the Wants and Interests of Corporate Man Under the Providence and Moral Government of God, Stated and Defended from Holy Writ and the Practice of the Apostles of Our Lord and Saviour Jesus Christ; and in these Days Revived in Britain by the Rev. Edward Irving; Exhibiting the Sole Means of National Reformation and Preservation.* Toronto, 1835.

Cartwright, R.D. *A Sermon, Preached in Saint George's Church, Kingston, on Thursday the 23rd of August, 1832, at the Visitation of the Hon'ble and Rt. Rev'd the Lord Bishop of the Diocese.* Kingston, 1832.

— "The Service for `The Thanksgiving of Women After Child-Birth.' A Sermon preached at the Carrying-Place, Murray, on Thursday, October 17th, before the Midland Clerical Association." The *Church*, 14 Dec. 1839.

— "St George's Day. A Sermon Preached in St. George's Church, Kingston on the 24th April 1837." The *Church*, 2 May 1840.

Clarke, James. *Address to a Large and Respectable Body of Freemasons, on their Laying the Corner Stone of St. George's Lodge, no. 15, and of Several Other Lodges.* St. Catherine's, U.C., 1835.

Cochran, John. *A Funeral Sermon, Preached in St. James' Church, St. John's, L.C. on the Occasion of the Death of Mrs. Alexr. Hamilton Peirce, on Sunday, December 28, 1834.* Montreal, 1835.

Cooper, H.C. *Characteristic Principles of the Church of England: Three Speeches of the Rev. H.C. Cooper, B.A., at the Annual Meetings of the London and Huron Branch Association of the Church Society of the Diocese of Toronto, in 1845, 1846 and 1847.* Toronto, 1847.

— *The Duty of the Members of the Church of England Respecting the Clergy Reserves: An Address Delivered in St. Peter's Church, Springfield, January 10, 1854.* Toronto, 1854.

Creen, Thomas. Excerpts from two sermons preached on the day of fasting and humiliation. The *Church*, 9 Feb. 1839.

— "Extract from a Discourse delivered in St. Mark's Church, Niagara, on occasion of the lamented deaths of the late Alexander Hamilton, Esquire, and Mrs. James Boulton." The *Church*, 30 March 1839.

Dade, Charles. "Notes on the Cholera Seasons of 1832 and 1834." *Canadian Journal of Industry, Science, and Art* (January 1962).

Darling, W.S. *A Conversation Between a Country Parson and One of His Flock, Upon the Subject of the Church Society.* Toronto, 1842.

— *Sketches of Canadian Life, Lay and Ecclesiastical, Illustrative of Canada and the Canadian Church.* London, 1849.

— "The Anglo-Saxon Race on the Continent of America." The *Church*, 24 April 1851.

— "Some Thoughts upon the Extension of the Church in the Remote Parts of this Diocese." The *Church*, 14 and 28 Aug. 1851.

Deacon, Job. "The Claims of the Church Society. A Sermon Preached Before the Parochial Association of Belleville, in Connexion with the Incorporated Church Society of the Diocese of Toronto, in the Parish Church of St. Thomas, on Thursday, 1st day of May 1845." The *Church*, 25 July and 1 Aug. 1845.

Denroche, Edward. *The Curate's Book.* London, 1832.

— *An Apology for the Doctrine of Scriptural Temperance, or the Church of Christ the True Temperance Society. A Sermon Preached in St. Peter's Church.* Brockville, 1840.

Elliot, Adam. "A Sermon, Preached in Christ Church, Hamilton, on the 13th May, 1840, before the Western Clerical Society." The *Church*, 25 July 1840.

Evans, Francis. Lecture on "the worship of the Virgin Mary, — Images, — the Invocation of Saints." The *Church*, 20 Feb. 1851.

Fidler, Isaac. *Observations on Professions, Literature, Manners, and Emigration, in the United States and Canada, Made During a Residence there in 1832.* New York, 1833.

Fletcher, John. *Letters to the Wesleyan Methodists of the Mission of Mono.* Toronto, 1854.

Fuller, T.B. *Thoughts on the Present State and Future Prospects of the Church of England in Canada, with Hints for some improvement in Her Ecclesiastical Arrangements; Humbly Addressed to the Rt. Rev. the Lord Bishop and the Rev. Clergy.* 1836.

Bibliography

— *Religious Excitements Tried by Scripture, and Their Fruits Tested by Experience. A Sermon, Preached in the Parish Church, on Sunday, the 13th February, 1842.* Toronto, 1842.

— *The Roman Catholic Church Not the Mother Church of England; or the Church of England, the Church Originally Planted in England.* 1844.

Givins, Salter. "A Sermon, Preached in St. Peter's Church, Cobourg, on Sunday, January 31, 1841, on behalf of the Newcastle District Committee of the Society for Promoting Christian Knowledge." The *Church*, 6 and 13 March 1841.

— "The Late John S. Cartwright, Esq. From a Sermon preached on occasion of his death ...." The *Church*, 2 May 1845.

Harris, J.H. *A Sermon, Preached at St. James's Church, York; on Sunday, March 17th, 1833, in aid of the Sunday School Society, for the Diocese of Quebec.* York.

— *A Letter to the Hon. & Ven. Archdeacon Strachan in Reply to Some Passages in his "Letter to Dr. Chalmers on the Life and Character of Bishop Hobart," Respecting the Principles and Effects of the Bible Society.* York, 1833.

— *Observations on Upper Canada College.* Toronto, 1836.

Hawkins, Ernest. *Annals of the Diocese of Toronto.* London, 1848.

Hooker, Richard. *Of the Laws of Ecclesiastical Polity* (1593-97). 2 vols. Reprinted, London, 1927.

Hudson, J. *A Sermon, on the Death of His Late Royal Highness the Duke of York, Commander in Chief of His Majesty's Forces. Preached in the Episcopal Church of York, Upper Canada, at the Garrison Service, on Sunday Morning, March 11, 1827.* York, 1827.

Knox, William. *Extra Official State Papers. Addressed to the Right Hon. Lord Rawdon, and the other Members of the Two Houses of Parliament, Associated for the Preservation of the Constitution and Promoting the Prosperity of the British Empire.* London, 1789.

Lett, Stephen. Sermon preached at St. George's Church, Toronto. The *Church*, 17 Jan. 1850.

McCaul, John. "*Love of God and of our Neighbour.*" *A Sermon, Preached in*

In His Name

the Cathedral Church of St. James, Toronto, on Tuesday, March 17, 1840, Before the Societies of St. George, St. Patrick, & St. Andrew. Toronto, 1840.

— *Emigration to a Better Country. A Sermon, Preached in the Cathedral Church of St. James, Toronto, on Saint Patrick's Day, 1842, before the Societies of St. George, St. Patrick, & St. Andrew.* Toronto, 1842.

— *The University Question Considered: By a Graduate.* Toronto, 1845.

— and John Macara. *Letters on King's College.* Toronto, 1848.

Macaulay, William. *A Sermon, Preached ... on Monday, March 20th, 1837, on occasion of the funeral of Mrs. Catherine Wright.* Picton, 1837.

— Excerpts from a sermon preached at the Visitation of the Archdeaconry of Kingston. The *Church*, 30 Sept. 1837.

— "Christ Alone Without Sin. A Sermon preached in St. Paul's Church, Cavan, before the Midland Clerical Association, on Thursday the 7th of February, 1839." The *Church*, 2 and 9 March 1839.

— "A Sermon, Preached in the Cathedral Church of St. James, Toronto, on Thursday, June 6th, 1844, on Occasion of the Visitation of the Lord Bishop of the Diocese." The *Church*, 28 June 1844.

— *The Harvest Blessing, or a Word to Prudent Men, Being A Sermon Preached in the Church of St. Mary Magdalene, Picton, C.W. ... August 28th, 1853.* Kingston.

MacGeorge, R.J. *The Perfect Law of Liberty: A Sermon, Preached at Trinity Church, Streetsville, on Sunday, XIIth, July, M.DCCC.XLVI.* Toronto, 1846.

Mackenzie, J.G.D. Sermon preached at St Paul's Church, Yorkville. The *Church*, 31 Jan. 1850.

— *A Sermon, on Occasion of the Death of Harriet, Wife of Lieut. Col. the Hon. Joseph Wells, Preached April 23rd, 1851, at St. Paul's Church, Toronto.* Weymouth, 1852.

— *A Sermon, on Occasion of the Death of Clarence Yonge Wells, Preached October 20th, 1850, at St. Paul's Church, Toronto.* Weymouth, 1852.

— *Selections from Sermons of the Late Rev. J.G.D. Mackenzie.* Toronto, 1882.

McMurray, William. *An Appeal to the Members of the Protestant Episcopal Church in the United States, in Behalf of Trinity College, Toronto, Canada West.* New York, 1852.

Bibliography

Mayerhoffer, V.P. *Twelve Years a Roman Catholic Priest*. Toronto, 1861.

Mountain, G.J. *A Sermon, Preached in the Parish Church of Fredericton, on the 14th January, 1816, Upon Occasion of a Collection Made in Aid of the Waterloo Subscriptions*. Fredericton, 1816.

— *A Valedictory Sermon, Preached in Christ Church, Fredericton, on the 29th June 1817*. Fredericton, 1817.

— *A Sermon Preached in the Cathedral Church of Quebec, on Sunday, the 12th September, 1819, after the Public Calamity Experienced in the Death of His Grace the Duke of Richmond, Governor in Chief*. Quebec, 1819.

— *A Sermon on the Education of the Poor, the Duty of Diffusing the Gospel, and, More Particularly, on the Importance of Family Religion. Preached before the Diocesan Committee of the Society for Promoting Christian Knowledge, in the Cathedral Church of Quebec, on the 24th February, 1822, Upon Occasion of the Annual Collection*. Quebec, 1822.

— *The Foundation and Constitution of the Christian Ministry and the General Outline of the Ministerial Character and Duties, Considered in an Ordination Sermon Preached in the Cathedral Church of Quebec on Sunday 30th July 1826*. Quebec, 1826.

— *Review of the Pastoral Letter of the Clergy of the Church of Scotland in the Canadas*. Montreal, 1828.

— *A Sermon Preached in the Parish Church of Montreal, on Thursday, the 9th of August, 1832. At the visitation of the Honourable and Right Reverend the Lord Bishop of Quebec*. Quebec, 1833.

— *A Retrospect of the Summer and Autumn of 1832; Being a Sermon Delivered in the Cathedral Church of Quebec, on Sunday, the 30th December, in that year*. Quebec, 1833.

— Extract of a sermon preached in the Cathedral Church of Quebec, Feb. 25, 1838. The *Church*, 19 May 1838.

— *Canadian Church Destitution. Reprint of the Report Made ... to the Right Hon. the Earl of Durham ... Upon the Insufficient State of the Church in the Provinces of Upper and Lower Canada*. Hexham, 1839.

— *A Charge Delivered to the Clergy of the Diocese of Quebec ... at His Primary Visitation, Completed in 1838*. Quebec, 1839.

— *A Sermon Preached in the Cathedral of Quebec, on the 24th November,*

In His Name

1839, and in Christ Church, Montreal, on the 12th January, 1840, Upon Occasion of the Annual Collections in those Churches Respectively, for the Society for Promoting Christian Knowledge. Cobourg, 1840.

— *The Soldier's Thanksgiving, a Sermon Preached in the Cathedral Church of Quebec, Upon Occasion of an Ordination, Immediately Before the Departure of the Author for the Red River, in Prince Rupert's Land.* N.p., n.d.

— *The Love of Country, Considered Upon Christian Principles, with a Special Application to the Case of Englishmen. A Sermon Preached in the Cathedral Church of Quebec, Before the St. George's Society of that City, on the 23rd of April, 1844.* Quebec, 1844.

— *A Circular Letter from the Bishop of Montreal, to the Clergy of His Diocese, on Church Vestments.* London, 1845.

— *A Charge Delivered to the Clergy of the Diocese of Quebec, in the Cathedral Church of Quebec, at the Triennial Visitation in 1845.* Quebec, 1845.

— *A Pastoral Letter to the Clergy and Laity of the Diocese of Quebec, Upon the Question of Affording the Use of Churches and Chapels of the Church of England, for the Purposes of Dissenting Worship.* Quebec, 1845.

— *A Charge Delivered to the Clergy of the Diocese of Quebec, in Christ-Church, at Montreal, Being the Parish Church of that City, at the Triennial Visitation, in 1848.* Quebec, 1848.

— *Thoughts on "Annexation," in Connection with the Duty and the Interest of Members of the Church of England; and as Affecting Some Particular Religious Questions ....* Quebec, 1849.

— *A Charge Delivered to the Clergy of the Diocese of Quebec, at the Triennial Visitation, Held in the Cathedral Church of Quebec, on the 2nd of July, 1851.* Quebec, 1851.

— *The House of the Lord God: Two Sermons Preached in Fredericton Cathedral: One in the Evening of the Day of its Consecration, Wednesday, 31st August, 1853, and the other on the Morning of the Sunday Following.* Fredericton, 1853.

— *A Charge Delivered to the Clergy of the Diocese of Quebec at the Triennial Visitation Held in the Cathedral Church of Quebec, on the 11th January, 1854.* Quebec, 1854.

Bibliography

— *The Duty of the Christian Minister in Following Christ. The Sermon Preached at an Ordination of Priests and Deacons, Held by the Provisional Bishop of New York, in Trinity Church, New-York, on the Third Sunday after Trinity, July 2, 1854*. New York, 1854.

Mountain, Jacob. *A Sermon Preached at Quebec, on Thursday, January 10th, 1799. Being the Day Appointed for a General Thanksgiving*. Quebec, 1799.

— *A Charge Delivered to the Clergy of the Diocese of Quebec in August, 1803*. Quebec, 1803.

— *A Sermon Preached at the Anniversary of the Royal Humane Society, in Christ Church, Surrey, on Sunday the 28th of March 1819*. London, 1819.

— Sermon preached at a confirmation service at York, probably in May 1820. The *Christian Recorder*, June 1820.

— Charge delivered at Kingston, 25 July 1820. The *Christian Recorder*, July 1820.

Mulock, J.A. *Methodism Unmasked, in a Review of "A Vindication of the Methodist Church" (so-called,) "In a Pastoral Address. By Benjamin Nankeville, Wesleyan Minister"*. Carleton Place, 1850.

Nelles, Abraham. *The Book of Common Prayer, According to the Use of the Church of England, Translated into the Mohawk Language*. Hamilton, 1842.

Norris, W.H. Extract from a sermon. The *Church*, 22 Aug. 1840.

Padfield, James. Sermon preached at a meeting of the Eastern Clerical Association in Williamsburg, 6 and 9 March 1839. The *Church*, 13 April 1839.

Paley, William. *Moral and Political Philosophy: Consisting of Evidences of Christianity, Moral and Political Philosophy, Natural Theology, and Horae Paulinae* (1785). Reprinted, London, 1835.

Palmer, Arthur. "On the Nature and Extent of Christian Unity." Sermon preached at a meeting of the Western Clerical Association in Hamilton, 1 Aug. 1838. The *Church*, 25 Aug. and 1 Sept. 1838.

— Address to the inhabitants of Guelph. Excerpt from Hamilton *Gazette*. The *Church*, 24 Nov. 1838.

In His Name

— "On the Difficulties and Encouragements of the Christian Ministry, with Some References to the Past and Present Condition of the Church in Western Canada. A Sermon, Preached in the Cathedral Church of St. James, Toronto, June 3rd, 1847, on the occasion of the Triennial Visitation of the Lord Bishop of the Diocese." The *Church*, 16 and 23 July 1847.

Patton, Henry. *Questions on the Chief Festivals and Holy Days*. Toronto, 1851.

— *Attachment to the Church of God. A Sermon Preached in the Cathedral Church of St. James, Toronto, on Wednesday, October 12th, 1853, at the Visitation of the Right Reverend the Lord Bishop of the Diocese of Toronto*. Toronto, 1853.

— *A Sermon on the Life, Labours, and Character, of the Late Honorable and Right Reverend John Strachan, D.D., L.L.D., Lord Bishop of Toronto ....* Montreal, 1868.

Phillips, Thomas. *The Canadian Remembrancer. A Loyal Sermon, Preached on St. George's Day, April 23, 1826; at the Episcopal Church in York*. York, 1826.

Published Correspondence and Papers Called Forth By a Canvas Among a Section of the Clergy of the Diocese of Toronto, Having in View the Recommendation of the Venerable the Archdeacon of York, in Said Diocese, as the Incumbent of the Proposed New Bishopric of Kingston, Canada West. 1854.

Pyne, Alexander. *Reminiscences of Colonial Life and Missionary Adventure in Both Hemispheres*. London, 1875.

Reid, James. *A Sermon, Preached in Trinity Church, in the Seigniory of St. Armand, Lower Canada, on the Twenty First Day of May, 1816. Being the Day Appointed by Proclamation. For a General Thanksgiving to Almighty God, "For His Great Goodness in Putting an End to the War in which we were Engaged Against France."* Montreal, 1816.

— *A Sermon Delivered in Trinity Church, St. Armand East, on the Death of the Hon. & Right Reverend Charles James Stewart, D.D., Lord Bishop of Quebec, on Sunday 10th September, 1837 .... To which is Added: A Sermon on the Same Occasion, Delivered at St. John's and Laprairie on the 17th September, 1837. By the Rev. Charles P. Reid*. Frelighsburg, 1837.

Bibliography

Rogers, R.V. *Schism. A Sermon Preached at Bytown, Before the Eastern Clerical Association, on Thursday, January 10th, 1839.* Cobourg, 1839.

— *Confidence in Death: A Sermon Preached in St. George's Church, Kingston, Canada West, on Sunday, January 26th, 1845, on the Occasion of the Death of John Solomon Cartwright* .... Kingston, 1845.

— "The Substance of a Sermon preached in St. James' Church, Stuartville, Kingston, November 14, 1847, on the occasion of the death of Mr. Micah Mason." The *Berean*, 16 Dec. 1847.

— "Sermon Preached at St. James' Church, Stuartville ... on the 5th of November, 1848." The *Berean*, 21 Dec. 1848.

Rose, A.W. *The Emigrant Churchman in Canada. By a Pioneer of the Wilderness* .... Ed. by Rev. Henry Christmas. 2 vols. London, 1849.

Salmon, George. *A Sermon Preached at the Village of Waterloo, Shefford, L.C. on Friday, 4th May, 1832. A Day Appointed for a General Fast.* Montreal, 1833.

Scadding, Henry. *The Eastern Oriel Opened. The Annual Address. Delivered Before the Societies of St. George, St, Andrew, and St. Patrick, in the Cathedral Church of St. James, Toronto, on St. George's Day, 1842* .... Toronto, 1842.

— *The Valedictory Address, Delivered Before the Athenaeum of Toronto, at the Close of their Annual Session, on Thursday, April 30, 1846.* Toronto, 1846.

— *A Memorial of the Reverend William Honywood Ripley ... Being ... the Sermon preached in Trinity Church ... Oct. the 28th, 1849.* Toronto, 1849.

Shortt, Jonathan. *"Peace in Believing." Exemplified in the Case of the Late Mary Anne Sophia Whitehead, Who Fell Asleep in Jesus on Sunday, the 7th March, 1847, in the 20th Year of her Age. The Substance of Sermons Preached in St. John's Church, Port Hope, on Sunday, March 14th, 1847.* Toronto, 1847.

— *The Gospel Banner! A Sermon Preached to the Loyal Orange Lodges, Assembled in St. John's Church, Port Hope, July 12th, 1853.* N.p., n.d.

Smithurst, John. *The Duke of Wellington, A Funeral Sermon, Preached on Sunday, the 21st of November, in the Morning, at St. John's Church, Elora, and in the Evening at St. George's, Guelph.* Elora, 1852.

In His Name

Spratt, George. *A Sermon Delivered at the Opening of St. John's Chapel in Quebec ... on 7th April, 1817.* Quebec, 1817.

Stewart, Charles. *Two Sermons, Preached in St. Armand, Lower Canada. Soon After the Decease of Mrs. Hannah Cooke, of that Place, with a Letter to her Husband.* Montreal 1810.

— *The Presence of God in His Holy House. A Sermon Preached at the Dedication of St. Paul's Church, in the Seigniory of St. Armand, Lower Canada, on the 28th July A.D. 1811.* Montreal, 1811.

— *Christ The Chief Cornerstone. A Sermon, Preached to the Members of the Select Surveyors' Lodge No. IX. Held in the Seigniory of St. Armand, Lower Canada, on their Celebration of the Festival of St. John the Apostle and Evangelist, A.D. 1811.* Montreal, 1812.

— *Two Sermons on Family Prayer, with Extracts from Various Authors; and a Collection of Prayers.* Montreal, 1814.

— *The Providence of God Manifested in the Events of the Last Year. A Sermon Preached on the First Day of January, A.D. 1815, in St. Paul's Church, in the Seigniory of St. Armand, Lower Canada.* Montreal, 1815.

— *A Short View of the Present State of the Eastern Townships in the Province of Lower Canada.* London, 1817.

— *A Charge to the Clergy of the Diocese of Quebec, Delivered at Montreal on the 9th August, and at York, Upper Canada, on the 30th August, 1826.* Quebec, 1827.

— *A Circular Letter Regarding Sunday Schools.* Quebec, 20th July 1830.

— *A Charge to the Clergy of the Diocese of Quebec, Delivered at the Visitation in Montreal, Lower Canada, 9th August, Kingston, Upper Canada, 23rd Aug., York, Upper Canada, 5th Sept, in the Year 1832.* Quebec, 1834.

— "Address from the Bishop of Quebec to the British Public ... received in July, 1834." Included in W.J.D. Waddilove, ed., *The Stewart Missions.* London, 1838.

Strachan, John. *The Christian Religion Recommended in a letter to his Pupils, Andrew Stuart & James Cartwright.* Montreal, 1807.

— *A Discourse on the Character of King George the Third. Addressed to the Inhabitants of British America.* Montreal, 1810.

— *A Sermon Preached at York Before the Legisl*r *Assembly, August 2nd, 1812.* York, 1812.

— *A Sermon Preached at York, Upper Canada, on the* 1... *Day Appointed for a General Thanksgiving.* Montreal, 1&.

— *A Sermon on the Death of the Honorable Richard Cartwright.* ... *Account of His Life. Preached at Kingston, on the 3d of Septembe*... Montreal, 1816.

— *A Letter to the Right Honourable the Earl of Selkirk on his Settlement at the Red River, near Hudson's Bay.* London, 1816.

— "A Sermon on the Death of the Late King." The *Christian Recorder*, May 1820.

— *A Visit to the Province of Upper Canada, in 1819.* Aberdeen, 1820. Written under the pseudonym of James Strachan.

— *Observations on the Policy of a General Union of all the British Provinces of North America.* London, 1824.

— *Observations on a "Bill for Uniting the Legislative Councils and Assemblies of the Provinces of Lower Canada and Upper Canada in one Legislature, and to Make Further Provision for the Government of the Said Provinces."* London, 1824.

— *A Sermon, preached at York, Upper Canada, third of July, 1825, On the Death of the Late Lord Bishop of Quebec.* Kingston, 1826.

— *Canada Church Establishment. Copy of a Letter addressed to R.J. Wilmot Horton, Esq. by the Rev. Dr. Strachan ... dated 16th May, 1827; respecting the State of the Church in that Province.* N.p., n.d.

— *Observations on the Provision Made for the Maintenance of a Protestant Clergy, in the Provinces of Upper and Lower Canada.* London, 1827.

— *An Appeal to the Friends of Religion and Literature, in behalf of the University of Upper Canada.* London, 1827.

— *A Speech of the Venerable John Strachan, D.D. Archdeacon of York, in the Legislative Council, Thursday Sixth March, 1828: On the Subject of the Clergy Reserves.* York, 1828.

— *A Letter to the Rev. A.N. Bethune, Rector of Cobourg, on the Management of Grammar Schools.* York, 1829.

— Letter from the Hon. and Venerable Dr. Strachan, Archdeacon of York, to Dr. Lee, D.D. Convener of a Committee of the General Assembly of the Church of Scotland. Kingston, 1829.

— A Letter, to the Right Honorable Thomas Frankland Lewis, M.P. 1830.

— Church Fellowship. A Sermon, Preached on Wednesday, September 5, 1832. At the Visitation of the Honorable and Right Rev. Charles James, Lord Bishop of Quebec. York, 1832.

— A Letter to the Rev. Thomas Chalmers, D.D. Professor of Divinity in the University of Edinburgh, on the Life and Character of the Right Reverend Dr. Hobart, Bishop of New York, North America. New York, 1832.

— The Cornwall Tribute: A Piece of Plate, Presented to the Honorable and Venerable John Strachan, D.D. Archdeacon of York, by Forty-Two of his Former Pupils, Educated by him at Cornwall. Presented Second July, MDCCCXXXIII. York, 1833.

— The Poor Man's Preservative Against Popery. Part. I. Containing an Introduction on the Character and Genius of the Roman Catholic Religion, and the Substance of a Letter to the Congregation of St. James' Church, Toronto, U.C. Occasioned by the Hon. J. Elmsley's Publication of the Bishop of Strasbourg's Observations on the 6th Chapter of St. John's Gospel. Toronto, 1834.

— A Letter, to the Congregation of St. James' Church, York, U. Canada, Occasioned by the Hon. John Elmsley's Publication, of the Bishop of Strasbourg's Observations, on the 6th Chapter of St. John's Gospel. York, 1834.

— The Church of the Redeemed. A Sermon Preached on Wednesday, 5th October, 1836, at a Meeting of the Clergy of the Established Church of Upper Canada. Under their Archdeacons Assembled. Toronto, 1836.

— Address to the Clergy of the Archdeaconry of York ... Delivered at Toronto on Wednesday the 13th September, 1837. N.p., n.d.

— Letters to the Honorable William Morris, Being Strictures on the Correspondence of that Gentleman with the Colonial Office, as a Delegate from the Presbyterian Body in Canada. Cobourg, 1838.

— Address and Report, of the Venerable the Archdeacon of York, Together with the Proceedings of a Meeting, of the Pew Holders and Persons Interested in St. James' Church, Held in the City Hall, January 9, 1839. Toronto, 1839.

Bibliography

— *Speeches of the Hon. Colonel Burwell, in the House of Assembly, the Right Rev. The Lord Bishop of Toronto, and the Hon. P. de Blaquière, in the Legislative Council.* Newcastle-upon-Tyne, 1840.

— *A Charge Delivered to the Clergy of the Diocese of Toronto, at the Primary Visitation, Held in the Cathedral Church of St. James, Toronto, on the 9th September, 1841.* Toronto, 1841.

— *Journal of the Visitation of the Diocese of Toronto, (Upper Canada,) in the Summer of 1840, by the Right Rev. The Lord Bishop of Toronto* .... London, 1841.

— *A Sermon Preached in the Cathedral Church of St. James, Toronto, Canada, on the 15th Day of May, 1842 ... on the Death of Elizabeth Emily, Wife of the Honourable Mr. Justice Hagerman.* Toronto, 1842.

— *The Church in Canada. A Journal of Visitation to the Western Portion of His Diocese by the Lord Bishop of Toronto, in the Autumn of 1842.* London, 1844.

— *A Pastoral Letter to the Clergy and Lay Members of the Established Church in Western Canada, 10 Dec., 1844.* N.p., n.d.

— *A Charge Delivered to the Clergy of the Diocese of Toronto, at the Triennial Visitation, held in the Cathedral Church of St. James, Toronto, on the 6th June, 1844.* Cobourg, 1844.

— *A Charge Delivered to the Clergy of the Diocese of Toronto, at the Visitation in June MD CCC XLVII.* Toronto, 1847.

— *Pastoral Letter to the Clergy and Laity of the Diocese of Toronto, on the Subject of the Cholera.* Toronto, 1848.

— *Thoughts on the Rebuilding of the Cathedral Church of St. James.* Toronto, 1850.

— *A Letter ... to the Rev. T.B. Murray, M.A., Secretary of the Society for Promoting Christian Knowledge, on the Subject of Establishing a Church University in Upper Canada.* London, 1850.

— *An Address to the Members of the Church of England... in behalf of the Upper Canada Church University.* London, 1850.

— *Secular State of the Church, in the Diocese of Toronto, Canada West.* N.p., n.d.

In His Name

— *A Letter to the Right Hon. Lord John Russell of [sic] the Present State of the Church in Canada.* Toronto, 1851.

— *Church University of Upper Canada. Pastoral Letter from the Lord Bishop of Toronto. Proceedings of the Church University Board. List of Subscribers, &c.* Toronto, 1851.

— *A Charge Delivered to the Clergy of the Diocese of Toronto, in May, MDCCCLI.* Toronto, 1851.

— *Pastoral Address, to the Clergy and Laity of the Diocese of Toronto.* Toronto, 1852.

— *The Report of the Bishop of Toronto, to the Most Hon. The Duke of Newcastle, Her Majesty's Secretary of State for the Colonies, on the Subject of the Colonial Church.* Toronto, 1853.

— *The Clergy Reserves. A Letter from the Lord Bishop of Toronto to the Duke of Newcastle, Her Majesty's Secretary for the Colonies.* Toronto, 1853.

— *A Charge Delivered to the Clergy of the Diocese of Toronto at the Visitation on Wednesday, Oct. 12, 1853.* Toronto, 1853.

— *Pastoral Letter to the Clergy and Laity of the Diocese of Toronto.* Toronto, 1854.

— *The Clergy Reserves. A Letter from the Bishop of Toronto, to the Honourable A.N. Morin, Commissioner of Crown Lands.* Toronto, 1854.

Stuart, G.O. *A Sermon, Preached at Kingston, Upper Canada, on Sunday, the 25th Day of November, 1827, on Occasion of Divine Service at Opening of St. George's Church.* Kingston, 1827.

— Extract from a charge to the clergy of the Archdeaconry of Kingston, 8 July 1836. The *Church*, 24 July 1836.

— Charge to the Clergy of the Archdeaconry of Kingston. The *Church*, 7 Oct. 1837.

— "A Discourse on the Occasion of the Death of the Late John Solomon Cartwright, Esquire, Delivered in St. George's Church, on Sunday, the 2nd of February, 1845." The *Church*, 28 Feb. 1845.

— "A Charge Delivered ... on the 15th December, in St. George's Church, Kingston, to the Clergy of his Archdeaconry...." The *Church*, 28 Dec. 1848.

Stuart, John. *A Sermon preached ... in St. George's, Kingston, April 1, 1793.* N.p., n.d.

Townley, Adam. *Ten Letters on the Church and Church Establishments, in Answer to Certain Letters of the Rev. Egerton Ryerson, by an Anglo-Canadian.* Toronto, 1839.

— "A Letter to a Friend, Occasioned by the Present State of Religious Parties in England." The *Church*, 2 and 9 Jan. 1851.

— *Seven Letters on the Non-Religious Common School System of Canada and the United States.* Toronto, 1853.

Usher, J.C. *A Sermon Preached to a Congregation, Assembled to Commemorate the Coming of Immanuel "in the likeness of Sinful Flesh," 25th December, 1835 ....* Hamilton, 1836.

Waddilove, W.J.D. *The Stewart Missions.* London, 1838.

Wade, C.T. "A Sermon, addressed to the Young, preached in St. John's Church, Peterboro', on Sunday, January 5, 1840." The *Church*, 1 Feb. 1840.

— "Childhood and Youth are vanity." Sermon preached on 12 Jan. 1840. The *Church*, 8 Feb. 1840.

Warburton, William. *The Works of the Right Reverend William Warburton ... Volume the Seventh.* London, 1811.

Wenham, John. *A Sermon Preached Before the Bishop of Quebec, and the Clergy of Upper Canada, at His Lordship's Primary Visitation, Held in York, on Wednesday, 30th Aug. 1826.* Brockville, 1826.

Whitaker, George. *A Sermon Preached in the Chapel of Trinity College, Toronto, on Sunday, June 27, 1852.* Toronto, 1852.

V. Secondary Sources

A. Books

Abbey, Charles J., and John H. Overton. *The English Church in the Eighteenth Century*. London, 1902.

Addison, James Thayer. *The Episcopal Church in the United States, 1789-1931*. New York, 1951.

Addleshaw, G.W.O. *The High Church Tradition: A Study in the Liturgical Thought of the Seventeenth Century*. 1941.

Akenson, Donald Harman. *The Irish in Ontario: A Study in Rural History*. Kingston and Montreal, 1984.

Allen, Richard. *The Social Passion: Religion and Social Reform in Canada 1914-28*. Toronto, 1973.

Arthur, Eric. *Toronto: No Mean City*. Toronto, 1964.

Balleine, F.R. *History of the Evangelical Party in the Church of England*. London, 1909.

Berger, Carl. *Science, God, and Nature in Victorian Canada*. Toronto, 1983.

Best, G.F.A. *Temporal Pillars: Queen Anne's Bounty, the Ecclesiastical Commissioners, and the Church of England*. Cambridge, 1964.

Bourne, E.C.E. *The Anglicanism of William Laud*. London, 1947.

Bowen, Desmond. *The Idea of the Victorian Church*. Montreal, 1968.

Brilioth, Yngve. *The Anglican Revival: Studies in the Oxford Movement*. London, 1933.

Buckner, Phillip A. *The Transition to Responsible Government: British Policy in British North America, 1815-1850*. Westport, Conn., and London, England, 1985.

Bull, William Perkins. *From Strachan to Owen: How the Church of England was Planted and Tended in British North America*. Toronto, 1938.

Burkholder, C.J. *A Brief History of the Mennonites in Ontario*. 1935.

Burt, A.L. *The Old Province of Quebec*. 2 vols. Toronto, 1933.

Bibliography

Burtniak, John, and Turner, Wesley B., eds. *Religion and Churches in the Niagara Peninsula: Proceedings, Fourth Annual Niagara Peninsula History Conference, Brock University, 17-18 April 1982.*

Carpenter, S.C. *Church and People, 1789-1889: A History of the Church of England from William Wilberforce to "Lux Mundi".* London, 1933.

— *Eighteenth Century Church and People.* London, 1959.

Carrington, Philip. *The Anglican Church in Canada: A History.* Toronto, 1963.

Chadwick, Owen. *The Victorian Church*, 2 vols. London, 1966.

Church, R.W. *The Oxford Movement, Twelve Years, 1833-45.* London, 1891.

Clark, J.C.D. *English Society, 1688-1832: Ideology, Social Structure and Political Practice During the Ancien Regime.* Cambridge, U.K., 1985.

Clark, S.D. *Church and Sect in Canada.* Toronto, 1968.

Cook, Ramsay. *The Regenerators: Social Criticism in Late Victorian English Canada.* Toronto, 1985.

Cornish, F.W. *The English Church in the Nineteenth Century.* 2 vols. London, 1910.

Cowan, Helen I. *British Emigration to British North America.* Toronto, 1961.

Cragg, Gerald R. *The Church and the Age of Reason, 1648-1789.* London, 1960.

— *From Puritanism to the Age of Reason.* Cambridge, 1950.

Craig, Gerald M. *Upper Canada, the Formative Years, 1784-1841.* Toronto, 1963.

Cronmiller, C.R. *A History of the Lutheran Church in Canada.* 1961.

Cross, Michael S., ed. *The Frontier Thesis and the Canadas: The Debate on the Impact of the Canadian Environment.* Toronto, 1970.

Crowfoot, A.H. *Benjamin Cronyn: First Bishop of Huron.* London, 1957.

— *This Dreamer: Life of Isaac Hellmuth, Second Bishop of Huron.* Toronto, 1963.

Cruikshank, E.A., ed. *The Correspondence of Lieut. Governor John Graves Simcoe.* 5 vols. Toronto, 1923-31.

Curtis, Bruce. *Building the Educational State: Canada West, 1836-1871.* London, Ont., 1988.

Cuthbertson, Brian. *The First Bishop: A Biography of Charles Inglis.* Halifax, 1987.

Davies, Horton. *Worship and Theology in England: From Watts and Wesley to Maurice, 1690-1850.* Princeton, 1961.

Dent, J.C. *The Story of the Upper Canadian Rebellion.* 2 vols. Toronto, 1885.

Dictionary of Canadian Biography. Vols. 4-12. Toronto, 1979-90.

Dictionary of Hamilton Biography. Vol. I. Hamilton, 1981.

Dorland, A.G. *A History of the Society of Friends (Quakers) in Canada.* Toronto, 1927.

Dunham, Aileen. *Political Unrest in Upper Canada.* London, 1927.

Earl, D.W.L., ed. *The Family Compact.* Toronto, 1967.

Elgee, William. *The Social Teachings of the Canadian Churches.* Toronto, 1964.

Elliott-Binns, L.E. *The Evangelical Movement in the English Church.* London, 1928.

— *Religion in the Victorian Era.* London, 1936.

Errington, Jane. *The Lion, the Eagle, and Upper Canada: A Developing Colonial Ideology.* Kingston and Montreal, 1987.

Faber, Geoffrey. *Oxford Apostles: A Character Study of the Oxford Movement.* London, 1933.

Ferguson, William. *Scotland; 1689 to the Present.* Edinburgh, 1968.

Fingard, Judith. *The Anglican Design in Loyalist Nova Scotia, 1783-1816.* London, 1972.

Flint, David. *John Strachan: Pastor and Politician.* Toronto, 1971.

French, G.S. *Parsons and Politics.* Toronto, 1962.

Bibliography

Glazebrook, G.P. de T. "The Church of England in Upper Canada, 1785-1867." Typescript, 1982, Robarts Library, University of Toronto.

Grant, John Webster. *A Profusion of Spires: Religion in Nineteenth-Century Ontario*. Toronto, Buffalo and London, 1988.

— ed. *The Church and the Canadian Experience*. Toronto, 1963.

Haller, William. *Foxe's Book of Martyrs and the Elect Nation*. London, 1963.

Harlow, Vincent T. *The Founding of the Second British Empire, 1763-1793*. 2 vols. London, 1964.

Harris, Reginald V. *Charles Inglis: Missionary, Loyalist, Bishop (1734-1816)*. Toronto, 1937.

Hayes, Alan L., ed. *By Grace Co-workers: Building the Anglican Diocese of Toronto, 1780-1989*. Toronto, 1989.

Henderson, J.L.H. *John Strachan: 1778-1867*. Toronto, 1969.

— *John Strachan: Documents and Opinions*. Toronto, 1969.

Hill, Christopher. *The Century of Revolution, 1603-1714*. London, 1961.

Hodgins, J.G., ed. *Documentary History of Education in Upper Canada ... 1791 to ... 1876*. 28 vols. Toronto, 1894-1910.

Houston, Susan E., and Alison Prentice. *Schooling and Scholars in Nineteenth-Century Ontario*. Toronto, 1988.

Hutton, W.H. *The English Church from the Accession of Charles I to the Death of Anne*. London, 1903.

Inge, W.R. *The Platonic Tradition in English Religious Thought*. London, 1926.

Ivison, Stuart, and Fred Rosser. *The Baptists in Upper and Lower Canada before 1820*. London, 1936.

Johnson, J.K., ed. *Historical Essays on Upper Canada*. Toronto, 1975.

Knox, R.A. *Enthusiasm: A Chapter in the History of Religion with Special Reference to the XVII and XVIII Centuries*. Oxford, 1950.

Landon, Fred. *Western Ontario and the American Frontier* (1941). Reprinted, Toronto, 1967.

Langtry, J. *History of the Church in Eastern Canada and Newfoundland.* London, 1892.

Lovejoy, Arthur O. *The Great Chain of Being: A Study of the History of an Idea.* Cambridge, Mass., 1942.

McKillop, A.B. *A Disciplined Intelligence: Critical Inquiry and Canadian Thought in the Victorian Era.* Montreal, 1979.

Marshall, John S. *Hooker and the Anglican Tradition.* London, 1963.

Masters, D.C. *Protestant Church Colleges in Canada: A History.* Toronto, 1966.

Mathieson, W.L. *English Church Reform, 1815-40.* London, 1923.

Millman, Thomas R. *Jacob Mountain, First Lord Bishop of Quebec: A Study in Church and State, 1793-1825.* Toronto, 1947.

— *The Life of Charles James Stewart.* London, Ont., 1953.

Mills, David. *The Idea of Loyalty in Upper Canada, 1784-1850.* Kingston and Montreal, 1988.

Mockridge, C.H. *The Bishops of the Church of England in Canada and Newfoundland.* Toronto, 1896.

Moir, J.S. *Church and State in Canada West: Three Studies in the Relation of Denominationalism and Nationalism, 1841-67.* Toronto, 1959.

— *The Church in the British Era.* Toronto, 1972.

— *Enduring Witness: A History of the Presbyterian Church in Canada.* Toronto, n.d.

— ed. *Church and State in Canada, 1627-1867: Basic Documents.* Toronto, 1967.

Moorman, John R.H. *A History of the Church of England.* New York, 1954.

Morris, Christopher. *Political Thought in England: Tyndale to Hooker.* London, 1953.

Mountain, Armine W. *A Memoir of George Jehosaphat Mountain.* Montreal, 1866.

Neatby, Hilda. *Quebec: The Revolutionary Age, 1760-91.* Toronto, 1966.

Nelson, W.H. *The American Tory*. New York, 1961.

Newman, John Henry. *Apologia Pro Vita Sua*. London, 1888.

Niebuhr, H. Richard. *The Social Sources of Denominationalism*. Connecticut, 1929.

Norman, E.R. *Church and Society in England, 1770-1970: A Historical Study*. London, 1976.

— *The Conscience of the State in North America*. Cambridge, 1968.

Norton, Mary Beth. *The British Americans: The Loyalist Exiles in England, 1774-1789*. Boston, 1972.

Overton, J.H. *The English Church in the Nineteenth Century*. London, 1894.

Palmer, R.R. *The Age of the Democratic Revolution, 1760-1800*. 2 vols. Princeton, 1959, 1964.

Phillips, Walter Alison, ed. *History of the Church of Ireland*. 3 vols. Vol. III: *The Modern Church*. London, 1933.

Playter, George F. *History of Methodism in Canada*. Toronto, 1862.

Prentice, Alison. *The School Promoters: Education and Social Class in Mid-Nineteenth Century Upper Canada*. Toronto, 1977.

Preston, Richard, ed. *Kingston before the War of 1812*. Toronto, 1959.

Radcliff, Thomas, ed. *Authentic Letters from Upper Canada*. Toronto, 1953.

Rea, J.E. *Bishop Alexander Macdonell and the Politics of Upper Canada*. Toronto, 1974.

Read, Colin. *The Rising in Western Upper Canada, 1837-8: The Duncombe Revolt and After*. Toronto, 1982.

Reed, T.A. *A History of the University of Trinity College*. Toronto, 1952.

Robertson, Thomas B. *The Fighting Bishop*. Ottawa, 1926.

Ruggle, Richard, ed. *Some Men and Some Controversies*. Erin, Ont., 1974.

Rupp, E.G. *Studies in the Making of the English Protestant Tradition*. Cambridge, 1947.

Sanderson, J.E. *The First Century of Methodism in Canada*. 2 vols. Toronto, 1908.

Scadding, Henry. *The First Bishop of Toronto*. Toronto, 1868.

Shortt, Adam, and A.G. Doughty, eds. *Documents Relating to the Constitutional History of Canada, 1759-1791*. 2 vols. Ottawa, 1918.

Sissons, C.B. *Egerton Ryerson: His Life and Letters*. 2 vols. Toronto, 1937.

Soloway, Richard A. *Prelates and People: Ecclesiastical Thought in England, 1783-1852*. London, 1969.

Spragge, George, ed. *The John Strachan Letter Book, 1812-34*. Toronto, 1946.

Storr. V.F. *The Development of English Theology in the Nineteenth Century, 1800-1860*. London, 1913.

Stromberg, Roland N. *Religious Liberalism in Eighteenth-Century England*. Oxford, 1954.

Stuart, H.C. *The Church of England in Canada, 1759-1793. From the Conquest to the Establishment of the See of Quebec*. Montreal, 1893.

Sykes, Norman. *Church and State in England in the Eighteenth Century*. Cambridge, 1934.

Taylor, Fennings. *The Last Three Bishops Appointed by the Crown for the Anglican Church of Canada*. Montreal, 1869.

Thompson, H.P. *Into All Lands: The History of the Society for the Propagation of the Gospel in Foreign Parts, 1710-1950*. London, 1951.

Troeltsch, Ernst. *The Social Teachings of the Christian Churches*. 2 vols. London, 1931.

Upton, L.F.S., ed. *The United Empire Loyalists: Men and Myths*. Toronto, 1967.

Vernor, C.W. *The Old Church in the New Dominion*. London, 1929.

Walker, F.A. *Catholic Education and Politics in Upper Canada*. Toronto, 1955.

Wallace, W.S. *The Family Compact*. Toronto, 1915.

— *A History of the University of Toronto, 1827-1927*. Toronto, 1927.

Walsh, H.H. *The Christian Church in Canada*. Toronto, 1956.

Ward, W.R. *Religion and Society in England, 1790-1850*. London, 1972.

Westfall, William. *Two Worlds: The Protestant Culture of Nineteenth-Century Ontario*. Kingston and Montreal, 1989.

Wilson, Alan. *The Clergy Reserves of Upper Canada: A Canadian Mortmain*. Toronto, 1968.

Wilson, Bruce G. *As She Began: An Illustrated Introduction to Loyalist Ontario*. Toronto and Charlottetown, 1981.

— *The Enterprises of Robert Hamilton: A Study of Wealth and Influence in Early Upper Canada, 1776-1812*. Ottawa, 1983.

Wise, S.F., and R.C. Brown. *Canada Views the United States: Nineteenth Century Political Attitudes*. Toronto, 1967.

Young, A.H. *The Revd. John Stuart, D.D., U.E.L. of Kingston, U.C. and His Family: A Genealogical Study*. Kingston, 1920.

— ed. *The Parish Register of Kingston, Upper Canada, 1785-1811*. Kingston, 1921.

Zaslow, Morris, ed. *The Defended Border: Upper Canada and the War of 1812*. Toronto, 1964.

B. Articles

Banks, John. "The Reverend James Magrath: Family Man and Anglican Cleric." *OH*, LV (September 1963), pp. 131-42.

Black, Robert Merrill. "The American Father of the Ontario Church: The Rev. John Stuart, U.E." *JCCHS*, XXVII (October 1985), pp. 55-62.

Boulton, William. "The Boulton Letters: Letters of the Rev. William Boulton, Master of U.C.C., to His Wife, 1833-34." Women's Canadian Historical Society of Toronto, *Transactions* no. 18, pp. 32-48.

Brooks, E.A. "The Little World of Robert Addison, First Priest of Niagara (1792-1829)." *JCCHS*, IV (November 1960), pp. 1-14.

Brown, George W. "The Formative Period of the Canadian Protestant Churches." In R. Flenley, ed., *Essays in Canadian History*. Toronto, 1939, pp. 346-72.

Bumsted, J.M. "Church and State in Maritime Canada, 1749-1807." *CHAR*, 1967, pp. 41-58.

Cameron, William J., George McKnight, and Michaele-Sue Goldblatt. "Robert Addison's Library." Hamilton, 1967.

Clemens, James M. "Taste Not; Touch Not; Handle Not: A Study of the Social Assumptions of the Temperance Literature and Temperance Supporters in Canada West Between 1839 and 1859." *OH*, LXIV (September 1972), pp. 142-60.

Clifford, N.K. "Religion and the Development of Canadian Society: An Historiographical Analysis." Canadian Society of Church History, *Papers*, 1969, pp. 14-32.

Cooke, William G. "The Diocese of Toronto and its Two Cathedrals." *JCCHS*, XXVII (October, 1985), pp. 98-115.

Cooper, J.I. "Irish Immigration and the Canadian Church before the Middle of the 19th Century." *JCCHS*, II (May 1955), pp. 1-16.

Cruikshank, Ernest A. "John Beverley Robinson and the Trials for Treason in 1814." *OHSPR*, XXV (1929), pp. 191-219.

Elliott, Bruce S. "Ritualism and the Beginnings of the Reformed Episcopal Movement in Ottawa." *JCCHS*, XXVII (April, 1985), pp. 18-41.

Fingard, Judith. "Charles Inglis and His `Primitive Bishoprick' in Nova Scotia." *CHR*, XLIX (September 1968), pp. 247-66.

Geddes, J.G. "Notes of Autobiography." *Journal and Transactions of the Wentworth Historical Society*, I (1892), pp. 44-47.

Gidney, R.D. "Centralization and Education: The Origins of an Ontario Tradition." *Journal of Canadian Studies*, VII (November 1972), pp. 33-48.

— "Elementary Education in Upper Canada: A Reassessment." *OH*, LXV (September 1973), pp. 169-85.

Gilmour, J.L. "The Baptists in Canada." In Adam Shortt and A.G. Doughty, eds., *Canada and Its Provinces*, vol. XI. Toronto, 1913, pp. 345-76.

Greenfield, Katherine. "Reference Sources for the History of the Church of England in Upper Canada, 1791-1867." *JCCHS*, IX (September 1967), pp. 50-74.

— "The Reverend John Gamble Geddes and Early Days at Christ's Church, Hamilton." *Wentworth Bygones*, no. 4 (1963), pp. 9-21.

Greer, Allan. "The Sunday Schools of Upper Canada." *OH*, LXVII (September 1975), pp. 169-84.

Gundy, H.P. "Strachan and Stuart Letters at Queen's." *Historic Kingston* (November 1959), pp. 34-39.

Hayes, Alan L. "The Struggle for the Rights of the Laity in the Diocese of Toronto, 1850-1879." *JCCHS*, XXVI (April 1984), pp. 5-17.

Headon, Christopher F. "Developments in Canadian Anglican Worship in Eastern and Central Canada, 1840-1868." *JCCHS*, XVII (June 1975), pp. 26-38.

Henderson, J.L.H. "The Abominable Incubus: The Church as by Law Established." *JCCHS*, XI (September 1969), pp. 58-66.

—"The Founding of Trinity College, Toronto." *OH*, XLIV (January 1952), pp. 7-14.

Horrall, S.W. "The Clergy and the Election of Bishop Cronyn." *OH*, LVIII (December 1966), pp. 205-20.

Houston, S.E. "Politics, Schools and Social Change in Upper Canada." *CHR*, LIII (September 1972), pp. 249-71.

Hunter, A.F. "The Probated Wills of Men Prominent in the Public Affairs of Early Upper Canada." *OHSPR*, XXIII (1926), pp. 328-59.

Kelley, A.R., ed. "From Quebec to Niagara in 1794: Diary of Bishop Jacob Mountain." *Rapport de l'Archiviste de la Province de Quebec* (1959-60), pp. 119-65.

Kenyon, John. "The Influence of the Oxford Movement upon the Church of England in Upper Canada." *OH*, LI (Spring 1959), pp. 79-94.

Kerr, W.B., and Mrs. Ada Brett Kerr. "Reverend William Leeming, First Rector of Trinity Church, Chippawa." *OHSPR*, XXXI (1936), pp. 135-54.

Lydekker, J.W. "The Rev. John Stuart, D.D., (1740-1811), Missionary to the Mohawks." *Historical Magazine of the Protestant Episcopal Church*, XI (March 1942), pp. 18-64.

MacLean, Hugh D. "An Irish Apostle and Archdeacon in Canada." *JCCHS*, XV (September 1973), pp. 50-65.

McMorine, Archdeacon. "Early History of the Anglican Church in Kingston." *OHSPR*, VIII (1907), pp. 92-102.

MacVean, William C. "The `Erastianism' of John Strachan." *Canadian Journal of Theology*, XIII (1967), pp. 189-204.

Masters, D.C. "The Nicolls Papers: A Study in Anglican Toryism." *CHAR*, 1945, pp. 42-48.

Mealing, S.R. "The Enthusiasms of John Graves Simcoe." *CHAR*, 1958, pp. 50-62.

Millman, T.R. "Beginnings of the Synodical Movement in Colonial Anglican Churches, with special reference to Canada." *JCCHS*, XXI (1979), pp. 3-19.

— "The Cathedral Church of St. James, Toronto." *Anglican*, 6 (August 1963), p. 3.

— "The Church of England in Western Ontario, 1785-1955." *Western Ontario Historical Notes*, XIII (March-June 1955), pp. 1-27.

— "The Forgotten Episcopal Visitation of Upper Canada, 1838." *JCCHS*, XXVII (October 1985), pp. 70-85.

Moir, J.S. "The Correspondence of Bishop Strachan and John Henry Newman." *Canadian Journal of Theology*, III (1957), pp. 219-25.

— "The Upper Canadian Religious Tradition." In *Profiles of a Province: Studies in the History of Ontario*. Toronto, 1967, pp. 189-95.

— "The Upper Canadian Roots of Church Disestablishment." *OH*, LX (June 1968), pp. 247-58.

Morton, W.L. "Review Essay: Strachan in the Round." *Journal of Canadian Studies*, IV (November 1969), pp. 46-50.

Norris, John M. "Proposals for Promoting Religion and Literature in Canada, Nova Scotia, and New Brunswick." *CHR*, XXXVI (1955), pp. 335-40.

Osmond, Oliver R. "The Churchmanship of John Strachan." *JCCHS*, XVI (September 1974), pp. 46-58.

Owram, Douglas. "Strachan & Ryerson: Guardians of the Future." *Canadian Literature*, LXXXIII (Winter, 1979), pp. 21-29.

Preston, R.A. "A Clash in St. Paul's Churchyard." *Historic Kingston* (October 1956), pp. 30-44.

Purdy, J.D. "John Strachan and the Diocesan Theological Institute at Cobourg, 1842-1852." *OH*, LXV (June 1973), pp. 113-23.

— "John Strachan's Educational Policies, 1815-41." *OH*, LXIV (March 1972), pp. 45-64.

Rawlyk, G.A. "The Reverend John Stuart: Mohawk Missionary and Reluctant Loyalist." In Esmond Wright, ed., *Red, White and True Blue: The Loyalists in the Revolution* (New York, 1976), pp. 55-71.

Rose, Elliot. "The Castle Builders: High Anglican Hopes of the Frontier in the Mid-Nineteenth Century." Canadian Society of Church History, *Papers*, 1975, pp. 42-63.

Ruggle, Richard E. "The Canadianization of the Church of England." Canadian Society of Church History, *Papers*, 1981, pp. 79-88.

— "Itinerant Clergy in Upper Canada." *JCCHS*, XXVII (October 1985), pp. 63-69.

Russell, Peter A. "Church of Scotland Clergy in Upper Canada: Culture Shock and Conservatism on the Frontier." *OH*, LXXIII (June 1981), pp. 88-111.

Scadding, Henry. "Church Annals at Niagara, from A.D. 1792-A.D. 1892." Toronto, 1892.

Scott, H.A. "The Roman Catholic Church East of the Great Lakes, 1760-1917." In Adam Shortt and A.G. Doughty, eds., *Canada and Its Provinces*, vol. XI. Toronto, 1913, pp. 11-112.

Smith, Alison. "John Strachan and Early Canada, 1799-1814." *OHSPR*, LII (September 1960), pp. 159-73.

Smith, C.H.E. "Rev. Robt. Addison, M.A." *Niagara Historical Society Transactions*, 35 (1923), pp. 61-71.

Spragge, George W. "The Cornwall Grammar School under John Strachan, 1803-12." *OHSPR*, XXXIV (1942), pp. 3-24.

— "Dr. Strachan's Motives for Becoming a Legislative Councillor." *CHR*, XIX (December 1938), pp. 397-402.

— "Elementary Education in Upper Canada, 1820-40." *OH*, XLIII (1951), pp. 107-22.

— "John Strachan's Connexion with Early Proposals for Confederation." *CHR*, XXIII (December 1942), pp. 363-73.

— "John Strachan's Contribution to Education, 1800-23." *CHR*, XXII (June 1941), pp. 147-58.

Stacey, C.P. "The War of 1812 in Canadian History." *OH*, L (Summer 1958), pp. 153-59.

Stanley, G.F.G. "John Stuart: Father of the Anglican Church in Upper Canada." *JCCHS*, III (June 1959), pp. 1-13.

Stimson, E.R. "Report of the Travelling Missionary of the Talbot District." *Western Ontario History Nuggets*, no. 3 (1944).

Talman, James J. "Church of England Missionary Effort in Upper Canada, 1815-40." *OHSPR*, XXV (1929), pp. 438-49.

— "The Position of the Church of England in Upper Canada, 1791-1840." *CHR*, XV (December 1935), pp. 361-74.

— "Report of a Missionary Journey Made by the Hon. and Rev. Charles James Stewart through Upper Canada in 1820." University of Western Ontario, 1942.

— "The Rev. Richard Flood, Indian Missionary and Rector of Delaware, 1834-65." *Transactions of the London and Middlesex Historical Society*, XII (1927), pp. 21-25.

— "Some Notes on the Clergy of the Church of England in Upper Canada Prior to 1840." *Royal Society of Canada Papers and Transactions*, II (1938), pp. 57-66.

— "Three Scottish-Canadian Newspaper Editor Poets." *CHR*, XXVIII (June 1947), pp. 166-77.

Tucker, L. Norman. "The Anglican Church and its Missions." In Shortt, Adam and A.G. Doughty, eds., *Canada and Its Provinces*, vol. XI. Toronto, 1913, pp. 199-246.

Walsh, H.H. "Research in Canadian Church History." *CHR*, XXXV (September 1954), pp. 208-16.

Wilson, Alan. "The Clergy Reserves: Economical Mischiefs or Sectarian Issue." *CHR*, XLII (1961), pp. 281-99.

Wise, S.F. "Conservatism: The Canadian Case." *South Atlantic Quarterly*, LXIX (Spring 1970), pp. 216-43.

— "God's Peculiar Peoples." In W.L. Morton, ed., *The Shield of Achilles: Aspects of Canada in the Victorian Age*. Toronto, 1968, pp. 36-61.

— "Sermon Literature and Canadian Intellectual History." *United Church Bulletin*, no. 18 (1965), pp. 3-18.

— "Upper Canada and the Conservative Tradition." In *Profiles of a Province: Studies in the History of Ontario*. Toronto, 1967, pp. 20-33.

Young, A.H. "The Bethunes." *OHSPR*, XXXVII (1931), pp. 553-74.

— "The Church of England in Upper Canada, 1791-1841." *Queen's Quarterly* (1930), pp. 145-66.

— "A Fallacy in Canadian History." *CHR*, XV (December 1934), pp. 351-60.

— "John Strachan." *Queen's Quarterly* (1928), pp. 386-407.

— "Lord Dorchester and the Church of England." *CHAR*, 1926, pp. 60-65.

— "More Langhorn Letters." *OHSPR*, XXIX (1933), pp. 47-71.

— "The Rev'd George Okill Stuart, M.A., LL.D. (Second Rector of York and of Kingston)." *OHSPR*, XXIV (1927), pp. 512-34.

— "The Revd. Richard Pollard, 1752-1824." *OHSPR*, XXV (1929), pp. 455-80.

— "The Rev. Robert Addison." *OHSPR*, XIX (1922), pp. 171-91.

— "The Rev. Robert Addison and St. Mark's Church, Niagara." *OHSPR*, XIX (1922), pp. 158-60.

— "The Revd. John Langhorn, Church of England Missionary, at Fredericksburgh and Ernesttown, 1787-1813." *OHSPR*, XXIII (1926), pp. 523-60.

C. Theses

Cross, Michael S. "The Dark Druidical Groves: The Lumber Community and the Commercial Frontier in British North America to 1854." Ph.D. Thesis, University of Toronto, 1968.

Fraser, Robert L. "Like Eden in Her Summer Dress: Gentry, Economy, and Society: Upper Canada, 1812-40." Ph.D. Thesis, University of Toronto, 1979.

Headon, Christopher F. "The Influence of the Oxford Movement upon the Church of England in Eastern and Central Canada, 1840-1900." Ph.D. Thesis, McGill University, 1974.

Henderson, J.L.H. "John Strachan as Bishop, 1839-1867." D.D. Thesis, General Synod of Canada, 1955.

McDermott, Mark C. "The Theology of Bishop John Strachan: A Study in Anglican Identity." Ph.D. Thesis, St. Michael's College, University of Toronto, 1983.

MacRae, Norma J. "The Religious Foundation of John Strachan's Social and Political Thought as Contained in His Sermons, 1803 to 1866." M.A. Thesis, McMaster University, 1978.

Patterson, Graeme H. "Studies in Elections and Public Opinion in Upper Canada." Ph.D. Thesis, University of Toronto, 1969.

Purdy, J.D. "John Strachan and Education in Canada, 1800-51." Ph.D. Thesis, University of Toronto, 1962.

Stagg, Ronald J. "The Yonge Street Rebellion of 1837: An Examination of the Social Background and a Re-assessment of the Events." Ph.D. Thesis, University of Toronto, 1976.

Thompson, A.N. "The Life of the Right Reverend Alexander Neil Bethune, D.D., D.L.L., Second Bishop of Toronto." Master of Sacred Theology Thesis, University of Toronto, 1957.

Turner, Harry Ernest. "The Evangelical Movement in the Church of England in the Diocese of Toronto, 1839-79." M.A. Thesis, University of Toronto 1959.

INDEX

Addison, Robert, 13, 15, 17, 26, 39, 40, 216
Alien Bill, 133
Allan, G.W., 185
American Episcopal Church, 203
American Revolution, 3–9, 12, 80, 115, 124, 127
Anglo-Catholicism. *See* High Church
Anne, Queen, 2
annexation movement, 168, 171-3
Anti-Slavery Association, 257
apostolic succession, 244, 246, 248, 251
Archbishop of Canterbury. See Canterbury
Archbishop of Dublin. *See* Dublin
Archbold, George, 42, 183
Ardagh, S.B., 257, 260-1, 268, 270
Armstrong, G.M., 249
Atkinson, A.F., 260, 262-3

Bagot, Sir Charles, 171, 173
Baker, Captain, 211
Baldwin, Edmund, 257
Baldwin, Robert, 171, 173
Bangs, Nathan, 15
Baptists, 9, 12-14, 38, 50, 77; clergy, 12-13, 38
Barclay, John, 106-7
Bartlett, T.M., 45
Bathurst, Lord, 67-8
Beaven, James, 184, 207, 211, 247-8; *Catechism on the Thirty-Nine Articles*, 248; *Help to Catechising*, 248; *Life and Writings of Saint Irenaeus*, 248
Berean, 260
Bethune, A.N., 42, 51, 79, 134, 138-9, 140, 142, 170, 182, 184-5, 199, 205, 214, 222, 225, 228, 245-6, 250-1, 256, 259, 261-5, 273-4; *The Christian Shepherd*, 251; *The Duty of Loyalty*, 168
Bethune, John, 129

In His Name

Bettridge, William, 132, 201-02; *Brief History of the Church in Upper Canada*, 179
Bible, distribution of, 26-7, 104; interpretation of, 91, 95-96, 104, 168, 241, 244, 246-8, 254, 258-9
Bible and Common Prayer Book Society of Upper Canada, 26, 103-4
Bible societies, 21, 104, 108. *See also* Bible and Common Prayer Society of Upper Canada, Bible Society of Upper Canada, British and Foreign Bible Society
Bible Society of Upper Canada, 27, 104
bishops: of England, 241, 244; of Upper Canada, 10, 63, 67, 76, 265-6; appointment of, 204-5, 210, 213, 265-7, 269. *See also* church: organization/government
Blake, Dominick, 45, 226, 268
Blakey, Robert, 41
Bleasdell, William, 270
Board of the General Superintendence of Education, 65-7, 77
Book of Common Prayer, 16, 22, 26, 27, 104, 187, 241, 257
Boomer, Michael, 272
Boswell, E.J., 183, 202, 268
Boulton, G.J., 185
Bovell, James, 211-2
Bower, E.C., 257
British and Foreign Bible Society, 26, 104-5, 256
Brockville Recorder, 105
Brooke, John, 4
Brough, C.C., 260, 268, 270
Brown, Dr, 15, 92, 94
Burke, Edmund, 126; *Reflections on the Revolution in France*, 126-7
Burwell, Adam, 120, 132, 134-5, 138, 165; *Doctrine of the Holy Spirit*, 120, 134, 165; *A Voice of Warning and Instruction Concerning the Signs of the Times*, 134

Calvinists, 14, 244, 254
Cambridge University, 2
Cameron, J.D., 44
Canada Committee (British House of Commons), 75-6, 79-80
Canada Company, 64, 67
Canadas, union of (1841), 62-3, 163, 171, 269
Canadian Conference (Methodist), 97

Index

Canterbury, archbishop of, 208, 263, 265
Carleton, Guy, 3-4
Cartwright, R.D., 138, 198-9, 219, 222, 255
Cartwright, Richard, 62
Catholic Church/Catholicism/Catholics. *See* Roman Catholics
Caulfield, A. St. George, 272
Champion, Thomas, 227
Chartists, 133
cholera epidemics, 113, 137-41, 143
Christian Recorder, 20, 25, 100-1, 103-5, 107, 122
church: buildings, 4, 11, 22, 45-6, 224, 249, 250; mission of, xv, 1, 8, 108, 136, 142, 164, 186-7, 228, 230, 253, 275, 295-6; organization/government, xiv, xv, xvi, 9, 37, 48, 49, 102, 105, 200-1, 203, 204, 206-7, 209, 210-4, 230, 246-7, 250-1, 254, 256, 265, 295, 297. *See also* synodical government; revenues, xv, 2, 5, 16-18, 20, 52, 63-4, 75, 126, 130, 200-2, 204, 214-5, 217, 222-25, 226; sufferings of, 135, 183-4, 187, 188, 209; as spiritual organization, xiv, 136, 142, 186-8, 190, 197, 239, 247, 253, 275, 295-6, 298
Church (newspaper), 49, 51, 132, 139-40, 164, 166-73, 177, 179-88, 202-5, 208-10, 212, 216, 218-22, 225-6, 239, 245-51, 253, 257-61, 265, 267, 271-3
Church and state, xiii, 8, 74, 114, 136, 163, 173, 186, 209, 252, 270, 274, 291, 292; alliance of, 1, 2, 18, 19, 125-8, 130, 176, 189, 208, 212, 241, 292, 295; separation of, xvi, 75-6, 98, 128, 134, 175, 177-8, 209, 229, 270, 292, 295
Churches: of the Holy Trinity, Toronto, 206; St. George's, Toronto, 229; St. James's, Toronto, 121, 128, 260; St. Mary's, Picton, 205; St. Peter's Church, Cobourg, 223; Trinity, New York, 6
church establishment: attack on, xvi, 8, 74, 75, 81, 135, 289, 290. *See also* disestablishment; defence of, xiii, xiv, xv, xvi, 2, 5, 8, 64, 80, 106, 114, 125-8, 132, 163, 176-7, 179, 187, 198, 209, 222, 228, 230, 270, 289, 297; idea of, xiv, xv, xvi, 1, 3, 7, 10, 11, 16, 18, 20, 28, 67, 107, 129, 178, 180, 182, 186, 188, 197, 199, 204, 218-9, 241, 275, 292-6
Church of Scotland, 38, 50, 69, 76-7, 79; claim to co-establishment, 7-8, 74-5, 107, 128-9, 174; clergy, 38, 74, 97, 106. *See also* Presbyterians
church-sect typology, 48, 50
Church Society, xv, 44, 197, 207, 221, 223-30, 266-9, 289-90, 295-6;

In His Name

    Central Board of Management, 224; Gore and Wellington District Association, 229; Lay Committee, 224; London District Branch, 266; St. Paul's Branch, 229; theological orientation, 227; Tract and Book Depository, 227
Church Union, 185

Clark, J.C.D., 113
Clark, S.D., xiii
Clarke, James, 250
clergy, xv, 3, 4, 6-8, 11, 13-16, 18, 20, 28, 39, 41-4, 50-3, 72, 82, 123, 126, 128-30, 188-9, 198-200, 210, 213, 218-9, 224, 228, 246, 265-7, 271, 275, 289-90, 298; appointment, 251, 266-9; discipline, 23, 245; education of, 20, 39, 62, 69, 90, 95, 104, 220, 224, 226; salaries, 5, 14, 18, 64, 126, 214-7, 219-26, 230. *See also under* church: revenues; social status of, 218-22, 230
clergy reserves, xiv, xv, 3, 5, 7, 8, 15, 18, 20, 41, 63-4, 74-5, 97, 107, 132, 174-5, 182-5, 208, 215, 217, 228, 270-1, 274, 298; secularization of, xvii, 63, 74-6, 78, 81, 89, 108, 136, 163, 175, 183-5, 187-8, 197, 207, 212, 256, 270-1, 291, 296-7
Clergy Reserves Corporation, 64, 123-4
Cobourg Theological Institute, 222, 228, 260-3
Colborne, Sir John, 76, 266
Colonial Advocate, 75
Colonial Church Regulation Bill, 210-13
common school legislation, 64-5, 67, 77-8, 177
Constitutional Act of 1791, xv, xvii, 6-9, 11, 28, 75, 127-30, 294
conversion, 92-4
Cooper, Mr. (layman at St. George's), 229
Cooper, Mr. (layman at St. Paul's), 229
Cooper, H.C., 177, 186, 205, 211-2, 258, 259
Corporation Act, 2, 74, 114, 134
Court of King's Bench, 64, 76
Cox, R.G., 185
Cromwell, Oliver, 2
Cronyn, Benjamin, 211, 214, 255-8, 261-3, 266, 268, 270, 272

Darling, W.S., 172, 188, 226, 273; *Sketches of Colonial Life*, 172
David, William, 257
Dawson, John, 221

Index

Deacon, Job, 225
de Blaquière, Peter Boyle, 204-5, 210, 226, 260, 272
Deists, 14
Delisle, David Chabrand, 4
disestablishment, xvi, 8, 135-6, 163, 177-8, 186-7, 189-90, 197, 201, 206, 209, 228, 230, 252-3, 271, 293, 295-6. *See also* establishment, attack on
dissenters. *See under* the various denominations and sectarian religion
Dublin, archbishop of, 255
Dundas, Henry, 10
Dunham, Darius, 13
Durham, Lord, *Report on the Affairs of British North America*, 170-1, 174

Eastern Clerical Association (Bytown), 183, 223, 249
Echo and Protestant Episcopal Recorder, 227, 260-1, 263-5, 269-71
education of clergy. *See under* clergy
educational system, 64-7, 70, 76-8, 104, 173, 177, 181, 207, 271, 291. *See also* university question
Elgin, Lord, 171
Elliot, Adam, 44-5, 52, 250
Ellis, Edward, 261-2
enthusiasm, religious. *See* sectarian religion
Episcopal Church (in United States), 99
Episcopal Church of Scotland, 99
establishment/established church. *See* church establishment
Evangelicals. *See* Low Church
Evangelical Alliance, 256
Evans, Francis, 257, 259, 272
Executive Council, 62, 64-5, 67, 70, 107

faith, 254; and good works, 90-4
Fenton, Rev., 27
Flanagan, Joseph, 248
Flood, John, 227, 272
Flood, Richard, 44, 182
French Canadians, 2-4, 171
French Revolution, 113-5, 133-4, 165, 178, 180

Friends of Religious Liberty, 75
frontierism, xiii, 48, 50-1
Froude, Richard Hurrell, 240; *Remains*, 242
Fuller, Thomas B., 182, 201, 247; *The Roman Catholic Church Not the Mother Church of England*, 248; *Thoughts on the Present State and Future Prospects of the Church of England in Canada*, 200

Geddes, J.G., 44
Genesee Conference (Methodist), 13
George I, 2
George II, 2
George III, 2, 115
Gibson, John, 44
Givins, Saltern, 44, 182, 223, 255
Glenelg, Baron Goderich, 76, 132
Glorious Revolution, 2
good society, vision of, 113, 163, 172, 189, 291, 294
Gore, Francis, 15, 63, 64
grace, 92, 186, 244, 247-8, 255
Grant, John Webster, xiii
Grasett, H.J., 78, 260
"Great Chain of Being", 117
Green, Thomas, 44-5, 47, 52-4, 272
Grenville, William, 6
Gribble, C.B., 269
Grieg, John, 257
Grier, John, 42, 227-8

Hackney Phalanx, 99
Hagerman, Christopher, 107
Haldimand, Frederick, 4
Hanoverian church, 9, 94, 99
Harper, W.F.S., 44-5, 52, 183
Harris, Joseph, 183, 257
Harris, Michael, 39, 41
Harrison, S.B., 78
Hawkins, Ernest, 188
Hellmuth, Isaac, 262
Henry VIII, 2

Index

Herchmer, William, 179, 219, 270
High Church/Anglo-Catholic/Tractarian, xiv, xv, xvi, xvii, 22, 99, 100-3, 213, 228, 239-59, 261-6, 268-9, 271-5, 296-7
Hill, B.C., 45, 257, 272
Hincks, Francis, 175
Hobart, John Henry, 99-100, 102-4
Hooker, Richard, 254
Horton, Robert Wilmot, 64
House of Assembly, xv, 7, 63, 69, 74-7, 173, 175, 185, 227, 270
House of Commons, 179, 210
House of Lords, 2
Hudson, John, 165
human nature, 120-1, 128, 167-8, 177
Hunter, Peter, 118
Huron, diocese of, 213, 255

immigration, 3, 12-13, 18, 38, 39, 41-3, 53-4, 180, 200, 289
imperial connection/patriotism, 124, 169, 170, 172-3, 176, 179, 182, 188-9, 293-4
Indian missions: Bay of Quinte, 39-40, 43-4; Grand River, 39-40, 43-5; Lake Huron, 43; Lake St. Clair, 43-4; Sault Ste. Marie, 44;
Inglis, Charles, 4, 6, 17-18, 23
inter-denominational relations, 18, 21-8, 37, 89-90, 102-6, 108, 256, 297
Irish Church Missions, 257

Johnson, J.K., xvii

Keble, John, *National Apostasy*, 239
Kennedy, T.S., 226, 249
Kent, John, 245, 251
King's College, xiv, 67-73, 76-7, 79, 81, 89, 163, 173-4, 181, 188, 261, 271-72
Kingston, diocese of. *See* Ontario, diocese of
Kingston Gazette, 25, 92, 124, 222
Knox, William, 5

Lafontaine, Louis-Hippolyte, 171
laity, xv, 16, 18, 43, 128, 185, 197-204, 207-8, 210, 213, 217, 222-5, 227-

343

In His Name

      30, 256, 265-9, 274-5, 289
Langhorn, John, 13-15, 17, 21-5, 39-40, 89, 216
Last Judgment, 122
Leeds, John, 131
Leeming, Ralph, 16, 40-41
Legislative Council, 7, 62-3, 69, 76-8, 97, 123, 182, 204
Lett, Stephen, 182, 185, 226
Lewis, John Travers, 273
Lewis, Thomas Frankland, 80
liberal Anglicanism, 21-2, 80, 99, 133, 163, 271
Lindsay, J.G.B., 183
liturgy. *See* worship
Locke, John, 121, 165-7
London Missionary Society, 105
Losee, William, 12-14
Low Church/Evangelical, xiv, xv, xvi, xvii, 26, 45, 202, 213-14, 228,
      239, 247, 254-61, 263-70, 272-4, 296, 297
Lower Canada, Church of England in, xvii, 2, 3, 9-10, 21, 105, 134-5
Loyalists, 5-7, 12, 17
Lundy, F.J., 182
Lutherans, 12, 14-15, 244, 254; clergy, 14, 16, 23

Macaulay, John, 107, 133, 198-9, 250
Macaulay, William, 39, 41, 80, 184, 199, 205, 219
Macdonell, Alexander, 13
MacGeorge, R.J., 177-8
Mack, Frederick, 44
Mackenzie, J.G.D., 182, 185
Mackenzie, William Lyon, 75, 80
MacNab, Allan, 175
Magrath, James, 217
Maitland, Sir Peregrine, 67, 74-5, 123, 127
Marriage Act of 1793, 9, 23-4
Marsh, Mr., 262
McCaul, John, 78, 261
McGill College, 66
McMurray, William, 182, 263
Mennonites, 12
messianism, xiv, xv, 100, 123

Index

Metcalfe, Charles Theophilus, 171
Methodists, 12-16, 19-20, 23-4, 38-9, 48, 50, 77, 90-7, 173, 217; clergy, 13-16, 25, 38, 39, 45, 48, 75, 90, 95-8, 132
Midland District Clerical Association, 184, 249
Midland District Grammar School, 15
missionary activity, xiv, xvi, 3, 12, 14-15, 37, 39-47, 49-50, 53, 61, 89, 104-5, 214, 218, 222, 224, 289; *See also* Indian missions
Montmollin, David-François de, 4
Moravians, 14
Morin, A.N., 175, 183
Morris, Ebenezer, 44-5
Morse, William, 45
Mortimer, George, 217
Mountain, George Jehoshaphat, 131, 199, 201, 203
Mountain, Jacob, 4, 9-11, 17, 20-5, 62-3, 65, 75, 89-90, 97, 124, 128-30, 221
Mountain, Salter J., 40
Mulkins, Hannibal, 257
Mulock, J.A., 250, 257
Municipalities Funds, 175
Murray, James, 3-4

Napoleonic Wars, 113-6, 123-4, 137, 165
natural theology, 116-7
Newman, John Henry, 240-3, 245-6
New York Conference (Methodist), 12-14
Nova Scotia, diocese of, 6, 259

O'Brian, J., 44
Ogilvie, John, 3
O'Meara, Frederick A., 45, 257, 272
O'Neill, H.H., 45, 52
Ontario, diocese of, 263-6, 273
Osler, F.L., 45-6, 53, 143, 216, 247, 259
Oxford movement, 99, 228, 239-48, 250-5, 259, 296. *See also* High Church/Anglo-Catholic/Tractarian
Oxford University, 2, 239-40

Padfield, James, 44, 183

In His Name

Paley, William, 126
Palmer, Arthur, 184-5, 211-12, 250
Paris, Treaty of (1763), 2, 12
parish system, 48-51
patriot raids, 139-41, 143, 166, 169
Patton, Henry, 183, 225, 243, 247, 273-5; *Questions on the Chief Festivals and Holy Days*, 249
Petrie, George, 44-5, 52, 54-5
Phillips, Thomas, 119-20
Pitt, William, 6, 127
Planet (Chatham), 270
political and social philosophy, xiv, xv, xvi, 2, 5, 8-10, 74, 114, 117-23, 125-7, 132, 134, 136, 163-8, 176-7, 182-3, 189, 295, 298
Pollard, Richard, 15, 19, 40
preaching, 48, 90, 95, 100, 165, 246, 258, 259
Presbyterians, 9, 12-16, 38, 105-7, 129, 132, 256; clergy, 13-14, 16, 23, 25. *See also* Church of Scotland
Price Resolutions, 175
puritanism, 2, 254
Pusey, Edward, 240, 245, 247, 264

Quakers, 12, 14
Quebec Act of 1774, 3
Quebec City resolutions (1851), 206
Quebec, diocese of, xvii, 4, 9-10, 20, 42, 67, 76, 214

Rebellion Losses Bill, 172
rebellions of 1837-38, 37, 41, 51, 108, 113, 121, 139, 140-1, 143, 164, 166, 174, 179-80, 188, 203
Recollets, 4
Record, 262
Reform Bill of 1832, 114, 133, 134
Reformation, English, 2, 218, 244, 248, 254
religious equality, 69-70, 74, 125, 129, 133, 135, 181, 187, 291, 293
Religious Tract Society, 256
representative government, 6
republicanism, 66, 71-2, 81, 97, 98, 164, 170, 172. *See also* revolution
reserves, clergy. *See* clergy reserves
responsible government, xvi, 163, 170-2, 189, 294

Index

revenues, church. *See under* church
revivals/revivalism, 92-5
revolution, 6, 7, 54, 81, 98, 114-6, 133-4, 137, 172, 189. *See also* American Revolution, French Revolution
Robinson, John Beverley, 62, 106
Rogers, R.V., 44, 183, 257, 260-4
Rolph, Romaine, 39
Roman Catholics, 2-3, 12-15, 19, 38-9, 63, 77, 80, 105, 133, 173, 177, 183, 240, 242, 244-6, 249; clergy, 13, 25, 38, 254-6, 260, 270; emancipation of, 74, 114,
rubrics, 22, 90, 244, 246, 248-9, 257. *See also* worship
Ryerson, Egerton, 75, 80, 173

sacraments, 101-2, 106, 246-8, 255, 258
St. James's Church, Toronto. *See under* churches
St. Mary's Church, Picton. *See under* churches
salvation, 91, 101, 186, 241, 250, 254, 275
Sampson, William, 16, 19
Sanson, Alexander, 257, 261
Scadding, Henry, 164-5, 176, 182, 250
SCCIPGDS. *See* Society for Converting and Civilizing the Indians and Propagating the Gospel Among the Destitute Settlers of Upper Canada
Scripture Readers Association, 256
sectarian religion, 2, 10, 14-15, 27, 37, 50-1, 55, 63, 72, 80, 89-90, 92, 93-94, 97, 100, 104, 108, 125, 129, 132-33, 180, 250-1, 261, 292. *See also under* individual denominations *and under* Strachan
secularization of clergy reserves. *See under* clergy reserves
sermons, xvi, 45, 100, 108, 119, 138, 140, 168, 176-8, 184, 216, 247, 249, 251, 255, 273
services. *See* worship
Shanklin, Robert, 262-3
Shaw, William, 249
Shortt, Jonathan, 257, 260-1
Simcoe, John Graves, 8-9
sin, 120, 134, 137-42, 178
Society for Converting and Civilizing the Indians and Propagating the Gospel Among Destitute Settlers of Upper Canada (SCCIPGDS), 43-4, 52, 105, 222-3, 225, 289

In His Name

Society for Promoting Christian Knowledge (SPCK), 26-7, 73, 103-6, 200
Society for the Propagation of the Gospel in Foreign Parts (SPG), 14-18, 20, 22, 24, 39, 42, 44, 51, 53-4, 105-6, 179, 184, 200, 201, 214-23, 225, 227, 265, 268, 272
SPCK. *See* Society for Promoting Christian Knowledge
SPG. *See* Society for the Propagation of the Gospel in Foreign Parts
Spratt, George, 42
Stanton, Robert, 107
Stennett, Walter, 182
Stewart, Charles, 20, 42, 44, 198-201, 203, 223
Stoughton, William, 39
Strachan, John, xiii, xvi, 12, 26-7, 61-2, 68-9, 74, 80-2, 89, 108, 113, 131, 134-5, 137, 143, 169, 170, 176, 179, 182, 184, 187, 189, 205-6, 208, 211, 214, 216, 218, 219, 222, 225, 255, 259, 260-1, 263, 266-8, 270, 274, 291, 293; as archdeacon of York, 62, 135-6, 201, 205; as bishop of Toronto, 50, 163, 184, 203-4, 206, 210, 220, 223-4, 241-4, 267, 269, 273; as clergyman at Cornwall, 15, 41, 62, 69, 70; as councillor, 62-3, 65, 69, 76, 77, 97, 107, 123, 182; as journalist, 20, 25, 103, 124; on church establishment, xiv, 20, 61, 64, 69, 72, 75, 80-2, 113, 116, 124-5, 127-31, 133-4, 136, 187, 189, 206, 209, 253, 291-2; on church organization/government, 19-20, 55, 63, 99-104, 198-205, 208, 210-1, 213, 223, 267; on clergy, 19-20, 42, 72, 96-7, 123, 215, 220-1, 223, 255, 267, 269; on clergy reserves, 61, 63-4, 89, 123-4, 128-9, 132, 136, 182-4, 187, 290; on education, xiii, xiv, 20, 61, 64-73, 76-9, 81, 89, 95-7, 117-8, 180, 182, 184, 204, 210, 272, 274, 290; on High Church doctrines, 99-103, 241-4, 246-50, 255, 257, 262-3; on human nature, 117, 120-2, 128, 142; on salvation, 91-4, 101-2, 136, 137; on sectarian religion, 19-20, 25-6, 69-70, 72, 75, 89-104, 107-8, 113, 128, 132, 250; on sin, 91, 101, 120-2, 137, 139-40, 142, 164; on worship, 20, 92, 94, 99-103, 248, 257; pastoral letters, 206; political and social philosophy, 12, 19-20, 62, 66, 72, 80-2, 97-8, 113-125, 127-8, 130, 133-7, 139-40, 142-3, 163-5, 169, 172, 178-9, 188; sermons, 25, 75, 93-5, 99-102, 114-6, 118-9, 121-4, 128, 131, 135-7, 139, 184, 254; visitations, 184, 206, 210-11, 213, 220, 247, 266, 270; *Appeal in Behalf of the University of Upper Canada*, 97; *Appeal to the Friends of Religion and Literature*, 71; *Church Fellowship*, 102; *Discourse on the Character of King George the*

Third, 115, 165; *Ecclesiastical Chart*, 75, 97, 124, 128, 131; *Letter to Dr. Lee*, 129; *Letter to the Right Hon. Lord John Russell on the Present State of the Church in Canada*, 208; *Letter to Thomas Frankland Lewis*, 80, 124, 128, 221; *Observations on the Provision Made for the Maintenance of a Protestant Clergy*, 128
Street, G.C., 44
Strong, S.S., 183
Stuart, George Okill, 15, 22, 40, 106-7, 199, 201, 205, 221, 225, 255, 261, 263
Stuart, John, 13-14, 17-19, 22-5, 39-41, 216
Sunday School Union, 256
Sweatman, Arthur, 274
Sydenham, Lord, 171, 174, 179, 182, 187
synodical government, xv, 197-213, 222-3, 229-30, 265-6, 269, 289-90, 295

temperance societies, 256, 297
Test Act, 2, 74, 114, 134
Thirteen Colonies, 4, 6, 115-6, 124, 127. *See also* United States
Thirty-Nine Articles, 68-9, 103, 241
Thompson, Joseph, 39, 41
tithes, 2
Toronto, diocese of, 215, 224. *See also* York
Toronto, University of, 173, 181-2, 204, 271. *See also* King's College
Townley, A.T., 171-2, 177, 185, 248, 264-5, 267
Tractarianism. *See* High Church
Tracts for the Times, 240, 245
Treaty of Paris. *See* Paris, Treaty of
Trinity, Church of, Toronto. *See under* churches
Trinity Church, New York. *See under* churches
Trinity College, Dublin, 255
Trinity College, Toronto, 181-2, 184, 205, 261, 272, 274

United Empire Loyalists. *See* Loyalists
United States, 133, 139, 169, 198, 294
Universalists, 14, 52
university legislation, 69-70, 76-7, 79, 173-4, 180-2, 185, 271, 291
University of Toronto. *See* Toronto, University of
university question, 9, 64, 66-8, 70-3, 76-7, 79, 173-4, 181, 182, 204,

In His Name

291. *See also under* university legislation
Upper Canada Bible Society. *See* Bible Society of Upper Canada
Upper Canada Clergy Society, 45
Upper Canada College, 76
Upper Canada, government. *See under* government
Upper Canadian Methodist Conference, 38, 174
Upper Canadian Travelling Missionary Fund, 44, 179, 218
Usher, James, 44
utilitarianism, 125-7, 130, 182

Veyssière, Leger-Jean-Baptiste-Noel, 4
virtue. *See* faith and good works
voluntarism, xiv, 75-7, 129-31, 173-6, 202, 217, 221-2, 225, 270, 274, 289, 295, 297

Waddilove, W.J.D., 44, 52-3
Wade, C.T., 44, 216
Wait, W.W., 183
Warburton, William, 125-7
War of 1812, 1, 11-13, 15, 61-2, 66, 115-6, 123-4, 140, 173
Weagant, John Gunther, 16, 40
Welby, T.E., 257
Wenham, John, 105-7
Wesleyan Methodists, 38, 171
Western Clerical Association, 201, 249
Westfall, William, xiii
Whig political tradition, 4-5
Widows and Orphans Fund, 224, 226-7
William and Mary, King and Queen, 2
Wilson, John, 15, 263, 265
Wilson, W. Carus, 262
Windsor Academy, 5-6
Wise, S.F., xiii, xvii, 293-4
works, good. *See* faith and good works
worship, 11, 17, 19, 41-2, 45-6, 90, 92, 99-102, 178, 180, 187, 226, 241, 244, 246-50, 255, 257-8, 274

York, archdeaconry of, 62, 67, 253; parish of, 15, 20, 40, 41, 61, 65. *See also* Toronto